INTERVIEW
WITH HISTORY

Books by *Oriana Fallaci*

INTERVIEW
WITH
HISTORY

—————◆◆—————

Oriana Fallaci

Translated by John Shepley

LIVERIGHT   NEW YORK

Library of Congress Cataloging in Publication Data

Fallaci, Oriana.
    Interview with history.

    Translation of Intervista con la storia.
    1. Statesmen—Interviews.   I. Title.
D412.6.F3313   920'.02   75-34022
ISBN 0-87140-590-3

Translation Copyright © 1976 by Liveright Publishing Corporation
                    FIRST EDITION
Originally published as *Intervista con la Storia* © 1974 Rizzoli Editore, Milano

PRINTED IN THE UNITED STATES OF AMERICA
            1 2 3 4 5 6 7 8 9

To my mother
TOSCA FALLACI
and to all those
who do not like power

Contents

Preface

---◆---

This book does not claim to be anything but what it is: I mean a direct witness to fourteen political figures of contemporary history. It does not want to promise anything more than it claims, I mean a document straddling journalism and history. Yet it also doesn't want to be considered as a simple collection of interviews for students of power and antipower. I do not feel myself to be, nor will I ever succeed in feeling like, a cold recorder of what I see and hear. On every professional experience I leave shreds of my heart and soul; and I participate in what I see or hear as though the matter concerned me personally and were one on which I ought to take a stand (in fact I always take one, based on a specific moral choice). So I did not go to these fourteen people with the detachment of the anatomist or the imperturbable reporter. I went with a thousand feelings of rage, a thousand questions that before assailing them were assailing me, and with the hope of understanding in what way, by being in power or opposing it, those people determine our destiny. For example: is history made by everyone or by a few? Does it depend on universal laws or on a few individuals and nothing else?

It is an old dilemma, I know, which no one has resolved and no one will ever resolve. It is also an old trap in which it is very dangerous to fall, since any answer carries within itself its own contradiction. It is not by chance that many try to compromise and maintain that history is made by everyone and by a few, that the few emerge as leaders because they were born at the right moment and are able to interpret that moment. Perhaps. But those who do not delude themselves about the absurd tragedy of life are led rather to follow Pascal when he says that if Cleopatra's nose had been shorter the whole aspect of the world would have been changed; they are led rather to fear what Bertrand Russell feared when he wrote, "Whether the populations of the world are to live or die rests with the decisions of Khrushchev, Mao Tse-tung and Mr. John Foster Dulles, not with ordinary mortals like ourselves. If they say 'Die', we shall die. If they say 'live', we shall live." * I cannot say he is wrong. In short, I cannot exclude the idea that our existence is decided by a few people, by their dreams and caprices, their initiative and will. Those few who through ideas, discoveries, revolutions, wars, or some quite simple gesture—the killing of a tyrant— change the course of events and the destiny of the majority.

Surely this is an atrocious hypothesis. It also is an offensive thought, for in that case what do we become? Impotent herds in the hands of now a noble shepherd, now an infamous one? Mere objects at hand, leaves blowing in the wind? And to deny this, you may even embrace some Marxist thesis by which everything is resolved by the class struggle: history-is-made-by-peoples-through-the-class-struggle. But you soon realize that everyday reality belies those Marxists, you soon object that without Marx Marxism would not exist (no one can demonstrate that if Marx had never been born or had not written *Das Kapital*, John Doe or Richard Roe would have written it). And discouraged, you conclude that those who make one turn instead of another are few, those who make us take one road instead of another are few, those who bring forth ideas, discoveries, revolutions, wars, and kill tyrants are few. Still more discouraged, you ask what those few are like: more intelligent than ourselves, stronger, more enlightened, more enterprising? Or individuals like ourselves, neither better nor worse, ordinary creatures who do not deserve our anger, our admiration, or our envy?

The question extends to the past, even a remote past of which we

---

* Bertrand Russell, *Portraits from Memory and Other Essays* (London: George Allen & Unwin, 1956).

know only what they have prescribed so that we would learn it obediently in school. Who is there to say that they did not teach us lies in school? Who can give us indisputable proof of the good faith of Xerxes, Julius Caesar, or Spartacus? We know everything about their battles and nothing about their human dimension, about their weaknesses and lies, about their intellectual and moral wavering. We have no evidence to show that Vercingetorix was a scoundrel. We do not even know whether Jesus Christ was tall or short, light or dark, educated or simple, whether he went to bed or not with Mary Magdalen, whether he really said the things that Matthew, Mark, Luke, and John assert. Ah, if only someone had interviewed him with a tape recorder so as to capture his voice, his ideas, his words! Ah, if only someone had taken down in shorthand what Joan of Arc declared at her trial before going to the stake! Ah, if only someone had questioned Cromwell and Napoleon in front of a movie camera! I do not trust news handed down by word of mouth, reports drawn up too late and that cannot be proved. Yesterday's history is a novel full of events that I cannot check, judgments that I cannot contest.

Not today's history. Because today's history is written the very moment it happens. It can be photographed, filmed, recorded on tape in interviews with the few people who control the world or change its course. It can be transmitted immediately through the press, radio, television. It can be interpreted, heatedly discussed. For this reason I like journalism. For this reason I fear journalism. What other profession allows you to write history at the very moment it happens and also to be its direct witness? Journalism is an extraordinary and terrible privilege. Not by chance, if you are aware of it, does it consume you with a hundred feelings of inadequacy. Not by chance, when I find myself going through an event or an important encounter, does it seize me like anguish, a fear of not having enough eyes and enough ears and enough brains to look and listen and understand like a worm hidden in the wood of history. I do not exaggerate, you see, when I say that on every professional experience I leave some of my soul. And it is not easy for me to say, Oh, come now, there's no need to be Herodotus; for better or worse you'll contribute a little stone to help compose the mosaic; you'll provide information to help make people think. And if you make a mistake, never mind.

The present book was born in this way, in the span of four years, those in which I did the fourteen interviews for my paper, *L'Europeo*. To the subjects here lined up, in short, I went in this spirit: each time seeking, together with information, an answer to the question of how they are different from ourselves. To meet them was often an exhausting chore. My request for an appointment was almost always met by cold silence or a refusal (the fourteen in the book are not the only ones I tried to meet), and if later they answered yes, I had to wait months for them to grant me an hour or half hour.

When I was finally in their presence, I had to exert myself to keep them for longer than an hour or half hour. Once there, however, it became a game to reach the truth and discover that not even a selective criterion justified their power. Those who determine our destiny are not really better than ourselves; they are neither more intelligent nor stronger nor more enlightened than ourselves. If anything, they are more enterprising, more ambitious. Only in the rarest cases did I have the certainty of finding myself face to face with a person born to lead us or to make us take one road instead of another. But these cases involved men who were not themselves in power; in fact they had fought it, and fought it at the risk of their own lives. As for those whom I liked or who charmed me in some way, the moment has come to confess that my mind remained reserved and my heart dissatisfied. Deep down I was sorry that they were sitting at the top of the pyramid. Since I was unable to believe them as I would have liked, I could not judge them innocent. So much the less as traveling companions.

Perhaps it is because I do not understand power, the mechanism by which men or women feel themselves invested or become invested with the right to rule over others and punish them if they do not obey. Whether it comes from a despotic sovereign or an elected president, from a murderous general or a beloved leader, I see power as an inhuman and hateful phenomenon. I may be mistaken but the earthly paradise did not end on the day that Adam and Eve were told by God that from now on they would work by the sweat of their brows and bring forth children in sorrow. It ended on the day that they realized that they had a master who tried to keep them from eating an apple, and, driven out over an apple, placed themselves at the head of a tribe where it was even forbidden to eat pork. Of course, to live in a group requires a governing authority; otherwise there is chaos. But the most tragic side of the human condition seems to me precisely that of needing an authority to govern, a chief. One can never know where a chief's power begins and ends; the only sure thing is that you cannot control him and that he kills your freedom. Worse: he is the bitterest demonstration that absolute freedom does not exist, has never existed, cannot exist. Even if it is necessary to behave as though it existed and to look for it. Whatever the price.

I feel I should warn the reader how much I am convinced of this, and also that apples are born to be picked, that meat can even be eaten on Friday. Still more to remind him or her that, to the same degree that I do not understand power, I do understand those who oppose power, who criticize power, who contest power, especially those who rebel against power imposed by brutality. I have always looked on disobedience toward the oppressive as the only way to use the miracle of having been born. I have always looked on the silence of those who do not react or who indeed applaud as the real death of a woman or a man. And listen: for me the most beautiful monument to human dignity is still the one I saw on a hill in the Peloponnesus. It was not a statue, it was not a flag, but three letters that in Greek signify No: oxi. Men thirsting for freedom had written them among the trees during the Nazi-Fascist occupation, and for thirty years that No had remained there, unfaded by the sun or rain. Then the colonels had obliterated it with a stroke of whitewash. But immediately, almost magically, the sun and rain had dissolved the whitewash. So that day by day the three letters reappeared on the surface, stubborn, desperate, indelible.

Truly, then, this book does not claim to be anything but what it is. It does not want to promise anything more than it claims, that is, a direct testimony by fourteen political figures of contemporary history, each with his or her symbolic meaning and alignment in a symbolic sequence. (Because of this, I did not want to bring any interview up to date, not even the older ones, nor to re-elaborate them, thereby spoiling their value as documents that crystallized the moments they were recorded. I wanted to leave them intact in their genuineness, without worrying over the fact that Golda Meir is no longer prime minister, Willy Brandt no longer chancellor, Thieu no longer dictator of South Vietnam, and Alexandros

Panagoulis no longer a persecuted hero of the Resistance to the Greek colonels. But while reading it, you should keep in mind that No that reappears, stubborn, desperate, indelible, among the trees on a hill in the Peloponnesus.

ORIANA FALLACI

INTERVIEW
WITH HISTORY

I

Henry Kissinger

This too famous, too important, too lucky man, whom they call Superman, Superstar, Superkraut, and who stitches together paradoxical alliances, reaches impossible agreements, keeps the world holding its breath as though the world were his students at Harvard. This incredible, inexplicable, unbearable personage, who meets Mao Tse-tung when he likes, enters the Kremlin when he feels like it, wakens the president of the United States and goes into his bedroom when he thinks it appropriate. This absurd character with horn-rimmed glasses, beside whom James Bond becomes a flavorless creation. He does not shoot, nor use his fists, nor leap from speeding automobiles like James Bond, but he advises on wars, ends wars, pretends to change our destiny, and does change it. But still, who is Henry Kissinger?

Books are written about him as about those great figures whom history has by now digested. Books like the ones illustrating his political and cultural background, written by admiring university colleagues, or like the one celebrating his talents as a seducer written by a French newspaperwoman with an unrequited passion. With his university colleagues he never cared to speak. With the French newspaperwoman he never cared to make love. He alludes to them all with a vexed grimace and dismisses them with a scornful wave of his plump hand. "They understand nothing," "None of what she says is true."

The story of his life is the object of research bordering on a cult, simultaneously paradoxical and grotesque, so everyone knows that he was born in Fürth, Germany, in 1923, son of Louis Kissinger, a high-school teacher, and Paula Kissinger, a housewife. Everyone knows that his family is Jewish, that fourteen of his relatives died in the concentration camps, that together with his father and mother and his brother Walter he fled in 1938 to London and then to New York, that at that time he was fifteen years old and was called Heinz, not Henry, nor did he know a word of English. But he learned it very quickly, and while his father worked as a post-office clerk and his mother opened a bakery shop, he did so well at his studies that he was admitted to Harvard, where he graduated with honors with a thesis on Spengler, Toynbee, and Kant, and later became a professor.

Everyone knows that at twenty-one he was a soldier in Germany, where he was one of a group of GI's selected by test and judged to have an IQ close to genius, that because of this (and despite his youth) he was entrusted with the job of organizing the government of Krefeld, a German city left without a government. Indeed it was in Krefeld that his passion for politics flowered, a passion that was to be gratified by his becoming an adviser to Kennedy and Johnson, later the presidential aide to Nixon, finally his secretary of state, until he came to be considered the second most powerful man in America. And already at that time, some maintained that he was much more, as is shown by the joke that for years made the rounds of Washington. "Just think what would happen if Kissinger died. Richard Nixon would become president of the United States!"

They used to call him Nixon's mental wet nurse. They had even coined a wicked and revealing surname for him and Nixon: Nixinger. They said that Nixon could not do without him; that he wanted him always at his side on every trip, for every ceremony, every official dinner, every vacation. Above all, for every decision. If Nixon decided to go to Peking, thereby dumbfounding both the right and left, it was Kissinger who had put the idea in his head. If Nixon determined to go to Moscow, thereby confounding East and West, it was Kissinger who had suggested it. If Nixon announced reaching an agreement with Hanoi that would abandon Thieu, it was Kissinger who had persuaded him to take this step. Thus Kissinger acted as an ambassador, a secret agent, a negotiator, a Mazarin, a

Metternich, a veritable president who used the White House as his own house.

Kissinger did not sleep there, since he wouldn't be allowed to bring in women, you would have said (he had not, as yet, married a former assistant of Nelson Rockefeller). For nine years he had created a myth of his amorous adventures and he carefully nourished it, always allowing himself to be seen with actresses, starlets, singers, models, women journalists, dancers, and millionairesses. Insatiable as a bull, though many did not believe such a myth and the skeptics claimed that he couldn't care less about these women, he behaved this way as a game, conscious of the fact that it increased his glamour, his popularity, his photographs in magazines. In this sense, too, he was the most talked-about man in America, and the most fashionable. His thick glasses had created a fashion, his curly hair, his gray suits and blue neckties, his deceptively ingenuous air of one who has discovered life's pleasures.

Then Nixon resigned in shame, unmasked and defeated by a secret *Putsch* that nobody will ever consider a *Putsch*. Some said, "This is the end of Kissinger too." Well, it was not. Kissinger remained where he was, still a powerful secretary of state and the new mental wet nurse of Ford, as unshakable and indestructible as a rock, or a cancer. Had he managed this devious *Putsch?* Was he irreplaceable, as the new president had intimated while begging him to stay? The mystery arose and is left to history.

After all, the whole Kissinger case is a mystery. The man himself, as well as his unparalleled success, is unexplained. As often happens when someone becomes very popular and very important, the more you know about him, the less you understand. Besides, he protects the incomprehensibility of his phenomenon so well that trying to explain it becomes a fatiguing exercise bordering on the impossible. Very rarely does he grant personal interviews; he speaks only at press conferences arranged by the administration. And I swear that I will never understand why he agreed to see me, scarcely three days after receiving my letter, in which I had entertained no illusions. He says it was because of my interview with General Giap in Hanoi in February 1969. It may be so. But the fact remains that after his extraordinary "yes," he changed his mind and decided to see me on one condition: that he would tell me nothing. During the meeting, I was to do the talking, and from what I said he would decide whether to grant me the interview or not. Assuming he could find the time. Yes, the time was found, the appointment made for Thursday, November 2, 1972, when I saw him arrive out of breath and unsmiling, and he said, "Good morning, Miss Fallaci." Then, still without smiling, he led me into his elegant office, full of books and telephones and papers and abstract paintings and photographs of Nixon. Here he forgot about me, turned his back, and began reading a long typewritten report. Indeed it was a little embarrassing to stand there in the middle of the room, while he had his back to me and kept reading. It was also stupid and ill-mannered on his part. However, it allowed me to study him before he studied me. And not only to discover that he wasn't attractive at all, so short and thickset and weighed down by a large head like a sheep, but to discover also that he is by no means carefree or sure of himself. Before facing someone, he needs to take time and protect himself by his authority, a frequent phenomenon in shy people who try to conceal their shyness and by this effort end by seeming rude. Or by really being rude.

After reading the typewritten report—meticulously and carefully, to judge by the time it took him—he finally turned to me and invited me to sit down on the couch. Then he took the adjacent armchair, higher than the couch, and from this privileged and strategic position began to ask me questions in the tone of a professor examining a pupil in whom he has little confidence. He reminded me of my mathematics and physics teacher at the Liceo Galilei in Florence, an individual I hated because he enjoyed frightening me by staring at me ironically from behind his spectacles. He even had the same baritone, or rather guttural, voice as this teacher, and the same way of leaning back in the armchair with his right arm outstretched, the gesture of crossing his legs, while his jacket was so tight over his stomach that it looked as though the buttons might pop.

If he intended to make me ill at ease, he succeeded perfectly. The nightmare of my schooldays assailed me to such a degree that, at each of his questions, I thought, Oh, God, will I know the answer? Because if I don't, he'll flunk me. His first question was about General Giap. "As I've told you, I never give personal interviews. The reason why I'm about to consider the possibility of granting you one is that I read your interview with Giap. Very interesting. What is Giap like?" He asked it with the air of having little time at his disposal, so I had to sum it all up in a single effective remark, and answered, "He seemed to me a French snob. Jovial and arrogant at the same time, but actually as boring as a rainy day. It was less an interview than a lecture. I couldn't get excited about him. Still what he told me turned out to be true."

To minimize the figure of Giap in the eyes of an American was almost an insult; they were all a little enamored of him as they were thirty years ago of Rommel. The expression "French snob" therefore left Kissinger bewildered. Perhaps he did not understand it. The revelation that he was "as boring as a rainy day" disturbed him; he knows that he himself carries the stigma of being a boring type, and his blue eyes flashed twice with hostility. The detail that struck him the most, however, was that I gave Giap credit for having predicted things correctly. Indeed he interrupted me: "Why true?" I replied that Giap had announced in 1969 what would happen in 1972. "For example?" For example the fact that the Americans would withdraw little by little from Vietnam and would end by abandoning a war that was costing them more and more money and had soon brought them to the brink of inflation. The blue eyes flashed again. "And what, in your opinion, was the most important thing that Giap told you?" His having essentially disavowed the Tet offensive by attributing it to the Vietcong alone. This time he did not comment. He only asked, "Does he think that the initiative was started by the Vietcong?" "Perhaps, yes, Dr. Kissinger. Even children know that Giap likes tank engagements à la Rommel. In fact the Easter offensive was carried out à la Rommel and . . ." "But he lost!" he protested. "Did he really lose?" I replied. "What makes you think that he didn't lose?" "The fact that you have accepted an agreement that Thieu doesn't like, Dr. Kissinger."

In an attempt to draw some information out of him, I added in a distracted tone, "Thieu will never give in." He fell into my little trap. He answered, "He'll give in. He has to." Then he concentrated on Thieu, his mare's-nest. He asked me what I thought of Thieu. I told him that I had never liked him. "And why have you never liked him?" "Dr. Kissinger, you know better than I. You tried for three days, or rather four, to get something out of him." This drew from him a sigh of assent and a grimace that, in retrospect, is surprising. Kissinger knows perfectly how to control his features; it seldom happens that his eyes or lips betray an idea or feeling. But during that first meeting, for some reason he made little effort to control himself. Every time I said something against Thieu, he nodded or smiled with complicity.

After Thieu he asked me about Nguyen Cao Ky and Do Cao Tri. Of the first he said that he was weak and talked too much. Of the second he said he was sorry not to have known him. "Was he really a great general?" Yes, I confirmed, a great general and a courageous one, the only general whom I had seen go to the front lines and into combat. For this too, I suppose, they had assassinated him. Here he pretended astonishment. "Assassinated? By whom?" "Certainly not by the Vietcong, Dr. Kissinger. The helicopter didn't crash because it was hit by mortar fire, but because someone had tampered with the blades. And certainly Thieu did not shed any tears over that crime. Nor did Cao Ky. A legend was being built up around Do Cao Tri, and he spoke so badly of Thieu and Ky. Even during my interview with him, he attacked them mercilessly." And this answer disturbed him more than the fact that I later criticized the South Vietnamese army.

This is what happened when he asked me about the last time I had been to Saigon, about what I had seen, and I replied that I had seen an army that wasn't worth a fig, and his face assumed a perplexed expression. Indeed, since I was sure that he was putting on an act, I joked. "Dr. Kissinger, don't tell me you need me to find out these things. You who are the most well-informed person in the world!" But he did not understand my irony and continued to question me as if the fate of the cosmos depended on my judgments, or as if he could not live without them. He knows how to flatter with diabolical, hypocritical—or should I say diplomatic?—finesse.

After fifteen minutes of conversation, when I was biting my nails for having accepted this absurd interview from the man I was supposed to interview, he forgot a little about Vietnam, and, in the tone of a zealous reporter, asked me which heads of state had impressed me most. (He likes the word "impress.") Resigned, I listed them. He agreed with me primarily on Bhutto. "Very intelligent, very brilliant." He did not agree about Indira Gandhi. "Did you really like her?" He didn't even try to justify the unfortunate choice he had suggested to Nixon during the Indo-Pakistani conflict, when he sided with the Pakistanis who were to lose the war against the Indians who were to win it. Of another head of state, of whom I had said that he did not seem to me highly intelligent but that I had liked him very much, he said, "It's not intelligence that's important in a head of state. The quality that counts in a head of state is strength. Courage, shrewdness, and strength."

I consider this remark one of the most interesting things he said to me, with or without the tape recorder. It illustrates his type, his personality. The man loves strength above all. Courage, shrewdness, and strength. Intelligence interests him much less, though he himself possesses it abundantly, as everyone says. (But is it a matter of intelligence or of erudition and cunning? The intelligence that counts, as far as I'm concerned, is the humane kind, that which is born from the understanding of men. And I wouldn't say that he has that kind of intelligence. So on this subject one ought to go a little deeper. Assuming it's worth the trouble.)

The last phase of my examination emerged from a question that I really didn't expect. "What do you think will happen in Vietnam with the cease-fire?" Taken by surprise, I told him the truth. I said what I had written in a dispatch just published in *L'Europeo:* there would be a great bloodbath, on both sides, and the war would go on. "And I'm afraid that the first to begin the bloodbath will be your friend Thieu." He jumped up, almost offended. "My friend?" "Well, anyway, Thieu." "And why?" "Because even before the Vietcong embark on their slaughter, he will carry out a secret massacre in his prisons and jails. There will not be many neutralists or many Vietcong to form part of the provisional government after the cease-fire. . . ." He frowned, looked perplexed, and finally said, "So you too believe in the bloodbath. . . . But there will be international supervisors!" "Dr. Kissinger, even in Dacca there were the Indians. But they didn't succeed in stopping the Mukti Bahini from slaughtering the Biharis." "I know, I know, and if . . . What if the armistice were delayed for a year or two?" "What, Dr. Kissinger?" "What if the armistice were delayed for a year or two?" he repeated. A perfect example of his shrewd use of flattery: he couldn't care less about my opinion. And yet, I fell for the ploy. I could have bitten my tongue, I could have wept. Indeed I think my eyes were wet when I looked at him again. "Dr. Kissinger, don't make me suffer from the thought that I've put a wrong idea in your head. Dr. Kissinger, the mutual slaughter will take place anyway—today, in a year, two years. And if the war goes on another year or two, besides the dead from that slaughter, we will have to count those from the bombing and fighting. Do I make myself clear? Ten plus twenty makes thirty. Aren't ten victims better than thirty?"

Stupidly unaware that he had made fun of me, I lost two nights of sleep over this, and when we met again for the interview I told him so. But he consoled me by saying that I shouldn't upset myself by feeling guilty, that my mathematical calculation was correct, better ten than thirty, and this episode too illustrates his type and personality. The man likes to be liked, so he listens to everything, records everything like a computer. And just when it seems that he has discarded some now old and useless piece of information, he brings it forth as though it were valid and up to date.

After about twenty-five minutes, he decided that I had passed my examination. But there remained one detail that bothered him a little: I was a woman. It was with a woman, the French journalist who had written the book, that he had had an unfortunate experience. Supposing, despite my good intentions, I too were to cause him embarrassment? At this point I got angry. Certainly I couldn't tell him what was on the tip of my tongue, namely that I had no intention of falling in love with him. But I could tell him other things, and I did. That I was not going to put myself in a situation like the one in which I found myself in Saigon in 1968 when, due to the poor figure cut by a cowardly Italian, I had had to put on a stupid display of heroics. That Mr. Kissinger should understand that I was not responsible for the bad taste of a lady who happened to be in the same profession as my own. So I shouldn't have to pay for that, but, if he liked, I would wear a false mustache the next time we met.

He agreed to let me interview him, without smiling, and announced that he would find an hour on Saturday. And at ten o'clock, Saturday, November 4, I was back at the White House. At ten-thirty I entered his office to begin perhaps the most uncomfortable and the worst interview that I have ever had. God, what a chore! Every ten minutes we were interrupted by the telephone, and it was Nixon who wanted something, asked something, petulant, tiresome, like a child who cannot be away from its mother.

Kissinger answered attentively, obsequiously, and the conversation with me was interrupted, making the effort to understand him still more difficult. Then, just at the high point, when he was setting forth for me the elusive essence of his personality, one of the telephones rang and again it was Nixon. Could Dr. Kissinger look in on him a minute? Of course, Mr. President. He jumped up, told me to wait, saying he would still try to give me a little time, and left. And thus ended our meeting. Two hours later, while I was still waiting, his assistant, Dick Campbell, came in all embarrassed and explained that the president was leaving for California and that Dr. Kissinger had to go with him. He would not be back in Washington before Tuesday evening, in time for the first election returns, but it was extremely doubtful that he would be able to conclude the interview at that time. If I could wait until the end of November, when many things would be clearer . . .

I couldn't, and anyway it wasn't worth the trouble. What was the point of trying to clarify a portrait that I already had before me? A portrait emerging from a confusion of lines, colors, evasive answers, reticent sentences, irritating silences. On Vietnam, obviously, he could not tell me anything more, and I am amazed that he had said as much as he had: that whether the war were to end or go on did not depend only on him, and he could not allow himself the luxury of compromising everything by an unnecessary word. About himself, however, he didn't have such problems. Yet every time I had asked him a precise question, he had wriggled out like an eel. An eel icier than ice. God, what an icy man! During the whole interview he never changed that expressionless countenance, that hard or ironic look, and never altered the tone of that sad, monotonous, unchanging voice. The needle on the tape recorder shifts when a word is pronounced in a higher or lower key. With him it remained still, and more than once I had to check to make sure that the machine was working. Do you know that obsessive, hammering sound of rain falling on a roof? His voice is like that. And basically his thoughts as well, never disturbed by a wish or fantasy, by an odd design, by a temptation of error. Everything in him is calculated, controlled as in the flight of an airplane steered by the automatic pilot. He weighs every sentence down to the last ounce, no unintentional words escape him, and whatever he says always forms part of some useful mechanism. Le Duc Tho must have sweated blood in those days, and Thieu must have found his cunning sorely tried. Kissinger has the nerves and brain of a chess player.

Naturally you will find explanations that take into consideration other aspects of his personality. For example, the fact that he is unmistakably a Jew and irreparably a German. For example, the fact that, as a Jew and German, transplanted to a country that still looks with suspicion on Jews and Germans, he carries on his back a load of knotted contradictions, resentments, and perhaps hidden humanity. In fact, they attribute to him boundless gifts of imagination, unappreciated talents for greatness. Could be. But in my eyes he remains an entirely common man and the most guilty representative of the kind of power of which Bertrand Russell speaks: "If they say 'Die', we shall die. If they say 'live', we shall live."

Let us not forget that he owes his success to the worst president that the United States has ever had: Nixon, trickster and liar, sick in his nerves and perhaps in his mind, who has come, despised by all, to an undignified end. Let us not forget that he was, and still is, Nixon's creature. If Nixon had not existed, probably we would never even have known that Kissinger had been born. For years Kissinger had been offering his services to two other presidents, neither of whom took him seriously. He was picked up by a governor who most certainly did not shine with acute brilliance and had arrived at political prominence only because of his billions: Nelson Rockefeller. Later Rockefeller had recommended him to Nixon, and the latter, in his ignorance, had been seduced by the pompous erudition of the German professor. Or was it by his totalitarian theses on the balance of the great powers, a laborious dusting-off of the Holy Alliance? Theirs was a meeting of two arrogant minds that believed neither in democracy nor in the changing world. And in that sense it was a successful meeting, so successful that the ease with which Kissinger abandoned Nixon when the latter fell into disgrace and shame seems truly astonishing. So far as I know, he did not even take the trouble to pay a visit to his Pygmalion who lay "dying" in a California hospital. He didn't even bother to say a few words in his defense, to assume any responsibility for the misdeeds of which he was surely not ignorant and that he had probably endorsed. He went over bag and baggage to his successor, Ford, and merrily continued his career as secretary of state.

Let's put it this way: he is an intellectual adventurer. And there would be nothing wrong in his being an intellectual adventurer (many great men and many great politicians have been—I would say almost all) if he succeeded in living in his own time and inventing something new, instead of going back to the decrepit concepts of his erudition or to personages who are in every sense defunct. Instead he is a man who lives in the past, without understanding the present and without divining the future. Much as he denies it, he really believes himself to be the reincarnation of Metternich, that is to say an individual who depended only on himself to arrange matters while basing his actions on secrecy, absolutism, and the ignorance of people not yet awakened to the discovery of their rights. And it is for this reason that Kissinger's successes always turn out to be brief and accidental: a flash in the pan or smoke in the eyes. It is for this reason that in the long run each of his undertakings, each of his expectations, fails, and he commits such gross errors. His peace in Vietnam did not resolve the problem or even the war. In Vietnam, after the armistice, the fighting and dying continued; in Cambodia (where he and Nixon had brought the war) there was never a moment of truce. And finally it ended as it did, because his peace accords were a fraud. A fraud to save Nixon's face, bring home the American boys, the POW's, withdraw the troops, and erase the uncomfortable word "Vietnam" from the newspapers.

And his mediation between the Arabs and Israelis? Extolled and publicized as it has been, it has not lightened the tragedy of the Middle East by an ounce and if anything has worsened matters for the protégés of the United States. Since he began meddling in that part of the world, the conflict has grown and a war has broken out, Arafat has been received at the UN as a head of state, and Hussein has been deprived of all rights to the West Bank. And the Cyprus drama? It was precisely under Kissinger that the Cyprus drama exploded, with all its consequences. Did Kissinger know or not know that the fascist junta in Athens was preparing that invasion? If he knew, he was a fool not to understand the mistake. If he didn't know, he was a bad secretary of state and even lacked the information that he boasts of having. And, in any case, the Cyprus drama deprived him of valuable allies: the Greek colonels. In abdicating they left Greece on the brink of war with Turkey. Constantine Karamanlis left NATO, and the Turks threatened to do likewise. What American, before Kissinger, has ever found himself with two NATO countries preparing to go to war and with the Atlantic Alliance made to look so ridiculous?

And then on Kissinger lies the horrible stain known as Chile. The documents that have appeared in the American press prove, beyond any possibility of denial, that it was Kissinger as well who wanted the overthrow of the democratic regime in Chile, the end of a democratically elected government. They also prove that Kissinger unleashed the CIA against Salvador Allende Gossens, that Kissinger financially helped those who were preparing the *coup d'état*. There are many who wonder if, like Macbeth, he is not troubled at night by a bloody ghost of Banquo: the ghost of Allende. No toasts with Chou En-lai and Leonid Brezhnev will ever be able to wash away the suspicions that lie on him for Allende's death. Nor does it help to see how generously Kissinger behaves with Franco and Franco's Spain, deaf to the future that a democratic Spain prepares for herself in spite of Ford's visits. It is almost unbelievable how this shaker of Communist leaders' hands shows his esteem and friendship only for the countries ruled by some form of Fascism. And it is poor consolation to go on saying that his star is declining, that perhaps it has already set, that it is history that will have the final say on this too famous, too important, too lucky man whom they called Superman, Superstar, Superkraut.

Published in its entirety in the weekly *New Republic*, quoted in its more salient moments in the Washington and New York dailies, and then by almost all the newspapers in the the United States, the interview with Kissinger kicked up a fuss that amazed me as much as its consequences. Obviously, I had underestimated the man and the interest that flourished around each of his words. Obviously, I had minimized the importance of that unbearable hour spent with him. In fact it immediately became the topic of the day. And the rumor soon spread that Nixon was enraged with Henry, that he therefore refused to see him, that in vain Henry telephoned him, asking for a hearing, and went to seek him out in his San Clemente residence. The gates of San Clemente remained closed, the hearing was not granted, the telephone went unanswered because the president did not care to answer. The president, among other things, did not forgive Henry for what Henry had said to me about the reason for his success: ". . . that I've always acted alone. Americans like that immensely. Americans like the cowboy who leads the wagon train by riding ahead alone on his horse, the cowboy who rides all alone into the town, the village, with his horse and nothing else. . . ." Even the press criticized him for this.

The press had always been generous with Kissinger, merciless toward Nixon. In this case, however, the sides were reversed and every newspaperman condemned the presumption, or at least the imprudence, of such a statement. How did Henry Kissinger dare to assume the whole credit for what he had achieved as Nixon's envoy? How did he dare to relegate Nixon to the role of spectator? Where was the president of the United States when the little professor entered the village to arrange things in the style of Henry Fonda in a Western film? The crueler newspapers published cartoons showing Kissinger dressed as a cowboy and galloping toward a saloon. Others showed a picture of Kissinger in cowboy hat and spurs, with the caption "Henry, the Lone Ranger." An exasperated Kissinger let himself be questioned by a reporter, to whom he said that receiving me had been "the stupidest thing in his life." Then he declared that I had garbled his answers, distorted his thoughts, embroidered on his words, and he did so in such a clumsy way that I became angrier than Nixon and took the offensive. I sent him a telegram to Paris, at the American embassy, where he happened to be at the moment, and in substance I asked him if he were a man of honor or a clown. I even threatened to make public the tapes of the interview. Mr. Kissinger should not forget that it had been recorded on tape and that this tape was at the disposal of everyone to refresh his memory and the exactness of his words. I made the same declaration to *Time* magazine, *Newsweek*, the CBS and NBC television networks, and to anyone who came to ask me about what had happened. And the altercation went on for almost two months, to the unhappiness of both of us, especially me. I could no longer stand Henry Kissinger; his name was enough to upset me. I detested him to such a point that I wasn't even able to realize that the poor man had had no other choice but to throw the blame on me. But certainly it would be incorrect to say that at that time I wished him all success and happiness.

The truth is that my anathemas have no effect. Very soon Nixon stopped looking askance at his Henry and the two of them went back to cooing like a pair of doves. Their cease-fire was accomplished. The American prisoners returned home. Those prisoners who were such a pressing issue for Mr. Nixon. And the reality of Vietnam became a period of waiting for the next war. Then, a year later, Kissinger became secretary of state in place of William Rogers. In Stockholm they even gave him the Nobel Peace Prize. Poor Nobel. Poor peace.

ORIANA FALLACI: I'm wondering what you feel these days, Dr. Kissinger. I'm wondering if you too are disappointed, like ourselves, like most of the world. Are you disappointed, Mr. Kissinger?

HENRY KISSINGER: Disappointed? Why? What has happened these days about which I should be disappointed?

O.F.: Something not exactly happy, Dr. Kissinger. Though you had said that peace was "at hand," and though you had confirmed that an agreement had been reached with the North Vietnamese, peace has not come. The war goes on as before, and worse than before.

H.K.: There will be peace. We have decided to have it and we will. It will come within a few weeks' time or even less; that is, immediately after the resumption of negotiations with the North Vietnamese for the final accord. This is what I said ten days ago and I repeat it. Yes, we will have peace within a reasonably short period of time if Hanoi agrees to another meeting before signing the accord, a meeting to settle the details, and if it accepts this in the same spirit and with the same attitude that it held in October. These "ifs" are the only uncertainty these days. But it is an uncertainty that I don't even want to consider. You're letting yourself succumb to panic, and in these matters there is no need to succumb to panic. Nor even to impatience. The fact is that . . . Well, for months we have been conducting these negotiations and you reporters haven't believed us. You've kept saying that they would come to nothing. Then, all of a sudden, you shouted about peace being already here, and now finally you say the negotiations have failed. In saying this, you take our temperature every day, four times a day. But you take it from Hanoi's point of view. And

. . . mind you, I understand Hanoi's point of view. The North Vietnamese wanted us to sign on October 31, which was reasonable and unreasonable at the same time and . . . No, I don't intend to argue about this.

O.F.: But you had committed yourselves to sign on October 31!

H.K.: I say and repeat that they were the ones to insist on this date, and that to avoid an abstract discussion about dates that at the time seemed entirely theoretical, we said that we would make every effort to conclude the negotiations by October 31. But it was always clear, at least to us, that we would not be able to sign an agreement whose details still remained to be clarified. We would not have been able to observe a date simply because, in good faith, we had promised to make every effort to observe it. So at what point are we? At the point where those details remain to be clarified and where a new meeting is indispensable. They say it's not indispensable, that it's not necessary. I say that it is indispensable and that it will take place. It will take place as soon as the North Vietnamese call me to Paris. But this is only November 4, today is November 4, and I can understand that the North Vietnamese don't want to resume negotiations just a few days after the date on which they had asked us to sign. I can understand their postponing things. But I, at least, cannot conceive their rejecting another meeting. Just now when we have covered ninety percent of the ground and are about to reach our goal. No, I'm not disappointed. I will be, certainly, if Hanoi should break the agreement, if Hanoi should refuse to discuss any changes. But I can't believe that, no. I can't even suspect that we've come so far only to fail on a question of prestige, of procedure, of dates, of nuances.

O.F.: And yet it looks as though they've really become rigid, Dr. Kissinger. They've gone back to a hard line, they've made serious, almost insulting, accusations against you. . . .

H.K.: Oh, that means nothing. It's happened before and we never gave it any importance. I would say that the hard line, the serious accusations, even the insults, are part of the normal situation. Nothing has changed essentially. Since Tuesday, October 31, that is ever since we've calmed down here, you reporters keep asking us if the patient is sick. But I don't see any sickness. And I really maintain that things are going to develop more or less as I say. Peace, I repeat, will come within a few weeks after the resumption of negotiations. Not within a few months. Within a few weeks.

o.f.: But when will the negotiations be resumed? That's the point.

h.k.: As soon as Le Duc Tho wishes to see me again. I'm here waiting. But without feeling anxious, I assure you. For God's sake! Before, two or three weeks used to go by between one meeting and another! I don't see why now we should be upset if a few days go by. The only reason that you're all so nervous is that people are wondering, "But will they resume these talks?" When you were all cynical and didn't believe that anything was happening, you never realized that time was passing. You were too pessimistic in the beginning, then too optimistic after my press conference, and now again you're too pessimistic. You can't get it into your heads that everything is proceeding as I had always thought it would from the moment I said that peace was at hand. It seems to me I then figured on a couple of weeks. But even if it should take more . . . That's enough, I don't want to talk any more about Vietnam. I can't allow myself to, at this time. Every word I say becomes news. At the end of November perhaps . . . Listen, why don't we meet again at the end of November?

o.f.: Because it's more interesting now, Dr. Kissinger. Because Thieu, for instance, has dared you to speak. Look at this clipping from *The New York Times*. It quotes Thieu as saying: "Ask Kissinger on what points we're divided, what are the points I don't accept."

h.k.: Let me see it. . . . Ah! No, I won't answer him. I won't pay any attention to this invitation.

o.f.: He's already given his own answer, Dr. Kissinger. He's already said that the sore issue is the fact that, according to the terms accepted by you, North Vietnamese troops will remain in South Vietnam. Dr. Kissinger, do you think you'll ever succeed in convincing Thieu? Do you think that America will have to come to a separate agreement with Hanoi?

h.k.: Don't ask me that. I have to keep to what I said publicly ten days ago . . . I cannot, I must not consider an hypothesis that I do not think will happen. An hypothesis that should not happen. I can only tell you that we are determined to have this peace, and that in any case we will have it, in the shortest time possible after my next meeting with Le Duc Tho. Thieu can say what he likes. That's his own business.

O.F.: Dr. Kissinger, if I were to put a pistol to your head and ask you to choose between having dinner with Thieu and having dinner with Le Duc Tho . . . whom would you choose?

H.K.: I cannot answer that question.

O.F.: And if I were to answer by saying that I'd like to think you'd more willingly have dinner with Le Duc Tho?

H.K.: I cannot, I cannot . . . I do not wish to answer that question.

O.F.: So can you answer this question: did you like Le Duc Tho?

H.K.: Yes. I found him a man very dedicated to his cause, very serious, very strong, and always polite and courteous. Also sometimes very hard, in fact difficult, to deal with, but this is something I've always respected in him. Yes, I have great respect for Le Duc Tho. Naturally our relationship has been very professional, but I think . . . I think I've noticed a certain niceness that shines through him. It's a fact, for instance, that at times we've even succeeded in making jokes. We said that one day I might go to teach international relations at the University of Hanoi and he would come to Harvard to teach Marxism-Leninism. Well, I would call our relations good.

O.F.: Would you say the same thing for Thieu?

H.K.: I have also had good relations with Thieu. At first . . .

O.F.: Exactly, at first. The South Vietnamese have said that you didn't greet each other like the best of friends.

H.K.: What did they say?

O.F.: That you didn't greet each other like good friends, I repeat. Would you care to state the opposite, Dr. Kissinger?

H.K.: Well . . . Certainly we had and have our own viewpoints. And not necessarily the same viewpoints. So let's say that we greeted each other as allies, Thieu and I.

O.F.: Dr. Kissinger, that Thieu was a harder nut to crack than anyone thought has now been shown. So as regards Thieu, do you feel that you've done everything you could or do you hope to be able to do something more? In short, do you feel optimistic about the problem of Thieu?

H.K.: Of course I feel optimistic! I still have things to do. A lot to do! I'm not through yet, we're not through yet! And I don't feel powerless. I don't feel discouraged. Not at all. I feel ready and confident. Optimistic. If I can't speak of Thieu, if I can't tell you what we're doing at this point in the negotiations, that doesn't mean I'm about to lose faith in being able to arrange things within the time I've said. That's why it's useless for Thieu to ask you reporters to make me spell out the points on which we disagree. It's so useless that I don't even get upset by such a demand. Furthermore I'm not the kind of person to be swayed by emotion. Emotions serve no purpose. Less than anything do they serve to achieve peace.

O.F.: But the dying, those about to die, are in a hurry, Dr. Kissinger. In the newspapers this morning there's an awful picture: a very young Vietcong dead two days after October 31. And then there was an awful piece of news: twenty-two Americans dead in a helicopter downed by a Vietcong mortar, three days after October 31. And while you advise against haste, the American Defense Department is sending fresh arms and ammunition to Thieu. Hanoi is doing the same.

H.K.: That was inevitable. It always happens before a cease-fire. Don't you remember the maneuvers that took place in the Middle East at the moment of the cease-fire? They went on for at least two years. You see, the fact that we're sending more arms to Saigon and that Hanoi is sending more arms to the North Vietnamese stationed in South Vietnam means nothing. Nothing. Nothing. And don't make me talk about Vietnam anymore, please.

O.F.: Don't you even want to talk about the fact that, according to many, the agreement accepted by you and Nixon is practically a sellout to Hanoi?

H.K.: That's absurd! It's absurd to say that President Nixon, a president who in the face of the Soviet Union and Communist China and on the eve of elections in his own country has assumed an attitude of aid and defense for South Vietnam against what he considered a North Vietnamese invasion . . . it's absurd to think that such a president could sell out to Hanoi. And why should he sell out just now? What we have done hasn't been a sellout. It has been to give South Vietnam an opportunity to survive in conditions that, today, are more political than military. Now it's up to the South Vietnamese to win the political contest that's awaiting them. As we've always said. If you compare the accepted agreement with our proposals of May 8, you'll realize that it's almost the same thing. There are no great differences between what we proposed last May and what the draft of the accepted agreement contains. We haven't put in any new clauses, we haven't made other concessions. I absolutely and totally reject the notion of a "sellout." But, really that's enough talk now about Vietnam. Let's talk about Machiavelli, about Cicero, anything but about Vietnam.

O.F.: Let's talk about war, Dr. Kissinger. You're not a pacifist, are you?

H.K.: No, I really don't think I am. Even though I respect genuine pacifists, I don't agree with any pacifist, and especially not with halfway pacifists: you know, those who are pacifists on one side and anything but pacifists on the other. The only pacifists that I agree to talk to are those who accept the consequences of nonviolence right to the end. But even with them I'm only willing to speak to tell them that they will be crushed by the will of the stronger and that their pacifism can only lead to horrible suffering. War is not an abstraction, it is something that depends on conditions. The war against Hitler, for example, was necessary. By that I don't mean that war is necessary in itself, that nations have to make war to maintain their virility. I mean that there are existing principles for which nations must be prepared to fight.

O.F.: And what do you have to say about the war in Vietnam, Dr. Kissinger? You've never been against the war in Vietnam, it seems to me.

H.K.: How could I have been? Not even before holding the position I have today . . . No, I've never been against the war in Vietnam.

O.F.: But don't you find that Schlesinger is right when he says that the war in Vietnam has succeeded only in proving that half a million Americans with all their technology have been incapable of defeating poorly armed men dressed in black pajamas?

H.K.: That's another question. If it is a question whether the war in Vietnam was necessary, a just war, rather than . . . Judgments of that kind depend on the position that one takes when the country is already involved in the war and the only thing left is to conceive a way to get out of it. After all, my role, our role, has been to reduce more and more the degree to which America was involved in the war, so as then to end the war. In the final analysis, history will say who did more: those who operated by criticizing and nothing else, or we who tried to reduce the war and then ended it. Yes, the verdict is up to history. When a country is involved in a war, it's not enough to say it must be ended. It must be ended in accordance with some principle. And this is quite different from saying that it was right to enter that war.

O.F.: But don't you find, Dr. Kissinger, that it's been a useless war?

H.K.: On this I can agree. But let's not forget that the reason why we entered this war was to keep the South from being gobbled up by the North, it was to permit the South to remain the South. Of course, by that I don't mean that this was our only objective. . . . It was also something more . . . But today I'm not in the position to judge whether the war in Vietnam has been just or not, whether our getting into it was useful or useless. But are we still talking about Vietnam?

O.F.: Yes. And, still speaking of Vietnam, do you think you can say that these negotiations have been and are the most important undertaking of your career and even of your life?

H.K.: They've been the most difficult undertaking. Also often the most painful. But maybe it's not even right to call them the most difficult undertaking. It's more exact to say that they have been the most painful undertaking. Because they have involved me emotionally. You see, to approach China was an intellectually difficult task but not emotionally difficult. Peace in Vietnam instead has been an emotionally difficult task. As for calling these negotiations the most important thing I have done . . . No, what I wanted to achieve was not only peace in Vietnam, it was three things. This agreement, the *rapprochement* with China, and a new relationship with the Soviet Union. I've always attached great importance to the problem of a new relationship with the Soviet Union. I would say no less than to the *rapprochement* with China and to ending the war in Vietnam.

O.F.: And you've done it. The coup with China has been a success, the coup with Russia has been a success, and the coup of peace in Vietnam almost. So at this point I ask you, Dr. Kissinger, the same thing I asked the astronauts when they went to the moon: "What next? What will you do after the moon; what else can you do besides your job as an astronaut?"

H.K.: Ah! And what did the astronauts say?

O.F.: They were confused and said, "We'll see . . . I don't know."

H.K.: Neither do I. I really don't know what I'll do afterward. But, unlike the astronauts, I'm not confused by it. I have found so many things to do in my life and I am sure that when I leave this post . . . Of course, I'll need some time to recuperate, a period of decompression. No one who is in the position I am can just leave it and start something else right away. But, as soon as I've been decompressed, I'm sure to find something that's worth doing. I don't want to think about it now, it could influence my . . . my work. We're going through such a revolutionary period that to plan one's own life, nowadays, is an attitude worthy of the nineteenth-century lower middle class.

O.F.: Would you go back to teaching at Harvard?

H.K.: I might. But it's very, very unlikely. There are more interesting things, and if, with all the experience I've had, I didn't find some way of keeping up an interesting life . . . it will really be my own fault. Furthermore, I've by no means decided to give up this job. I like it very much, you know.

O.F.: Of course. Power is always alluring. Dr. Kissinger, to what degree does power fascinate you? Try to be frank.

H.K.: I will. You see, when you have power in your hands and have held it for a long period of time, you end up thinking of it as something that's due you. I'm sure that when I leave this post, I'll feel the lack of power. Still power as an instrument in its own right has no appeal for me. I don't wake up every morning saying, my God, isn't it extraordinary that I can have an airplane at my disposal, that a car with a chauffeur is waiting for me at the door? Who would ever have said it was possible? No, such thoughts don't interest me. And if I should happen to have them, they certainly don't become a determining factor. What interests me is what you can do with power. Believe me, you can do wonderful things. . . . Anyway it wasn't a desire for power that drove me to take this job. If you look at my political past, you'll see that President Nixon couldn't have figured in my plans. I've been against him in a good three elections.

O.F.: I know. You once even stated that Nixon "wasn't fit to be president." Has this ever made you feel embarrassed with Nixon, Dr. Kissinger?

H.K.: I don't remember the exact words I may have said against Richard Nixon. But I suppose I must have said something more or less like that since people go on repeating the phrase in quotation marks. Anyway if I did say it, that's the proof that Nixon wasn't included in my plans for gaining a high government position. And as for feeling embarrassed with him . . . I didn't know him at that time. I had toward him the usual attitude of intellectuals, do you see what I mean? But I was wrong. President Nixon has shown great strength, great ability. Even by calling on me. I had never approached him when he offered me this job. I was astonished by it. After all he knew I had never shown much friendship or sympathy for him. Oh, yes, he showed great courage in calling me.

O.F.: He didn't lose anything by it, Dr. Kissinger. Except for the accusation that's made against you today, that you're Nixon's mental wet nurse.

H.K.: That's a totally senseless accusation. Let's not forget that before he knew me, President Nixon had been very active in foreign policy. It had always been his consuming interest. Even before he was elected, it was obvious that foreign policy was a very important matter for him. He has very clear ideas on the subject. He's a strong man. Furthermore, you don't become president of the United States, you don't get nominated twice as a presidential candidate, you don't survive so long in politics, if you're a weak man. You can think what you like of President Nixon, but one thing is certain: you don't twice become president by being someone else's tool. Such interpretations are romantic and unfair.

O.F.: Are you very fond of him, Dr. Kissinger?

H.K.: I have great respect for him.

O.F.: Dr. Kissinger, people say that you care nothing about Nixon. They say that all you care about is this job and nothing else. They say you would have done it under any president.

H.K.: Instead I'm not at all sure that I would have been able to do with another president what I've done with him. Such a special relationship, I mean the relationship there is between me and the president, always depends on the style of the two men. In other words, I don't know many leaders, and I've met several, who would have had the courage to send their aide to Peking without saying anything to anybody. I don't know many leaders who would leave to their aide the task of negotiating with the North Vietnamese, while informing only a tiny group of people about it. Certain things really depend on the type of president; what I've done has been possible because he made it possible for me.

O.F.: And yet you were also an adviser to other presidents. Even presidents who were Nixon's opponents. I'm speaking of Kennedy, Johnson . . .

H.K.: My position toward all presidents has always been to leave to them the job of deciding if they wanted to know my opinion or not. When they asked me for it, I gave it to them, telling them, indiscriminately, what I thought. It never mattered to me what party they belonged to. I answered questions from Kennedy, Johnson, and Nixon with the same independence. I gave them the same advice. It's true that it was more difficult with Kennedy. In fact people like to say that I didn't get along with him. Well . . . yes, it was mostly my fault. At that time I was much less mature than now. And then I was a part-time adviser; you can't influence the day-by-day policy of a president if you see him only twice a week when others see him seven days a week. I mean . . . with Kennedy and Johnson I was never in a position comparable to the one I have now with Nixon.

O.F.: No Machiavellianism, Dr. Kissinger?

H.K.: No, none. Why?

O.F.: Because at certain moments, listening to you, one might wonder not how much you have influenced the president of the United States, but how much Machiavelli has influenced you.

H.K.: In no way at all. There is really very little of Machiavelli that can be accepted or used in the modern world. The only thing I find interesting in Machiavelli is his way of considering the will of the prince. Interesting, but not to the point of influencing me. If you want to know who has influenced me the most, I'll answer with the names of two philosophers: Spinoza and Kant. So it's curious that you choose to associate me with Machiavelli. People rather associate me with the name of Metternich. Which is actually childish. On Metternich I've written only one book, which was to be the beginning of a long series of books on the construction and disintegration of the international order of the nineteenth century. It was a series that was to end with the First World War. That's all. There can be nothing in common between me and Metternich. He was chancellor and foreign minister in a period when, from the center of Europe, you needed three weeks to go from one continent to another. He was chancellor and foreign minister in a period when wars were conducted by professional soldiers and diplomacy was in the hands of aristocrats. How can you compare that with today's world, a world where there is no homogenous group of leaders, no homogenous internal situation, no homogenous cultural reality?

O.F.: Dr. Kissinger, how do you explain the incredible movie-star status you enjoy, how do you explain the fact that you're almost more famous and popular than a president? Have you a theory on this matter?

H.K.: Yes, but I won't tell you. Because it doesn't match most people's theories. The theory of intelligence, for example. And then intelligence is not all that important in the exercise of power, and often actually doesn't help. In the same way as a head of state, a fellow who does my job doesn't need to be too intelligent. My theory is completely different, but, I repeat, I won't tell you. Why should I as long as I'm still in the middle of my work? Rather, you tell me yours. I'm sure that you too have a theory about the reasons for my popularity.

O.F.: I'm not sure, Dr. Kissinger. I'm looking for one through this interview. And I don't find it. I suppose that at the root of everything there's your success. I mean, like a chess player, you've made two or three good moves. China, first of all. People like chess players who checkmate the king.

H.K.: Yes, China has been a very important element in the mechanics of my success. And yet that's not the main point. The main point . . . Well, yes, I'll tell you. What do I care? The main point arises from the fact that I've always acted alone. Americans like that immensely. Americans like the cowboy who leads the wagon train by riding ahead alone on his horse, the cowboy who rides all alone into the town, the village, with his horse and nothing else. Maybe even without a pistol, since he doesn't shoot. He acts, that's all, by being in the right place at the right time. In short, a Western.

O.F.: I see. You see yourself as a kind of Henry Fonda, unarmed and ready to fight with his fists for honest ideals. Alone, courageous . . .

H.K.: Not necessarily courageous. In fact, this cowboy doesn't have to be courageous. All he needs is to be alone, to show others that he rides into the town and does everything by himself. This amazing, romantic character suits me precisely because to be alone has always been part of my style or, if you like, my technique. Together with independence. Oh, that's very important in me and for me. And finally, conviction. I've always been convinced that I had to do whatever I've done. And people feel it, and believe in it. And I care about the fact that they believe in me—when you sway or convince somebody, you shouldn't confuse them. Nor can you even simply calculate. Some people think that I carefully plan what are to be the consequences, for the public, of any of my initiatives or efforts. They think this preoccupation is always on my mind. Instead the consequences of what I do, I mean the public's judgment, have never bothered me. I don't ask for popularity, I'm not looking for popularity. On the contrary, if you really want to know, I care nothing about popularity. I'm not at all afraid of losing my public; I can allow myself to say what I think. I'm referring to what's genuine in me. If I were to let myself be disturbed by the reactions of the public, if I were to act solely on the basis of a calculated technique, I would accomplish nothing. Look at actors. The really good ones don't rely only on technique. They perform by following a technique and their own convictions at the same time. Like me, they're genuine. I don't say that all this has to go on forever. In fact, it may evaporate as quickly as it came. Nevertheless for the moment it's there.

O.F.: Are you trying to tell me you're a spontaneous man, Dr. Kissinger? My God, if I leave out Machiavelli, the first character with whom it seems to me natural to associate you would be some cold mathematician, painfully self-controlled. Unless I'm mistaken, you're a very cold man, Dr. Kissinger.

H.K.: In tactics, not in strategy. In fact, I believe more in human relations than in ideas. I use ideas but I need human relations, as I've shown in my work. After all, didn't what happened to me actually happen by chance? Good God, I was a completely unknown professor. How could I have said to myself: Now I'm going to maneuver things so as to become internationally famous? It would have been pure folly. I wanted to be where things were happening, of course, but I never paid a price for getting there. I've never made concessions. I've always let myself be guided by spontaneous decisions. One might then say it happened because it had to happen. That's what they always say when things have happened. They never say that about things that don't happen—the history of things that didn't happen has never been written. In a certain sense, however, I'm a fatalist. I believe in destiny. I'm convinced, of course, that you have to fight to reach a goal. But I also believe that there are limits to the struggle that a man can put up to reach a goal.

O.F.: One more thing, Dr. Kissinger: but how do you reconcile the tremendous responsibilities that you've assumed with the frivolous reputation you enjoy? How can you get Mao Tse-tung, Chou En-lai, or Le Duc Tho to take you seriously and then let yourself be judged as a carefree Don Juan or simply a playboy? Doesn't it embarrass you?

H.K.: Not at all. Why should it embarrass me when I go to negotiate with Le Duc Tho? When I speak to Le Duc Tho, I know what I have to do with Le Duc Tho, and when I'm with girls, I know what I must do with girls. Besides, Le Duc Tho doesn't at all agree to negotiate with me because I represent an example of moral rectitude. He agrees to negotiate with me because he wants certain things from me in the same way that I want certain things from him. Look, in the case of Le Duc Tho, as in the case of Chou En-lai and Mao Tse-tung, I think that my playboy reputation has been and still is useful because it served and still serves to reassure people. To show them that

I'm not a museum piece. Anyway, this frivolous reputation amuses me.

O.F.: And to think I believed it an undeserved reputation, I mean playacting instead of a reality.

H.K.: Well, it's partly exaggerated, of course. But in part, let's face it, it's true. What counts is not to what degree it's true, or to what degree I devote myself to women. What counts is to what degree women are part of my life, a central preoccupation. Well, they aren't that at all. For me women are only a diversion, a hobby. Nobody spends too much time with his hobbies. And that I spend only a limited time with them you can see by taking a look at my schedule. I'll tell you something else: it's not seldom that I'd rather see my two children. I see them often, in fact, though not as much as before. As a rule, we spend Christmas together, the important holidays, and several weeks during the summer, and I go to Boston once a month. Just to see them. You surely know that I've been divorced for some years. No, the fact of being divorced doesn't bother me. The fact of not living with my children doesn't give me any guilt complexes. Ever since my marriage was over, and it was not the fault of either of us that it ended, there was no reason not to get divorced. Furthermore, I'm much closer to my children now than when I was their mother's husband. I'm also much happier with them now.

O.F.: Are you against marriage, Dr. Kissinger?

H.K.: No. The dilemma of marriage or no marriage is one that can be resolved as a question of principle. It could happen that I'll get married again . . . yes, that could happen. But, you know, when you're a serious person, as, after all, I am, to live with someone else and survive that living together is very difficult. The relationship between a woman and a fellow like me is inevitably so complex. . . . One has to be careful. Oh, it's difficult for me to explain these things. I'm not a person who confides in reporters.

O.F.: So I see, Dr. Kissinger. I've never interviewed anyone who evaded questions and precise definitions like you, anyone who defended himself like you from any attempt by others to penetrate to his personality. Are you shy, Dr. Kissinger?

H.K.: Yes. Fairly so. But as compensation I think I'm pretty well

balanced. You see, there are those who depict me as a mysterious, tormented character, and those who depict me as an almost cheerful fellow who's always smiling, always laughing.
Both these images are incorrect. I'm neither one nor the
other. I'm . . . I won't tell you what I am. I'll never tell anyone.

Washington, November 1972

2

Nguyen Van Thieu

———◆·◆———

The appointment with Nguyen Van Thieu was for eight in the morning in the presidential palace in Saigon, where the president invited me to have breakfast with him. And at eight on the dot Nguyen Van Thieu entered the room where I, along with his special adviser Hoang Duc Nha and the photographer Gianfranco Moroldo, was waiting for him. A great smile on his round and shining face, an unexpected cordiality in his voice and eyes, Thieu came forward extending me his open hand and immediately began with a joke. "Which of you two is the chief?" he asked, indicating with his short index finger Moroldo and me. "Both," replied Moroldo. "Not at all," I joked back. "I'm the chief, even if he's tall and I'm short." And, perhaps because the dictator is so short, even shorter than I, he liked the answer. In fact, he exploded in a laugh full of approbation and exclaimed, "Right. I absolutely agree. Power should not be divided. There should be only one, that's all." Precisely the concept he was to repeat at the end of the interview, when, all excited, he was to say, "Ask me who's the chief here." And I, "Who's the chief here?" And he, "I am! I'm the chief! *Moi! C'est moi le chef!*" He had been described to me as a very closed man, and I was therefore dumbfounded. I actually wondered if what had made him so cheerful and extroverted might not be the bombings of Hanoi, which had been going on implacably for days. He had not yet received the news that the Americans had again suspended them and that Kissinger would again meet with Le Duc Tho.

Thieu was wearing a gray suit with a light shirt. Two days before, he had sent me a message asking whether I preferred him in full uniform or in civilian clothes, and I had answered, "I always prefer civilian clothes." But as with many military men, civilian clothes do not suit him, and this produced a certain clumsiness in him that communicated itself in all his gestures. His effort to make me feel welcome, for example, or so that I would judge him a perfect host. Goodness, wasn't it too early an hour for me? Had I already had coffee? Would I like his little breakfast? Please, follow me to this other room. Please sit here. He sat down at the head of the table, his napkin tucked into the collar of his shirt, and when Moroldo made the gesture of taking the first photograph, Nha began a little dance of winks and black looks by which he begged him to remove the napkin from the collar of his shirt, for God's sake. He didn't understand. And with his imploring gaze, he seemed to reply, "But what are you saying? What do you want?" Then in the end he understood. And took it off. Confused, blushing. But his sulky face seemed to comment, "But why? What's wrong with it? Now I'll get spots on my suit and my wife will get angry." Nha was seated to his left, watching out for any error. I, to his right. The table was carefully set, the breakfast excessive. Fish soup, vegetables, meat rolls, sweets, tea, coffee, solicitude: "Eat, eat. It's good, you know? It's good when it's hot. Come on, aren't you hungry?"

The conversation flourished as soon as I asked the first question: "But do you always wake up so early, Mr. President?" He was waiting impatiently for me to say something. His answer burst out. "Oh, yes! Almost always." Just think, at six-thirty, to hear the news on the radio. But he stayed in bed until seven-thirty—to reflect a little. And at eight he was ready to meet with generals, ministers, and smoke his cigar. "Just one, eh?" "That's enough for the whole day. For two years I've been doing it, two and a half, I mean ever since I gave up smoking a pipe. In fact, it's not a good thing at all for a president to smoke a pipe, do you think? A cigar is better for a president, right?" Whoever told him that a president smokes cigars, not a pipe, God only knows. In any case, it could only have been an American, and this prattle immediately made you feel a little sorry for him. "Of course, Mr. President. That's true."

In the evening, he went on, he went to bed very late. Until two in the morning he never slept. Falling asleep, he left the radio on, and so the radio stayed on even while he slept. He was so used to sleeping with the radio on, even to distinguishing music from words in his sleep, that when the music stopped and the news began, he immediately opened his eyes and listened with a clear mind. By that I shouldn't think, however, that he didn't know how to enjoy life. Sometimes he played tennis, went horseback riding, and three or four times a week he had them show a film for him. Love stories, Westerns, judo, and karate. The only thing he didn't have time to do was read. Takes too much attention, doesn't it? "Of course, Mr. President. I understand."

Eating with appetite, even voracity, he told me stories of his youth, of his military career, of his participation in the *coup d'état* against Diem, and the name of Diem evoked in him an unexpected sadness. "They promised me not to kill him. I had said to them, 'All right, I'll join you on condition that he's not killed.' Instead they killed him, those idiots. Irresponsible madmen. It gave me a pain that I still have, here between my head and my heart. Each anniversary of his death I have a Mass said, here in my chapel. And I always pray for him, for his soul."

He seemed to be sincere. Nothing in him betrayed the diabolical shrewdness thanks to which he was to remain a tyrant protected by an army of a million men and by a police corps that carried out massacres. Little by little, you were even surprised to find yourself wondering if he was really as perfidious as they said. And you thought: maybe he doesn't have that contented look because the bombs are falling on Hanoi; so much joviality is a comedy whose aim is to disguise his shyness as a former peasant. Maybe he didn't start off with that business about power not being divisible, his *le chef c'est moi*, because he is overbearing, but simply because he's afraid of not being taken seriously. And strange, perhaps paradoxical, even naïve as it sounds: even knowing that he was a dark dictator, even knowing that the prisons of South Vietnam were full of Vietcong, even hating him and having always hated everything he represents, stolen and undeserved power, ignorance, corruption, obedience to the strongest, abuse, in spite of yourself and with anger you ended by feeling a human sympathy for him.

He seemed so small, so lost, so alone. He seemed the very sym-

bol of a crushed, exploited country, humiliated by the interests of
those who make and unmake the destiny of others like a toy: the
global strategies of Dr. Kissinger. His minuet with China and Russia. The cynicism of those who tell you one day, "You must make
war on the communists! The communists are bad! You must kill
them!" And the next day tell you, "Why are you making war on
the communists? The communists are not bad. There's no need to
kill them, don't you understand? Sign here and have a cigar. Don't
smoke a pipe. American presidents have always smoked cigars." He
had rebelled through having realized that he had lost his friends and
perhaps had never had friends, only masters. And now he was looking for friends. Even for an hour, for a morning, with a foreign
newspaperwoman whom he had never seen and whom he knew
was no friend of his. "Oh, Mademoiselle! Sometimes I feel as
though there's nothing left to do except pray to God, Mademoiselle!"

When breakfast was over—with all the discomfort that a European can feel eating fish soup at eight in the morning—he asked
me courteously if I would care to continue the interview in his office. Perhaps Mr. Moroldo would prefer another background for his
photographs. So we went into his office and there we stayed until
half-past twelve. We spoke almost always in French, the language
in which he studied. Only when he wanted to clarify an idea, in
his desperate need to explain himself and to be understood at least
by someone, he repeated the sentence in English. But his English
is not good and so he asked Nha to come to his aid. Sometimes
he had tears in his eyes. Sometimes his voice broke in a sob that
was immediately choked back. And he trembled with rage, with
pain, with passion. And also with dignity. "*Messieurs les Américains*, I told them. I have nothing to be sold to Russia and China!
For me it is a question of life and death! To be or not to be!" In
short, there was a certain dignity in him and in his tragedy. Had we
understood him well? That, at least at that particular moment, he
was no longer the ridiculous puppet of the Americans that we had
believed him to be? And, since it is always good to redeem a man,
any man, even a bad man, I was now glad to offer him some compassion and a certain respect.

Was I wrong? I'm afraid so, today. In fact, almost every time that
I have tried to give compassion and respect to a government leader,

almost every time that I have tried to absolve even partially some famous son of a bitch, I have later been bitterly sorry. Despite all his chatter, Thieu soon signed what Kissinger wanted. And, once having signed, he kept his prisons full, refused to call the elections he had promised, and never opened negotiations with the Vietcong. So the war went on and now he has finally lost it, as he deserved to.

ORIANA FALLACI: Mr. President, it is no longer a secret that between you and the Americans today there exists more emnity than friendship. The harshness with which in October you rejected the agreement accepted by Kissinger, the coldness with which you received General Haig at Christmas, everything shows that you are now at swords' points. And people are wondering what Thieu thinks of this drama.

NGUYEN VAN THIEU: Mademoiselle, I am not the mysterious type that many believe. On the contrary, I'm a very open man. I never hide anything, even in politics, and I don't listen to those who advise me not to say what I think or to say the opposite. In fact, I always answer, "Instead one should say it. Loud and clear." But when we come to a subject like this, I have to remember that I represent South Vietnam. As President Thieu, I cannot allow myself the luxury of being an open enemy of the United States, which for better or worse is still my friend, my ally. Besides I promised Nixon that, even if conflicts should arise, we would still be allies and not consider ourselves enemies. Mademoiselle, can't there perhaps be quarrels between husbands and wives? And do they become enemies for that? Not only that, quarrels between a husband and wife should take place in the bedroom and after the door has been locked. Children should never see their parents in a hair-pulling match. It's the same for friends. And it's in my interest, in the interest of the United States, to avoid any public row that serves the communists.

O.F.: I understand. But when I interviewed Dr. Kissinger, I had the impression that there was no love lost between you two and I'm a little surprised at your caution, Mr. President.

N.V.T.: Vous savez, Mademoiselle, one must know how to forget. Yes, forget. When you're running a country, you can't afford to nourish rancor. My discussions with Dr. Kissinger have been very frank. At times, actually harsh. I'd go so far as to say very harsh. Nevertheless, basically they remained discussions between friends and—well, I must treat him as a friend. After his departure, all the journalists in Saigon asked me, "How goes the disagreement?" And I answered, "When you talk about disagreement, you must talk about agreement. Between the two of us there are agreements and disagreements." Mademoiselle, I have said "no" to the Americans. What more do you want? When I say no, I mean no. But the moment hasn't come to announce to the world that everything is over. There is still hope for peace. I still have faith that peace will come. It may come even in a few weeks, in a month. It's no time to give up in desperation.

O.F.: Then it's true that your "no" is a "no" à la vietnamienne. That is, a no that could mean yes.

N.V.T.: Not at all. I repeat, when I say no, I mean no. And when I say, "I don't agree with you at all, Messieurs les Américains, though I remain your friend," I mean that and nothing else. I have always maintained that Dr. Kissinger, as Nixon's representative and negotiator, has the sacred duty of consulting me and reconciling my point of view with the American point of view. I have always expected the government of the United States to uphold my views and to help me convince the communists to modify their demands. And, so as not to be vague about it, I will tell you that there are two fundamental points accepted by Kissinger and rejected by me. One is the presence of North Vietnamese troops in South Vietnam. The other is the political formula that the North Vietnamese would like to impose on our future. Like the whole agreement, these two points have been conceived by the communists in Paris. So I explained to Dr. Kissinger that to accept them would mean to bow to the demands of the North Vietnamese. What the North Vietnamese demand is the loss of South Vietnam, the end of South Vietnam. Voilà.

O.F.: Couldn't you explain yourself better, Mr. President?

N.V.T.: Mais vous savez, Madenoiselle, c'est très simple! The Americans say that in South Vietnam there are 145,000 North Vietnamese, I say there are 300,000, and anyway there's no need to quibble. Whether the exact figure is theirs or mine (but it's mine), to tolerate the presence of 300,000 North Vietnamese, sanctioned by a juridical agreement, ratified by an international conference and therefore by the whole world, is absolutely unacceptable. Because it's like recognizing their right to call themselves liberators, their right to maintain that Vietnam is one country from Hanoi to Saigon, but belonging to Hanoi and not to Saigon. Do I make myself clear, Mademoiselle? I maintain that to accept an army of 300,000 soldiers in a country means to recognize the sovereignty of such an army over that country. It means to consider the North Vietnamese as liberators instead of aggressors. And consequently it means to consider the South Vietnamese army as a mercenary army of the Americans. In short, turning everything upside down. And this is what I said to Kissinger: "But, Dr. Kissinger, don't you understand that by doing this you place the legal government of South Vietnam in the position of a puppet government installed by the Americans?"

O.F.: But after the armistice, the North Vietnamese would withdraw from South Vietnam, wouldn't they?

N.V.T.: *Eh bien*, the agreement doesn't say so at all. No, it doesn't say so. That's why I say to the North Vietnamese: "Let's be honest. If you don't have something at the back of your minds, if you really don't intend to renew your aggression against South Vietnam, why do you insist so much on this business of leaving an army here? After all! You demand that the American troops withdraw within sixty days, you demand that I kick out our allies, and then you want me to keep the aggressor here. *Mais c'est fou!* It's senseless, crazy!"

O.F.: Mr. President, let's be realistic. What is there to fear with an army of a million soldiers at your command?

N.V.T.: *Voilà la question.* Everybody asks me the same thing. "Mr. President, if you are so strong from the military and political standpoint, what are you worried about?" I'll tell you what I'm worried about. It's not at all difficult for a North Vietnamese to learn the accent of the South and pass himself off as a South Vietnamese. They too are Vietnamese. Among us they're not at all recognizable like the Americans. Haven't they already played that little trick in Laos with the Pathet

Lao? In 1962, when the Americans withdrew from Laos, the North Vietnamese were also supposed to withdraw. But do you know that happened? The Americans went to the airport, and one by one, from the first general to the last soldier, they recorded their departure. We even knew the number: forty-eight persons. Instead the North Vietnamese stayed in the jungle speaking as Pathet Lao, disguised as Pathet Lao, and no control commission was ever able to find out how many there were. Mademoiselle, that's their system. Exactly the same thing would happen here. Isn't it happening already? They learn the accent of the South, they spread through the villages, they infiltrate Vietcong units and so become 300,000 activists ready to come together again as an army. *Messieurs les Américains,* I say, does that sound acceptable to you? And then how come you've changed your minds?

O.F.: Changed their minds about what?

N.V.T.: Mademoiselle, I'll give you an example. When a thief breaks into your house, there are two things you can do: either call the police or get rid of him yourself. But if you call the police, and the police come, and instead of arresting the thief say to you: "Come on, make peace with this thief, you must accept the fact that he's already in your house, cheer up, sign this paper to legalize his presence in your house . . . ," then I get mad. And I answer, "Eh, Mr. Policeman, have we gone crazy? First you tell me that we must arrest thieves, that we must call the police, that we must defend ourselves, and now you tell me that I must accept the thief in writing? How come? First you were so afraid of the thief, and now you aren't any more? Now you actually authorize him to steal my things? *Monsieur le policier! Mais alors!*"

O.F.: It really drives you out of your mind, doesn't it, Mr. President?

N.V.T.: *Bien sûr!* Because, Mademoiselle, what kind of peace is a peace that gives the North Vietnamese the right to keep their troops here? What kind of treaty is a treaty that legalizes their presence here *de facto?* I proposed another solution, even though it was to my disadvantage. I said, "Let the North Vietnamese troops withdraw simultaneously with the American troops, then I promise to demobilize the same number of soldiers. If the North Vietnamese, for example, withdraw 145,000 soldiers, I demobilize 145,000 soldiers. If they withdraw 300,000, I demobilize 300,000." They didn't accept. Why? I know why. They need all their troops so as to have a fine bloodbath.

O.F.: Mr. President, do you think that the ceasefire will bring about a bloodbath?

N.V.T.: *Oui bien sûr!* It's inevitable. There's no need to take seriously what Pham Van Dong says in interviews and in his propaganda. He keeps saying that the North Vietnamese don't want a communist government in South Vietnam, they don't want a bloodbath in South Vietnam, they don't want to take over South Vietnam, but he only keeps saying it to quiet the Americans who are afraid of a bloodbath. Are we perhaps supposed to forget the massacres around Quang Tri, at An Loc, on Highway One, which is now called Horror Road? Are we supposed to forget what they did in 1968 in Hue, during the Tet offensive? And what did they do in Hanoi after they took power? I talked about this with Kissinger too. I told him: "Dr. Kissinger, so should we have fought for eighteen years, should we have sacrificed hundreds of thousands of human lives in order to have a million heads cut off after the cease-fire? I too want to go down in history as a man who brought peace. I too! If I sign what you want, within six months there'll be a bloodbath. And I care nothing for the applause of the moment, the people who cry, 'Bravo, bravo, bravo! *Vive la paix!*' I care about what happens afterward."

O.F.: So, in your opinion, Nixon and Kissinger made a mistake. Mr. President, how do you explain the fact that they made a mistake?

N.V.T.: It's simple; they were too impatient to make peace, too impatient to negotiate and sign. When you deal with the communists, you mustn't set a deadline. You mustn't tell them that you want to repatriate prisoners as soon as possible and conclude peace as soon as possible—otherwise they take advantage of you. It's dangerous to tell them candidly, "The prisoners must be home by Christmas. Peace must be reached before the end of the presidential mandate, before the new elections, before the New Year . . ." It's a huge mistake because they know the Western mentality, Western democracy, and so they blackmail you. They know very well that if the president of the United States sets a deadline, the whole Congress will be after him to make him keep his promise. And what are they able to show? That President Nixon is incapable of bringing peace by the date that he himself set. He himself! And they exploit the opposition, discredit the government, and . . . I told the Americans, "Be patient, one must be patient with the communists, more patient than they." No use.

O.F.: In other words, Mr. President, you expected just what has happened.

N.V.T.: Mademoiselle! North or South, we are all Vietnamese, and I know the Vietnamese a little better than the Americans. In 1968, when the peace talks opened in Paris, many people asked me, "Mr. Thieu, when do you think the talks will end?" And I answered, "*Vous savez* . . . If the communists agree to negotiate, it means that they need to negotiate. Not that they want peace. What they want is a bombing halt in order to catch their breath and launch another offensive. By taking advantage of this pause, they'll try to inflict another Dien Bien Phu on us." More or less what they did during the Geneva Conference of 1954. In Geneva they did nothing but waste time and they played the same game that they've been playing for four years in Paris. But when they won at Dien Bien Phu, they were quick to come to an agreement. If it hadn't been for Dien Bien Phu, the Geneva Conference would still be going on.

O.F.: Mr. President, allow me to think that this talk about patience wasn't the only thing you said to Kissinger. What else did you tell him?

N.V.T.: *Voilà*. You are a giant, I told him. You don't care about anything because you have nothing to be afraid of. You weigh two hundred pounds, and if you swallow the wrong pill you don't even notice it. Your organism neutralizes it. But I'm just a little man, maybe even a little sick. I weigh hardly a hundred pounds, and if I swallow the same pill I can die of it. You are a great boxer. You walk through the streets with your broad shoulders, your big muscles, and if someone punches you in the stomach, you don't even notice it. At the most, you turn around and look at him with a contemptuous smile. Instead I'm a little boxer, and maybe I'm not even a boxer because my physical constitution won't allow me such sport. If someone gives me the same punch, I fall on the ground like a rag. So you can allow yourself the luxury of accepting such an agreement. I can't. To you a bad agreement blows neither hot nor cold. For me it's a question of life and death. *Allons, donc!* What are 300,000 North Vietnamese to you? Nothing. What is the loss of South Vietnam to you? Not even a speck on the map of the world. What's more, the loss of South Vietnam might even be to your convenience. It helps to contain China, it helps your world strategy. But for me, *Messieurs les Américains,* for me it's not a question of choosing between Moscow and Peking. It's a question of choosing between life and death.

O.F.: I'd like to know what he answered!

N.V.T.: Mademoiselle, his strategic idea of the world is very brilliant. A Southeast Asia controlled by the Russians, or an Indochina controlled by the Russians, in order to control and contain China. The Russians are less dangerous than the Chinese, so it's necessary to ask the Russians to contain the Chinese and oppose Indochina to them as a threat on the southern borders of China, et cetera, et cetera, amen. Good, very good! It's like a general who looks at the map and marks the strategic points. But for the poor captain leading his company through rivers and woods, for the poor captain climbing hills under enemy fire and sleeping in trenches, in mud, it isn't so good at all. He doesn't have any global interests on this planet. He doesn't even have anything to give in exchange. He doesn't have the Middle East to exchange for Vietnam, Germany for Japan, Russia for China! He has only the question of life or death for seventeen and a half million inhabitants. And what he risks is to fall under the aegis of Hanoi. Or of Moscow and Peking, which is the same thing.

Voilà le problème, Messieurs les Américains! You look very far, too far; we can't allow ourselves to do that. You're not only a great boxer, a giant, you're also a very powerful businessman and can afford the luxury of saying, "I've spent a dollar but now I must make an exchange, and business is business, money doesn't count, and *allez hop!* I don't mind getting back only ten cents. The ninety I lose . . . who gives a damn? Ninety cents are nothing!" For me it's not like that. If I buy a cigar and pay a dollar for it, I must resell it for a dollar ten. I need those ten cents to eat. I am a little country, my dear American friends. I don't have your global interests; my only interest is in survival. Ah, these great powers who divide the world among themselves! They have an open market everywhere and what does it matter if this market costs the life of a small country?

O.F.: In other words, Mr. President, you think that Kissinger was about to sell Vietnam in the name of his world strategy.

N.V.T.: *Eh bien,* I don't know if that was exactly his intention. It may even be that he believed, in good faith, that it was a good agreement. Anyway I told him: "Doctor . . . to be or not to be. That is the question for us!"

O.F.: And so you won. At least for the moment. Your "no" prevented the agreement. At least for the moment. But for how long? Where does it put you, Mr. President, if the Americans sign without you? Kissinger said it clearly in his last press conference: "With respect to Saigon, if we reach an agreement that the president considers just, we will go ahead."

N.V.T.: *Allons donc!* To sign what? If they wanted to sign by themselves, they would have already signed. They certainly wouldn't have waited until today! The fact that they haven't signed by the date set by themselves, with or without the consent of South Vietnam, allows me to think that President Nixon has thought it over and understood that such a signing would have meant abandoning South Vietnam.

But I want to answer you in a more direct way, Mademoiselle, because you are not the first person to ask me: "If the United States abandons you, what do you do?" Here's my answer: "I suppose we'll fight until the last cartridge and that then the communists will conquer us." It's certain. There can be no doubt. The French abandoned us in 1954, and as a result, half of Vietnam fell into communist hands. If the United States repeats what the French did, the other half of Vietnam will end up the same way. Because once the Americans have gone away with a signed agreement, the Russians and Chinese won't leave us in peace. And where is there another power that could help us like the United States has helped us? Maybe we'll find other countries ready to give us a hand, but none of them would have the means of the United States. No, no, if America abandons us, for us it's the end. The complete, absolute end, and there's no use discussing it any more. Remember Tibet? No one intervened in Tibet, not even the United Nations, and now Tibet is communist. When a country cannot resist an invasion, there is nothing it can do but let itself be invaded.

O.F.: Mr. President, doesn't it seem to you that you've counted too much on the Americans?

N.V.T.: I still can't make such a judgment, Mademoiselle! The moment still hasn't come for me to say, "I've been abandoned." I have to go on explaining myself to the Americans, who look too far ahead, if you see what I mean. Maybe I've counted on them too much, it's true. But in my place you would have done the same. A small country like mine, to keep its independence, needs everything—from military aid to economic. Oh, sure I counted a lot on the Americans, sure! I still count on them, despite everything! If you don't trust your friends, then who should you trust? A friend is like a wife. Until the day she abandons you or you abandon her, until the day you get a divorce, there has to be trust, doesn't there?

O.F.: Well, a little trust must have come back to you when the Americans resumed the bombing of Hanoi. Here in Saigon we said: "Thieu must have toasted the news with champagne!"

N.V.T.: Let's get one thing straight. Nobody loves war. I certainly don't love war. Having to make war gives me no joy. So the bombing of Hanoi doesn't make me drink champagne, just as the rockets falling on Saigon don't make me drink champagne. But frankly, and since this war exists, we have to do it. And on the day when these bombings are again suspended, I'll ask Mr. Nixon: "Why? What do you hope to achieve that way? What do you think you've achieved?" No, I won't be the one to pray for the bombings to end. They have a purpose, and if we want to achieve that purpose, we have to bomb. Mademoiselle, speaking as a soldier, I tell you that the shorter the war the less atrocious it is.

o.f.: That's what advocates of the atomic bomb say, Mr. President.

n.v.t.: I'm not an advocate of the atomic bomb. I'm not talking about the atomic bomb. I'm talking about . . . Have you ever heard of gradualism? Well, in my opinion, gradualism is no way to cure an illness. Especially when the illness has been going on a long time, it should be cured in a hurry, with drastic medicine. Mademoiselle, war is an illness. Nobody likes it, but when it gets a grip on you, it has to be cleared up quickly. Without gradualism. The gradualism of President Johnson was untenable. He never realized this simple truth: either you fight a war or you don't. And the gradualism pursued by the Americans after Johnson has been the same. The Americans have been bombing for years, not bombing, bombing again, reducing, escalating, above the twentieth parallel, below the twentieth parallel . . . But what is all this? War? That's not war, it's half a war. *C'est une demi-guerre.* So far we have fought half a war, *une demi-guerre.* And I tell you that had we attacked North Vietnam with a classical war, had we continually bombed North Vietnam, had we landed troops in North Vietnam, the war would be over today. And let me add that if peace negotiations fail, there is only one way to end this war: to carry the war to North Vietnam. In every sense, including landing troops.

o.f.: Do you mean to say that landing troops is still under consideration?

n.v.t.: Why not, if the Americans are ready to do it? If the Americans can't do it, nobody can! But let me explain better. When I was defense minister and the Americans began bombing in June 1965, one of them asked me, "*Monsieur le Ministre,* do you think these bombings will end the war in three months?" And I answered, "It depends on you Americans." Then I repeated the example of the boxer. "You are a big boxer and North Vietnam is a little boxer. If you want to, you can knock him down in the first round. If you don't want to and you prolong the match until the ninth round, the public may get discouraged and demand its money back. But even worse: if while prolonging the match you get a cramp, that little opponent might even beat you. *Allons, donc! Soyez de grands boxeurs!* Knock him down in the first round. You'll never get anywhere by bombing gradually. On the contrary, you'll furnish Giap with an argument to maintain that a small country like North Vietnam can resist American might. They are putting you to the test, *Messieurs les Américains!* Don't go through the motions of bombing, don't fight a psychological war, fight a war!"

Mademoiselle, all of us have been through American bombardments. I've been through them myself, in 1942, when the Japanese were here. And I remind you that it's not so difficult to endure bombing—after a while you get in the habit, especially if you have good shelters. Thus, after the first bombings, the North Vietnamese were completely discouraged. And the morale of the population was low, and in Hanoi they were expecting a landing. But the Americans didn't insist, and . . . The Americans kill for five minutes, then they give four minutes breathing space, then they kill again. . . .

O.F.: Mr. President, allow me to be naïve. Or simply human. Don't you feel uneasy at the thought that those poor wretches on whom the bombs are falling in Hanoi are Vietnamese like yourself?

N.V.T.: Mademoiselle! I know very well that they're Vietnamese like myself. Deep in my heart, I don't enjoy it at all. But I also know that to end a war you have to bomb them, and I know that the end of the war in South Vietnam means the end of the war in North Vietnam. Don't you think that they've had enough of it too? Do you think that they suffer only from the bombings? Can you imagine what it means to sustain the burden of an expeditionary force to the South? They have nothing to eat because of that expeditionary force. And they've had so many dead by now! Together with the Vietcong, from 1964 to today, they have had 1,057,000 dead. Look, I have it here in my secret documents. And then they suffer from something else, the North Vietnamese. They suffer from a regime that isn't suited to their mentality, to their way of life. Communism is no good for the Vietnamese. They are too individualistic, and I assure you that only a few million out of twenty million in the North are communists. I assure you that the great majority of them would rise up if there were a landing.

O.F.: Which seems to me unlikely with all the problems that Nixon has to face with Congress, the Senate, with public opinion that has had enough of this war and demands that he give it up, Mr. President.

N.V.T.: That's another matter. I know Nixon's problems; it's no accident that I was the first to applaud his doctrine. In June 1969, when I made that trip to Taiwan and South Korea, Chiang Kai-shek and Chung Hee Park asked me, "But what's going on? Is it true that the Americans want to withdraw their troops from Vietnam? Why do you accept such a thing? Why don't you ask them to stay until the end of the war?" And I answered, "It's not a matter of preventing the Americans from withdrawing their troops. It's a matter of resolving the problem by replacing their troops with an army of my own. Namely, the army they should have given me a long time ago." Yes, Mademoiselle. In 1954, when the French pulled out, the Americans had already foreseen that the North Vietnamese would attack us just as the North Koreans had attacked South Korea. And if they had furnished us with an army, there would have been no need to ask for their help. We asked them to come in order to resolve an immediate problem, not forever. And when I realized that, by their presence in South Vietnam, two American presidents risked being sent to the devil, I said, "Help me to help you. Give us a strong army. We'll fight alone." And I agreed with Nixon on Vietnamization, and Nixon began to withdraw his troops, and when in the history of war has anyone seen an army of over a half million men withdrawn in four years? The only thing American that's left is the air force. And Vietnamization has worked splendidly, as everyone recognizes, and things have gone just as I said. I had even said that there would be an attack before the American elections, another in 1973 . . .

O.F.: Mr. President, allow me one observation. I'm not at all sure that everyone recognizes the success of Vietnamization. If it hadn't been for the American air force, the North Vietnamese would have won their Easter offensive.

N.V.T.: *Oui. D'accord.* But Vietnamization couldn't be done in a day, Mademoiselle. Not even in a year. We knew it would take from five to seven years, and so it's not yet finished. It's true that we would have lost in the face of Giap's attack, if it hadn't been for American air power. But who took Quang Tri and Binh Dinh? Who stopped the North Vietnamese at An Loc and Kontum? The Americans maybe? Vietnamization will be complete only when our air force has been strengthened.

O.F.: Strengthened, Mr. President? But you have plenty of planes, helicopters, reconnaissance planes, cargo planes, while the North Vietnamese have nothing but two or three MiGs! When one arrives at the Saigon airport . . .

N.V.T.: We have the planes but we don't have the pilots, Mademoiselle. We don't have the technicians. We still have to teach them, to train them. And that takes a year or two. Why didn't we do it before? Because first we had to see to the army! I always said that we wouldn't be ready before 1973. That's why the communists demand the suppression of the Vietnamization program and are afraid of it. Do you know how long it takes to create a modern army?

O.F.: Mr. President, I don't understand anything any more. We started talking more or less about peace, and here we are talking again about war. Do you want to end the war or win the war?

N.V.T.: I want to end it, Mademoiselle. I'm not looking for victories like Giap. And speaking as a soldier, not a politican, let me say, what do we have to win by this war? If we sign a peace treaty tomorrow, what will we have won in South Vietnam? I'll tell you what. Inflation, hundreds of thousands of dead, God know how many cities destroyed, a million refugees, a million soldiers to be paid each month . . . Fighting the war in your own country really means to have lost the war, even if the victory is set down in black and white in an armistice. In fact, the art of war is to carry the war into enemy territory, to destroy in enemy territory, as Giap could explain to you very well. In that sense, he has every right to say that he's won the war. And again I ask you: If we sign a peace treaty tomorrow, what have we won? Have we perhaps conquered a square inch of territory in North Vietnam? Have we perhaps won a seat in the North Vietnamese parliament? We have won nothing, nothing. We have lost in order to exchange our defeat for a peace treaty. Mademoiselle! They've called me intransigent.

How can a man be called intransigent who is ready to negotiate with the NLF, a man who is ready to step down a month before the elections? Are the various Pham Van Dongs, Le Duans, Vo Nguyen Giaps ready to negotiate with me? Are they ready to step down?

O.F.: So how long will this war last, Mr. President? Years, months, weeks?

N.V.T.: Did you ever put that question to Giap?

O.F.: Yes, but almost four years ago.

N.V.T.: And what did he answer?

O.F.: He told me the war might even go on for twenty years.

N.V.T.: *Voilà la réponse.* This war will go on for as long as Giap wants, that is for as long as he wants to impose it on us. If I were able to carry the war to the North, as he has brought it to the South, then you would have every right to put such a question to me and insist on an answer. But now I can only give you an opinion. Either peace will come within a few weeks, let's say a month, or the war will go on for another three or four years. It's too difficult to stop a war based on guerrillas. How many guerrillas were there in Malaya? Ten thousand? And how long did it take the British to beat them? Twelve years. It's hard to fight a war being waged by hooligans.

O.F.: Did you tell that to General Haig when he came here? Because from what I understand, you didn't exactly throw your arms around each other, you and Haig.

N.V.T.: *Eh bien,* Mademoiselle, *vous savez* . . . He calls me Mr. President, I call him Mr. General, or rather General, so . . . We didn't have much to say to each other. I said to him, "So here you are, General. Tell me in what capacity you're here." And he answered, "I'm here to explain President Nixon's point of view." Then I pointed out to him that he wasn't even here as a negotiator, he was here only as a messenger. "Let's hear this point of view, General." He explained it to me. I listened and then told him only that I would answer Nixon directly, by a personal letter. And I would give this letter to him, Haig, in his capacity as messenger. Haig went away, next day he came back, and I gave him the letter. *"Voilà la lettre, mon général. Bon voyage. Au revoir."* I keep explaining myself to the Americans. And I go on and on, in the hope that they'll understand me. The day that they tell me, "We don't understand you, Mr. Thieu, and so we abandon you . . ." *Bon!* You'll see me react to their peace. Until that day . . . Of course I'm ready to receive Kissinger again! I'm always expecting him to come to Saigon to see me. I don't understand why he hasn't yet come. Maybe he thought it wasn't the right moment. . . . Maybe he's about to reach an agreement that to him seems just. . . . Maybe he's about to come and tell me, "Mr. President, in my opinion the moment has come to sign a peace treaty." Then I'll tell him, "Have a seat. Let's take a look at what kind of peace you're talking about."

O.F.: And are you ready to invite him to breakfast, as you've invited me?

N.V.T.: Why not? If the North Vietnamese offered him tea and biscuits, why shouldn't I offer him breakfast? My manners are as good as Le Duc Tho's. And you can always try to discuss things while eating, as long as it doesn't ruin your digestion. I'm not an enemy of Dr. Kissinger. I'm not even an enemy of the North Vietnamese as North Vietnamese. My only enemies are the communists when they want to bring communism here. They can keep it in their own house for as long as they like. Mademoiselle, when the war is over, I'll be more than ready to shake hands with Giap. And even go to have supper in his home. And say to him, "*Alors, mon général!* Let's talk a little. You're from the North, I'm from the South. You have a lot of coal and I have a lot of rice. Let's build a beautiful railroad from Hanoi to Saigon and exchange our goods. Now thanks for the supper, and when will I have the honor of receiving you as my guest in Saigon?"

O.F.: How many times you've mentioned the name of Giap, Mr. President! One would say that you always have that name in mind! What do you think of Giap?

N.V.T.: Mademoiselle, I think he's been a good general but by no means the Asian Napoleon that he thinks he is. Giap's greatness was invented by the French press after Dien Bien Phu. And Dien Bien Phu is still his only great victory, though it wasn't the extraordinary victory he thinks it was and that the French have always maintained in their newspapers. From a military standpoint, Dien Bien Phu was an easy battle for Giap. The French had nothing at Dien Bien Phu: neither planes, nor tanks, nor artillery. Giap had only to use waves of assault troops and the tactic of rotating his divisions. Let's be honest. What did the French really lose at Dien Bien Phu? Not even a tenth of their army. Any French general who was in Indochina at the time will tell you that the French army was by no means completely defeated; if Paris had sent them reinforcements, they would have been able to defend even North Vietnam.

The French didn't lose the war at Dien Bien Phu because of Giap. The war was lost at Dien Bien Phu because it had already been lost in France, politically, psychologically, morally. It's Giap who's got the idea in his head that he did something militarily decisive at Dien Bien Phu. And ever since he's done nothing but look for his new Dien Bien Phu, without understanding that a modern army today hasn't much in common with the French army in the 1950s. Giap's error, in this war, has been not to recognize the extraordinary strength of the American army and also to underestimate my army.

O.F.: Mr. President, we've been talking about the North Vietnamese and nothing else. So I think the moment has come to talk about the Vietcong and the other disagreement you had with Kissinger.

N.V.T.: *Très bien.* I maintain that the political formula accepted by the Americans in October is an untrustworthy formula by which the North Vietnamese are trying to impose a coalition government on us. I maintain that we'll never accept such a formula, no matter how it's disguised, since I'm not imposing any government on Hanoi and I don't want Hanoi to impose something on Saigon. The constitution of North Vietnam says that Vietnam is one, indivisible, from Lao Kai to Ca Mau. The constitution of South Vietnam says the same. Vietnam is one from Ca Mau to Lao Kai, and so forth. But there is still a *de facto* situation: two states within this nation. The state of North Vietnam and the state of South Vietnam, each with its own government, its own parliament, its own constitution. Therefore each of the two states must decide its political future without the other interfering. Like Germany. Like Korea. Do

I make myself clear? I said two states, two states, two states. Like Korea. Like Germany. Two states waiting for reunification. When such a reunification will come, God only knows. Personally I can't see it happening before another twenty years or so, and for this reason I have always asked that North Vietnam and South Vietnam be admitted to the United Nations.

O.F.: But the Vietcong exist, Mr. President, and they are South Vietnamese. They should participate in the political life of South Vietnam.

N.V.T.: Yes, but without interference on the part of North Vietnam. So I say: let the political future of South Vietnam be decided by ourselves and the communists of South Vietnam. I agree to negotiate with the NLF, I agree to organize elections with them, I agree to having them as a political party in the future. But this is a matter of South Vietnamese politics, not North Vietnamese politics! I don't want impositions by Hanoi; I want to negotiate freely with the NLF! But how can I do so if the North Vietnamese stay here disguised as Vietcong? Mademoiselle, not even the Liberation Front could negotiate freely with me while having three hundred thousand North Vietnamese armed with artillery weapons on its back! So I repeat: leave us alone, us and the Vietcong. We'll understand each other better, and more quickly. We are all South Vietnamese and I know that most of the Vietcong who have been fighting for twenty years don't want to invade South Vietnam! How could they if they are South Vietnamese? I know that they only want to participate in the political life of the country and . . .

O.F.: Have you ever tried to open talks with them, Mr. President?

N.V.T.: But how can I if the North Vietnamese are here? How can they if the North Vietnamese are here? This is what I keep on repeating to the Americans and what they don't understand. Let's suppose that I want to meet with Madame Binh, something by the way that I might even like to do. How can I? How can she? Madame Binh isn't free to speak to me; her spokesmen are the North Vietnamese! I tell you, Mademoiselle, that only when the North Vietnamese leave will the Vietcong feel free to come and speak with me. And they'll come. Because I'll invite them, and because they will no longer be controlled

by others. The fact is that . . . Mademoiselle, two or three
years ago we had something here called the "Chu Hoi movement." Chu Hoi means, more or less, "Vietcong deserter."
Well, at a certain point their number was very high: about two
hundred thousand. And this worried the North Vietnamese
immensely, because, obviously, if you let the Chu Hoi continue there'd be no NLF left. So what did the North Vietnamese do? They scattered themselves through the villages and in
Vietcong units to replace the Vietcong or keep them from
deserting. And . . . don't you understand that this second disagreement with Dr. Kissinger is a result of the first? Don't you
understand that the main problem is still the presence of those
three hundred thousand North Vietnamese?

O.F.: Yes, Mr. President, but you go a little further by rejecting *ipso
facto* a coalition government. If you are ready to accept the
Vietcong in the politics of South Vietnam, why do you reject
the idea of a coalition government?

N.V.T.: Because what I said so far doesn't at all mean a coalition
government, it simply means Vietcong participation in the
elections! Because what I reject is the demand by other people
for a coalition government! A government is the result of elections—yes or no? So even if one day there should even be a
government in Saigon completely controlled by the communists, this will have to come about through elections. Yes or
no? Not a prefabricated government. Not a government imposed by Hanoi. What am I basically asking for? Three
months for discussions with the NLF, plus three months to
come to an agreement with the NLF and organize the elections, and finally the elections on a one-man-one-vote basis.
Allons, donc! But what do they expect of me? What, more
than this? I represent a legal government, and I submit to
holding discussions with those who would like illegally to take
my place, I agree to having them in the elections . . . God
damn it! I even accept the possibility that they may win,
though I'm ready to bet that won't happen; I'll cut my throat if
they win . . . No, no, Mademoiselle. They represent too
small a percentage of the population. Their number is around
one hundred thousand. From fifty thousand to one hundred
thousand and . . .

O.F.: Plus those who are now in prison. Mr. President, your analysis may even be convincing, at first. But examined in the light of those facts you don't mention, it's less convincing. How can you organize real elections with the thousands of Vietcong and suspected Vietcong who fill the prisons and concentration camps of South Vietnam?

N.V.T.: I'll answer that reproach right away. When you're at war, it's obvious that you put in prison anyone working for the enemy who is making war on you. It happens in every country. *C'est las normalité*, Mademoiselle. And those who today are in prison are those who have participated in acts of murder or other atrocities. And there are less of them than you think. Nevertheless, when peace comes, even their problem will be resolved. I ask nothing better than an exchange of prisoners. Civilians, military, everybody. Well, the North Vietnamese have refused this too. And I say, how come? I am ready to exchange ten thousand North Vietnamese prisoners of war and some thousands of civilian detainees for five hundred American POWs. I'm ready to give free passage to all of them, North Vietnamese, Cambodians, Laotians, Vietcong, civilians, all of them, and they're still not happy! Certainly such an exchange would have to take place when the war is over, not before! Do you know what the real problem is? It's that the Americans have shown too much anxiety, too much concern about those five hundred prisoners in Hanoi, and now the North Vietnamese use them as though they were merchandise to impose their political conditions. It's disgusting.

O.F.: And the neutralists, Mr. President? From what I understand, they constitute the majority of a population that's had enough of everything: Thieu, the Vietcong, the Americans, the North Vietnamese, the war . . .

N.V.T.: They're not the majority of the population. If it were as you say, Mademoiselle, I wouldn't be here. Believe me, the great majority of the South Vietnamese has great fear of the communists. A fear that was crystallized by the Tet offensive and by the massacres that took place around the time of the Easter offensive. There's no other way to explain what happened here during the flag campaign. All I had to do was say the word and everybody bought a flag or painted the colors of our flag on the façades of their houses. Do you really think that certain things can be imposed by an order? Mademoiselle . . . I look on the neutralists as poor innocents, or rather poor idiots, and don't let myself worry about them. I feel very sorry for them, the neutralists, because they lend themselves to the communist game. They're so naïve. They think they're acting politically and they let the communists lead them by the nose. It would be better if they joined the Vietcong units and fought with weapons. I'd have much more respect for them. This way they are neither politicians nor soldiers, they take risks on one side or the other, and . . . *Soyons sérieux*, Mademoiselle! How can anyone be a neutralist in Vietnam?

O.F.: Is this why you've issued a decree suppressing opposition parties in Vietnam, Mr. President?

N.V.T.: *Mon Dieu!* The decree isn't to suppress them. It's to encourage them to unite. There are twenty-seven legal political parties in South Vietnam, plus forty illegal ones. Such an abundance would be a luxury even in peacetime—just imagine in time of war. And let's not forget that our constitution encourages the two-party system. Now let's suppose that the peace agreement is signed in Paris, let's suppose that in three months we arrive at an understanding with the NLF—what happens? What happens is that, at the moment when we are fighting the communists in the game called democracy, an electoral battle takes place where the communists are on one side and twenty-seven legal political parties and forty illegal ones are on the other. Isn't it better to regroup a little, if we want to win? So I said, let's regroup our minor parties into no more than six major parties. Mademoiselle, *ça suffit!* It seems to me enough for a country of seventeen and a half million inhabitants! Politics doesn't have to be irresponsibility. *Allons, donc!*

O.F.: Mr. President, we've been talking a lot about democracy and elections. So I feel entitled to ask you a disagreeable question. What do you have to say to those who call you the dictator of South Vietnam?

N.V.T.: *Tiens!* I knew you'd ask that! Mademoiselle, I don't know if we should take this down too on your tape recorder, but . . . take a look at the countries of Southeast Asia and then tell me which ones can be called democratic according to your concept of democracy. Thailand? Korea? The Philippines? Mademoiselle! . . . In all sincerity, it seems to me that South Vietnam is still the most democratic country. Maybe not as democratic as you would like, but democracy is not a standard that can be applied in an identical way everywhere. Democracy as they have it in America, or as you have it in Europe, cannot exist here yet. We're not yet ready for it. Don't forget that Vietnam has never known a democratic life in the sense that you give to this expression. Up until 1945 we were a French colony. Until 1954 we were dominated by the Vietminh. Until 1963 we were under President Diem. So I allow myself to state that democracy, here, only began to exist in 1963 when Thieu became president.

O.F.: But what kind of democracy is a democracy that offers only a single candidate in elections? In the 1971 elections you didn't even have an opponent, Mr. President!

N.V.T.: *Tiens, tiens.* Mademoiselle! We must judge these things in the context of South Vietnam. We must remember that the president elected in 1971 would be the president who would discuss peace. We must remember that just at that time, that is when there was no longer any political stability because my opponents had withdrawn their candidacies, the North Vietnamese were grouping their divisions beyond the demilitarized zone and along the frontier with Cambodia, in preparation for launching a new offensive. Well, while this was happening, a lot of people came to me and said, "Mr. Thieu, if the others withdraw their candidacies, you too must withdraw. Otherwise it's not democracy." And I answered, "Our constitution doesn't stipulate that the elections are annulled if there is only one candidate. It doesn't even say that a single candidate must step aside or look for an opponent. That takes at least six or seven months. In six or seven months the North Vietnamese have all the time they need to complete their preparations for an offensive and to attack us I say. To attack us just at the time when we are without military and political leadership. Good-by South Vietnam. So say what you like. I'm staying. What's your next question, Mademoiselle?

O.F.: A brutal question, Mr. President. I hate to be brutal, especially since you've been so nice to me, inviting me to breakfast and so forth, but I have in mind a series of brutal questions. Here's the first: What have you to say about the fact that you're called an "American puppet" or the "man of the Americans"?

N.V.T.: Who says that?

O.F.: Everyone. Almost everyone. Does it really surprise you?

N.V.T.: Do the Americans say so too?

O.F.: Yes, many Americans.

N.V.T.: Ah! *Tiens!* Uhm . . . Mademoiselle! I am the man of the Vietnamese, not the man of the Americans. Even less am I an American puppet, as I think I've recently shown. Even in this interview. I'm an ally of the Americans, that's all. Go on, please.

O.F.: I'll go on. Question number two. What do you have to say to those who accuse you of being corrupt, the most corrupt man in Vietnam?

N.V.T.: Mademoiselle, it's not even worth the trouble to answer. What should I answer? Once the machine to throw slander on a president starts going, there's no stopping it. Such accusations don't happen by error—they happen for a precise purpose. You can correct an error, but not a purpose. I say to you only: have you ever seen a president's daughter living in a boardinghouse run by nuns in London? That's where mine lives.

O.F.: Well, then let's put it another way, Mr. President. Is it true that you were born very poor?

N.V.T.: Very true. My father was an orphan at the age of ten. And when he got married, my mother supported the family by bringing baskets of rice and coconuts to the village market. Thirteen days after the birth of her first child, she had to sell their hut and move to the other side of the river, because she had no money. And, thanks to her, my elder brother was able to study in Paris. My younger brother was able to study in Hue. But I had to study in the village school. We're a family of self-made men—today my brothers are ambassadors. But my sisters still carry chickens and baskets of rice to the market to sell like my mother did. *Oui, c'est vrai.*

O.F.: And is it true that today you're immensely rich, with bank accounts and houses in Switzerland, London, Paris, and Australia?

N.V.T.: It's not true. I swear to you on the head of my daughter and of my son that I own nothing abroad. Neither a house in London, nor a house in Paris, nor a house in Australia, nor a house in Switzerland. I heard the story about the house in Switzerland some time ago through some Americans. And I answered, "*Messieurs les Américains,* you have all the necessary technology to discover this house, all the necessary cameras to photograph it. Bring me photographs of this house."

I only own something in Vietnam, and you want to know what? An apartment in General Headquarters where, being a general, I am entitled to two small bachelor apartments. So I've combined them into one. I've modernized it a little, and I keep it as a place to go on weekends. But it doesn't really belong to me, it belongs to the army. And I'll give it back to the army, transformed into a museum. Then I have a wooden house on the river, where I go when I want to water-ski. It's a prefabricated house, very cheap. It was given to me by the lumbermen's union. Then I have the house where I was born, which is the poorest in the village. People go by it and laugh. "Look at the house of President Thieu!" Finally I own a little land where I enjoy making agricultural experiments. And there I grow rice and melons; I raise chickens, geese, pigs, and even fish, since there's a pond. That's all.

Since I've been president, I haven't even bought a car—instead I use President Diem's. It's an old Mercedes with an engine that's always breaking down. Can you imagine the president of Vietnam returning solemnly from some trip, getting off the plane, and getting into this Mercedes that starts and all of a sudden stops? So that the military police have to push it in the hope of starting up the motor, and bang! bang! bang! While the president is cursing, "God damn it! I must buy a car!" Go on, Mademoiselle.

O.F.: I'm going on, Mr. President. Question number four. Aren't you afraid of being killed? For instance, assassinated like President Diem?

N.V.T.: No. Frankly, no. I believe in God and in the fact that he protects me. Mind you, it's not that I'm a one-hundred-per-

cent fatalist. In other words, I don't believe that God is always
there to protect you and that it's therefore useless to protect
yourself. On the contrary, I think that one should do everything possible to give God a hand and help him to protect
you. But there's a limit to everything, and in the end I conclude, "I do my duty and defend myself from the risks that
such duty involves. The rest is up to God. Even he should
take some responsibility for me, *n'est-ce-pas?* After all, it's a
question of mutual trust!" Joking aside, Mademoiselle, it
wouldn't be at all difficult to kill me. I shake hands with everybody and don't pay much attention; my security agents do
nothing but complain. And I keep insisting, *"Messieurs les
agents, qu'est-ce que c'est que ça?!* I do my job, you do yours.
If you can't do it, so much the worse for you and me. I don't
give a damn. *Je m'en fous."* I don't give a damn because . . .
how can you avoid being killed if someone really wants to do
it? Last week I reviewed five thousand men of the defense
forces. Each one had a loaded rifle and all that was needed to kill
me was a single bullet from a single rifle. Nothing is simpler
than to assassinate a president of Vietnam. But why should
they since I've told them that it's not worth the trouble, that I
prefer to go away alive rather than dead? Furthermore, I'm not
obsessed by the idea of dying. And I've shown it by participating in God knows how many battles until 1965, even recently
facing the North Vietnamese artillery and Vietcong gunfire.
No one forced me to go to Quang Tri, to Binh Long, or Kontum. I was a president, not a general at the front! And still I
went. I prayed to the Holy Virgin and then I went.

O.F.: You're very religious, eh?

N.V.T.: *Oui, oui, oui! Beaucoup! Beaucoup!* Every Sunday I hear
Mass in my chapel and every evening I pray. I also prayed that
my troops would retake Quang Tri without spilling too much
blood. I even prayed when Dr. Kissinger came here to try to
get me to accept things I couldn't accept. I'm a true Catholic.
I was converted after thinking about it for eight years. My wife
was already a Catholic when I married her in 1951, and since
the Church insisted that the marriage was valid only if I converted, I went to the priest and told him, "Monseigneur, I'm
an officer and I'm fighting a war. I have no time to study the

catechism. Give me time. When the war is over, I promise you, I'll study the catechism and convert." Then the war ended and I kept my promise. But it wasn't as easy as I thought. I wanted to understand everything and I drove that poor priest crazy with my questions. He was a country priest, he didn't know how to answer. I had to find me a Dominican father and . . . *Voyez bien*, Mademoiselle, anything I do I like to do well. Whether it's being converted, or playing tennis, or riding a horse, or holding the office of president. I like responsibility more than power. That's why I say that power should never be shared with others. That's why I'm always the one to decide! Always! I may listen to others suggest some decision, and then make the opposite decision. *Oui, c'est moi qui décide*. If one doesn't accept responsibility, one isn't worthy to be the chief and . . . Mademoiselle, ask me this question, "Who's the chief here?"

O.F.: Who's the chief here?

N.V.T.: I am! I'm the chief! *Moi! C'est moi le chef!*

O.F.: Thank you, Mr. President. Now I think I can go.

N.V.T.: Are you leaving? Have we finished? Are you satisfied, Mademoiselle? Because if you're not satisfied, you must tell me. Mademoiselle, I hope you're satisfied because I've hidden nothing from you and I've spoken to you with complete frankness. I swear. I didn't want to in the beginning. But then . . . what can I do? That's the way I am. Come on, tell me. Did you ever expect to find such a fellow?

O.F.: No, Mr. President.

N.V.T.: *Merci*, Mademoiselle. And, if you can, pray for peace in Vietnam. Peace in Vietnam means peace in the world. And sometimes I feel as though there's nothing left to do except pray to God.

Saigon, January 1973

3

General Giap

He was the man whose name was most often heard during the Vietnam war. And not because he was minister of defense in Hanoi, commander in chief of the armed forces, deputy prime minister, but because it was he who had defeated the French at Dien Bien Phu. The Americans lived in the nightmare of a Dien Bien Phu, and as soon as things began going badly, they said, "It's Giap getting ready for a new Dien Bien Phu." Or else, simply, "It's Giap." They spoke of Giap in February 1968, when the Vietcong unleashed the Tet offensive. They spoke of Giap in March and April, when the North Vietnamese took Hue and besieged Khe San. They spoke of Giap in May and June, when the Vietcong launched the second offensive on Saigon and the central highlands. They would go on speaking of Giap for years. The name, short and dry as a slap in the face, was a threat forever suspended in the air, a bugbear from the seventeenth parallel on down. You frighten children by whispering, "I'll send for the bogeyman." You frightened the Americans by whispering, "Giap is coming." Furthermore, hadn't they inflated him themselves, with their mania for legends? They hadn't even asked themselves if the legend might not be premature.

At Dien Bien Phu, Giap had of course won a triumph, but it was yet to be seen if he were really an Asian Napoleon, a genius in military strategy, a perennial victor. Had not the Tet offensive perhaps failed, as well as the May offensive? Had not Hue fallen and the siege of Khe San been lifted in the end? The war, in that February of 1969, had gone more in favor of the Americans and South Vietnamese. Hanoi's only real victory had been the abdication of Johnson and the suspension of the bombings over North Vietnam. In Saigon, Thieu had consolidated his power.

But Giap was still Giap. And anyone who was a journalist wanted to interview Giap. It was obvious why. Ho Chi Minh was too old by now, too sick. He shook the hands of visitors, made some exclamation about final victory, and then withdrew coughing. A meeting with Ho Chi Minh was good only from a human and personal point of view, that is, you could say, "I've met Ho Chi Minh." But it didn't give you much else to say. But a meeting with Giap! Giap had plenty of things to say, and he hadn't been saying them since 1954. More unapproachable than even Ho Chi Minh, he had not turned up even at official functions; every so often a rumor circulated that he was dead.

So as soon as I had arrived in Hanoi in that February of 1969, I had asked to see Giap and with stubborn hope was getting ready for the meeting, carefully reading up on his biography. And such a fascinating biography. Son of a landowner reduced to poverty, he had been raised in a rich French family, a far cry from a Marxist education. Like a good bourgeois, he had studied at the imperial college in Hue, then at the University of Hanoi, where he had taken his degree in jurisprudence and philosophy; finally he had been a teacher of literature and history at the French *lycée* in Hanoi, tormenting his pupils with the campaigns of Napoleon. On the blackboard he used to draw the details of battles, analyzing them at length, and his colleagues made fun of him. "Do you want to become a general?"

But as a revolutionary, he had begun very early—at the age of fourteen. At eighteen, moreover, he had already been in prison; at twenty he aligned himself with Ho Chi Minh. For his thundering rages and stony silences, Ho Chi Minh used to call him Volcano Covered with Snow, and for his courage he used to call him Kui, or Devil. In 1935 he had joined the Communist party and married one of his comrades, Minh Tai. In 1939, the year when the communists had been outlawed, he had escaped to China, and Minh Tai had covered his flight by getting herself arrested in his place.

Because of this she had died in 1941, in a rat-infested cell. Many believe that as a result of this Giap had learned to hate and become closed to all pity, open to all cruelty. Didn't the French find it out when, between 1945 and 1954, they had fallen into his traps full of poisonous bees, his pits full of snakes, or were blown up by booby traps hidden under corpses abandoned by the wayside?

A master of sabotage, he liked to say that guerrilla warfare would always win out over modern weapons. And it goes without saying that at Dien Bien Phu he had won with cannons. A hundred cannons transported by the Vietminh piece by piece, on their backs, on bicycles, by forced marches and without rations. If Dien Bien Phu had cost the French twelve thousand dead, it had cost Giap a good forty-five thousand. And it goes without saying that he would mention it with indifference, detachment. "Every two minutes three hundred thousand people die on this planet. What are forty-five thousand for a battle? In war death doesn't count." His harshness was not free of cynicism, and indeed he had little in common with the austere Marxists of Hanoi. He always wore new and well-pressed uniforms; he lived in a beautiful colonial villa built by the French and furnished in French taste; he owned a limousine with curtains, and was remarried to a beautiful girl many years younger than himself. In short, he certainly did not lead the life of a monk or a Ho Chi Minh.

In Hanoi my request to interview Giap had been received with many reservations by the North Vietnamese. "Why does it have to be Giap? Giap isn't the only one in this war. And besides Giap doesn't receive visitors." But, three days before my departure, my female guide and interpreter, An The, brought me the news that yes, I could see Giap, "Tomorrow at three-thirty in the afternoon. Not for an official interview, mind you: for a *causerie*, a chat. And not alone: together with the other women of the delegation." The other women of the delegation were two communists and a socialist from the PSIUP (Partito Socialista Italiano d'Unità Proletaria), together with whom I had been invited to North Vietnam. Their names were Carmen, Giulia, and Marisa: intelligent, friendly women. They understood the difficulty that this collective appointment gave me and promised not to open their mouths so that I could question Giap as comfortably as possible. They also promised to yield their place should he choose one of them to sit next to him, and to take notes if he were to forbid the use of the tape recorder.

Next day they dressed carefully and were already ready by noon. And I as well—tense and nervous. In fact I don't remember what happened from noon on. I remember only that we left escorted by An The, her assistant Huan, and the interpreter Ho, and that staff officers were waiting for us at the entrance to the War Ministry, all grave and smartly dressed in their olive-green uniforms. Then one by one they bowed with broad smiles and escorted us along a corridor to a large room with a divan and many armchairs along the walls. In the center of the room, stiff as a lead soldier, was Vo Nguyen Giap. The legendary Giap.

I was astonished first of all at how short he was. I knew he was less than five feet tall, but, seen in this way, he looked even shorter. He had short legs, short arms, and a very short neck that immediately disappeared inside his jacket. His body was squat, even fat. His face was swollen and covered with little blue veins that made him look purple. No, it was not an extremely likable face. Perhaps because of that purple color, perhaps because of those uncertain outlines, it cost you some effort to keep from looking at him, where the things you found were scarcely interesting. The huge mouth full of tiny teeth, the flattened nose enlarged by two huge nostrils, the forehead that stopped at the middle of his skull in a mop of black hair . . .

But his eyes! His eyes were perhaps the most intelligent eyes I had ever seen. Sharp, shrewd, laughing, cruel—everything. They shone like two drops of light, pierced you like two sharp knives, and conveyed such sureness, such authority. I even asked myself incredulously: Is it possible that these eyes wept one night in the Lam Son mountains? One night, in the Lam Son mountains, where he was organizing guerrilla warfare against the French, someone had brought Giap the news that Ho Chi Minh was dead. And, in one of his books, he had recounted the episode as follows: "I felt everything whirl around me. I collected his things in the straw basket he used as a suitcase and asked Tong to pronounce the funeral oration. It was very cold and millions of stars illumined the immensity of the sky. But an infinite sadness twisted my heart, and with my eyes full of tears I looked at the stars and all of a sudden wept." Who knows! Perhaps in some remote past these eyes had really wept, but nothing in the world could have made them weep again.

He came toward me with his hand extended in a worldly, free-and-easy manner. There was even something worldly in his smile. He asked me if I spoke French and his voice was shrill, his tone so inquisitorial that I was intimidated and answered *"Oui, Monsieur"* instead of *"Oui, mon Général."* But this didn't irritate him, and in fact it seemed to me that he liked hearing himself called Monsieur instead of "Comrade," the appellation used by Giulia, Carmen, and Marisa. He led us to the back of the room so that we could sit down, asked Giulia and Marisa to take the armchairs, and invited Carmen to sit down next to him on the divan. True to her word, Carmen demurred and moved so that I could take her place. But this took time, and several minutes went by before everyone was settled: my friends, An The, Huan, and Ho in the armchairs on our right and the staff officers to our left. The shoes of one of the officers were too tight. He loosened the laces from one hook, then from another, and still another, and soon both his shoes were completely unlaced. Then another officer did the same, and then even a third, while I kept wondering how to conduct the interview.

It was certainly not an ideal situation for me, with all these people seated in a row as though in school or at the theater. There was no way of knowing what the proper ceremony was and what would happen in the first ten minutes: an exchange of compliments, refreshments? In front of the divan where I was seated with Giap was a table loaded with delicacies: fried cheese balls, rice sweets, meat croquettes, comfits, cookies, and little glasses of red liqueur. But no one touched them except myself, and something happened that made me win the match. It happened that Giap saw my tape recorder and was alarmed. *"Je vous prie, pas celui-là, ça sera seulement une causerie entre nous, vous savez."* I tried to argue, a discussion ensued at the end of which we agreed on the necessity of at least taking notes. And, in the wake of this conversation, I was able to get him to speak.

I must confess that it wasn't even difficult. Giap loves to talk and he talked for forty-five minutes, without letting up, in the pedantic tone of a professor lecturing some rather unintelligent pupils. To interrupt to ask a question was a hopeless undertaking. Giulia, Carmen, Marisa, An The, Ho, all those who were taking notes couldn't keep up with him. It was even pathetic to see those heads

bent over their notebooks and those hands writing, writing, writing
so breathlessly. I was the only one not writing, but how could I have
done so while his terrible eyes sought mine?

Giap in his turn questioned me, reproached me, challenged me,
and it was not seldom that he abandoned himself to passionate outbursts. As when I said to him that the Tet offensive had failed, and
he got up nervously, walked around the table, and with outstretched arms exclaimed, "Tell that to the Liberation Front!"
(Thus disclaiming any responsibility for the offensive that everyone
attributed to him.) His little hands moved ceaselessly, he showed
the satisfaction of one who likes to hear the sound of his own voice,
and he let up only when he realized that the time limit set for the
interview had been passed. He stopped suddenly. And immediately
jumped to his feet, which made everyone else rise. The officers
who had unlaced their shoes did not know what to do. Red in the
face, they arranged the laces that had been left in a tangle on the
floor. And one, getting to his feet, stumbled and almost ended up
on the floor.

In the hotel we transcribed word for word the notes made by
Giulia, Carmen, Marisa, An The, Huan, and Ho; then we compared them and composed the text of the interview, without omit-
ting so much as a comma. But a surprise was in store for me next
morning. An The arrived with three sheets of typewritten onionskin,
which she gave to me saying that this, only this, was the text of the
conversation I had had with the general. The general would not
recognize any other text and I must promise to publish it. I read the
sheets. There was no longer anything of what I had heard and that
the others had transcribed. There was not his answer to the question about the Tet offensive, there was not his answer to the one
about the Paris peace talks, and not even the one on the end of the
war. There was nothing except a series of vague and rhetorical sentences—good at the most for a political rally. "I repeat, the general
insists on the publication of this text," said An The, her forefinger
raised. "I'll publish it," I replied. "But together with the true text."
And I did.

Giap never forgave me, and the North Vietnamese who had
given me a visa even less. Independence of judgment, as we know,
is a virtue that many communists don't like. Or they like it only in

cases where you are prompted to write something in their favor. In Hanoi they had accepted me for what I had written in 1968 from Saigon, attacking the Americans and praising the Vietcong. But now that I was explaining, in the same spirit, where they were wrong in Hanoi, all their tender feelings for me vanished, together with their good memories of me. They insulted me and called me stupid names. They said that I had wronged General Giap in order to render a service to the Americans, even that it was the Americans who had sent me to North Vietnam: "obviously I belonged to the CIA!" But I did not get more upset than necessary, least of all was I surprised, and this interview remained a document that is still talked about today. Published all over the world, it even landed on the desk of Henry Kissinger, who, thanks to it (as I have explained elsewhere), agreed to see and talk to me.

ORIANA FALLACI: General Giap, in many of your writings you pose the following question: Who after all will win the war in Vietnam? So I ask you: Today, here in the first months of 1969, do you think you can say that the Americans have lost the war in Vietnam, that they have been militarily defeated?

VO NGUYEN GIAP: They recognize it themselves. But now I'll show you why the Americans have already been defeated—militarily and politically. And to show you their military defeat, I go back to their political defeat, which is at the bottom of everything. The Americans have committed a very grave error in choosing South Vietnam as a battlefield. The reactionaries in Saigon are too weak—even Taylor, McNamara, and Westmoreland knew this. What they didn't know is that, being so weak, they would not know how to profit from American aid. Because what was the goal of the American aggression in Vietnam? Clearly, a neocolony based on a puppet government. But to create a neocolony you need a stable government, and the government of Saigon is an extremely unstable one. It has no effect on the population, people don't believe in it. So in what paradox do the Americans find themselves? The paradox of not being able to withdraw from South Vietnam even if they want to, because in order to withdraw they must leave behind a stable political situation. That is, a few servants capable of taking their places. Servants yes, but strong ones. Servants yes, but serious ones. The puppet government of Saigon is neither strong nor serious; it's worth nothing even as a servant; it can't stand on its feet even when propped up with tanks. And so how can the Americans leave? And yet they must leave—they can't keep six hundred thousand men in Vietnam for another ten, fifteen years! This then is their political defeat: to achieve nothing from a political standpoint despite the enormous military apparatus at their disposal.

O.F.: General, this doesn't mean that militarily they've lost the war.

V.N.G.: Be patient, don't interrupt me. Of course it means that. If they didn't feel themselves beaten, the White House wouldn't be talking about peace with honor. But let's go back awhile, to the times of Geneva and Eisenhower. How did the Americans begin in Vietnam? With their usual methods, namely, military and economic aid to puppet governments. Together with the dollar. Because they always believe they can solve anything with the dollar. Even a free and independent government, they thought they could set it up with the dollar: that is, with an army of puppets bought with the dollar, with thirty thousand advisers paid in dollars, with the invention of strategic hamlets built on dollars. But the people intervened, and the American plan failed. The strategic hamlets failed, the advisers failed, the army of puppets failed. And the Americans found themselves forced to intervene militarily, as Ambassador Taylor had already recommended.

So the second phase of their aggression began: the special war. They were certain of being able to conclude it by 1965, at the most by 1966—with a hundred and fifty thousand men and eighteen billion dollars. But in 1966 the war was by no means over, and in fact had risen to another two hundred thousand men, and they were talking about the third phase, namely limited war. The famous two-pronged policy of Westmoreland: on one side to win over the population and on the other to exterminate the Liberation forces. But the two prongs didn't take hold and Westmoreland lost the war. As a general he lost it in 1967, when he wanted additional troops sent and made that optimistic report to Washington, announcing that 1968 would be a good year for the war in Vietnam, it would

allow Johnson to win re-election. In Washington, Westmoreland was greeted as a hero, but he certainly knew that
this war was beginning to cost a little too much. Taylor had
understood that from the beginning. Come on now! Korea
cost the Americans twenty billion dollars, Vietnam has already
cost them more than a hundred billion. Korea cost them more
than fifty-four thousand dead, Vietnam has already surpassed
this figure . . .

o.f.: The Americans say thirty-four thousand dead, General.

v.n.g.: Hm . . . I'd say at least double. The Americans always
give figures lower than the truth: when it suits them, three instead of five. They can't have had only thirty-four thousand
dead. And when we've shot down more than thirty-two
hundred of their planes! And when they admit that one out of
every five of their planes has been shot down! Look: in five
years of war they've certainly lost no less than seventy thousand men. And maybe that's too low.

o.f.: General, the Americans also say that you have lost half a
million.

v.n.g.: The exact number.

o.f.: Exact?

v.n.g.: Exact. But to get back to what I was saying, 1968 arrives
and in that year the Americans were really certain of winning.
Then just look, all of a sudden there was the Tet offensive and
the Liberation Front shows that it is able to attack them whenever it wants, wherever it wants. Including the most well-
defended cities, including Saigon. And the Americans finally
admit that this war is a strategic error. Johnson admits it, Mc-
Namara admits it. They recognize that it was the wrong time,
the wrong place, that Montgomery was right in saying that the
army must not be brought onto the Asian continent. The victorious Tet offensive . . .

o.f.: General, everyone agrees that the Tet offensive was a great
psychological victory. But from a military standpoint don't you
think it was a failure?

v.n.g.: Failure?

o.f.: I would say so, General.

v.n.g.: Tell that to, or rather ask, the Liberation Front.

o.f.: First I'd like to ask you, General.

v.n.g.: You must understand that this is a delicate question, that I cannot express judgments of this kind, that I cannot meddle in the affairs of the Front. It's a delicate thing . . . very delicate . . . Anyway you surprise me, since the whole world has recognized that, from a military and political standpoint, the Tet offensive . . .

o.f.: General, even from a political standpoint it was not a huge victory. The population did not rise up, and after two weeks the Americans regained control. Only in Hue did we see a saga that went on for a month. In Hue, where there were North Vietnamese.

v.n.g.: I don't know if the Front foresaw or desired the population to rise up, though I would think that without the help of the population the forces of the Front would not have been able to enter the city. And I won't discuss the Tet offensive, which didn't depend on me, didn't depend on us; it was conducted by the Front. But it's a fact that, after the Tet offensive, the Americans passed from the attack to the defense. And defense is always the beginning of defeat. I say beginning of defeat without contradicting myself. In fact our final victory is still to come and one cannot yet speak of the definite defeat of the Americans. Actually the Americans are still strong, who can deny it? It will still take much effort on our part to beat them completely. The military problem . . . now I speak as a soldier . . . yes, the Americans are strong, their weapons are strong. But that won't do them any good because the war in Vietnam is not only a military war, and so military strength and military strategy are not enough either to win it or understand it.

o.f.: Yes, General. But . . .

v.n.g.: Don't interrupt me. The United States, I was saying, is waging war by arithmetical strategy. They ask their computers, make additions and subtractions, extract square roots, and on that they act. But arithmetical strategy doesn't work here—if it did, they would have exterminated us already. With their airplanes, for example. It was no accident that they thought they could subdue us in a few weeks by unloading on us all those billions of explosives. Because, as I've already told you, they figure everything in billions, in dollars. And they underestimate the spirit of a people that knows how to fight for a just cause, to save its homeland from the invader. They can't get it in their heads that the war in Vietnam can be understood only by the strategy of a people's war, that the war in Vietnam is not a question of numbers and well-equipped soldiers, that all that doesn't solve the problem. For example. They said that to win it was necessary to have a ratio of twenty-five to one. Then they realized that figure was impossible and reduced it to six to one. Then they came down to three, maintaining that was a dangerous ratio. No, something more is needed than an equation of three to one, six to one, twenty-five to one, and this something is a whole people against them. When a whole people rebels, there's nothing you can do. And there's no wealth in the world that can liquidate it. This is the reason for our strategy, our tactics, which the Americans can't understand.

O.F.: Since you're so sure that they'll ultimately be defeated, General, when do you think this will happen?

V.N.G.: Oh, this isn't a war that you resolve in a few years. In a war against the United States, you need time, time . . . The Americans will be defeated in time, by getting tired. And in order to tire them, we have to go on, to last . . . for a long time. That's what we've always done. Because, you know, we're a small nation. We're scarcely thirty million, half of Italy, and we were hardly a million at the beginning of the Christian era, when the Mongols came. After conquering Europe and Asia, the Mongols came here. And we, who were scarcely a million, defeated them. They came here three times, the Mongols, and three times we defeated them. We didn't have their means, yet still we resisted and endured and repeated to ourselves: all the people must fight. What was valid in 1200 is still valid in the twentieth century. The problem is the same. We are good soldiers because we are Vietnamese.

O.F.: General, the Vietnamese in the South who are fighting alongside the Americans are also Vietnamese. What do you think of them as soldiers?

V.N.G.: They can't be good soldiers. They aren't good soldiers. Because they don't believe in what they're doing and therefore they lack any combat spirit. The Americans know this too, and they're very much better. If the Americans hadn't known that puppet-soldiers are bad soldiers, they would have had no need to bring so many of their own troops into Vietnam.

O.F.: General, let's talk about the Paris Conference. Do you think that peace may come from the Paris Conference or from a military victory like the one you had at Dien Bien Phu?

V.N.G.: Dien Bien Phu . . . Dien Bien Phu . . . The fact that we've gone to Paris proves our good intentions. And it can't be said that Paris is useless, since not only ourselves but also the Liberation Front is in Paris. In Paris we must translate to a political level what is happening in Vietnam and . . . Madame! Paris, Madame, *vous savez* . . . is something for the diplomats.

O.F.: So are you saying, General, that the war will not be resolved in Paris, that it can only be resolved militarily, never diplomatically, that the Dien Bien Phu of the Americans must still come and will come?

V.N.G.: Dien Bien Phu, Madame, Dien Bien Phu . . . Look, it's not always true that history repeats itself. But this time it will repeat itself. And just as we beat the French militarily, we will beat the Americans militarily. Yes, Madame, their Dien Bien Phu is still to come. And it will come. The Americans will definitely lose the war at the moment when their military strength reaches its height, and the great machine they've put together no longer succeeds in moving. We'll beat them, that is, at the moment when they have the most men, the most weapons, the most hope of winning. Because all that wealth, that strength, will become a millstone around their necks. It's inevitable.

O.F.: Am I mistaken, General, or did you already try a second Dien Bien Phu at Khe San?

V.N.G.: Oh, no. Khe San didn't try to be, nor could it have been, a Dien Bien Phu. Khe San wasn't that important to us. Or it was only to the extent that it was important to the Americans—in fact at Khe San their prestige was at stake. Because just look at the usual paradox that you always find with the Americans: as long as they stayed in Khe San to defend their prestige, they said Khe San was important. When they aban-

doned Khe San, they said Khe San had never been important.
Besides, don't you think we won at Khe San? I say yes and
. . . but do you know that journalists are curious? Too
curious. And since I'm a journalist too, I'd like to reverse roles
and put a couple of questions to you. First question. Do you
agree on the fact that the Americans have lost the war in the
North?

O.F.: I'd say yes, General. If by war in the North you mean the
bombings, I think the Americans have lost. Since they've
achieved nothing substantial and then have had to suspend
them.

V.N.G.: Second question. Do you agree on the fact that the Americans have lost the war in the South?

O.F.: No, General. They haven't lost it. Or not yet. You haven't really kicked them out. They're still there. And they're staying.

V.N.G.: You're mistaken. They're still there, but in what condition?
Stranded, paralyzed, in the expectation of new defeats that
they try to avoid without knowing how. Defeats that have and
will have disastrous consequences for them—from an economic, political, historical point of view. They're there with
their hands tied, locked in their own strength; they can only
place their hopes in the Paris peace talks. But even there
they're so stubborn, they don't give up their positions.

O.F.: General, you say that the Americans are stubborn in Paris.
But the Americans say the same thing about you. So what good
are these Paris peace talks?

V.N.G.: Madame, *vous savez* . . .

O.F.: General, here we do nothing but talk about peace but it seems
that nobody really wants it. So how long will these Paris peace
talks last?

V.N.G.: A long time! Especially if the United States doesn't give up
its position. A long time. All the more since we won't give up
ours, we're not in a hurry, we have patience. Because while
the delegations are discussing, we go on with the war. We love
peace but not peace at any price, not peace by compromise.
Peace for us can only mean total victory, the total departure of
the Americans. Any compromise would be a threat of slavery.
And we prefer death to slavery.

O.F.: So then, General, how long will the war go on? How long will this poor people be asked to sacrifice itself, to suffer, and die?

v.n.g.: As long as necessary: ten, fifteen, twenty, fifty years. Until we achieve total victory, as our president, Ho Chi Minh, said. Yes! Even twenty, even fifty years! We're not in a hurry, we're not afraid.

Hanoi, February 1969

4

Golda Meir

The story of this interview is quite special. It is the story of an interview that was mysteriously stolen and had to be done all over again. I had met Golda Meir twice, for more than three hours, before the theft occurred. I again saw Golda Meir twice, for about two hours, after the theft had occurred. So I think I can say I'm the only journalist to have talked four times and for a good six hours with this fantastic woman whom you can praise or revile as you like but who cannot be denied the adjective fantastic. Am I mistaken? Am I guilty of optimism, or let's even say feminism? Maybe. But while I admit that I have nothing against feminism, I must add that I will never be objective about Golda Meir. I will never succeed in judging her with the disenchantment I would like to impose on myself when I say that a powerful personage is a phenomenon to be analyzed coldly, surgically.

In my opinion, even if one is not at all in agreement with her, with her politics, her ideology, one cannot help but respect her, admire her, even love her. I almost loved her. Above all, she reminds me of my mother, whom she somewhat resembles. My mother too has the same gray curly hair, that tired and wrinkled face, that heavy body supported on swollen, unsteady, leaden legs. My mother too has that sweet and energetic look about her, the look of a housewife obsessed with cleanliness. They are a breed of women, you see, that has gone out of style and whose wealth consists in a disarming simplicity, an irritating modesty, a wisdom that comes from having toiled all their lives in the pain, discomfort, and trouble that leave no time for the superfluous.

All right, Golda Meir is also something else, something more. For example: for years it was she who could have lighted or extinguished the fuse of a world conflict. For years she was the most authoritative representative of a doctrine that many people condemn and whose tenets I reject: Zionism. But this we know. And I'm not interested in telling what we know about Golda Meir. I'm interested in telling what we don't know. So here is the story of this interview. Or rather my story with Golda Meir, at that time prime minister.

My first meeting took place at the beginning of October, in her Jerusalem residence. It was a Monday, and she had dressed herself in black, as my mother does when she's expecting visitors. She had also powdered her nose, as my mother does when she's expecting visitors. Seated in the drawing room, with a cup of coffee and a pack of cigarettes, she seemed concerned only to make me feel at ease and to minimize her authority. I had sent her my book on Vietnam and a bouquet of roses. The roses were in a vase and the book in her hands. Before I could ask any questions, she began to discuss the way in which I had viewed the war, and so it was not difficult to get her to speak about her war: of terrorism, of the Palestinians, of the occupied territories, of the conditions that she would put to Sadat and Hussein should she come to negotiate with the Arabs. Her voice was warm and vibrant, her expression smiling and jovial. She charmed me at once, without effort. Her conquest was complete when, an hour and a quarter later, she said she would see me again.

The second meeting took place three days later, in her prime ministerial office. Two highly interesting hours. Abandoning political questions, on which I followed her at times with reservations, in the second meeting she talked exclusively about herself: about her childhood, her family, her trials as a woman, her friends. Pietro Nenni, for instance, for whom she feels boundless admiration and a touching affection. At the moment of saying good-by, we ourselves had become friends. She even gave me a photograph for my mother, with the most flattering dedication in the world. She begged me to come back and visit her soon. "But without that thing there, eh? Only for a chat between ourselves over a cup of tea!" That thing there was the tape recorder, on which I had taken down every sentence, every reply. Her aides seemed astonished; it was the first time she had spoken with such candor in front of that-thing-there. One of them asked me to send him a copy of the tapes to give to a kibbutz that is preserving documents on Golda Meir.

The tapes. As I said at the beginning of this book, for my work nothing is more precious than tapes. There are no stenographic records, memories, notes that can take the place of a person's live voice. The tapes were two minicassettes of ninety minutes each, plus a third of five or six minutes. Of the three, only the first had been transcribed. So I put them in my purse with the care reserved for a jewel, and left next day, arriving in Rome about eight thirty in the evening. At nine-thirty I checked into a hotel. A famously good hotel. And here, as soon as I was in my room, I took the three minicassettes out of my purse and put them in an envelope. Then I put the envelope on the desk, placing on top of it a pair of glasses, a valuable compact, and other objects, and left the room. I locked the door, of course, gave the key to the desk clerk, and went out. For about fifteen minutes: time to go across the street and eat a sandwich.

When I came back, the key had disappeared. And when I went upstairs, the door to my room was open. Only the door. Everything else was in order. My suitcases were locked, the valuable compact and other objects were still where I had left them—at first glance it seemed that nothing had been touched. And it took a couple of seconds for me to realize that the envelope was empty, that Golda's tapes were gone. Even my tape recorder, which contained another tape with a few sentences, was missing. They had taken it out of a traveling bag, ignoring a jewel box, and then had carefully rearranged the contents of the bag. Finally they had taken two necklaces that I had left on the table. To throw us off the track, the police said.

The police came immediately and stayed until dawn. Even the political division came, represented by sad and unpleasant young men who take no interest in ordinary thefts but only in more delicate matters. Even the scientific division came, with the cameras and instruments that are used to find clues in murder cases. But they found only my fingerprints: the thieves had operated with kid gloves, in every sense. Then the sad and unpleasant young men concluded that it was a political theft, as I myself already knew. What I couldn't understand was why it had been done and by whom. By an Arab looking for information? By some personal enemy of Golda's? By a jealous journalist? Everything had been done with precision, speed, lucidity—à la James Bond. And surely I had been followed; nobody knew I would arrive in Rome that day, at that hour, in that hotel. What about the key? Why had the key disappeared from its pigeonhole?

The next day something strange happened. A woman with two airline bags appeared at the hotel and asked to see the police. She had found the bags in the bushes of the Villa Borghese and wanted to turn them over to the police. What did the bags contain? Some twenty minicassette tapes like mine. She was seized at once and taken to the police station. Here, one by one, the tapes were played. All that was on them were popular songs. A warning? A threat? A hoax? The woman was unable to say why she had gone to look for the police in that particular hotel.

To get back to Golda. Golda learned of the theft the next evening, when she was at home with friends and was telling about our interview: "The day before yesterday I had an experience; I enjoyed being interviewed by . . ." She was interrupted by one of her aides, who handed her my telegram. "Everything stolen repeat everything stop try to see me again please." She read it, they told me, put her hand to her breast, and for several minutes didn't say a word. Then she raised two distressed, determined eyes, and said with careful enunciation, "Obviously somebody doesn't want this interview to be published. So we'll have to do it over. Find me a couple of hours for a new appointment." This is just what she said, they assure me, and I can't believe that any other government leader would have reacted in this way. I'm sure that any other, in her place, would have given a shrug. "So much the worse for her. I already gave her more than three hours. Let her write what she can remember, manage the best she can." The fact is that Golda, before being a statesman, is one of that breed of women that has gone out of style. The only condition she made was that we wait a month, and the new appointment was set for Thursday, November 14. And so it happened. Certainly, returning to her that day, I didn't imagine I would discover how much I could love her in spite of all. But, to explain such a serious statement, I must tell what moved me still more.

Golda lives alone. At night there is not even a dog to watch over her sleep in case she feels ill; there is her bodyguard on duty at the entrance to her villa and that's all. During the day, to help her around the house, she has only a girl who comes in to make the bed, dust, and do the ironing. If she invites you to dinner, for example, Golda herself does the cooking, and after cooking, she cleans up: so that tomorrow the girl doesn't find everything dirty. Well, the evening before my appointment, she had guests to dinner and they stayed until two in the morning, leaving a shambles of dirty dishes, dirty glasses, overflowing ashtrays, disorder. So that tomorrow the girl wouldn't find everything dirty, at two in the morning Golda began washing dishes and glasses, sweeping, and tidying, and she did not get to bed before three-thirty. At seven, she got up, as always, to read the papers and listen to the news on the radio. At eight she conferred with certain generals. At nine she conferred with certain ministers. At ten . . . she felt ill. At the age of seventy-four, three and a half hours of sleep are not enough.

When I heard about it, I was ashamed to come in. I kept saying, "Let's put off the appointment, it doesn't matter, I swear it doesn't matter!" But she wanted to keep her engagement: "Yes, poor thing, she came all this way and it's the second time she's come and they stole her tapes." After resting for twenty minutes on the divan in her office, she appeared behind her desk, pale, worn out, and very sweet. I wasn't to worry about the delay; she would give me as much time as I needed. And the interview was resumed—like the time before, better than the time before. In October she had been unable to speak of her husband, of what had been the tragedy of her life. This time she did even this, and since to speak of it is so painful for her, when she found that she couldn't go on, she reassured me: "Don't worry, we'll finish tomorrow!"

Then she gave me a fourth appointment, the splendid hour in which we spoke of old age, youth, and death. God, how alluring she looked when she talked of these things! Many maintain that Golda is ugly and rejoice in doing cruel caricatures of her. I answer: Certainly beauty is an opinion, but to me Golda seems like a beautiful old woman. Many maintain that Golda is masculine and enjoy spreading vulgar jokes about her. I answer: Certainly femininity is an opinion, but to me Golda seems a woman in every way. That gentle modesty, for instance. That almost incredible candor when you remember how crafty and clever she can be when she swims among the whirlpools of politics. That torment in conveying the anguish of a woman for whom childbearing is not enough. That tenderness in evoking the testimony of her children and grandchildren. That involuntary flirting. The last time I saw her she was wearing a sky-blue pleated blouse, with a pearl necklace. Stroking it with her short, pink-manicured nails, she seemed to be asking, "So do I look all right?" And I thought, a pity she's in power, a pity she's on the side of those who command. In a woman like this, power is an error in taste.

I won't repeat that she was born in Kiev in 1898, with the name of Golda Mabovitz, that she grew up in America, in Milwaukee, where she married Morris Meyerson in 1917, that in 1918 she emigrated with him to Palestine, that the surname Meir was urged on her by David Ben-Gurion because it sounded more Hebrew, that her success began after she had served as ambassador to Moscow in the times of Stalin, that she smokes at least sixty cigarettes a day, that she keeps going mainly on coffee, that her working day lasts eighteen hours, that as prime minister she earns the miserable sum of about four hundred dollars a month. I'm not about to look for the secret of her legend. The interview that follows explains it with all her good and her flaws. I composed it following the chronology of the meetings.

Naturally the police never got to the core of the mystery surrounding the theft of those tapes. Or, if they did get to the core of it, they took care not to inform me. But a clue that soon became more than a clue offered itself. And it's worth the trouble to relate it, if only to give another idea of those in power.

At about the same time as my interview with Golda Meir, I had asked for one with Muammar el-Qaddafi. And he, through a high official of the Libyan Ministry of Information, had let me know that he would grant it. But all of a sudden, a few days after the theft of the tapes, he sent for the correspondent of a rival weekly of *L'Europeo*. The correspondent rushed off to Tripoli and, by some coincidence, Qaddafi regaled him with sentences that sounded like answers to what Mrs. Meir had told me. The poor journalist, needless to say, was ignorant of this detail. But I, needless to say, realized it at once. And I raised a more than legitimate question: how was it possible for Mr. Qaddafi to answer something that had never been published and that no one, other than myself, knew? Had Mr. Qaddafi listened to my tapes? Had he actually received them from someone who had stolen them from me? And immediately my mind recalled an unforgotten detail. The day after the theft I had played amateur detective and gone on the sly to rummage in the trash collected on the floor of the hotel where the crime had taken place. Here, and though they swore in the hotel that no Arab had gone up for days, I had discovered a piece of paper written in Arabic. I had given it, along with my statement, to the political division of the police.

That's all. And, of course, I might be mistaken. Of course, the thief might well have been some American tourist or some Frenchman. Qaddafi never granted me the promised interview. He never called me to Tripoli to dispel the shameful suspicion that I still feel justified in nourishing.

About Golda, well, she isn't involved any more in that error of taste called power. She is no longer prime minister. In a sudden, somehow brutal way, history took her off the job and sent her home. But home was the kibbutz where she had been longing to live and, I bet, that brutality was the nicest gift she could dream of. Nobody will ever convince me that she is not much happier now, far from power, than she ever was when I met her. After all, she deserves to end her days as she always dreamed. You will understand it from her own words.

GOLDA MEIR: Good morning, dear, good morning. I was just looking at your book on the war. And I was asking myself if women really react differently to war than men. . . . I'd say no. In these last years and during the war of attrition, I've so often found myself having to make certain decisions: for instance, to send our soldiers to places from where they wouldn't come back, or commit them to operations that would cost the lives of who knows how many human beings on both sides. And I suffered . . . I suffered. But I gave those orders as a man would have given them. And now that I think of it, I'm not at all sure that I suffered any more than a man would have. Among my male colleagues I have seen some oppressed by a darker sadness than mine. Oh, not that mine was little! But it didn't influence, no, it didn't influence my decisions. . . . War is an immense stupidity. I'm sure that someday all wars will end. I'm sure that someday children in school will study the history of the men who made war as you study an absurdity. They'll be astonished, they'll be shocked, just as today we're shocked by cannibalism. Even cannibalism was accepted for a long time as a normal thing. And yet today, at least physically, it's not practiced any more.

ORIANA FALLACI: Mrs. Meir, I'm glad you were the first to bring up this subject. Because it's just the one with which I meant to begin. Mrs. Meir, when will there be peace in the Middle East? Will we be able to see this peace in our lifetimes?

G.M.: You will, I think. Maybe . . . I certainly won't. I think the war in the Middle East will go on for many, many years. And I'll tell you why. Because of the indifference with which the Arab leaders send their people off to die, because of the low estimate in which they hold human life, because of the inability of the Arab people to rebel and say enough.

Do you remember when Khrushchev denounced Stalin's crimes during the Twentieth Communist Congress? A voice was raised at the back of the hall, saying, "And where were you, Comrade Khrushchev?" Khrushchev scrutinized the faces before him, found no one, and said, "Who spoke up?" No one answered. "Who spoke up?" Khrushchev asked again. And again no one answered. Then Khrushchev exclaimed, "Comrade, I was where you are now." Well, the Arab people are just where Khrushchev was, where the man was who reproached him without having the courage to show his face.

We can only arrive at peace with the Arabs through an evolution on their part that includes democracy. But wherever I turn my eyes to look, I don't see a shadow of democracy. I see only dictatorial regimes. And a dictator doesn't have to account to his people for a peace he doesn't make. He doesn't even have to account for the dead. Who's ever found out how many Egyptian soldiers died in the last two wars? Only the mothers, sisters, wives, relatives who didn't see them come back. Their leaders aren't even concerned to know where they're buried, if they're buried. While we . . .

O.F.: While you? . . .

G.M.: Look at these five volumes. They contain the photograph and biography of every man and woman soldier who died in the war. For us, every single death is a tragedy. We don't like to make war, even when we win. After the last one, there was no joy in our streets. No dancing, no songs, no festivities. And you should have seen our soldiers coming back victorious. Each one was a picture of sadness. Not only because they had seen their brothers die, but because they had had to kill their enemies. Many locked themselves in their rooms and wouldn't speak. Or when they opened their mouths, it was to repeat like a refrain: "I had to shoot. I killed." Just the opposite of the Arabs. After the war we offered the Egyptians an exchange of prisoners. Seventy of theirs for ten of ours. They answered, "But yours are officers, ours are fellahin! It's impossible." Fellahin, peasants. I'm afraid . . .

O.F.: Are you afraid that war between Israel and the Arabs may break out again?

G.M.: Yes. It's possible, yes. Because, you see, many say that the Arabs are ready to sign an agreement with us. But, in these dictatorial regimes, who is to say that such an agreement would be worth anything? Let's suppose that Sadat signs and is then assassinated. Or simply eliminated. Who's to say that his successor will respect the agreement signed by Sadat? Was the truce that all the Arab countries had signed with us respected? Despite that truce, there was never peace on our borders and today we're still waiting for them to attack us.

O.F.: But there's talk of an agreement today, Mrs. Meir. Even Sadat is talking about it. Isn't it easier to negotiate with Sadat than it was to negotiate with Nasser?

G.M.: Not at all. It's exactly the same. For the simple reason that Sadat doesn't want to negotiate with us. I'm more than ready to negotiate with him. I've been saying it for years: "Let's sit down at a table and see if we can arrange things, Sadat." He flatly refuses. He's not a bit ready to sit down at a table with me. He goes on talking about the difference between an agreement and a treaty. He says he's ready for an agreement, but not a peace treaty. Because a peace treaty would mean recognition of Israel, diplomatic relations with Israel. See what I mean? Sadat doesn't mean definite talks that would put an end to the war, but a kind of cease-fire. And then he refuses to negotiate with us directly. He wants to negotiate through intermediaries. We can't talk to each other through intermediaries! It's senseless, useless! In 1949 too, in Rhodes, after the War of Independence, we signed an agreement with the Egyptians, Jordanians, Syrians, and Lebanese. But it was through an intermediary, through Dr. Bunche, who on behalf of the United Nations met first with one group, then with another. . . . Great results.

O.F.: And the fact that Hussein is talking about peace—that isn't a good sign either?

G.M.: I've said nice things about Hussein lately. I congratulated him for having talked about peace in public. I'll go further and say I believe Hussein. I'm sure that by now he's realized how futile it would be for him to embark on another war. Hussein has understood that he made a terrible mistake in 1967, when he went to war with us without considering the message Eshkol had sent him: "Stay out of the war and nothing will happen to you." He's understood that it was a tragic piece of foolishness to listen to Nasser and his lies about bombing Tel Aviv. So now he wants peace. But he wants it on his conditions. He claims the left bank of the Jordan, that is the West Bank, he claims Jerusalem, he invokes the United Nations Resolution. . . . We once accepted a United Nations resolution. It was when we were asked to divide Jerusalem. It was a deep wound in our hearts, but still we accepted. And we all know the consequences. Were we maybe the ones to attack the Jordanian army? No, it was the Jordanian army that entered Jerusalem! The Arabs are really strange people: they lose wars and then expect to gain by it. After all, did we or didn't we win the Six Day War? Do we or don't we have the right to set our conditions? Since when in history does the one who attacks and loses have the right to dictate terms to the winner? They do nothing but tell us: restore this, restore that, give up this, give up that . . .

O.F.: Will you ever give up Jerusalem, Mrs. Meir?

G.M.: No. Never. No. Jerusalem no. Jerusalem never. Inadmissible. Jerusalem is out of the quastion. We won't even agree to discuss Jerusalem.

O.F.: Would you give up the West Bank of the Jordan?

G.M.: On this point there are differences of opinion in Israel. So it's possible that we'd be ready to negotiate about the West Bank. Let me make myself clearer. I believe the majority of Israelis would never ask the Knesset to give up the West Bank completely. However, if we should come to negotiate with Hussein, the majority of Israelis would be ready to hand back part of the West Bank. I said part—let that be clear. And for the moment the government hasn't decided either yes or no. Nor have I. Why should we quarrel among ourselves before the head of an Arab state says he's ready to sit down at a table with us? Personally, I think that if Hussein should decide to negotiate with us, we might give him back a part of the West Bank. Either after a decision by the government or parliament, or after a referendum. We could certainly hold a referendum on this matter.

O.F.: And Gaza? Would you give up Gaza, Mrs. Meir?

G.M.: I say that Gaza must, should be part of Israel. Yes, that's my opinion. Our opinion, in fact. However, to start negotiating, I don't ask Hussein or Sadat to agree with me on any point. I say, "My opinion, our opinion, is that Gaza should remain part of Israel. I know you think otherwise. All right, let's sit down at a table and start negotiating." Do I make myself clear? It's by no means indispensable to find ourselves in agreement before the negotiations: we hold negotiations precisely in order to reach an agreement. When I state that Jerusalem will never be divided, that Jerusalem will remain in Israel, I don't mean that Hussein or Sadat shouldn't mention Jerusalem. I don't even mean that they shouldn't mention Gaza. They can bring up anything they like at the time of negotiations.

O.F.: And the Golan Heights?

G.M.: It's more or less the same idea. The Syrians would like us to come down from the Golan Heights so that they can shoot down at us as they did before. Needless to say, we have no intention of doing so, we'll never come down from the plateau. Nevertheless, we're ready to negotiate with the Syrians too.

On our conditions. And our conditions consist in defining a border between Syria and Israel that stabilizes our presence up there. In other words, the Syrians today find themselves exactly where the border ought to be. On this I don't think we'll yield. Because only if they stay where they are today can they be kept from shooting down at us as they did for nineteen years.

O.F.: And the Sinai?

G.M.: We've never said that we wanted the whole Sinai or most of the Sinai. We don't want the whole Sinai. We want control of Sharm El Sheikh and part of the desert, let's say a strip of desert, connecting Israel with Sharm El Sheikh. Is that clear? Must I repeat it? We don't want most of the Sinai. Maybe we don't even want half of the Sinai. Because it's not important to us to be sitting along the Suez Canal. We're the first to realize that the Suez Canal is too important to the Egyptians, that to them it even represents a question of prestige. We also know that the Suez Canal isn't necessary for our defense. We're ready to give it up as of today. But we won't give up Sharm El Sheikh and a strip of desert connecting us with Sharm El Sheikh. Because we want our ships to be able to enter and leave Sharm El Sheikh. Because we don't want to find ourselves again in the conditions we found ourselves in the other time, when we gave up Sharm El Sheikh. Because we don't want to take the risk of waking up again some morning with the Sinai full of Egyptian troops. On these terms, and only on these terms, are we ready to negotiate with the Egyptians. To me they seem very reasonable terms.

O.F.: And so it's obvious that you'll never go back to your old borders.

G.M.: Never. And when I say never, it's not because we mean to annex new territory. It's because we mean to ensure our defense, our survival. If there's any possibility of reaching the peace you spoke of in the beginning, this is the only way. There'd never be peace if the Syrians were to return to the Golan Heights, if the Egyptians were to take back the whole Sinai, if we were to re-establish our 1967 borders with Hussein. In 1967, the distance to Natanya and the sea was barely ten miles, fifteen kilometers. If we give Hussein the possibility of covering those fifteen kilometers, Israel risks being cut in two and . . . They accuse us of being expansionists, but, believe me, we're not interested in expanding. We're only interested in new borders. And look, these Arabs want to go back to the 1967 borders. If those borders were the right ones, why did they destroy them?

O.F.: Mrs. Meir, so far we've been talking about agreements, negotiations, treaties. But since the 1967 cease-fire, the war in the Middle East has taken on a new face: the face of terror, of terrorism. What do you think of this war and the men who are conducting it? Of Arafat, for instance, of Habash, of the Black September leaders?

G.M.: I simply think they're not men. I don't even consider them human beings, and the worst thing you can say of a man is that he's not a human being. It's like saying he's an animal, isn't it? But how can you call what they're doing "a war"? Don't you remember what Habash said when he had a bus full of Israeli children blown up? "It's best to kill the Israelis while they're still children." Come on, what they're doing isn't a war. It's not even a revolutionary movement because a movement that only wants to kill can't be called revolutionary.

Look, at the beginning of the century in Russia, in the revolutionary movement that rose up to overthrow the czar, there was one party that considered terror the only means of struggle. One day a man from this party was sent with a bomb to a street corner where the carriage of one of the czar's high officials was supposed to pass. The carriage went by at the expected time. But the official was not alone, he was accompanied by his wife and children. So what did this true revolutionary do? He didn't throw the bomb. He let it go off in his hand and was blown to pieces. Look, we too had our terrorist groups during the War of Independence: the Stern, the Irgun. And I was opposed to them, I was always opposed to them. But neither of them ever covered itself with such infamy as the Arabs have done with us. Neither of them ever put bombs in supermarkets or dynamite in school buses. Neither of them ever provoked tragedies like Munich or Lod airport.

O.F.: And how can one fight such terrorism, Mrs. Meir? Do you really think it helps to bomb Lebanese villages?

G.M.: To a certain extent, yes. Of course. Because the fedayeen are in those villages. The Lebanese themselves say, "Certain areas are Al Fatah territory." So certain areas should be cleaned up. It's the Lebanese who should think of cleaning them up. The Lebanese say they can't do anything. Well, that's what Hussein used to say at the time when the fedayeen were encamped in Jordan. Even our American friends said it: "It's not that Hussein doesn't want to get rid of them! It's that he doesn't have enough strength to get rid of them." But in September 1970, when Amman was in danger and his palace was in danger and he himself found himself in danger, Hussein realized that he could do something. And he liquidated them. If the Lebanese go on doing nothing, we'll respond, "Very well. We realize your difficulties. You can't do anything. But we can. And just to show you, we'll bomb those areas that shelter the fedayeen."

Maybe more than any other Arab country, Lebanon is offering hospitality to the terrorists. The Japanese who carried out the Lod massacre came from Lebanon. The girls who tried to hijack the Sabena plane in Tel Aviv had been trained in Lebanon. Are we supposed to sit here with our hands folded, praying and murmuring, "Let's hope that nothing happens"? Praying doesn't help. What helps is to counterattack. With all possible means, including means that we don't necessarily like. Certainly we'd rather fight them in the open. But since that's not possible . . .

O.F.: Mrs. Meir, would you be ready to talk with Arafat or Habash?

G.M.: Never! Not with them! Never! What is there to discuss with people who haven't even the courage to risk their own skins and consign the bombs to someone else? Like those two Arabs in Rome, for example. The ones who handed the record player with a bomb to the two stupid English girls. Listen, we want to arrive at peace with the Arab states, with responsible governments of the Arab states, whatever their regime, since their regime isn't our concern. But to people like Habash, Arafat, Black September, we have nothing to say. The people to talk to are others.

O.F.: Do you mean us Europeans, Mrs. Meir?

G.M.: Exactly. The Europeans, and not only the Europeans, must

decide to stop this business that you call war. Up to now
there's been too much tolerance on your part. A tolerance, let
me say, that has its roots in unextinguished anti-Semitism.
But anti-Semitism is never exhausted in the suffering of just
Jews. History has shown that anti-Semitism in the world has
always brought on disaster for everyone. It begins by tormenting the Jews and ends by tormenting anybody. To give you a
trite example, there was that first airplane that was hijacked. It
was an El Al plane, remember? They hijacked it to Algeria.
Well, some people said it was too bad, others were happy
about it, and no pilot dreamed of declaring, "From now on I
don't fly to Algeria." If he had said this, if they had said it, this
nightmare of air piracy wouldn't exist today. Instead no one
reacted, and today air piracy is a custom of our times. Any
madman can hijack a plane to indulge his madness, any criminal can hijack a plane to extort money. You don't need political reasons.

But let's get back to Europe and the fact that terrorism has
its headquarters in Europe. In every European capital there
are offices of so-called liberation movements, and you know
very well it's not a matter of harmless offices. But you do
nothing against them. You'll be sorry. Thanks to your inertia
and your indulgence, terror will be multiplied and you'll pay
the price of it too. Haven't the Germans already done so?

O.F.: Yes, you were very hard on the Germans after they released
the three Arabs.

G.M.: Oh, you must try to understand what the Munich tragedy
meant to us! The very fact that it happened in Germany . . .
I mean, postwar Germany is not Nazi Germany. I know Willy
Brandt; I always meet him at socialist conferences; he was
once here too, when he was mayor of Berlin, and I'm well
aware that he fought the Nazis. Not for a moment did I think
that he was glad to release those Arabs. But Germany . . .
You see, I've never been able to set foot in Germany. I go to
Austria and can't bring myself to enter Germany. . . . For us
Jews, relations with Germany are such a conflict between
mind and heart. . . . Don't make me say such things. I'm
prime minister, I have certain responsibilities . . . Look, let

me conclude by saying that my harsh judgment couldn't be helped. The statements made by the Germans were like adding insult to injury. After all it was a matter of Arabs who had participated in the killing of eleven unarmed Israelis and who now will try to kill others.

O.F.: Mrs. Meir, do you know what many people think? That Arab terrorism exists and will always exist as long as there are Palestinian refugees.

G.M.: That's not so, because terrorism has become a kind of international evil—a sickness that strikes people who have nothing to do with Palestinian refugees. Take the example of the Japanese who carried out the Lod massacre. Are the Israelis occupying any Japanese territory? As for the refugees, listen: wherever a war breaks out there are refugees. Palestinian refugees aren't the only ones in the world; there are Pakistani, Hindu, Turkish, German ones. For heaven's sake, there were millions of German refugees along the Polish border that's now inside Poland. And yet Germany assumed the responsibility for these people, who were its own people. And the Sudeten Germans? Nobody thinks the Sudeten Germans should go back to Czechoslovakia—they themselves know they'll never go back. In the ten years I attended United Nations meetings, I never heard anyone talk about the Sudeten Germans who were thrown out of Czechoslovakia. Why does everyone get so emotional about the Palestinians and no one else?

O.F.: But the case of the Palestinians is different, Mrs. Meir, because . . .

G.M.: It certainly is. Do you know why? Because when there's a war and people run away, they usually run away to countries with a different language and religion. The Palestinians instead fled to countries where their own language was spoken and their own religion observed. They fled to Syria, Lebanon, Jordan— where nobody ever did anything to help them. As for Egypt, the Egyptians who took Gaza didn't even allow the Palestinians to work and kept them in poverty so as to use them as a weapon against us. That's always been the policy of the Arab countries: to use the refugees as a weapon against us. Hammarskjöld had proposed a development plan for the Middle East, and this plan provided first of all for the resettlement of the Palestinian refugees. But the Arab countries said no.

O.F.: Mrs. Meir, don't you at least feel a little sorry for them?

G.M.: Of course I do. But pity is not responsibility, and the responsibility for the Palestinians isn't ours, it's the Arabs'. We in Israel have absorbed about 1,400,000 Arab Jews: from Iraq, from Yemen, from Egypt, from Syria, from North African countries like Morocco. People who when they got here were full of diseases and didn't know how to do anything. Among the seventy thousand Jews who came here from Yemen, for example, there wasn't a single doctor or a single nurse, and almost all of them had tuberculosis. And still we took them, and built hospitals for them, and took care of them, we educated them, put them in clean houses, and turned them into farmers, doctors, engineers, teachers . . . Among the 150,000 Jews who came here from Iraq, there was only a very small group of intellectuals, and yet today their children go to the university. Of course, we have problems with them—all that glitters is not gold—but the fact remains that we accepted and helped them. The Arabs, on the other hand, never do anything for their own people. They make use of them and that's all.

O.F.: Mrs. Meir, what if Israel let the Palestinian refugees come back here?

G.M.: Impossible. For twenty years they've been fed on hatred for us; they can't come back among us. Their children weren't born here, they were born in the camps, and the only thing they know is that they must kill Israelis, destroy Israel. We found arithmetic books in the Gaza schools that put problems like this: "You have five Israelis. You kill three of them. How many Israelis are left to be killed?" When you teach such things to children of seven or eight, there's no more hope. Oh, it would be a great misfortune if there were no other solution for them but to return here! But there is a solution. It was demonstrated by the Jordanians when they gave them citizenship and called on them to build a country called Jordan. Yes, what Abdullah and Hussein did was much better than what the Egyptians did. But did you know that in the good old days in Jordan, Palestinians were holding office as prime minister and foreign minister? Did you know that after the partition of 1922 Jordan had only three hundred thousand Bedouins and that Palestinian refugees were in the majority? Why didn't they accept Jordan as their country, why . . . ?

O.F.: Because they don't recognize themselves as Jordanians, Mrs. Meir. Because they say they are Palestinians and that their home is in Palestine, not Jordan.

G.M.: Then we have to understand what we mean by the word Palestine. We must remember that when England assumed the mandate over Palestine, Palestine was the land included between the Mediterranean and the borders of Iraq. This Palestine covered both banks of the Jordan, and was even governed by the same high commissioner. Then in 1922 Churchill partitioned it, and the territory west of the Jordan became Cisjordania, and the territory east of the Jordan became Transjordania. Two names for the same people. Abdullah, Hussein's grandfather, had Transjordania and later he also took over Cisjordania, but, I repeat, it was still the same people. The same Palestine. Before liquidating Israel, Arafat should liquidate Hussein. But Arafat is so ignorant. He doesn't even know that, at the end of the First World War, what now is Israel wasn't called Palestine: it was called Southern Syria. And then . . . after all! If we must talk about refugees, I'll remind you that for centuries the Jews were refugees par excellence! Dispersed in countries where their language wasn't spoken, their religion not observed, their customs not recognized . . . Russia, Czechoslovakia, Poland, Germany, France, Italy, England, Arabia, Africa . . . Shut up in ghettos, persecuted, exterminated. And yet they survived, and they never stopped being a people, and they came together again to found a nation. . . .

O.F.: But that's just what the Palestinians want, Mrs. Meir: to form a nation. It's just for this reason that some people say they should have their state on the West Bank.

G.M.: Look, I've already explained that to east and west of the Jordan you find the same people. I've already explained that once they were called Palestinians and later were called Jordanians. If they now want to call themselves Palestinians or Jordanians, I couldn't care less. It's none of my business. But it is my busi-

ness that they don't set up another Arab state between Israel
and what is now called Jordan. In the stretch of land between
the Mediterranean and the borders of Iraq, there's room for
only two countries: one Arab and one Jewish. If we sign a
peace treaty with Hussein and define our borders with Jordan,
whatever happens on the other side of the border won't concern Israel. The Palestinians can come to any arrangement
they like with Hussein; they can call that state what they like,
give it any regime they like. The important thing is that a third
Arab state doesn't emerge between us and Jordan. We don't
want it. We can't allow it. Because it would come to be used
as a dagger against us.

O.F.: Mrs. Meir, I'd like to take up another subject. And here it is.
When one has a dream, this dream feeds on utopia. And
when the dream is realized, one discovers that . . . utopia is
utopia. Are you satisfied with what Israel is today?

G.M.: I'm a frank woman. I'll answer you frankly. As a socialist, no.
I can't say that Israel is what I dreamed. As a Jewish socialist
who has always laid great stress on the Jewish component in
her socialism, well, Israel is more than what I dreamed. Now
I'll explain. For me, the realization of Zionism is part of socialism. I know that other socialists won't agree with me, but
that's how I think of it. I'm not objective about this, and I
think there are a couple of gross injustices in the world: the
one oppressing black Africans and the one oppressing Jews.
And besides I think these two injustices can only be corrected
by socialist principles. To see justice for the Jewish people has
been the purpose of my life and . . . to cut it short, forty or
fifty years ago, I had no hopes at all that the Jews would have a
sovereign state. We do have one now, so it doesn't seem to me
right to worry too much about its faults and defects. We have
a soil where we can put our feet, where we can realize our
ideals of socialism that before were just hanging in the air.
That's already a lot. Of course, if I were really to examine my
thoughts . . .

O.F.: What is it you don't like in Israel? What is it that's disappointed you?

G.M.: Oh . . . I think that none of us dreamers realized in the beginning what difficulties would come up. For example, we hadn't foreseen the problem of bringing together Jews who had grown up in such different countries and remained divided from each other for so many centuries. Jews have come here from all over the world, as we wanted, yes. But each group had its own language, its own culture, and to integrate it with other groups has been much more difficult than it seemed in theory. It's not easy to create an homogenous nation with people so different. . . . There was bound to be a clash. And it gave me disappointment and grief. Also . . . you'll think me foolish, naïve, but I thought that in a Jewish state there wouldn't be the evils that afflict other societies. Theft, murder, prostitution . . . I thought so because we had started out well. Fifteen years ago in Israel there were almost no thefts, and there were no murders, there was no prostitution. Now instead we have everything, everything. . . . And it's something that breaks your heart; it hurts more than to discover that you still haven't created a more just, a more equal society.

o.f.: Mrs. Meir, but do you still believe in socialism as you did forty years ago?

g.m.: Essentially, yes. That's still the basic idea. . . . But to be honest, one must look at things realistically. One must admit that there's a big difference between socialist ideology and socialism as put to a practical test. All socialist parties that have come to form governments and assumed the responsibilities for a country have had to stoop to compromise. Not only that, ever since socialists have been in power in individual countries, international socialism has declined. It was one thing to be an international socialist when I was a girl, that is when no socialist party was in power, and quite another now. The dream I had, the dream of a just world united in socialism, has gone to the devil. National interests have prevailed over international interests, and the Swedish socialists have shown themselves to be first of all Swedes, the English socialists first of all Englishmen, the Jewish socialists first of all Jews. . . . This I began to understand during the war in Spain. In a lot of countries there were socialists in power. But they didn't lift a finger for the Spanish socialists.

O.F.: But what socialism are we talking about, Mrs. Meir? I mean, do you agree with Nenni when he says that he's come to prefer Swedish socialism?

G.M.: Of course! Because, you see, you can have all the dreams you like, but when you're dreaming, you're not awake. And when you wake up, you realize that your dream has very little in common with reality. To be free, to be able to say what you think, that's so necessary. . . . Soviet Russia isn't poor, it isn't illiterate, and yet there the people don't dare speak. And privilege still exists. . . . At the United Nations I never saw any difference between the foreign ministers of socialist countries and the foreign ministers of reactionary countries. A year ago, by abstaining from voting, they even let a resolution pass calling us war criminals. And I told my socialist colleagues when I met them at the Vienna Conference: "Your country abstained from voting. So that makes me a war criminal, eh?" But you were speaking of Pietro Nenni . . . Nenni is something else. Nenni's a separate chapter in the history of socialism. Nenni's one of the best individuals existing in the world today. Because he's so honest, there's such rectitude in him, such humanity, such courage of his convictions! I admire him like no one else. I'm proud to be able to call him a friend. And . . . of course I think the same as he does about socialism!

O.F.: Mrs. Meir, do you know what I've been thinking, listening to you? I've been wondering if so much sadness hasn't made you cynical, or at least disillusioned.

G.M.: Oh, no! Me, I'm not at all cynical! I've lost my illusions, that's all. For example, forty or fifty years ago, I thought that a socialist was always an honest person, incapable of telling lies. Now I know instead that a socialist is a human being like anyone else, capable of lying like anyone else, and behaving dishonestly like anyone else. That's sad, of course, but it's not enough to make you lose your faith in man! Not enough to conclude: man is fundamentally bad. No, no! Look, when I meet someone, I always think that this is an honest person and I go on thinking so until I have proof to the contrary. If later I do have proof to the contrary, I still don't say that that person is bad. I say that he or she has behaved badly with me. After all, I'm not suspicious. I never expect the worst from people.

And . . . I don't know if I'd call myself an optimist. At my age, optimism is too much of a luxury. But, look, in my long life I've seen so much evil, that's true. In return, I've also seen so much good. So very much. . . . And if in my memory I go over the many individuals I've known, believe me, there are very few I can judge in a completely negative way.

O.F.: But are you religious, Mrs. Meir?

G.M.: No! Oh, no! I never have been. Not even when I was a little girl. No, this attitude of mine doesn't come from a religious faith. It comes from my instinctive faith in men, from my stubborn love for humanity. Religion . . . You know, my family was traditional but not religious. Only my grandfather was religious, but with him you go very far back in time, you go back to the days when we lived in Russia. In America, you see . . . we spoke Hebrew among ourselves, we observed the holidays, but we went to temple very seldom. I only went for the New Year, to go with my mother and find her a place to sit. The only time I've followed the prayers in a synagogue was in Moscow. And you know what I say? If I'd stayed in Russia, I might have become religious. Maybe.

O.F.: Why?

G.M.: Because in Russia the synagogue is the only place where Jews can express themselves. Listen to what I did when I was sent to Moscow in 1948 by my government, as head of the diplomatic mission. Before leaving I gathered all the people who were going with me and said, "Take all your prayer books, prayer shawls, yarmulkes, everything. I'm sure we'll meet Jews only in the synagogue." Well, that's just how it happened. Of course, the first Saturday no one knew I'd go to the synagogue and I found hardly two hundred people there. Or a little more. But for Rosh Hashana, the Jewish New Year, and for Yom Kippur, the Day of Atonement, they came in thousands. I stayed in the synagogue from morning to night, and at the moment when the rabbi intoned the last sentence of the prayer of atonement, the one that says "*Leshana habaa b'Yerusha-laym*, next year in Jerusalem," the whole synagogue seemed to tremble. And I, who am an emotional woman, prayed. Really. You understand, it wasn't like being in Buenos Aires or New York and saying, "Next year in Jerusalem." From

Buenos Aires, New York, you take a plane and you go. There
in Moscow, the invocation took on a special meaning. And
while praying, I said, "God, make it really happen! If not next
year, in a few years." Does God exist and did he listen to me?
It's really happening.

O.F.: Mrs. Meir, don't you feel some sentimental tie with Russia?

G.M.: No, none. You know, many of my friends who left Russia as
adults say that they feel attached to that country, to its scenery,
its literature, its music. But I didn't get time to appreciate
those things. I was too little when I left Russia; I was only
eight, and of Russia I only have bad memories. No, from Russia I didn't take with me even a single moment of joy—all my
memories up to the age of eight are tragic memories. The
nightmare of pogroms, the brutality of the Cossacks charging
down on young socialists, fear, shrieking—that's the luggage I
packed in Russia and carried to the United States. Do you
know what's the first memory in my life? My father nailing up
the door and windows to keep the Cossacks from breaking into
our house and killing us. Oh, that sound of the hammer
pounding nails into the wooden planks! Oh, the sound of
horses' hoofs when the Cossacks are advancing along our
street!

O.F.: How old were you, Mrs. Meir?

G.M.: Five or six. But I remember everything so vividly. We lived
in Kiev, and the day my father left Kiev to go to the United
States . . . We were very poor, we didn't even have enough
to eat, and he thought of going to America for a year or two,
saving a little money and coming back. In the early 1900s, to
the Jews America was a kind of bank where you went to pick
up the dollars scattered on the sidewalks and came back with
your pockets full. So my father left Kiev, but Kiev was a city
forbidden to Jews who didn't have a job, for example a job like
my father's, he being a craftsman, and once he had left, we
had to leave too.

And we went to Pinsk, I, my mother, my two sisters. That
was in 1903. We stayed in Pinsk until 1905, when the brutality of the czarist regime reached its height. The Constitution
of 1905, in fact, was a dirty lie—a trick to gather the socialists
together and arrest them more easily. And my elder sister, who

was nine years older than I, belonged to the socialist movement. Her political activities kept her out late at night, and it
used to drive my mother crazy because our house was next to
a police station where they brought the young socialists they'd
arrested and . . . They beat them to death and every night
you heard such cries! My mother always thought she could
recognize my sister's voice. "It's she! It's she!" Oh, we were so
happy when my father wrote us to join him in America because in America things were good!

O.F.: You're very attached to America, aren't you?

G.M.: Yes, and not only because I grew up in America, because in
America I went to school, and lived there until I was almost
twenty. Because . . . well, because in America I lost my terror of Pinsk, of Kiev. How can I explain the difference for me
between America and Russia? Look, when we arrived, I was a
little more than eight years old, my elder sister was seventeen,
and my younger one four and a half. My father was working
and belonged to the union. He was very proud of his union,
and two months later, on Labor Day, he said to my mother,
"Today there's a parade. If you all come to the corner of such
and such a street, you'll see me marching with my union!"
My mother took us along, and while we were there waiting for
the parade, along came the mounted police to clear a path for
the marchers—do you see? But my little four-and-a-half-year-
old sister couldn't know that, and when she saw the police on
horseback, she began to tremble and then to cry, "The Cossacks! The Cossacks!" We had to take her away, without giving
my father the satisfaction of seeing him marching with his
union, and she stayed in bed for days with a high fever, repeating: "The Cossacks! The Cossacks!" So, look, the America
I knew is a place where men on horseback protect a parade of
workers, the Russia I knew is a place where men on horseback
massacre Jews and young socialists.

O.F.: That's not exactly how it is, Mrs. Meir, but anyway . . .

G.M.: Oh, listen! America is a great country. It has many faults,
many social inequalities, and it's a tragedy that the Negro
problem wasn't resolved fifty or a hundred years ago, but it's
still a great country, a country full of opportunity, of freedom!
Does it seem to you nothing to be able to say what you like, to

write what you like, even against the government, the Es-
tablishment? Maybe I'm not objective, but for America I feel
such gratitude! I'm fond of America, okay?

O.F.: Okay. We've finally come to the figure of Golda Meir. So
shall we talk about the woman Ben-Gurion called "the ablest
man in my cabinet"?

G.M.: That's one of the legends that's grown up around me. It's also
a legend I've always found irritating, though men use it as a
great compliment. Is it? I wouldn't say so. Because what does
it really mean? That it's better to be a man than a woman, a
principle on which I don't agree at all. So here's what I'd like
to say to those who make me such a compliment: And what if
Ben-Gurion had said, "The men in my cabinet are as able as a
woman"? Men always feel so superior! I'll never forget what
happened at a congress of my party in New York in the 1930s.
I made a speech, and in the audience there was a writer friend
of mine. An honest person, a man of great culture and refine-
ment. When it was over, he came up to me and exclaimed,
"Congratulations! You've made a wonderful speech! And to
think you're only a woman!" That's just what he said, in such
a spontaneous, instinctive way. It's a good thing I have a sense
of humor. . . .

O.F.: The Women's Liberation Movement will like that, Mrs.
Meir.

G.M.: Do you mean those crazy women who burn their bras and go
around all disheveled and hate men? They're crazy. Crazy.
But how can one accept such crazy women who think it's a
misfortune to get pregnant and a disaster to bring children into
the world? And when it's the greatest privilege we women have
over men! Feminism . . . Listen, I got into politics at the
time of the First World War, when I was sixteen or seventeen,
and I've never belonged to a women's organization. When I
joined the Zionist labor movement, I found only two other
women—ninety percent of my comrades were men. I've lived
and worked among men all my life, and yet to me the fact of
being a woman has never, never I say, been an obstacle. It's
never made me uncomfortable or given me an inferiority complex. Men have always been good to me.

O.F.: Are you saying you prefer them to women?

G.M.: No, I'm saying that I've never suffered on account of men because I was a woman. I'm saying that men have never given me special treatment but neither have they put obstacles in my way. Of course I've been lucky, of course not all women have had the same experience, but be that as it may, my personal case doesn't prove that those crazy women are right. There's only one point on which I agree with them: to be successful, a woman has to be much more capable than a man. Whether she dedicates herself to a profession or dedicates herself to politics. There aren't many women in our parliament, something that bothers me a lot. And these few women, let me assure you, are by no means less capable than men. In fact, they're often much more capable. So it's ridiculous that toward women there still exist so many reservations, so many injustices, that when a list is being drawn up for the elections, for example, only men's names get chosen. But is it all the fault of men? Wouldn't it be, at least partly, the fault of women too?

O.F.: Mrs. Meir, you've just said that to be successful a woman has to be much more capable than a man. Doesn't that perhaps mean it's more difficult to be a woman than a man?

G.M.: Yes, of course. More difficult, more tiring, more painful. But not necessarily through the fault of men—for biological reasons, I'd say. After all, it's the woman who gives birth. It's the woman who raises the children. And when a woman doesn't want only to give birth, to raise children . . . when a woman also wants to work, to be somebody . . . well, it's hard. Hard, hard. I know it from personal experience. You're at your job and you think of the children you've left at home. You're at home and you think of the work you're not doing. Such a struggle breaks out in you, your heart goes to pieces. Unless you live in a kibbutz, where life is organized in such a way that you can both work and have children. Outside the kibbutz, it's all running around, trying to be in two places at once, getting upset, and . . . well, all this can't help but be reflected on the structure of the family. Especially if your husband is not a social animal like yourself and feels uncomfortable with an active wife, a wife for whom it's not enough to be only a wife. . . . There has to be a clash. And the clash may even break up the marriage. As happened to me. Yes, I've paid for being what I am. I've paid a lot.

O.F.: In what sense, Mrs. Meir?

G.M.: In the sense of . . . pain. Because, you see, I know that my children, when they were little, suffered a lot on my account. I left them alone so often. . . . I was never with them when I should have been and would have liked to be. Oh, I remember how happy they were, my children, every time I didn't go to work because of a headache. They jumped and laughed and sang, "Mamma's staying home! Mamma has a headache!" I have a great sense of guilt toward Sarah and Menahem, even today when they're adults and have children of their own. And still . . . still I have to be honest and ask myself, Golda, deep in your heart do you really regret the fact that you behaved as you did with them? No. Not deep in my heart. Because through suffering I gave them a life that's more interesting, less banal than the ordinary. I mean, they didn't grow up in a narrow family environment. They met important people, they heard serious discussions, they took part in big things. And if you talk to them, they'll tell you the same thing. They'll tell you: "Yes, Mamma neglected us too much, she made us suffer by her absence, her politics, by not paying attention to us, but we can't bear her a grudge because, being the way she was, she gave us so much more than any other mother!"

If you knew how proud I felt the day that . . . In 1948, the time when we were fighting the British, I was writing the handbills that the boys and girls in the movement pasted on the walls at night. My daughter didn't know I was the one who was writing those handbills, and one day she said to me, "Mamma, I'll be back late tonight. And maybe I won't come back." "Why?" I asked, alarmed. "I can't tell you, Mamma." Then she went out with a package under her arm. Nobody could know better than I what was in that package, and putting up handbills at night was very dangerous. I stayed up till dawn waiting for Sarah, cursing myself in the fear that something had happened to her. But at the same time I was so proud of her!

O.F.: Mrs. Meir, that sense of guilt that you feel toward your children, did you also feel it toward your husband?

G.M.: Let's not talk about that . . . I don't want to talk about it . . . I never talk about it . . . Well, all right, let's try. You see, my husband was an extraordinarily nice person. Educated, kind, good. Everything about him was good. But he was also a person who was only interested in his family, his home, his music, his books. He was aware of social problems, of course, but when it came to his home and the unity of his family, they lost whatever interest they had for him. I was too different from him. I had always been. Domestic bliss wasn't enough for me, I had to be doing what I was doing! To give it up would have seemed to me an act of cowardice, of dishonesty with myself. I would have become set in my discontent, in sadness. . . .

I met my husband when I was just fifteen. We got married very soon, and from him I learned all the beautiful things like music and poetry. But I wasn't born to be satisfied with music and poetry, and . . . He wanted me to stay home and forget about politics. Instead I was always out, always in politics and . . . Of course I have a sense of guilt toward him too. . . . I made him suffer so much, him too. . . . He came to Israel because I wanted to come to Israel. He came to the kibbutz because I wanted to be on a kibbutz. He took up a way of life that didn't suit him because it was the kind of life that I couldn't do without. . . . It was a tragedy. A great tragedy. Because, as I say, he was a wonderful person and with a different woman he could have been very happy.

O.F.: Didn't you ever make an effort to adapt yourself to him, to please him?

G.M.: For him I made the biggest sacrifice of my life: I left the kibbutz. You see, there was nothing I loved so much as the kibbutz. I liked everything about the kibbutz: the manual work, the comradeship, the discomforts. Ours was in the valley of Jezreel, and in the beginning it had nothing to offer but swamps and sand, but soon it became a garden full of orange trees, fruits, and just to look at it gave me such joy that I could have spent my whole life there. Instead he couldn't stand it, neither psychologically nor physically. He couldn't stand eating at the communal table with the rest of us. He couldn't stand the hard work. He couldn't stand the climate and the feeling of being part of a community. He was too individualistic, too introverted, too delicate. He got sick and . . . we had to leave, go back to the city, to Tel Aviv. It was a feeling of pain that still goes through me like a needle. It was really a tragedy for me, but I put up with it, thinking that in the city the family would be more tranquil and more united. But it wasn't like that. And in 1938 we separated. Then in 1951 he died.

O.F.: Wasn't he proud of you, at least in the last years?

G.M.: I don't know . . . I don't think so. I don't know what he thought in the last years, and besides he was so withdrawn that nobody would have been able to guess it. Anyway his tragedy didn't come from the fact of not understanding me—he understood me very well. It came from the fact that he did understand me, and at the same time realized he couldn't change me. In short, he knew I had no choice, that I had to be what I was. But he didn't approve, that's it. And who knows if he wasn't right.

O.F.: But you never thought of getting a divorce, Mrs. Meir, you never thought of getting married again when he died?

G.M.: Oh, no! Never! Such an idea never entered my head, never! I've always gone on thinking of myself as married to him! After the separation we still saw each other. Sometimes he came to see me in my office. . . . Maybe you haven't understood one important thing: even though we were so different and incapable of living together, there was always love between us. Ours was a great love; it lasted from the day we met till the day he died. And a love like that can't be replaced.

O.F.: Mrs. Meir, is it true you're very modest? How should I say it . . . very puritanical, very concerned with morality?

G.M.: Look, as I said before, I've always lived among men. And never, never has a man allowed himself to tell a dirty joke in my presence, to say anything disrespectful or proposition me. Do you know why? Because I've always said that if I'm given a glass of water, that water must be clean. Otherwise I don't drink it. That's the way I am; I like things to be clean. A dear friend of mine once said to me, "Golda, don't be so rigid. There are no moral or immoral things. There are only beautiful or ugly things." I suppose he was right. What's more, I suppose that the same thing can be beautiful and ugly. Because to some it looks beautiful and to others ugly. However . . . I don't know how to explain. . . . Maybe this way: love is always beautiful, but the act of love with a prostitute is ugly.

O.F.: They say too that you're very hard, inflexible . . .

G.M.: I, hard? No. There are a few points, in politics, on which they might think me hard. In fact, I'm not one to compromise and I say so adamantly. I believe in Israel, I don't yield when it comes to Israel—period. Yes, in that sense the word inflexible applies to me. But otherwise, I mean in private life, with people, with human problems . . . it's foolish to say I'm hard. I'm the most sensitive creature that you'll ever meet. It's no accident that many accuse me of making political decisions on the basis of my feelings instead of my brain. Well, what if I do? I don't see anything bad in that, quite the contrary. I've always felt sorry for people who are afraid of their feelings, of their emotions, and who hide what they feel and can't cry wholeheartedly. Because anyone who can't cry wholeheartedly can't laugh wholeheartedly either.

O.F.: Do you sometimes really cry?

G.M.: Do I! And how! And yet if you were to ask me, "Tell me, Golda, have you had more laughter or tears in your life?" I'd answer, "I think I've laughed more than I've cried." Aside from my family dramas, my life has been so lucky. I've known such fine people, I've had the friendship of such interesting people—especially in the fifty years I've spent in Israel. I've always moved within a circle of intellectual giants; I've always been appreciated and loved. And what else can you ask of fortune? I'd really be ungrateful if I didn't know how to laugh.

O.F.: Not bad for a woman who's considered the symbol of Israel.

G.M.: I, a symbol?! Some symbol! Are you maybe pulling my leg? You didn't know the great men who were really the symbol of Israel, the men who founded Israel and by whom it was influenced. Ben-Gurion is the only one of them left, and I swear to you on my children and grandchildren that I've never put myself in the same category as a Ben-Gurion or a Katznelson.

I'm not crazy! I've done what I've done, that's true. But I can't say that if I hadn't done what I've done, Israel would have been any different.

O.F.: Then why do they say that you're the only one who can hold the country together?

G.M.: Nonsense! Now I'll tell you something that'll convince you. When Eshkol died in 1969, they conducted a poll to find out how much popularity his possible successors had. And you know how many people came out for me? One percent. Maybe one and a half percent. All right, there was a crisis in my party and even as foreign minister I'd felt the effects of it—but still one, one and a half percent! And a woman so unpopular up until three years ago should today be the one holding the country together? Believe me, the country holds together by itself; it doesn't need a prime minister named Golda Meir. If the young people were to say, "Enough fighting, enough war, let's surrender," no Golda Meir could do anything about it. If in the kibbutzim of Beth Shean, they had said, "Enough of living under the rockets of the fedayeen, enough sleeping in shelters, let's go away," no Golda Meir would have been able to do anything about it. What's more, it was by accident that Golda Meir got to lead the country. Eshkol was dead, someone had to take his place, and the party thought I might replace him because I was acceptable to all factions and . . . that's all. In fact, I didn't even want to accept. I had got out of governmental politics, I was tired. You can ask my children and grandchildren.

O.F.: Mrs. Meir, don't try to tell me that you're not aware of your success!

G.M.: Of course I am! I don't suffer from delusions of grandeur, but neither am I troubled by an inferiority complex. When I deny being a symbol and holding the country together, I'm not saying I'm a failure! I may not always have been perfect but I don't see that I've failed in my career, either as labor minister, or foreign minister, or party secretary, or head of the government. Indeed I must admit that, in my opinion, women can be good government leaders, good heads of state. Oh, Lord, maybe I would have functioned just as well if I'd been a man. . . . I don't know, I can't prove it, I've never been a man.

. . . But I think that women, more than men, possess a capacity that helps in doing this job. It's that of going right to the essence of things, of taking the bull by the horns. Women are more practical, more realistic. They don't dissipate themselves in mystifications like men, who always beat around the bush trying to get to the heart of the matter.

O.F.: And yet you sometimes speak as though you didn't like yourself. Do you like yourself, Mrs. Meir?

G.M.: What person with any sense likes himself? I know myself too well to like myself. I know all too well that I'm not what I'd like to be. And to give you an idea what I'd like to be, I'll tell you who I like: my daughter. Sarah is so good, so intelligent, so intellectually honest! When she believes in something, she goes all the way. When she thinks something, she says it without mincing words. And she never gives in to others, to the majority. I really can't say the same for myself. When you're doing the job I'm doing, you always have to stoop to compromises, you can never let yourself remain one hundred percent faithful to your ideas. Of course, there's a limit to compromise, and I can't say I always stoop to them. However, I stoop enough. And that's bad. That's another reason why I can't wait to retire.

O.F.: Will you really retire?

G.M.: I give you my word. Listen, in May next year I'll be seventy-five. I'm old. I'm exhausted. My health is essentially good, my heart functions, but I can't go on with this madness forever. If you only knew how many times I say to myself: To hell with everything, to hell with everybody, I've done my share, now let the others do theirs, enough, enough, enough! There are days when I'd like to pack up and leave without telling anyone. If I've stayed this long, if for the moment I'm still here, it's out of duty and nothing else. I can't just throw everything out the window! Yes, many don't believe that I'll leave. Well, they'd better believe it, I'll even give you the date: October 1973. In October of '73 there'll be elections. Once they're over, good-by!

O.F.: I don't believe it. And everyone says you'll change your mind because you aren't able to sit still and do nothing.

G.M.: Look, there's another thing that people don't know about me.

By nature, I'm a lazy woman. I'm not one of those people who has to fill up every minute or else get sick. I like to be with nothing to do, even just sitting in an armchair, or wasting time with little things I enjoy. Cleaning the house, ironing, cooking a meal . . . I'm an excellent cook, an excellent housewife. My mother used to say, "But why do you want to study? You're such a good housewife!" And then I like to sleep. Oh, I like it so much! I like to be with people, to talk about this and that—to hell with serious talk, political talk! I like to go to the theater. I like to go to the movies, without my bodyguard underfoot. How did it happen that whenever I want to see a film, they even send the Israeli army reserves along with me? This is a life? It's been years that I haven't been able to do what I like, to sleep, to talk about trivial things, to sit with my hands folded. I'm always tied to this piece of paper that lists what I have to do, what I have to say, half hour by half hour.

Ah! And then there's my family. I don't want my grandchildren to say, "Grandma behaved badly with her children and neglected them, and later she behaved badly with us and neglected us." I'm a grandmother. I don't have many more years to live. And I intend to spend those years with my grandchildren. I also intend to spend them with my books. I have shelves full of books that I've never read. At two in the morning when I go to bed, I take one of them in my hand and try to read it, but after two minutes—pff!—I fall asleep and the book drops. Finally I want to go to Sarah's kibbutz when I like. For a week, a month, not rush there Friday evening to rush back on Saturday evening. I should be the master of the clock, not the clock the master of me.

O.F.: So you're not afraid of old age.

G.M.: No, it's never frightened me. When I know I can change things, I become as active as a cyclone. And almost always I succeed in changing them. But when I know I can't do anything, I resign myself. I'll never forget the first time I flew in an airplane—in 1929, from Los Angeles to Seattle. For my work, eh, not for fun! It was a little plane and the moment it took off, I thought: How crazy! Why did I do it? But right after that I calmed down—what good would it do to get frightened?

Another time I flew from New York to Chicago with a friend
of mine, and we got caught in an awful storm. The plane was
bouncing and swaying, and my friend cried like a baby. So I
said to him, "Stop it, why are you crying, what good does it
do?" My dear, old age is like an airplane flying in a storm.
Once you're in it, there's nothing you can do. You can't stop a
plane, you can't stop a storm, you can't stop time. So you
might as well take it easy, with wisdom.

O.F.: Is it this wisdom that sometimes makes you severe with young
people?

G.M.: Listen, you'd have to be crazy not to realize that the younger
generations think differently and that that's the way it should
be. It would really be dreary if every generation was a copy of
the previous one; the world wouldn't go forward any more. I
accept the fact with joy that young people are different from
me. What I condemn in them is their presumption in saying,
"Everything you've done is wrong so we'll redo it all from the
beginning." Well, if they were to do it all over again better, I
wouldn't even mind, but in many cases they're no better than
us old people and can even be worse. The calendar isn't the
standard for good and evil! I know selfish and reactionary
young people and generous and progressive old ones. And
then there's another thing I condemn in young people: their
mania for copying whatever comes from outside. Their fashions irritate me. Why that music that isn't music and is only
good to give you a headache? Why that long hair, those short
skirts? I hate fashions, and I've always hated them. Fashion is
an imposition, a lack of freedom. Somebody in Paris decides
for some reason that women should wear miniskirts, and here
they all are in miniskirts: long legs, short legs, skinny legs, fat
legs, ugly legs. . . . Never mind as long as they're young.
When they're fifty, I really get mad. Have you seen those old
men who grow a bunch of little curls on the back of their
necks?

O.F.: The fact is, Mrs. Meir, that yours was a heroic generation,
while the one of today . . .

G.M.: So is the one of today. Like my children's generation. When
I see men of forty-five or fifty who've been fighting the war for
twenty, thirty years . . . But you know what I say? Even the

young people of today are a heroic generation. At least in Israel. When I think that at eighteen they've already been soldiers, and that to be a soldier here doesn't just mean training and that's all . . . I feel my heart bursting. When I go among high-school students and think that a whim of Sadat's could tear them away from their desks, I get a lump in my throat. For the moment I often get impatient with them. I argue with them. But after five minutes I say to myself, Golda, in a month they could be at the front. Don't be impatient with them. So let them be conceited, arrogant. So let them wear miniskirts, long hair. Last week I was at a kibbutz in the north. In the office they were shocked, they said, "To make such a trip! So tiring! You're crazy!" But you know why I went? Because the granddaughter of one of my old comrades was getting married. And in the Six Day War he had lost two grandsons.

O.F.: Mrs. Meir, have you ever killed anyone?

G.M.: No . . . I've learned to shoot, of course, but I've never happened to kill anyone. I don't say it as consolation—there's no difference between killing and making decisions by which you send others to kill. It's exactly the same thing. And maybe it's worse.

O.F.: Mrs. Meir, how do you look on death?

G.M.: I can tell you right away: my only fear is to live too long. You know, old age is not a sin and not a joy—there are plenty of disagreeable things about old age. Not to be able to run up and down the stairs, not to be able to jump. . . . And yet you get used to some things without difficulty. It's just a matter of physical troubles, and physical troubles aren't degrading. What is degrading is to lose your mental lucidity, to become senile. Senility . . . I've known people who died too soon, and that hurt me. I've known people who died too late, and that hurt me just as much. Listen, for me, to witness the decay of a fine intelligence is an insult. I don't want that insult to happen to me. I want to die with my mind clear. Yes, my only fear is to live too long.

Jerusalem, November 1972

5

Yasir Arafat

When he arrived, on the dot for the appointment, I remained for a moment uncertain, telling myself no, it couldn't be he. He seemed too young, too innocuous. At least at first glance, I noticed nothing in him that showed authority, or that mysterious fluid that always emanates from a leader to assail you like a perfume or a slap in the face. The only striking thing about him was his mustache, thick and identical with the mustaches worn by almost all Arabs, and the automatic rifle that he wore on his shoulder with the free-and-easy air of one who is never separated from it. Certainly he loved it very much, that rifle, to have wrapped the grip with adhesive tape the color of a green lizard: somehow amusing. He was short in height, five feet three, I'd say. And even his hands were small, even his feet. Too small, you thought, to sustain his fat legs and his massive trunk, with its huge hips and swollen, obese stomach.

All this was topped by a small head, the face framed by a kassiah, and only by observing this face were you convinced that yes, it was he, Yasir Arafat, the most famous guerrilla in the Middle East, the man about whom people talked so much, to the point of tedium. A very strange, unmistakable face that you would have recognized among a thousand in the dark. The face of an actor. Not only for the dark glasses that by now distinguished him like the eyepatch of his implacable enemy Moshe Dayan, but for his mask, which resembles no one and recalls the profile of a bird of prey or an angry ram. In fact, he has almost no cheeks or forehead. Everything is summed up in a large mouth with red and fleshy lips, then in an aggressive nose, and two eyes that though screened by glass lenses hypnotize you: large, shining, and bulging. Two ink spots. With those eyes he was now looking at me, courteously and absentmindedly. Then in a soft, almost affectionate voice, he murmured in English, "Good evening, I'll be with you in two minutes." His voice had a kind of funny whistle in it. And something feminine.

Those who had met him by day, when the Jordanian headquarters of Al Fatah was thronged with guerrillas and other people, swore they had seen around him a stirring excitement, the same as he aroused every time he appeared in public. But my appointment was at night, and at that hour, ten o'clock, there was almost no one. This helped to deprive his arrival of any dramatic atmosphere. Not knowing his identity, you would have concluded that the man was important only because he was accompanied by a bodyguard. But what a bodyguard! The most gorgeous piece of male flesh I had ever seen. Tall, slender, elegant: the type who wears camouflage coveralls as though they were black tie and tails, with the chiseled features of a Western lady-killer. Perhaps because he was blond and with blue eyes, I had the spontaneous thought that the handsome bodyguard was a Westerner, even a German. And perhaps because Arafat brought him along with such tender pride, I had the still more spontaneous thought that he was something more than a bodyguard. A very loving friend, let's say. In addition to him, who soon turned on his heel and disappeared, there was an ugly individual in civilian clothes who gave you dirty looks as though to say: "Touch my chief and I'll drill you full of holes." Finally there was the escort who was to act as interpreter, and Abu George, who was to write down questions and answers so that they could later be checked with my text.

These last two followed us into the room chosen for the interview. In the room there were a few chairs and a desk. With a provocative, exhibitionist gesture, Arafat put his automatic rifle on the desk and sat down with a smile of white teeth, pointed as the teeth of a wolf. On his windbreaker, of gray-green cloth, a badge stood out with two Vietnam Marines and the inscription "Black Panthers against American Fascism." It had been given to him by two kids from California who called themselves American Marxists and had come with the pretext of offering him the alliance of Rap Brown, but in reality to do a film and make money. I told him so. He was struck by my judgment but not offended. The atmosphere was relaxed, cordial, but unpromising. I knew that an interview with Arafat is never good for obtaining memorable responses. And even less for getting any information out of him.

The most famous man in the Palestinian resistance is also the most mysterious; the curtain of silence surrounding his private life is so thick as to make you wonder if it doesn't constitute a trick to increase his publicity, a piece of coquetry to make him more precious. Even to obtain an interview with him is very difficult. With the excuse that he is always traveling, now to Cairo and now to Rabat, now to Lebanon and now to Saudi Arabia, now to Moscow and now to Damascus, they keep you waiting for days, for weeks, and if then they give it to you, it is with the air of presenting you with a special privilege or an exclusive right of which you're not worthy.

In the meantime, you try, of course, to gather information on his character, on his past. But wherever you turn, you find an embarrassed silence, only partly justified by the fact that Al Fatah maintains the greatest secrecy about its leaders and never supplies you with their biographies. Under-the-table confidences will whisper that he's not a communist, that he never would be even if Mao Tse-tung himself were personally to indoctrinate him; he is a soldier, they repeat, a patriot, and not an ideologue.

Indiscretions by now widespread will confirm that he was born in Jerusalem, sometime in the late twenties, that his family was noble and his youth spent in easy circumstances: his father owned an old fortune still largely unconfiscated. Such confiscation, which took place over the course of a century and a half, had been imposed by the Egyptians on certain land estates and on certain property in the center of Cairo. And then? Let's see. . . . Then in 1947 Yasir had fought against the Jews who were giving birth to Israel and had enrolled in Cairo University to study engineering. In those years he had also founded the Palestinian Student Association, the same from which the nucleus of Al Fatah was to emerge. Having obtained his degree, he had gone to work in Kuwait; here he had founded a newspaper in support of the nationalist struggle, and he had joined a group called the Muslim Brothers. In 1955 he had

gone back to Egypt to take an officers' training course and special-
ize in explosives; in 1963 he had helped especially in the birth of Al
Fatah and assumed the name of Abu Ammar. That is, He Who
Builds, Father Builder. In 1967 he had been elected president of
the PLO, the Palestinian Liberation Organization, a movement
that now includes the members of Al Fatah, of the Popular Front,
of Al Saiqa, and so forth; only recently he had been chosen as the
spokesman of Al Fatah, its messenger.

At this point, if you asked why, they spread their arms and answered, "Well, someone has to do that too, one person or another,
it doesn't make any difference." Of his daily life they told you
nothing, except for the detail that he didn't even have a house. And
it was true. When he wasn't staying with his brother in Amman, he
slept on the bases or wherever he happened to be. It was also true
that he was not married. There were no known women in his life,
and despite the gossip of a platonic flirtation with a Jewish woman
writer who had embraced the Arab cause, it really seemed that he
could do without them: as I had suspected seeing him arrive with
the handsome bodyguard.

You see, my suspicion is that, except for whatever details might
serve to correct any inexactness, there is nothing more to say about
Arafat. When a man has a tumultuous past, you feel it even when
he conceals it, since his past is written on his face, in his eyes. But
on Arafat's face you find only that strange mask placed there by
Mother Nature, not by any experience for which he has paid.
There is something unsatisfactory about him, something un-
realized. Furthermore, if you stop to think about it, you realize that
his fame burst out more through the press than through his ex-
ploits. Even worse, it was pulled out of the shadows by Western
journalists and particularly by the Americans, who are always so
skillful in inventing personalities or building them up. Just think of
what they did with the bonzes in Vietnam, and with that nobody
called the venerable Tri Quang. Of course, Arafat cannot be compared to Tri Quang. He is truly a creator of the Palestinian resistance, or one of its creators, and a strategist. Or one of its strategists. But this doesn't mean, all the less did it mean when I met
him, that he was the leader of the Palestinians in war. (The real
brains of the movement, at the time, was Farolik El Kaddoumi,

called Abu Lotuf.) And, in any case, among all the Palestinians I met, Arafat remains the one who impressed me least of all.

Or should I say the one I liked least of all? One thing is certain: he is not a man born to be liked. He is a man born to irritate. It is difficult to feel sympathy for him. First of all for the silent refusal that he opposes to anyone attempting a human approach: his cordiality is superficial, his politeness (when it exists) is formal, and a trifle is enough to make him hostile, cold, and arrogant. He warms up only when he gets angry. And then his soft voice becomes a loud one, his eyes become pools of hatred, and he looks as though he would like to tear you to pieces along with all his enemies.

Then, a lack of originality and charm characterizes all his replies. In my opinion, it is not the questions that count in an interview but the answers. If a person has talent, you can ask him or her the most banal thing in the world: he or she will always find the way to answer you brilliantly or profoundly. If a person is mediocre, you can put the most acute questions in the world to him or her: he or she always answer you as a mediocrity. If then you apply such a law to a man struggling between calculation and passions, watch out. After listening to him, you're likely to end up empty-handed. With Arafat I really found myself left empty-handed. He almost always reacted with indirect or evasive discourses, turns of phrase that contained nothing beyond his rhetorical intransigence, his constant fear of not persuading me.

He had no wish to consider, even as part of a dialectical game, the point of view of others. Nor is it enough to observe how the encounter between an Arab who believes in the war and a European who no longer believes in it is an immensely difficult encounter. Also because the latter remains imbued with her Christianity, with her hatred for hatred, and the other instead remains muffled inside his law of an eye for an eye, and a tooth for a tooth, which is the epitome of any mistaken pride. But there comes a point at which such pride fails, and it is there where Yasir Arafat invokes the understanding of others or insists on dragging anyone who is disturbed by doubts behind his own barricade. To be interested in his cause, to admit its fundamental justice, to criticize its weak points, and therefore risk one's own physical and moral safety, are not enough for him. Even to this he reacts with the arrogance that I mentioned, the most unjustified haughtiness, and that absurd inclination to pick a quarrel. And aren't these the characteristics of mediocrity, of insufficient intelligence?

The interview lasted ninety minutes, a great part of which was wasted in translating the answers that he gave me in Arabic. He insisted on this himself—so as to ponder each word, I suppose. And each of those ninety minutes left me dissatisfied on the human level as well as on the intellectual or political. But I was amused to discover that he doesn't wear dark glasses in the evening because he needs them to see. He wears them to be noticed. In fact, whether by day or night, he sees very well. With blinkers, but very well. Hasn't he even made a career in recent years? Hasn't he got himself elected head of the whole Palestinian resistance and doesn't he travel around like a chief of state? As such, doesn't he go to the UN where he shouts, "An olive branch in one hand and a gun in the other hand," thus disturbing the best friends of the Palestinian cause? Nobody could ever accuse me of denying the rights of the Palestinians. I'm convinced that they will win because they must win. Yet it is bitter to see their rights advanced by inadequate people. And here is my personal judgment on Arafat: someone that history will inevitably reassess, like Kissinger, and restore to his real proportions.

ORIANA FALLACI: Abu Ammar, people talk of you so much but almost nothing is known about you and . . .

YASIR ARAFAT: The only thing to say about me is that I'm a humble Palestinian fighter. I became one in 1947, along with the rest of my family. Yes, that was the year when my conscience was awakened and I understood what a barbarous invasion had taken place in my country. There had never been one like it in the history of the world.

O.F.: How old were you, Abu Ammar? I ask because there's some controversy about your age.

Y.A.: No personal questions.

O.F.: Abu Ammar, I'm only asking how old you are. You're not a woman. You can tell me.

Y.A.: I said, no personal questions.

O.F.: Abu Ammar, if you don't even want to tell your age, why do you always expose yourself to the attention of the world and let the world look on you as the head of the Palestinian resistance?

Y.A.: But I'm not the head of it! I don't want to be! Really, I swear it. I'm just a member of the Central Committee, one of many, and to be precise the one who has been ordered to be the spokesman. That is to report what others decide. It's a great misunderstanding to consider me the head—the Palestinian resistance doesn't have a head. We try in fact to apply the concept of collective leadership and obviously the matter presents difficulties, but we insist on it since we believe it's indispensable not to entrust the responsibility and prestige to one man alone. It's a modern concept and helps not to do wrong to the masses who are fighting, to our brothers who are dying. If I should die, your curiosity will be exhausted—you'll know everything about me. Until that moment, no.

O.F.: I wouldn't say your comrades could afford to let you die, Abu Ammar. And, to judge by your bodyguard, I'd say they think you're much more useful if you stay alive.

Y.A.: No. Probably instead I'd be much more useful dead than alive. Ah, yes, my death would do much to help the cause, as an incentive. Let me even add that I have many probabilities of dying—it could happen tonight, tomorrow. If I die, it's not a tragedy—someone else will go around in the world to represent Al Fatah, someone else will direct the battles. . . . I'm more than ready to die. I don't care about my safety as much as you think.

O.F.: I understand. On the other hand, you cross the lines into Israel once in a while yourself, don't you, Abu Ammar? The Israelis are convinced that you've entered Israel twice, and just escaped being ambushed. And they add that anyone who succeeds in doing this must be very clever.

Y.A.: What you call Israel is my home. So I was not in Israel but in my home—with every right to go to my home. Yes, I've been there, but much more often than only twice. I go there continually, I go when I like. Of course, to exercise this right is fairly difficult—their machine guns are always ready. But it's less difficult than they think; it depends on circumstances, on the points chosen. You have to be shrewd about it, they're right about that. It's no accident that we call these trips "trips of the fox." But you can go ahead and inform them that our boys, the fedayeen, make these trips daily. And not always to attack the enemy. We accustom them to crossing the lines so they'll know their own land, and learn to move about there with ease. Often we get as far, because I've done it, as the Gaza Strip and the Sinai Desert. We even carry weapons there. The Gaza fighters don't receive their arms by sea—they receive them from us, from here.

O.F.: Abu Ammar, how long will all this go on? How long will you be able to resist?

Y.A.: We don't even go in for such calculations. We're only at the beginning of this war. We're only now beginning to prepare ourselves for what will be a long, a very long, war. Certainly a war destined to be prolonged for generations. Nor are we the first generation to fight. The world doesn't know or forgets that in the 1920s our fathers were already fighting the Zionist invader. They were weak then, because too much alone against adversaries who were too strong and were supported by the English, by the Americans, by the imperialists of the earth. But we are strong—since January 1965, that is since the day that Al Fatah was born, we're a very dangerous adversary for Israel. The fedayeen are acquiring experience, they're stepping up their attacks and improving their guerrilla tactics; their numbers are increasing at a tremendous rate. You ask how long we'll be able to resist—that's the wrong question. You should ask how long the Israelis will be able to resist. For we'll never stop until we've returned to our home and destroyed Israel. The unity of the Arab world will make this possible.

O.F.: Abu Ammar, you always invoke the unity of the Arab world. But you know very well that not all the Arab states are ready to go to war for Palestine and that, for those already at war, a peaceful agreement is possible, and can even be expected. Even Nasser said so. If such an agreement should take place, as Russia too expects, what will you do?

Y.A.: We won't accept it. Never! We will continue to make war on Israel by ourselves until we get Palestine back. The end of

Israel is the goal of our struggle, and it allows for neither compromise nor mediation. The issues of this struggle, whether our friends like it or not, will always remain fixed by the principles that we enumerated in 1965 with the creation of Al Fatah. First: revolutionary violence is the only system for liberating the land of our fathers; second: the purpose of this violence is to liquidate Zionism in all its political, economic, and military forms, and to drive it out of Palestine forever; third: our revolutionary action must be independent of any control by party or state; fourth: this action will be of long duration. We know the intentions of certain Arab leaders: to resolve the conflict with a peaceful agreement. When this happens, we will oppose it.

O.F.: Conclusion: you don't at all want the peace that everyone is hoping for.

Y.A.: No! We don't want peace. We want war, victory. Peace for us means the destruction of Israel and nothing else. What you call peace is peace for Israel and the imperialists. For us it is injustice and shame. We will fight until victory. Decades if necessary, generations.

O.F.: Let's be practical, Abu Ammar. Almost all the fedayeen bases are in Jordan, others are in Lebanon. Lebanon has little wish to fight a war, and Jordan would very much like to get out of it. Let's suppose that these two countries, having decided on a peaceful agreement, decide to prevent your attacks on Israel. In other words, they prevent the guerrillas from being guerrillas. It's already happened and will happen again. In the face of this, what do you do? Do you also declare war on Jordan and Lebanon?

Y.A.: We can't fight on the basis of "ifs." It's the right of any Arab state to decide what it wants, including a peaceful agreement with Israel; it's our right to want to return home without compromise. Among the Arab states, some are unconditionally with us. Others not. But the risk of remaining alone in fighting Israel is a risk that we've foreseen. It's enough to think of the insults they hurled at us in the beginning; we have been so maltreated that by now we don't pay any attention to maltreatment. Our very formation, I mean, is a miracle. The candle that was lighted in 1965 burned in the blackest darkness. But now we are many candles, and we illuminate the whole Arab nation. And beyond the Arab nation.

O.F.: That's a very poetic and very diplomatic answer, but it's not the answer to what I asked you, Abu Ammar. I asked you: If Jordan really doesn't want you any more, do you declare war on Jordan?

Y.A.: I'm a soldier and a military leader. As such I must keep my secrets—I won't be the one to reveal our future battlefields to you. If I did, Al Fatah would court-martial me. So draw your own conclusions from what I said before. I told you we'll continue our march for the liberation of Palestine to the end, whether the countries in which we find ourselves like it or not. Even now we are in Palestine.

O.F.: We're in Jordan, Abu Ammar. And I ask you: But what does Palestine mean? Even Palestine's national identity has been lost with time, and its geographical borders have also been lost. The Turks were here, before the British Mandate and Israel. So what are the geographical borders of Palestine?

Y.A.: We don't bring up the question of borders. We don't speak of borders in our constitution because those who set up borders were the Western colonialists who invaded us after the Turks. From an Arab point of view, one doesn't speak of borders; Palestine is a small dot in the great Arabic ocean. And our nation is the Arab one, it is a nation extending from the Atlantic to the Red Sea and beyond. What we want, ever since the catastrophe exploded in 1947, is to free our land and reconstruct the democratic Palestinian state.

O.F.: But when you talk of a state, you have to say too within what geographical limits this state is formed or will be formed! Abu Ammar, I ask you again: what are the geographical borders of Palestine?

Y.A.: As an indication, we may decide that the borders of Palestine are the ones established at the time of the British Mandate. If we take the Anglo-French agreement of 1918, Palestine means the territory that runs from Naqurah in the north to Aqaba in the south, and then from the Mediterranean coast that includes the Gaza Strip to the Jordan River and the Negev Desert.

O.F.: I see. But this also includes a good piece of land that today is part of Jordan, I mean the whole region west of the Jordan. Cisjordania.

Y.A.: Yes. But I repeat that borders have no importance. Arab unity is important, that's all.

O.F.: Borders have importance if they touch or overlap the territory of a country that already exists, like Jordan.

Y.A.: What you call Cisjordania is Palestine.

O.F.: Abu Ammar, how is it possible to talk of Arab unity if from now on such problems come up with certain Arab countries? Not only that, but even you Palestinians are not in agreement. There is even a great division between you of Al Fatah and the other movements. For example, with the Popular Front.

Y.A.: Every revolution has its private problems. In the Algerian revolution there was also more than one movement, and for all I know, even in Europe during the resistance to the Nazis. In Vietnam itself there exist several movements; the Vietcong are simply the overwhelming majority, like we of Al Fatah. But we of Al Fatah include ninety-seven percent of the fighters and are the ones who conduct the struggle inside the occupied territory. It was no accident that Moshe Dayan, when he decided to destroy the village of El Heul and mined 218 houses as a punitive measure, said, "We must make it clear who controls this village, we or Al Fatah." He mentioned Al Fatah, not the Popular Front. The Popular Front . . . In February 1969 the Popular Front split into five parts, and four of them have already joined Al Fatah. Therefore we're slowly being united. And if George Habash, the leader of the Popular Front, is not with us today, he soon will be. We've already asked him to join us; there's basically no difference in objectives between us and the Popular Front.

O.F.: The Popular Front is communist. You say that you're not set up that way.

Y.A.: There are fighters among us representing all ideas; you must have met them. Therefore among us there is also room for the Popular Front. Only certain methods of struggle distinguish us from the Popular Front. In fact we of Al Fatah have never hijacked an airplane, and we have never planted bombs or caused shooting in other countries. We prefer to conduct a

purely military struggle. That doesn't mean, however, that we
too don't have recourse to sabotage—inside the Palestine that
you call Israel. For instance, it's almost always we who set off
bombs in Tel Aviv, in Jerusalem, in Eilat.

O.F.: That involves civilians, however. It's not a purely military
struggle.

Y.A.: It is! Because, civilians or military, they're all equally guilty of
wanting to destroy our people. Sixteen thousand Palestinians
have been arrested for helping our commandos, eight thousand houses of Palestinians have been destroyed, without
counting the tortures that our brothers undergo in their
prisons, and napalm bombings of the unarmed population.
We carry out certain operations, called sabotage, to show
them that we're capable of keeping them in check by the same
methods. This inevitably hits civilians, but civilians are the
first accomplices of the gang that rules Israel. Because if the
civilians don't approve of the methods of the gang in power,
they have only to show it. We know very well that many don't
approve. Those, for example, who lived in Palestine before the
Jewish immigration, and even some of those who immigrated
with the precise intention of robbing us of our land. Because
they came here innocently, with the hope of forgetting their
ancient sufferings. They had been promised Paradise, here on
earth, and they came to take over Paradise. Too late they discovered that instead it was hell. Do you know how many of
them now want to escape from Israel? You should see the emi-
gration applications that pile up at the Canadian embassy in
Tel Aviv, or the United States embassy. Thousands.

O.F.: Abu Ammar, you never answer me directly. But this time you
must do so. What do you think of Moshe Dayan?

Y.A.: That's a very embarrassing question. How can I answer? Let's
say this: I hope that one day he'll be tried as a war criminal,
whether he's really a brilliant leader or whether the title of
brilliant leader is something he's bestowed on himself.

O.F.: Abu Ammur, I seem to have read somewhere that the Israelis
respect you more than you respect them. Question: Are you
capable of respecting your enemies?

Y.A.: As fighters, and even as strategists . . . sometimes yes. One
must admit that some of their war tactics are intelligent and

can be respected. But as persons, no, because they always behave like barbarians; there's never a drop of humanity in them. People often talk of their victories; I have my own ideas about their victory of 1967 and the one in 1956. The one in 1956 shouldn't even be called a victory; that year they only queued up after the British and French aggressors. And they won with the help of the Americans. As for their 1967 victory, they owe it to the help of the Americans. Money comes in lavish and uncontrolled donations from the Americans to Israel. And besides money, they also get lavish shipments of the most powerful weapons, the most advanced technology. The best the Israelis possess comes from outside—this story of the wonders that they have achieved in our country ought to be re-examined with a greater sense of reality. We know very well what the wealth of Palestine is and is not: you don't get more than just so much out of our land; you don't create gardens out of the desert. Therefore the major part of what they possess comes from outside. And from the technology with which the imperialists supply them.

O.F.: Let's be honest, Abu Ammar. They've put and are putting technology to good use. And as soldiers, they come off well.

Y.A.: They have never won by their positive aspects; they've always won through the negative aspects of the Arabs.

O.F.: That too is part of the game of war, Abu Ammar. Besides, they've also won because they're brave soldiers.

Y.A.: No! No! No! No, they're not! In hand-to-hand combat, face to face, they're not even soldiers. They're too afraid of dying, they show no courage. That's what happened in the battle of Karameh and that's what happened the other day in the battle of El Safir. Crossing the lines, they came down on Wadi Fifa with forty tanks, on Wadi Abata with ten tanks, on Khirbet el Disseh with ten tanks and twenty jeeps with 106-caliber machine guns. They preceded the advance with a heavy artillery bombardment and after ten hours sent in their planes, which bombed the whole area indiscriminately, and then helicopters to fire missiles against our positions.

Their objective was to reach the valley of El Nmeiri. They never reached it; after a twenty-five-hour battle, we drove them back across the lines. Do you know why? Because we used more courage than they did. We surrounded them, we attacked them in the rear with our rifles, with our bazookas—face to face, without fear of dying. It's always the same story with the Israelis. They're good at attacking with planes because they know we have no planes, with tanks because they know we have no tanks, but when they run into face-to-face resistance, they don't risk any more. They run away. And what good is a soldier who takes no risks, who runs away?

O.F.: Abu Ammar, what do you say of the operations carried out by their commandos? For example, when their commandos go to Egypt to dismantle a radar station and carry it away? You need a little courage for something like that.

Y.A.: No, you don't. Because they always look for very weak, very easy objectives. Those are their tactics, which, I repeat, are always intelligent but never courageous in that they consist in employing enormous forces in an undertaking of whose success they're a hundred percent sure. They never move unless they're certain that everything will go well, and if you take them by surprise, they never fully commit themselves. Every time they've attacked the fedayeen in strength, the Israelis have been defeated. Their commandos don't get by us.

O.F.: Maybe not by you, but they do get by the Egyptians.

Y.A.: What they're doing in Egypt is not a military action, it's a psychological war. Egypt is still their strongest enemy, and so they're trying to demoralize it and undermine it through a psychological war incited by the Zionist press with the help of the international press. Their game consists in propagandizing an action by exaggerating it. Everybody falls for it because they possess a powerful press agency. We have no press agency, nobody knows what our commandos are doing, our victories go unnoticed because we have no wire service to transmit the news to newspapers that anyway wouldn't publish it. So no one knows, for example, that on the same day that the Israelis were stealing the radar station from the Egyptians, we entered an Israeli base and carried off five large rockets.

O.F.: I wasn't talking about you, I was talking about the Egyptians.

Y.A.: There's no difference between Palestinians and Egyptians. Both are part of the Arab nation.

O.F.: That's a very generous remark on your part, Abu Ammar.

Especially considering that your family was actually expropriated by the Egyptians.

Y.A.: My family was expropriated by Farouk, not by Nasser. I know
the Egyptians well because I went to the university in Egypt,
and I fought with the Egyptian army in 1951, 1952, and 1956.
They're brave soldiers and my brothers.

O.F.: Let's get back to the Israelis, Abu Ammar. You say that with
you they always suffer huge losses. How many Israelis do you
think you've killed up to this date?

Y.A.: I can't give you an exact figure, but the Israelis have confessed
to having lost, in the war against the fedayeen, a percentage of
men that is higher than that of the Americans in Vietnam—in
proportion, of course, to the population of the two countries.
And it's indicative that, after the 1967 war, their traffic deaths
increased ten times. In short, after a battle or a skirmish with
us, it comes out that a lot of Israelis have died in automobile
accidents. This observation has been made by the Israeli newspapers themselves, because we know that the Israeli generals
never admit to losing men at the front. But I can tell you that,
going by the American statistics, in the battle of Karameh they
lost 1247 men between dead and wounded.

O.F.: And do you pay an equally heavy price?

Y.A.: Losses to us don't count, we don't care if we die. Anyway,
from 1965 to today, we have had slightly over nine hundred
dead. But you must also consider the six thousand civilians
dead in air raids and our brothers who die in prison under torture.

O.F.: Nine hundred dead can be many or few, depending on the
number of combatants. How many fedayeen are there al-
together?

Y.A.: To tell you that figure, I would have to ask permission from
the Military Council, and I don't think they would give it to
me. But I can tell you that at Karameh we were only 392
against 15,000 Israelis.

O.F.: Fifteen thousand? Abu Ammar, maybe you mean 1500.

Y.A.: No! No! No! I said 15,000, 15,000! Including, of course, the
soldiers employed with the heavy artillery, the tanks, the
planes, the helicopters, and the parachutists. As troops alone,
they had four companies and two brigades. What we say is

never believed by you Westerners, you listen to them and that's all, you believe them and that's all, you report what they say and that's all!

O.F.: Abu Ammar, you're an unfair man. I am here and I'm listening to you. And after this interview I'll report word for word what you've told me.

Y.A.: You Europeans are always for them. Maybe some of you are beginning to understand us—it's in the air, one can sense it. But essentially you're still for them.

O.F.: This is your war, Abu Ammar, not ours. And in this war of yours we are only spectators. But even as spectators you can't ask us to be against the Jews and you shouldn't be surprised if in Europe the Jews are often loved. We've seen them persecuted, we've persecuted them. We don't want it to happen again.

Y.A.: Sure, you have to pay your debts to them. And you want to pay them with our blood, with our land, rather than with your blood, your land. You go on ignoring the fact that we have nothing against the Jews, we have it against the Israelis. The Jews will be welcome in the democratic Palestinian state. We'll offer them the choice of staying in Palestine when the moment arrives.

O.F.: But, Abu Ammar, the Israelis are Jews. Not all Jews can identify themselves with Israel, but Israel can't help identifying itself with the Jews. And you can't ask the Jews of Israel to go wandering around the world once more and thereby end up in extermination camps. That's unreasonable.

Y.A.: So you want to send us wandering around the world.

O.F.: No. We don't want to send anybody. You least of all.

Y.A.: But wandering around is what we're doing now. And if you're so anxious to give a homeland to the Jews, give them yours— you have a lot of land in Europe, in America. Don't presume to give them ours. We've lived on this land for centuries and centuries; we won't give it up to pay your debts. You're committing an error even from a human point of view. How is it possible that the Europeans don't recognize it even while being such civilized people, so advanced, and perhaps more advanced than on any other continent? And yet you too have fought wars of liberation, just think of your Risorgimento.

Therefore your error is on purpose. You can't claim ignorance about Palestine because you know Palestine well. You sent us your Crusades, and it's a country right under your nose. It's not Amazonia. I believe that someday your conscience will awaken. But till that day it's better that we don't see each other.

o.f.: Is that the reason, Abu Ammar, that you always wear dark glasses?

y.a.: No. I wear them so as not to let people know whether I'm asleep or awake. But, between ourselves, I'm always awake behind my glasses. I sleep only when I take them off, and I sleep very little. I had said, no personal questions.

o.f.: Only one, Abu Ammar. You aren't married, and there are said to be no women in your life. Do you want to be like Ho Chi Minh, or is the idea of living with a woman at your side repugnant to you?

y.a.: Ho Chi Minh. . . . No, let's say that I've never found the right woman. And now there's no more time. I've married a woman called Palestine.

Amman, March 1972

6

Hussein of Jordan

The king was the picture of bitterness, of wounded pride devoid of all illusions. You couldn't look at him without feeling a need to do something for him, perhaps whisper to him, "Give up everything, Majesty. Go away, save yourself. If you stay here, they'll kill you. If they kill you, no one will pardon you. It's not worth it, Majesty; you've taken too many risks already. You're only in your thirties." Or rather than whisper it to him, you would have shouted it at him, and it wasn't the fear of insulting him that restrained you. It was the knowledge that he knew. It was written on that face whose mustache was already sprinkled with gray, whose lines already covered the memory of a remote youth. Have you ever seen a sadder face than the face of Hussein? His lips are strips of disheartenment; he looks as though he's about to cry even when he smiles or laughs. Besides I don't think that he's able to laugh—except perhaps at rare moments when he plays with his children.

Wherever and however you find him, he has the air of a man to whom you can't say that life is a gift of God. He lives it, yes, and certainly not as an ascetic or saint. He likes women, motorcycles, racing cars, seaside vacations, and violent emotions. He defends it, yes, and certainly not as a weakling; for this reason he has learned to shoot and his aim is deadly. But with detachment, with anger I would say, and the suspicion that each day may be his last.

The king was seated in an armchair in his office in the royal palace, wearing a greenish, not very elegant suit, with a shirt that instead suited him well, and a necktie chosen with taste. The armchair was huge and this made him look smaller than his actual size—about five feet three inches. In fact, when he leaned back, his feet hardly touched the carpet. But he leaned back all the same, resting his elbows on the arms of the chair and clasping his hands over his stomach, almost as though to show you that his short stature gave him no complexes, and indeed he carried it with great dignity, aided by a well-developed body. Wide shoulders, bulging biceps, solid thighs, and muscular calves—the body of a young bull ever in search of a brawl or a female to mount.

The comparison came to you spontaneously if you forgot his face; he had the desperate strength of a young bull that never gives up. You rope him and he gets away, then he comes charging back. You catch him again, shut him up in a cage, and he shakes it until you let him out into the arena. Where he fights. The more you prod him, the more you torment him, the more you wound him, the more he fights. Albeit in an uncertain, confused, mistaken way: a thrust of the horns here, of the head there, a stamp of the hoof. The politics of Hussein. And one can only wonder if his bitterness and sadness are not chiefly born of this: of the realization of being only a young bull flung into a corrida from which he can only emerge dead. Picadors, banderilleros, toreros, friends, enemies, Israelis, Egyptians, Syrians, Palestinians, all are united against him in what is basically a very simple conspiracy. In his case, power is anything but comfortable. Just think of the attempts that have been made on his life ever since his youth.

To say Hussein is to say assassination attempts. To say conspiracies, pistol shots, bombs, poison. He himself has written that the plots against him have been so numerous, varied, and continous that he sometimes feels like the hero of a detective story. The first time, as we know, was when he was sixteen and before his eyes they killed his grandfather, King Abdullah. It was on the steps of the Aksa Mosque in Jerusalem, and the revolver shots were not only fired at Abdullah—one also hit him, aimed at the heart. He was saved by a heavy medal that his grandfather had pinned on his uniform; the bullet smashed against it. The episode of the Syrian MiGs took place in 1958. He was flying his plane toward Europe when two of them attacked him, and he only escaped thanks to his skill as a pilot, going into a dive and then rising again, zigzagging, and running the risk of crashing in the mountains and hills.

In 1960 they tried to do him in by a more insidious method. He had developed sinus trouble and the doctor was treating him with nose drops. One day Hussein opened a new bottle and a drop fell on the washbasin, the washbasin began to sizzle, and a hole soon appeared in place of the drop. Someone had substituted sulphuric acid for the medicine. And what to say of the servant who tried to stab him in his sleep? Or of the cook who put poison in his food? It was discovered because one of his orderlies tested the food on the palace cats and the cats died. And the bomb placed in the office of his prime minister, Hazza Majali, on the day when Hussein was to pay him a visit? Hussein did not die because the bomb exploded in advance, killing only the prime minister and eight other persons. And the four bursts of machine-gun fire against what looked like his automobile and instead was the automobile of his uncle? And the military revolt organized by the supreme commander of his army, Abu Nuwar? The troops had been quartered at Zerqa; Hussein jumped in a jeep and overtook them. Descending from the jeep, he saw a revolver pointed at him; this time he was saved because he fired more quickly than the other man. He always goes around with a Colt .38 stuck in his belt; when he goes to bed he puts it under his pillow.

The most extraordinary fact about Hussein is that the more his life is in danger, the more he exposes himself. The day I arrived in Amman, I had noticed on the runway a sturdy young man with a mustache who very much resembled Hussein. He had helped a pleasant lady and two children to board an airliner on its way to London. Then he had gone to a Mercedes parked near the gate, taken the wheel, and driven off by himself, taking the road that leads into the city. I had exclaimed, "That looks like Hussein!" And someone had answered, "Yes, it was Hussein. He always goes without an escort, unguarded." Furthermore, it's even absurd to insist that Hussein is courageous. He is so in a rash, irritating way. In 1967, when the Israelis were advancing on Jordan, he was the only head of state to go to the front. Alone, in his jeep. His soldiers fled, in tatters, and he went forward, under the whistle of bombs and mortar shells. When the Israelis crossed the frontier at El Sifa and attacked with fifty tanks, he rushed off there and began following the battle. Certain things were done by the *condottieri* of the past; today not even the generals participate in combat.

So you can only conclude that he likes physical danger. And I emphasize the word physical—which is his great limitation. As in bulls. The very sports he practices represent a physical danger and nothing else. He enjoys parachuting, shutting off the engines of his helicopter and letting it fall, to resume control only at the last moment, racing in his Porsche up to 180 miles an hour, doing reckless stunts with his Hawker Hunter jet. There was a time when he also liked to disguise himself as a taxi driver and look for passengers at night in the streets of Amman, so as to ask them what they thought of the new king named Hussein.

The king did not stand out in any particular gesture I have mentioned so far. On the contrary, his attitude was quiet, cordial, his smile carefree. It had been so from the moment he had thrown open the door and shaken my hand, asking if things were going all right for me in Jordan and if anyone had given me trouble. If anything happened, I was to let him know immediately. It was obvious to whom he was alluding. His tone was that of the master of the house who wants to remind you that the master of the house is himself and not the fedayeen you've just met. Having made this point, the king had offered me a Jordanian cigarette and had leaned forward to light it, enjoying the remark by which I had stressed my ignorance of protocol. "They told me to address you as 'Your Majesty,' and for the second time I forget . . . Majesty." "Never mind," he had answered. "Nowadays a king is nothing but an employee of the state; it doesn't seem to me appropriate to stand on ceremony. I never do it."

This is quite true when you remember that he often received journalists in his shirt sleeves, that he lived in a small villa of a few rooms where the servants were few, and that his wife Muna did the cooking. At that time his wife was Muna, the nice British former stenographer whose name before marrying him was Tony Gardiner. At the time, and even while unfaithful to her in countless affairs, Hussein loved her. What accounted for this love, it seems, was really the simplicity of a woman who did not feel diminished by cooking for him and who refused the title of queen, and only reluctantly accepted that of princess. So no one suspected that he would repudiate her, two years later, for a younger and more beautiful wife. His family life had been like that of any little bourgeois opposed to divorce.

I asked the king if I might begin the interview. He nodded and at the same moment his carefree attitude disappeared. His voice, which before had sounded masculine, authoritarian, sank and gave out in a polite murmur: "Please, go ahead." This led me to suspect something the possibility of which I hadn't even considered: that he was timid. He is. Quite in the same way as fighting bulls when they discover you're not hurting them and, overtaken by embarrassment, retreat, bowing their necks. But still I was surprised. You're not surprised, however, by the showman's instinct with which he antic- ipates your questions, the serpentine skill with which he parries them. In fact, if his education is Western (we must not forget that Hussein studied in a Swiss school and was molded by Glubb Pasha, Sir John Bagot Glubb, the Englishman who set up his army), his blood is Arab a thousand percent, laden with astuteness, with de- viousness.

At my first question, his jaws closed, his arms jerked in an im- perceptible shudder, and this reaction was to be repeated several times in the course of our conversation. Or rather, every time I may have asked him something uncomfortable. He does not enjoy being interviewed, and for this reason my interview was not a long one. He had promised me forty minutes. When forty-five were over, he looked at his watch and, scarcely concealing his relief, murmured, "I'm sorry, we must stop. I have another appoint- ment." Nor was there any way to keep him longer. We parted at the door with the promise to complete the interview a few days later. Instead, I didn't see him again.

Perhaps because he did not want to resume a conversation that he knew had not been sincere? Or because actually what he had told me about the Palestinians was one big lie? That day, sitting in that engulfing armchair, he had shown himself so solid with them, so tolerant, so desirous of peace. He had chewed the word peace with the same wholeheartedness with which one masticates chew- ing gum. Five months later, instead, he was to unleash his Bedouins against the fedayeen and decimate them in a frightful bloodbath, the massacre that today goes under the name of Black September. The fedayeen defended themselves; the battle raged for several days. But in vain. They had been taken too much by surprise, and could not hold out against an entire army. Even in the refugee camps there were thousands of dead. Those who saw the dead state that Hussein's troops were merciless. Some had had their genitals, legs, arms cut off—after being tied up. Others had been decapitated. And among the victims there were old women and children. . . . An ugly, brutal story.

Indeed the whole civilized world reacted with disgust and condemned Hussein. And many said that by such a gesture he had pushed the situation to the extreme, that from now on it would be much worse. Nor were they wrong, for the survivors took refuge in Lebanon and there regained strength by redoubling their terrorism. What we now have to suffer in Europe, with such episodes as Munich and Fiumicino, with carnage that is not our business, with blackmail and . . .

Should I despise Hussein because he lied to me? I don't know; I wouldn't say so. Anyone who is at the head of a country so tormented as his certainly cannot reveal his strategy to the enemy, much less confide in a journalist. Since his way of freeing himself from the fedayeen was based on a sudden about-face and an unanticipated massacre, he had no other choice but to lie to me. But he lied too well, and that lie depicts a man who is tragic, yes, but also treacherous. Tragic by destiny, treacherous by necessity. As I could convince myself when I met him again almost three years later.

I met him again in November of 1974, one month after the Arab Summit in Rabat. The summit where, unanimously, the Arab leaders had taken from him Cisjordania and his right to negotiate on the Palestinians' behalf. This time Hussein looked destroyed, a living portrait of defeat and humiliation. And indeed, the humiliation had been burning, as it had been the fruit of a vengeance wanted and organized by Arafat. Seen under such circumstances, Hussein aroused sympathy, almost a need to absolve him and choose his side of the barricade. But let us not forget the following truth: Those who hold power and shape the destiny of others should never be judged in a moment of misfortune or defeat. If seen as a corpse hung by the feet, even Mussolini could arouse some pity. Those who hold power and shape the destiny of others must be judged when they are alive. So, in my opinion, the real portrait of Hussein remains the one that I painted in my first, and by now old, interview.

It is that interview that I prefer to offer for the verdict of today and of tomorrow.

ORIANA FALLACI: Majesty, but who is in command in Jordan? At the check points people are stopped by the fedayeen, at the borders the fedayeen attack, in the villages it's the fedayeen who decide. It's no longer paradoxical to say they've set up a state within your state.

HUSSEIN OF JORDAN: Many things are not going well, I know. Excesses, a taking of positions that I can't allow. Sometimes this provokes friction. I've talked at length with their leaders. I cited the agreements they bound themselves to observe and that often they haven't observed—Jordan is a sovereign state. And Jordan is the country that pays for the Israeli reprisals. Their leaders have reacted to my words like reasonable people and I think that certain things will change. But we're far from saying that everything is going as I'd like. And still . . . when I'm asked why I don't stop the fedayeen, why I don't throw the fedayeen out . . . I answer: I won't stop them, I won't throw them out. Not because I can't but because I don't want to. It's not true that I'm a prisoner of the fedayeen; that's what Israeli propaganda says. It's not true that I can't control them. Because they have every right to fight, to resist. They've suffered for twenty years, and the Israelis are occupying their land. That land is also Jordanian territory—who should help them if not Jordan? Don't forget that a good part of my population is Palestinian, don't forget that the tragedy of the refugees is more evident here than elsewhere. I have to be with them.

O.F.: But they aren't with you, Majesty. I haven't found much friendship toward you among the fedayeen. And I've often found, so to speak, hostility.

H.: When men suffer oppression and have anger in their hearts, their actions have uncontrolled consequences. This grieves me but doesn't discourage me. We will reach an agreement—their leaders aren't fools and I'm an optimist. Certainly it's difficult, at times painful. But in life one must make choices and then keep faith with them. I've chosen to keep the fedayeen and I keep faith with my choice. Even if my position may seem quixotic or naïve . . . one day we'll have to arrive at a peaceful solution.

O.F.: Majesty, do you really believe in a peaceful solution?

H.: Yes, I do. I've always accepted the resolution offered by the UN Security Council; I've always fought for it and will go on fighting for it. My position is clear: I say and repeat that all the Israelis have to do is to withdraw from the territories occupied in 1967. There's no other way to achieve peace. But the Israelis don't want to withdraw; they don't want peace.

O.F.: By accepting the Security Council resolution, you grant Israel the right to exist. In short, you don't deny that Israel is an historical reality that cannot be eradicated.

H.: No, I don't deny it. To accept that resolution automatically includes the recognition of Israel. And that means I believe in the possibility of living in peace with Israel.

O.F.: But this is exactly the opposite of what the fedayeen want, Majesty! The fedayeen want to destroy Israel; they don't recognize Israel's right to exist. The fedayeen consider as an enemy, or rather a traitor, anyone who accepts the resolution offered by the UN Security Council. They reject every peaceful compromise, they don't exclude war, they're calling for war. Majesty, how can you reconcile your position with that of the fedayeen?

H.: In appearance they can't be reconciled, but I'm sure that sooner or later the fedayeen will end by being persuaded that it's necessary to reach a peaceful compromise. Because other Arab states as well will convince them of this necessity. And then, when you stop to think of it, there's no great difference between my search for peace and their desire for war. In the West that may seem a paradox, but for us who have a more elastic mentality, there's no paradox. Both the fedayeen and myself want to see our rights recognized. And I would never accept a peace that didn't recognize our rights, their rights. I tell you if Israel were to accept the resolution of the Security Council, the commando attacks would cease—the commandos would no longer have any reason to exist. It's the stubbornness of the Israelis that brings about the existence of the commandos, not vice versa.

O.F.: Allow me to disagree, Majesty. The fedayeen wouldn't at all

be satisfied with Israel's withdrawal from the occupied territories. If the Israelis were to withdraw their troops, the
fedayeen would pursue their attacks still farther. That's another reason why the Israelis don't withdraw.

H.: I must believe, I want to believe that that's not so. I must
believe in peace, someone must believe . . .

O.F.: Majesty, in speaking of the Palestinian state they want to set
up, the leaders of the fedayeen always repeat that it will include the territory on the left bank of the Jordan, in short the
West Bank. But doesn't this territory belong to the kingdom of
Jordan?

H.: Yes, but it's almost completely inhabited by Palestinians—it's
Palestine. So it's normal for the Palestinians to want to regain
possession sooner or later. And, to keep faith with the choices
I've made, it's likewise normal that I don't oppose it. When
the time comes, I'll ask the Palestinians of the West Bank to
decide whether they want to remain with Jordan or become
independent. I'll say to them: Decide your future for yourselves. Then I'll accept what they've decided.

O.F.: But then Jordan . . . what will be left of it?

H.: There'll be left . . . what's left. I know very well that the West
Bank constitutes the most fertile territory in Jordan. By occupying it, the Israelis have caused us immense economic
harm. But once again there arises the necessity for a choice:
either interests or conscience. When a king, anyway a head of
state, says that he recognizes the right of self-determination of
a people, he must carry it through to the end. It's very easy to
be liberal in words, very difficult to be so in deeds. And also
when this war is over, Jordan will turn out to be the country
that has paid most cruelly and most bitterly of all.

O.F.: That part of Jordan you're ready to give up includes Jerusalem, Majesty.

H.: Yes . . . but Jerusalem should never be anyone's private property. Jerusalem is as sacred to the Muslims as it is to the Christians and Jews—on this we Arabs are all in agreement. The
immediate problem, therefore, is for the Israelis to realize it as
well and recognize our rights over the Arab part of Jerusalem.
And not insist on annexing it to Israel. You emphasize the future conflicts in the Arab world and forget that it's the Israelis
who want to crush us by their expansionism.

O.F.: Majesty, these conflicts don't belong to the future, they belong to the present. Arab unity doesn't exist—we saw that in Rabat.

H.: The Rabat conference wasn't useful, but I've always known that Arab unity wouldn't be achieved at the conference table by gathering the heads of the various Arab states in one room. It can be reached only through separate contacts between state and state—slowly, patiently. Syria and ourselves, Egypt and ourselves . . . I've been to Egypt several times, and I'll go back again because each meeting is more fruitful than you imagine. Corners get smoothed away, details are clarified . . .

O.F.: Even with Egypt, with Nasser? And speaking of Nasser, it's always you who went to him, Majesty. It's never Nasser who comes to you. Is one permitted to draw conclusions?

H.: Those who have less fear of traveling are the ones who travel. Some people are bothered by airplanes because they cling too much to life. Let's put it this way: airplanes don't bother me; I have no fear of traveling in search of friends.

O.F.: Not even when those friends try to make you crash, as happened with those Syrian MiGs? Am I wrong, Majesty, or is it always your Arab friends like Nasser who want to kill you?

H.: I don't want to talk about that. . . . There's no need to talk about it. . . . The Arabs are my allies, my friends. . . .

O.F.: I know, Majesty. But we Italians have a proverb that in your case should be reversed as follows: God protect me from my enemies, I'll look after my friends. In fact, when you go to see your friends, you always carry a pistol. Are you sure that a pistol is enough to guarantee your safety?

H.: Westerners are always afraid I'll be killed. The first thing they ask me is, but aren't you afraid of being killed? No, I don't even think about it. I swear it. I've looked death in the face so many times that by now I'm as accustomed to the risk as to day and night. Besides, if I let myself be obsessed by the idea of death, I'd no longer go out of my house and wouldn't even feel safe there. I'm an Arab, I believe in fate. God's will be done, and what will be will be.

O.F.: All those who enjoy taking physical risks speak of fatalism, Majesty.

H.: No, it's not true that I enjoy risks—no intelligent person likes to gamble with his life. But for me risk has become the natural element in which to live—what water is to a fish. A fish doesn't even realize it's living in water because it couldn't live elsewhere. I like sports, it's true, and sports always offer a margin of risk or else they're not sports. But I don't do them for that; I do them because I have to move, to take exercise. Someone once asked me if the gift I admire most in a man was courage. I hesitated before answering yes. Certainly I admire courage; a man without courage isn't a man. But physical courage isn't enough if it's not accompanied by intelligence, and what I most admire in a man is intelligence. Only with that do you resolve things, and with determination.

O.F.: Not even with that, Majesty. And your case shows it. Majesty, you've just told me of some fine plans, but I'd like to reply with a realistic question. Don't you ever get fed up and dream of something more practical, I mean telling it all to go to hell and retiring to live in peace?

H.: Yes . . . I'm afraid so. There are days when a man who does my job really thinks of it. He wakes up in the morning and says enough. . . . Every morning is a dilemma—to keep going or not. And every morning I end up resolving the dilemma by saying to myself: Keep going, you have to keep going. You see, I wasn't born to do a king's job. When I was a boy and the prospect of becoming king was still remote because I knew that when my grandfather died, the kingdom would pass to my father, I thought of choosing a profession. And I hesitated between the law profession and that of being a pilot. The study of law is beautiful if you believe in the law as I do. And then law is a search for all the whys—I would have made an excellent lawyer, I know it. The dialectical play of just and unjust, of right and wrong. . . . Yes, still better than being a pilot. Though for me flying a plane is an overwhelming joy: the open spaces, the technology. . . . When I fly my plane, I never let the copilot take the controls. And instead my grandfather died so soon and . . . my father got sick, and it was my turn to become king. So young. Hardly seventeen. Early, too early. If only you knew how tough it was for me. I knew nothing and I kept making mistakes. . . . For so many years I made mistakes. I've learned very late.

o.f.: And once you'd learned, did you like it, Majesty? Or rather, let's put the question in the most brutal and honest terms: as of today, do you think it's worth it, Majesty?

h.: What a difficult, embarrassing question. I've already told you that I didn't choose this job and that, if I could have, perhaps I wouldn't have chosen it. Because, if being head of state is a term in prison, being a king is a life sentence. But I shouldn't consider the problem of whether I like it or not, I should consider the problem of doing it even if I don't like it. In any job you get days of weariness, of nausea—but if we give in to them, we'd be like those misfits who are always changing jobs and end by doing all of them badly. No, so long as my people want me, or so long as I'm alive among a people who want me, I'll never give up the job of king. I've sworn it to myself before swearing it to others. And not only as a question of pride, believe me. Because I love this land of mine. And I think that to give it up and live on the Riviera would be an act of cowardice, of treason. So I stay. Whether it's worth it or not, cost what it may. I'm ready to face anyone, anyone who tries to send me away.

Amman, April 1972

7

Indira Gandhi

This incredible woman who governed almost half a billion people and won a war in the face of the opposition of the United States and China. You looked at her and thought no one would succeed in driving her from the throne she had democratically conquered, at that time. Some said she would go on being prime minister of India for twenty years, and since she was only in her fifties she might stay there for the rest of her life. When you came to think of it, she was the only true queen and one of the few remarkable rulers in the world, a thoroughbred horse, at that time. I liked her so, at that time. I used to choose her as an example to show how good women can be when they govern a country. I admired her. And I refused to listen to those who warned me, saying, "Maybe you shouldn't trust her that much." I judged them envious of her talent and her success. Then, suddenly, this changed.

It was in the spring of 1975, when she gave up democracy and became a dictator. It was when she forgot what her father had done and what she had lasted for, freedom. All happened with the quickness of a blow, in a few days, a few hours. We know the story, as it is so recent. She had been tried and convicted, maybe wrongly, maybe excessively, for illicit behavior in the electoral campaign (some minor fault that all politicians commit in her country and in the world) and she had been put in the situation of having to consider resigning her power, like Nixon had done. Resignation was imperative. Yet she would not resign. She refused to do what even Nixon had done. And, with a coup to be compared to the coups of the most ruthless tyrants, she gave up being Prime Minister Indira to become Dictator Indira. Overnight she had all the opposition arrested, the constitution violated, and freedom assassinated. In the name of democracy, of course, and of law and of order. It always takes place that way. I said this in a report that I will not summarize; people know it. But it's worth recalling that because of the coup, I rejected her and my admiration for her. I didn't hide my regret and shame at having portrayed her in the past as a woman to love and respect.

It is true that doing a portrait of her had been a disturbing task at that time too. Her personality eluded any attempt to fix it in any precise shape or color. It was too many things at once, and all in conflict among themselves. Many people didn't like her. And they called her arrogant, cynical, ambitious, ruthless. They accused her of ideological inconsistency, of demagoguery, of playing a double game. Many, on the other hand, liked her, to the point of falling in love with her. And they called her strong, courageous, generous, brilliant. They extolled her good sense, her equilibrium, her honesty. Among those who didn't like her, you often found men. Among those who did, you often found women. Indeed it's hard to be a man and accept the remark that circulated in India: "She wears the trousers all right." In other words, it was impossible to be a woman and not feel redeemed, vindicated, by her enormous success, which belied all the banalities used to justify patriarchy and male rule in any society. Being a woman, justifications of her wrongs came much easier. In fact, at that time, I liked to point out that to rule a country and especially a country like India, so quarrelsome, so complex, one must not be a saint. Whatever Henry Kissinger may say about power ("It's not intelligence that's important in a head of state. The quality that counts in a head of state is strength. Courage, shrewdness, and strength"), to rule a country like India one must be intelligent. She is truly not a saint, she knows in every sense how to drink from the cup of life, I used to say, on the other hand, she is intelligent. And, while admitting that interviewing her was easier than understanding her, I gave judgments that even now I don't withdraw. For instance, even now I must recognize that on personal matters, she is spontaneous.

She hides nothing, she unveils herself—in a caressing, modulated, highly pleasant voice. Her face too is pleasant. She has beautiful hazel eyes, a little sad, and a strange, indulgent, enigmatic smile that awakens curiosity. She resembles no one, not even in her black curls that on the right side are lightened by an odd streak of gray hair, almost a flash of silver. I also must recognize that she bursts out with modern ideas. Note her answer to my question about religion. When one is the leader of the most religious people on earth, it takes guts to say that you don't believe in the gods but in man.

Also, I cannot forget that she is not an ordinary woman with an ordinary destiny and an ordinary past. First of all, she is the daughter of Jawaharlal Nehru; second, she is a disciple of Mohandas K. (Mahatma) Gandhi—the two legendary figures who dared to challenge the British Empire and started its breakup. In their shadow she grew up, was educated and shaped. And if today Nehru is mentioned as Indira's father, until yesterday Indira was known as Nehru's daughter. If today the name of Gandhi creates confusion with Indira's surname (she has it from her husband, who was not related to the Mahatma), until yesterday Indira owed part of her popularity to the fact of being called Gandhi. Hers is the case of a person born among exceptional people in exceptional times. The Nehru family had been immersed in politics for generations. A grandfather had been among the founders of the Congress Party, to which Indira belongs. Her parents were members of the executive committee, and also her aunt—Vijayalakshmi Pandit, who was to be the only woman called to preside over the UN. As a child, Indira not only sat on the lap of the Mahatma, she sat on the laps of all the important men who were to create India.

The struggle for independence took place before her eyes, her first school of life being the police who descended on them at night to make arrests. There is a story of her opening the door to friends and saying, "I'm sorry, there's no one at home. My father, mother, grandfather, grandmother, and aunt are all in prison." Also for this reason she was sent to study in Switzerland at the age of eight. But at thirteen she came back and founded a corps of little guerrillas, the Monkey Brigade. Six thousand children who did not always restrict themselves to carrying messages—sometimes they attacked the British barracks. Led by her. The letters that Nehru wrote her from prison are of this period. "Do you remember how fascinated you were when you first read the story of Jeanne d'Arc, and how your ambition was to be something like her? . . . In India today we are making history, and you and I are fortunate to see this happening before our eyes and to take some part ourselves in this great drama." Today the letters are collected in two volumes and used in the schools.

She too was in prison—for thirteen months, but according to the sentence of the special tribunal, it should have been seven years. She was there with her husband. Returning to Europe to attend Somerville College at Oxford, she had joined the Labour Party and met a young lawyer from Bombay—Feroze Gandhi. He too was up to his neck in politics. They were married in Delhi in February 1942. Six months later the British authorities had them both arrested and charged with subversion, and this was the beginning of a difficult, and certainly not happy, marriage.

In 1947, when Nehru became prime minister, Indira practically went to live with her father, who was a widower and needed a woman at his side. Feroze Gandhi could never accept this choice. He opposed it until the day he died, in 1960, of a heart attack. But he didn't blunt her decision. Driven likewise by resentment over the excessive attentions that, so they say, Feroze paid to other women, for seventeen years Indira spent more time with her father than with her husband. They called her "the first lady of India," "the daughter of the nation." Together with him she traveled, received heads of state, held rallies. In 1956, she joined the executive committee of the party. In 1958, she became head of the party and expelled the men she had admired as a child. On Nehru's death, in 1964, it seemed inevitable that she would take his place. And in the elections of 1966 she did so, carrying off 355 seats as against 169. Later, in the 1970 elections, her triumph was doubled and didn't end till the day she betrayed democracy, the memory of her father, herself. So, until that day, one could say that her political biography had something in common with that of Golda Meir, who also came to power through a party career. And the parallel between the two women did not end there, since Golda too had an unhappy marriage, Golda too sacrificed to power the husband she loved and by whom she had had two children. Their lives confirmed with chilling exactness how difficult it is for a woman of talent to realize her talent and at the same time save her happiness. More than difficult, actually impossible to the point of tragedy. Paradoxically, I mean, the strain and injustice of being a woman were demonstrated precisely by the two women who had arrived at the top of the pyramid. And it was painful ind infuriating to discover that a man with a destiny can follow it without giving up his family, without giving up love. A woman cannot. For her, the two things don't coexist. Or they coexist only in tragedy. And such truth doesn't end because Indira's belief in democracy has ended. It remains a bitter reality on which men should meditate a lot. I say more: in that sense, I'm still on the side of Indira. My refusal of the woman as politician is not accompanied by my refusal of the woman as such. Even during the hours that followed the arrest of the opposition leaders and her coup, that is even during the burst of my indignation against her, I couldn't help thinking how alone she was and how much more unhappy than a man who puts himself in the same situation.

I met Indira Gandhi in her office in the government palace. The same office that had been her father's—large, cold, and plain. She was sitting, small and slender, behind a bare desk. When I entered, she got up and came forward to give me her hand, then sat down again and cut the preliminaries short by fixing me with a gaze that meant: Go ahead with the first question, don't waste time, I really have no time to waste. She answered cautiously at first. Then she opened up like a flower and the conversation flowed along without obstacles, in mutual sympathy. We were together for more than two hours, and when the interview was over, she left the office to accompany me to the taxi waiting for me in the street. Along the corridors and going down the stairs, she held me by the arm, as though she had always known me and talked about this and that, responding with an absent-minded nod to the bows of officials. She looked tired that day, and all of a sudden I exclaimed, "Deep down I don't envy you, and I shouldn't like to be in your place." And she said, "The problem is not in the problems I have, it's in the idiots around me. Democracy, you know . . ." I now wonder what she meant by that unfinished phrase. And sometimes I ask myself whether she had, even then, a certain contempt for the system she represented and, years later, would overthrow.

Forty-eight hours later, having found some gaps in the interview, I wanted to see her again, but without standing on ceremony I went to her house, a modest bungalow that she shares with her sons Rajiv and Sanjay. No one is more accessible than Indira Gandhi when she is home, and you realize this in the morning when she receives people who come with petitions, protests, wreaths of flowers. I rang the bell, the secretary came to open the door, and I asked her if the prime minister could give me another half hour. The secretary answered, "Let's see," then went away and came back with Indira. "Come, sit down, let's have a cup of tea." We sat down in the living room opening on the garden and talked for another hour. Besides the things I asked her, she told me about her son Rajiv, who is married to an Italian girl and is a pilot for Air-India, then of her younger son Sanjay, who is an automobile designer and still a bachelor. Finally she called a beautiful dark little boy who was playing on the lawn, and embracing him tenderly, murmured, "This is my grandchild; this is the man I love most in the world." It was a strange sensation to watch this very powerful woman embracing a child. It brought back to mind the injustice I spoke of, the solitude that oppresses women intent on defending their own destinies, their own dreams, their own mistakes.

The interview with Indira had a sequel. The fact is that Bhutto read it, lost his temper, and feeling jealous, sent for me so that I might hear his side. But this is a story I will save for later, in the chapter on Bhutto. What I care for, instead, is to make clear that this interview must be read recalling that it took place when she wasn't what she is today, and I saw her as I don't today. Usually I do not change my mind about people whom I met and judged. The first impression remains valid. But sometimes I do, with pride. Because having a mind means also using it to recognize a mistake and correct it. Especially when history is involved. And history is something in movement, in process, like life. History is life.

ORIANA FALLACI: Mrs. Gandhi, I have so many questions to ask you, both personal and political. The personal ones, however, I'll leave for later—once I've understood why many people are afraid of you and call you cold, indeed icy, hard . . .

INDIRA GANDHI: They say that because I'm sincere. Even too sincere. And because I don't waste time in flowery small talk, as people do in India, where the first half hour is spent in compliments: "How are you, how are your children, how are your grandchildren, and so forth." I refuse to indulge in small talk. And compliments, if at all, I save for after the job is done. But in India people can't stomach this attitude of mine, and when I say, "Hurry up, let's get to the point," they feel hurt. And think I'm cold, indeed icy, hard. Then there's another reason, one that goes with my frankness: I don't put on an act. I don't know how to put on an act; I always show myself for what I am, in whatever mood I'm in. If I'm happy, I look happy; if I'm angry, I show it. Without worrying about how others may react. When one has had a life as difficult as mine, one doesn't worry about how others will react. And now go ahead. You can ask anything you like.

O.F.: Fine. I'll begin with the most brutal question. You have won, more than won, a war. But quite a few of us consider this victory a dangerous one. Do you really think that Bangladesh will be the ally you hoped for? Aren't you afraid it may turn out instead to be a most uncomfortable burden?

I.G.: Look, life is always full of dangers and I don't think one should avoid dangers. I think one should do what seems right. And if what seems right involves danger . . . well, one must risk the danger. That's always been my philosophy—I've never thought of the consequences of a necessary action. I examine the consequences later, when a new situation arises and I then face the new situation. And that's it. You say this victory is dangerous. I say that today no one can yet tell if it's dangerous, that today I don't see the risks you mention. If, however, those risks should become reality . . . I'll act in accordance with the new reality. I hope that sounds like a positive statement. I want to answer you in a positive way. I want to state that there will be friendship between Bangladesh and ourselves. And not a one-sided friendship, of course—no one does anything for nothing; each has something to give and something to take. If we offer something to Bangladesh, it's obvious that Bangladesh is offering something to us. And why shouldn't Bangladesh be able to keep its promises? Economically it's full of resources and can stand on its feet. Politically it seems to me led by trained people. The refugees who took shelter here are going home. . . .

O.F.: Are they really going home?

I.G.: Yes, two million have already gone back.

O.F.: Two million out of ten. That's not much.

I.G.: No, but give them time. They're going back fast. Fast enough. I'm satisfied. More than I expected.

O.F.: Mrs. Gandhi, in mentioning the dangers of your victory, I wasn't referring only to Bangladesh. I was also referring to West Bengal, which is India, and which is now clamoring for its independence. I've heard the Naxalites in Calcutta . . . And there's a sentence of Lenin's that says, "The world revolution will pass through Shanghai and Calcutta."

I.G.: No. That's not possible. And you know why? Because a revolution is already taking place in India. Things are changing here already—peacefully and democratically. There's no danger of communism. There would be if we had a rightist government instead of mine. In fact the communists gained strength in India when the people thought my party was moving to the right. And they were correct. In the face of such a threat, they had no other choice but to throw themselves to the far left. But now that the people are conscious of our efforts, now that they see us resolving problems, the communists are losing strength. As for the Naxalites in West Bengal, they are completely under control, and I'm sure that the ones in Bangladesh will also be brought under control. No, I don't expect trouble.

O.F.: They've already given you some trouble, in Bangladesh. I saw fearful lynchings in Dacca after the liberation.

I.G.: They happened in the first five days and were few in comparison with the massacres that the others carried out, in comparison with the million people the others killed. There were some unfortunate incidents, it's true, and we tried to prevent them. If you only knew how many people we saved! But we couldn't be everywhere, we couldn't see everything, and it was inevitable that some things would escape us. In all communities you find groups that behave badly. But you must understand them too. They were so enraged, blinded by resentment.

To be just, one should not consider what you saw in a few days but what they saw and suffered for many months.

O.F.: Mrs. Gandhi, you know the accusation that it was you Indians who provoked this war and attacked first. What do you say to that?

I.G.: I'd answer by admitting that, if you want to go way back, we helped the Mukti Bahini. So, if you consider it all as beginning with that aid and from that moment, yes—we were the ones to start it. But we couldn't do otherwise. We couldn't keep ten million refugees on our soil; we couldn't tolerate such an unstable situation for who knows how long. That influx of refugees wouldn't have stopped—on the contrary. It would have gone on and on and on, until there would have been an explosion. We were no longer able to control the arrival of those people, in our own interest we had to stop it! That's what I said to Mr. Nixon, to all the other leaders I visited in an attempt to avert the war.

However, when you look at the beginning of the actual war, it's not hard to recognize that the Pakistanis were the ones to attack. They were the ones who descended on us with their planes, at five o'clock that afternoon when the first bombs fell on Agra. I can prove it to you by the fact that we were taken completely by surprise. The weekend is the only time when we in the government can leave Delhi, and, well, almost no one was in Delhi. I had gone to Calcutta. The defense minister had gone to Patna and from there he was to go to Bangalore in the south. The finance minister had gone to Bombay and was about to go to Poona. The head of the armed forces was somewhere else; I don't remember where. We all had to rush back to Delhi, and for this reason our troops went on the counteroffensive only the next day, instead of in a few hours. For this reason the Pakistanis succeeded in occupying some areas. Naturally we were prepared; we knew that something would happen. But we were only really ready for air attacks. If it hadn't been for that, they would have knocked us out.

O.F.: Mrs. Gandhi, you mentioned the trip you took to Europe and America to avert the conflict. Can you tell the truth today about what happened? How did things go with Nixon?

I.G.: I made the trip knowing I was like the child putting his finger into the hole in the dike. And there are things that . . . I don't know . . . one can't . . . oh, why not! The truth is that I spoke clearly to Mr. Nixon. And I told him what I had already told Mr. Heath, Mr. Pompidou, Mr. Brandt. I told him, without mincing words, that we couldn't go on with ten million refugees on our backs, we couldn't tolerate the fuse of such an explosive situation any longer. Well, Mr. Heath, Mr. Pompidou, and Mr. Brandt had understood very well. But not Mr. Nixon. The fact is that when the others understand one thing, Mr. Nixon understands another. I suspected he was very pro-Pakistan. Or rather I knew that the Americans had always been in favor of Pakistan—not so much because they were in favor of Pakistan, but because they were against India.

However, I had recently had the impression they were changing—not so much by becoming less pro-Pakistan as by becoming less anti-India. I was wrong. My visit to Nixon did anything but avert the war. It was useful only to me. The experience taught me that when people do something against you, that something always turns out in your favor. At least you can use it to your advantage. It's a law of life—check it and you'll see it holds true in every situation of life. Do you know why I won the last elections? It was because the people liked me, yes, because I had worked hard, yes, but also because the opposition had behaved badly toward me. And do you know why I won this war? Because my army was able to do it, yes, but also because the Americans were on the side of Pakistan.

O.F.: I don't understand.

I.G.: Let me explain. America always thought it was helping Pakistan. But if it hadn't helped Pakistan, Pakistan would have been a stronger country. You don't help a country by supporting a military regime that denies any sign of democracy, and what defeated Pakistan was its military regime. That regime supported by the Americans.˙ Sometimes friends are dangerous. We must be very careful about the help friends give us.

O.F.: And the Chinese? The Chinese too were on Pakistan's side, and unless I'm mistaken, China is the largest potential enemy of India.

I.G.: No. I don't see why we and the Chinese should have to be enemies. We don't want to be their enemies. If that's what they want, we can't do anything about it, but I don't think they really want it because I don't think that in the final analysis it would do them any good. As for the position they held in this war . . . well, I think they've been more skillful than the Americans. Certainly they've had a lighter touch—had they wanted to, they could have done more for Pakistan. Isn't that so? It was the Americans who sent the Seventh Fleet into the Bay of Bengal, not the Chinese. So as to take no chances, I didn't remove our troops from the Chinese border, but I never believed the Chinese would intervene by making a false move. In other words, I never believed in the danger of a third world war. Naturally, if the Americans had fired a shot, if the Seventh Fleet had done something more than sit there in the Bay of Bengal . . . yes, the Third World War would have exploded. But, in all honesty, not even that fear occurred to me.

O.F.: It feels so strange to talk about war with you who were brought up in the cult of nonviolence, Mrs. Gandhi! I wonder how you've felt in these days of conflict.

I.G.: You must keep in mind that it wasn't my first war; I've had to face others. And anyway I'll tell you a little story about nonviolence. India had barely become independent, in 1947, when Pakistan invaded Kashmir, which at the time was ruled by a maharajah. The maharajah fled, and the people of Kashmir, led by Sheikh Abdullah, asked for Indian help. Lord Mountbatten, who was still governor general, replied that he wouldn't be able to supply aid to Kashmir unless Pakistan declared war, and he didn't seem bothered by the fact that the Pakistanis were slaughtering the population. So our leaders decided to sign a document by which they bound themselves to go to war with Pakistan. And Mahatma Gandhi, apostle of nonviolence, signed along with them. Yes, he chose war. He said there was nothing else to do. War is inevitable when one must defend somebody or defend oneself.

O.F.: The point is I persist in seeing this war as a war between brothers. I even said so to General Aurora and General Niazi. And both of them answered, "Basically we are brothers."

I.G.: Not basically—entirely. The Indians and Pakistanis are literally brothers. I know you were surprised when, after the fall of

Dacca, Pakistani and Indian officers shook hands. But do you realize that, up until 1965, in our army and the Pakistani one you could come across generals who were brothers? Blood brothers, sons of the same father and the same mother. Or you found an uncle on one side and a nephew on the other, a cousin here and a cousin there. Besides it's still true today. I'll tell you something else. There was a time when even two ambassadors to Switzerland, the one from India and the one from Pakistan, were two blood brothers. Oh, the Partition imposed on us by the British was so unnatural! It served only to divide families, to break them up. I remember harrowing episodes. People who emigrated, people who didn't want to emigrate. . . . Many Muslims didn't want to leave India to go to live in Pakistan, but the propaganda was that there they'd have greater opportunities and so they left. Many Hindus, on the other hand, didn't want to stay in Pakistan, but they had ties there or property and so they stayed.

To become our enemies—what an absurdity. A crazy absurdity when you stop to think that we, Muslims and Hindus, had conducted the struggle for independence together. Yes, even under the British there were hostile groups. There were clashes. But, as we found out later, these were clashes provoked by those who had no wish to let us live together—on the eve of the Partition. The policy of keeping us divided was always followed by foreigners, even after the Partition. If Indians and Pakistanis had been together . . . I don't say as confederated countries but as neighboring and friendly countries . . . like Italy and France, for example . . . believe me, both of us would have progressed much further. But, it would seem that it was not in the interest of "someone" for us to make progress. It was in "someone's" interest that we be always at war, that we tear each other to pieces. Yes, I'm inclined to absolve the Pakistanis. How should they have behaved? Someone encouraged them to attack us, someone gave them weapons to attack us. And they attacked us.

O.F.: Bhutto says that he would be ready to set up a confederation with India. What do you think of that, Mrs. Gandhi?

I.G.: You know . . . Bhutto is not a very balanced man. When he talks, you never understand what he means. What does he mean this time? That he wants to be friends with us? We've wanted to be friends with him for some time; I've always wanted to. Here's something that Westerners don't know. The Western press has always insisted that India was Pakistan's enemy and vice versa, that the Hindus were against the Muslims and vice versa. They've never said, for instance, that my party has been fighting this attitude ever since we were dismembered into two countries. Since then we have maintained that religious hostilities are wrong and absurd, that minorities cannot be eliminated from a country, that people of different religions must live together.

But how is it possible for people in the modern world to go on killing each other for religion? The problems we should be concerned with nowadays are quite different! They're the problems of poverty, of the rights of the individual, of the changes brought about by technology. They're the ones that count, more than religion! Because they're universal problems, because they pertain in equal measure to Pakistan and ourselves. I can't take it seriously when people get excited and scream that religion is in danger, and similar stupidities. Unfortunately even in India there are people who talk like that. And they're the same ones who say, "We should never have accepted the existence of Pakistan. Now that it exists, it ought to be destroyed." But these are only a few madmen who have no following among the masses.

In India you don't find propaganda against Pakistan. During the war there was a little of it, naturally, but even during the war we were able to control it. In fact the Pakistanis were astonished by this. There were prisoners in the camp hospitals who exclaimed, "What? You're a Hindu doctor and you want to cure me?" Look, I can only reply to Bhutto that, if he knows what he's saying, he's saying the only thing to be said. And if he didn't say that, what would his future be? I'm told Bhutto is ambitious. I hope he's very ambitious; ambition may help him see reality.

O.F.: To digress a moment, Mrs. Gandhi. You're not religious, are you?

I.G.: Well . . . it depends on what you mean by the word religion. Certainly I don't go to temples and pray to the gods or anything like that. But if by religion we mean a belief in humanity rather than the gods, an effort to make man better and a little happier, then yes, I'm very religious.

O.F.: I hope that wasn't an embarrassing question, Mrs. Gandhi.

I.G.: No, why?

O.F.: This one is embarrassing, however. You've always proclaimed a policy of nonalignment, then last August you signed the Indo-Soviet friendship pact. Isn't there a conflict between the two things?

I.G.: No, I wouldn't say so. Because what does nonalignment mean? It means we don't belong to any military bloc and that we reserve the right to be friends with any country, independently of the influence of any country. All this has remained unchanged after the signing of the Indo-Soviet treaty, and others can say or think what they like—our policy won't change because of the Soviet Union. We know very well that India's destiny is linked to world peace. However, the treaty exists, you say, and it puts us in a different position toward the Soviet Union than the one we have toward other countries. Yes, the treaty exists. Nor does it exist on only one side. Look how we're situated geographically and you'll see that India is very important for the Soviet Union. Still, in international matters, the treaty changes nothing. That is, it doesn't prevent us from being friends with other countries, which indeed we are. It doesn't prohibit us from practicing the same nonalignment, as indeed we do. And I assure you we'll go on making our decisions without worrying whether it pleases or displeases the Soviet Union, China, America, France, or anyone else. Do you want to know something else? A month after the signing someone asked Chou En-lai what he thought of it. And Chou En-lai answered, "It makes no difference. I don't see why it should make any difference."

O.F.: Opening an Indian embassy in Hanoi in the near future does make a difference, however. In fact, you are head of the International Control Commission for Vietnam. What does this mean? That you'll give up membership on the commission and your chairmanship?

I.G.: I don't know. . . . Obviously the problem arises. . . . But I still haven't thought about how to resolve it. And to talk about this. . . . Let's talk about it anyway. Listen, the International Control Commission isn't doing anything, it's never done anything. What good does it do to be on it or not? Before opening the embassy in Hanoi, I gave it a lot of thought, but it wasn't really a painful decision. American policy in Vietnam is what it is, in Saigon the situation is anything but normal, and I'm happy to have done what I did.

O.F.: So are people right to think you're more on the left than your father was?

I.G.: Look, I don't see the world as something divided between right and left. And I don't at all care who's on the right or left or in the center. Even though we use them, even though I use them myself, these expressions have lost all meaning. I'm not interested in one label or the other—I'm only interested in solving certain problems, in getting where I want to go. I have certain objectives. They're the same objectives my father had: to give people a higher standard of living, to do away with the cancer of poverty, to eliminate the consequences of economic backwardness. I want to succeed. And I want to succeed in the best way possible, without caring whether people call my actions leftist or rightist.

It's the same story as when we nationalized the banks. I'm not for nationalization because of the rhetoric of nationalization, or because I see in nationalization the cure-all for every injustice. I'm for nationalization in cases where it's necessary. When we were first considering it, my party was disturbed by one trend in favor and one against. So as not to split the party, I suggested a compromise: to give the banks a year's time and see if they succeed in showing us that nationalization wasn't necessary. The year went by and we realized it hadn't done any good, that the money still ended up in the hands of the rich industrialists or friends of the bankers. So I concluded that it was necessary to nationalize the banks. And we did. Without considering it a socialist gesture or an antisocialist gesture, just a necessary one. Anyone who nationalizes only so as to be considered on the left to me is a fool.

O.F.: However, you've used the word socialist on various occasions.

I.G.: Yes, because it's the closest to what I want to do. And because in all societies that have applied a form of socialism, a certain degree of social and economic equality has been achieved. But by now even the word socialism has so many meanings and interpretations. The Russians call themselves socialists, the Swedes call themselves socialists. And let's not forget that in Germany there was also a national socialism.

O.F.: Mrs. Gandhi, what does the word socialism mean to you?

I.G.: Justice. Yes, it means justice. It means trying to work in a more egalitarian society.

O.F.: But in the pragmatic sense, free of ideologies.

I.G.: Yes. Because what good does it do to remain tied to an ideology if you don't achieve anything by it? I have an ideology myself—you can't work in a vacuum; you have to have faith in something. As my father said, you have to keep an open mind, but you have to pour something into it—otherwise ideas slip away like sand between your fingers. The fact that I have an ideology, however, doesn't mean I'm indoctrinated. Nowadays you can no longer let yourself be indoctrinated— the world is changing so fast! Even what you wanted twenty years ago is no longer relevant today; it's outdated.

Look, for me the only point that has remained unchanged through the years is that in India there is still so much poverty. A great part of the people still don't enjoy the benefits they should have derived from independence—and so then what good does it do to be free? After all, why did we want to become free? Not just to throw out the British. About this we were always clear. We always said that our struggle was not only against the British as representatives of colonialism, it was against all the evil that existed in India. The evil of the feudal system, the evil of the system based on caste, the evil of economic injustice. Well, that evil has not been uprooted. After twenty years we're politically free, yes, but very far from having reached the objective we set for ourselves.

O.F.: So then what point have you reached?

I.G.: That's difficult to say because the point of arrival is continually shifting. Have you ever climbed a mountain? You see, once you arrive at the top of a mountain, you think you've reached the highest point. But it's only an impression that doesn't last long. You soon realize that the peak you've climbed was one of the lowest, that the mountain was part of a chain of mountains, that there are still so many, so many mountains to climb. . . . And the more you climb, the more you want to climb—even though you're dead tired.

I mean, poverty assumes so many aspects here in India. There aren't only the poor that you see in the cities, there are the poor among the tribes, the poor who live in the forest, the poor who live on the mountains. Should we ignore them as long as the poor in the cities are better off? And better off with reference to what? To what people wanted ten years ago? Then it seemed like so much. Today it's no longer so much. So look, when you govern a country, and especially a country so vast and complex as India, you never arrive at anything. Just when you think you've achieved something, you realize you've achieved nothing. And still you have to go forward just the same—toward a dream so distant that your road has neither beginning nor end.

O.F.: And you, Mrs. Gandhi—at what point have you arrived on this road?

I.G.: At no point, at a very important point: that of having convinced the Indians that they can do things. At first people asked us, "Can you do it?" And we kept silent because we didn't believe in ourselves, we didn't believe that we could do things. Today people no longer say to us, "Can you?" They say, "When can you?" Because the Indians finally believe in themselves, they believe they can do things. Oh, the word "when" is so important for a people, for an individual! If an individual thinks he won't do it, he'll never do it. Even if he's highly intelligent, even if he has countless talents. To become capable, one must have faith in oneself. Well, as a nation, I believe we've acquired faith in ourselves. And I like to think I've provided this faith. I also like to think that by providing faith, I've focused their pride. I say focused because pride isn't something you give. It doesn't even break out suddenly; it's a feeling that grows very slowly, very confusedly. Our pride has grown in the last twenty-five years, though others don't understand it and underestimate it. You've never been very generous, you Westerners, toward us Indians. You should have seen that things were changing, albeit slowly. You should have seen that something was happening. Not much, but something.

O.F.: Have you really not also given your people pride, Mrs. Gandhi? You yourself are so proud.

I.G.: No. On the contrary, I'm not. No.

O.F.: Of course you are. Wasn't it an act of pride to refuse the aid the world offered you during the famine of 1966? I remember a ship loaded with grain, with food, that never left the port of Naples. And everything spoiled, while the people of India were dying.

I.G.: I never heard about it. No, I didn't know that the ship was loaded and ready to sail—otherwise I wouldn't have refused it. But it's true that I refused foreign aid. It's true. It wasn't my personal decision, however—it was the whole country that said no. And believe me, it happened by itself, all of a sudden. Yes, all of a sudden inscriptions appeared on walls. Signs appeared. And that "no" exploded all over India, in an act of pride that surprised even me. Then even the political parties, all of them, even the deputies in Parliament, said no: it's better to die of hunger than be taken for a nation of beggars. I had to make myself the interpreter of that no, repeat it to those who wanted to help us. And it was hard for you, I understand. I think you were hurt by it. Sometimes we hurt one another without realizing it.

O.F.: We didn't want to hurt you.

I.G.: I know. I repeat, I understand. But you must also understand us—always undervalued, underestimated, not believed. Even when we believed, you didn't believe us. You said, "How is it possible to fight without violence?" But without violence we obtained our freedom. You said, "How is it possible for democracy to work with an illiterate people who are dying of hunger?" But with that people we made a democracy work. You said, "Planning is something for communist countries; democracy and planning don't go together!" But, with all the errors we committed, our plans succeeded. Then we announced that there'd be no more starvation in India. And you responded, "Impossible. You'll never succeed!" Instead we succeeded; today in India no one dies of hunger any more;

food production far exceeds consumption. Finally we promised to limit the birth rate. And this you really didn't believe; you smiled scornfully. Well, even in this things have gone well. The fact is that we have grown by over seventy millions in ten years, but it's also true that we have grown less than many other countries, including the countries of Europe.

O.F.: Often through dreadful methods, like the sterilization of men. Do you approve of that, Mrs. Gandhi?

I.G.: In India's distant past, when the population was low, the blessing given a woman was, "May you have many children." Most of our epics and literature stress this wish, and the idea that a woman should have many children hasn't declined. I myself, in my heart, say that people should have all the children they want. But it's a mistaken idea, like many of our ideas that go back thousands of years, and it must be rooted out. We must protect families, we must protect children, who have inalienable rights and should be loved, should be taken care of physically and mentally, and should not be brought into the world only to suffer. Do you know that, until recently, poor people brought children into the world for the sole purpose of making use of them? But how can you change, by force or all of a sudden, an age-old habit? The only way is to plan births, by one means or another. And the sterilization of men is one method of birth control. The surest, most radical method. To you it seems dreadful. To me it seems that, properly applied, it's by no means dreadful. I see nothing wrong in sterilizing a man who has already brought eight or ten children into the world. Especially if it helps those eight or ten children to live better.

O.F.: Have you ever been a feminist, Mrs. Gandhi?

I.G.: No, never. I've never had the need to; I've always been able to do what I wanted. On the other hand, my mother was. She considered the fact of being a woman a great disadvantage. She had her reasons. In her day women lived in seclusion—in almost all Indian states they couldn't even show themselves on the street. Muslim women had to go out in purdah, that heavy sheet that covers even the eyes. Hindu women had to go out in the *doli,* a kind of closed sedan chair like a catafalque. My mother always told me about these things with bitterness and rage. She was the oldest of two sisters and two brothers, and she grew up with her brothers, who were about her age. She grew up, to the age of ten, like a wild colt, and then all of a sudden that was over. They had forced on her her "woman's destiny" by saying, "This isn't done, this isn't good, this isn't worthy of a lady."

At a certain point the family moved to Jaipur, where no woman could avoid the *doli* or purdah. They kept her in the house from morning to night, either cooking or doing nothing. She hated doing nothing, she hated to cook. So she became pale and ill, and far from being concerned about her health, my grandfather said, "Who's going to marry her now?" So my grandmother waited for my grandfather to go out, and then she dressed my mother as a man and let her go out riding with her brothers. My grandfather never knew about it, and my mother told me the story without a smile. The memory of these injustices never left her. Until the day she died, my mother continued to fight for the rights of women. She joined all the women's movements of the time; she stirred up a lot of revolts. She was a great woman, a great figure. Women today would like her immensely.

O.F.: And what do you think of them, Mrs. Gandhi? Of their liberation movement, I mean.

I.G.: I think it's good. Good. Because, you see, until today the rights of people have always been put forward by a few individuals acting in the name of the masses. Today instead people no longer want to be represented; each wants to speak for himself and participate directly—it's the same for the Negroes, for the Jews, for women. So not only Negroes and Jews, but also women are part of a great revolt of which one can only approve. Women sometimes go too far, it's true. But it's only when you go too far that others listen. This is also something I've learned from experience. Didn't they perhaps give us the vote because we went too far? Yes, in the Western world, women have no other choice. In India, no. And I'll explain the reason. It's a reason that also has to do with my own case. In India women have never been in hostile competition with men—even in the most distant past, every time a woman emerged as a leader, perhaps as a queen, the people accepted her. As something normal and not exceptional. Let's not forget that in India the symbol of strength is a woman: the goddess Shakti. Not only that—the struggle for independence here has been conducted in equal measure by men and by women. And when we got our independence, no one forgot that. In the Western world, on the other hand, nothing of the kind has ever happened—women have participated, yes, but revolutions have always been made by men alone.

O.F.: Now we come to the personal questions, Mrs. Gandhi. Now I'm ready to ask them. And here's the first: Does a woman like you find herself more at ease with men or with women?

I.G.: For me it's absolutely the same—I treat one and the other in exactly the same way. As persons, that is, not as men and women. But, even here, you have to consider the fact that I've had a very special education, that I'm the daughter of a man like my father and a woman like my mother. I grew up like a boy, also because most of the children who came to our house were boys. With boys I climbed trees, ran races, and wrestled. I had no complexes of envy or inferiority toward boys. At the same time, however, I liked dolls. I had many dolls. And you know how I played with them? By performing insurrections, assemblies, scenes of arrest. My dolls were almost never babies to be nursed but men and women who attacked barracks and ended up in prison. Let me explain. Not only my parents but the whole family was involved in the resistance—my grandfather and grandmother, my uncles and aunts, my cousins of both sexes. So ever so often the police came and took them away, indiscriminately. Well, the fact that they arrested both my father and mother, both my grandfather and grandmother, both an uncle and an aunt, made me accustomed to looking on men and women with the same eyes, on an absolute plane of equality.

O.F.: And then there's that story about Joan of Arc, isn't there?

I.G.: Yes, it's true. It's true that Joan of Arc was my dream as a little girl. I discovered her toward the age of ten or twelve, when I went to France. I don't remember where I read about her, but I recall that she immediately took on a definite importance for me. I wanted to sacrifice my life for my country. It seems like foolishness and yet . . . what happens when we're children is engraved forever on our lives.

O.F.: Yes indeed. And I'd like to understand what it is that's made you what you are, Mrs. Gandhi.

I.G.: The life I've had, the difficulties, the hardships, the pain I've suffered since I was a child. It's a great privilege to have led a difficult life, and many people in my generation have had this privilege—I sometimes wonder if young people today aren't deprived of the dramas that shaped us. . . . If you only knew what it did to me to have lived in that house where the police were bursting in to take everyone away! I certainly didn't have a happy and serene childhood. I was a thin, sickly, nervous little girl. And after the police came, I'd be left alone for weeks, months, to get along as best I could. I learned very soon to get along by myself. I began to travel by myself, in Europe, when I was eight years old. At that age I was already on the move between India and Switzerland, Switzerland and France, France and England. Administering my own finances like an adult.

People often ask me: Who has influenced you the most? Your father? Mahatma Gandhi? Yes, my choices were fundamentally influenced by them, by the spirit of equality they infused in me—my obsession for justice comes from my father, who in turn got it from Mahatma Gandhi. But it's not right to say that my father influenced me more than others, and I wouldn't be able to say whether my personality was formed more by my father or my mother or the Mahatma or the friends who were with us. It was all of them; it was a complete thing. It was the very fact that no one ever imposed anything on me or tried to impose himself on the others. No one ever indoctrinated me. I've always discovered things for myself, in marvelous freedom. For instance, my father cared very much about courage, physical courage as well. He despised those who didn't have it. But he never said to me, "I want you to be courageous." He just smiled with pride every time I did something difficult or won a race with the boys.

O.F.: How much you must have loved that father!

I.G.: Oh, yes! My father was a saint. He was the closest thing to a saint that you can find in a normal man. Because he was so good. So incredibly, unbearably good. I always defended him, as a child, and I think I'm still defending him—his policies at least. Oh, he wasn't at all a politician, in no sense of the word. He was sustained in his work only by a blind faith in India—he was preoccupied in such an obsessive way by the future of India. We understood each other.

O.F.: And Mahatma Gandhi?

I.G.: A lot of mythology arose after his death. But the fact remains that he was an exceptional man, terribly intelligent, with tremendous intuition for people, and a great instinct for what was right. He said that the first president of India ought to be a *harijan* girl, an untouchable. He was so against the class system and the oppression of women that an untouchable woman became for him the epitome of purity and benediction. I began to associate with him when he came and went in our house—together with my father and mother he was on the executive committee. After independence I worked with him a lot—in the period when there were the troubles between Hindus and Muslims, he assigned me to take care of the Muslims. To protect them. Ah, yes, he was a great man. However . . . between me and Gandhi there was never the understanding there was between me and my father. He was always talking of religion. . . . He was convinced that was right. . . . The fact is, we young people didn't agree with him on many things.

O.F.: Let's go back to you, Mrs. Gandhi, to your history as an unusual woman. Is it true that you didn't want to get married?

I.G.: Yes. Until I was about eighteen, yes. But not because I felt like a suffragette, but because I wanted to devote all my energies to the struggle to free India. Marriage, I thought, would have distracted me from the duties I'd imposed on myself. But little by little I changed my mind, and when I was about eighteen, I began to consider the possibility of getting married. Not to have a husband, but to have children. I always wanted to have children—if it had been up to me, I would have had eleven. It was my husband who wanted only two.

And I'll tell you something else. The doctors advised me not to have even one. My health was still not good, and they said that pregnancy might be fatal. If they hadn't said that to me, maybe I wouldn't have got married. But that diagnosis provoked me, it infuriated me. I answered, "Why do you think I'm getting married if not to have children? I don't want to hear that I can't have children; I want you to tell me what I have to do in order to have children!" They shrugged their shoulders and grumbled that perhaps if I were to put on weight that would protect me a little—being so thin, I would never succeed in remaining pregnant. All right, I said, I'll put on weight. And I started having massages, taking cod-liver oil, and eating twice as much. But I didn't even gain an ounce. I'd made up my mind that on the day the engagement was announced I'd be fatter, and I didn't gain an ounce. Then I went to Mussoorie, which is a health resort, and I ignored the doctors' instructions; I invented my own regime and gained weight. Just the opposite of what I'd like now. Now I have the problem of keeping slim. Still I manage. I don't know if you realize I'm a determined woman.

O.F.: Yes, I've realized that. And, if I'm not mistaken, you even showed it by getting married.

I.G.: Yes, indeed. No one wanted that marriage, no one. Even Mahatma Gandhi wasn't happy about it. As for my father . . . it's not true that he opposed it, as people say, but he wasn't eager for it. I suppose because the fathers of only daughters would prefer to see them get married as late as possible. Anyway I like to think it was for that reason. My fiancé, you see, belonged to another religion. He was a Parsi. And this was something nobody could stand—all of India was against us. They wrote to Gandhi, to my father, to me. Insults, death threats. Every day the postman arrived with an enormous sack and dumped the letters on the floor. We even stopped reading them; we let a couple of friends read them and tell us what was in them. "There's a fellow who wants to chop you both into little pieces. There's someone who's ready to marry you even though he already has a wife. He says at least he's a Hindu." At a certain point the Mahatma got into the controversy—I've just found an article he wrote in his newspaper, imploring people to leave him in peace and not be so narrowminded. In any case, I married Mr. Feroze Gandhi. Once I get an idea in my head, no one in the world can make me change my mind.

O.F.: Let's hope the same thing didn't happen when your son Rajiv married an Italian girl.

I.G.: Times have changed; the two of them didn't have to go through the same anguish I did. One day in 1965 Rajiv wrote me from London, where he was studying, and informed me, "You're always asking me about girls, whether I have a special girl, and so forth. Well, I've met a special girl. I haven't proposed yet, but she's the girl I want to marry." A year later, when I went to England, I met her. And when Rajiv returned to India, I asked him, "Do you still think about her in the same way?" And he said yes. But she couldn't get married until she was twenty-one, and until she was sure she'd like to live in India. So we waited for her to be twenty-one, and she came to India, and said she liked India, and we announced the engagement, and two months later they were husband and wife. Sonia is almost completely an Indian by now, even though she doesn't always wear saris. But even I, when I was a student in London, often wore Western clothes, and yet I'm the most Indian Indian I know. If you only knew, for instance, how much I enjoy being a grandmother! Do you know I'm twice a grandmother? Rajiv and Sonia have had a boy and a girl. The girl was just born.

O.F.: Mrs. Gandhi, your husband has now been dead for some years. Have you ever thought of remarrying?

I.G.: No, no. Maybe I would have considered the problem if I'd met someone with whom I'd have liked to live. But I never met this someone and . . . No, even if I had met him, I'm sure I wouldn't have got married again. Why should I get married now that my life is so full? No, no, it's out of the question.

O.F.: Besides I can't imagine you as a housewife.

I.G.: You're wrong! Oh, you're wrong! I was a perfect housewife. Being a mother has always been the job I liked best. Absolutely. To be a mother, a housewife, never cost me any sacrifice— I savored every minute of those years. My sons . . . I was crazy about my sons and I think I've done a super job in bringing them up. Today in fact they're two fine and serious men. No, I've never understood women who, because of their children, pose as victims and don't allow themselves any other activities. It's not at all hard to reconcile the two things if you organize your time intelligently. Even when my sons were little, I was working. I was a welfare worker for the Indian Council for Child Welfare. I'll tell you a story. Rajiv was only four years old at that time, and was going to kindergarten. One day the mother of one of his little friends came to see us and said in a sugary voice, "Oh, it must be so sad for you to have no time to spend with your little boy!" Rajiv roared like a lion: "My mother spends more time with me than you spend with your little boy, see! Your little boy says you always leave him alone so you can play bridge!" I detest women who do nothing and then play bridge.

O.F.: So there was a long period in your life when you stayed out of politics. Didn't you believe in it any more?

I.G.: Politics. . . . You see, it depends on what kind of politics. What we did during my father's generation was a duty. And it was beautiful because its goal was the conquest of freedom. What we do now, on the other hand . . . Don't think that I'm crazy about this kind of politics. It's no accident that I've done everything to keep my sons out of it, and so far I've succeeded. After independence I retired immediately from politics. My children needed me, and I liked my job as a social worker. I said, "I've done my share. Leave the rest to the others." I went back into politics only when it was clear that things weren't going as they should have in my party. I was always arguing, I argued with everyone—with my father, with the leaders I had known since I was a child . . . and one day, it was in 1955, one of them exclaimed, "You do nothing but criticize! If you think you can correct things, correct them. Go ahead, why don't you try?" Well, I could never resist a challenge, so I tried. But I thought it was something temporary, and my father, who had never tried to involve me in his activities, thought so too. People who say it was her father who prepared her for the post of prime minister, it was her father who launched her, are wrong. When he asked me to help him, I really didn't suspect the consequences.

O.F.: And yet everything began because of him.

I.G.: Obviously. He was prime minister, and to take care of his home, to be his hostess, automatically meant to have my hands in politics—to meet people, to know their games, their secrets. It also meant to fall sooner or later into the trap of direct experience. And this came in 1957, a weekend when my father had to go north for a rally. I went with him, as always, and when we got to Chamba, we discovered that the lady who had charge of his schedule had also set up a meeting for him someplace else—for Monday morning. So if my father had given up the rally in Chamba, we'd have lost the elections in Chamba; if he gave up the one in the other city, which was near Pathankot, we'd lose the elections there. "And if I went?" I suggested. "If I spoke, and explained that you couldn't be in two places at once?" He answered it was impossible. I'd have had to cover three hundred miles of bad road through the hills. And it was already two o'clock Monday morning. So I said good night and murmured, "A pity, it seemed to me a good idea." At five-thirty, when I woke up, I found a note under the door. It was from my father. It said, "A plane will take you to Pathankot. From there it's only three hours by car. You'll arrive in time. Good luck." I arrived in time and held the rally. It was a success and I was asked for others. That was the beginning of . . . everything.

O.F.: Were you still married at that time, or were you already separated?

I.G.: But I always stayed married to my husband! Always, until the day he died! It's not true that we were separated! Look, the truth is otherwise and . . . why not say it for once and for all? My husband lived in Lucknow. My father lived in Delhi, of course. So I shuttled between Delhi and Lucknow and . . . naturally, if my husband needed me on days when I was in Delhi, I ran back to Lucknow. But if it was my father who needed me, on days when I was in Lucknow, I ran back to Delhi. No, it wasn't a comfortable situation. After all there's quite a distance between Delhi and Lucknow. And . . . yes, my husband got angry. And he quarreled. We quarreled. We quarreled a lot. It's true. We were two equally strong types, equally pigheaded—neither of us wanted to give in. And . . . I like to think those quarrels made us better, that they enliv-

ened our life, because without them we would have had a normal life, yes, but banal and boring. We didn't deserve a normal, banal, and boring life. After all, ours had not been a
forced marriage and he had chosen me. . . . I mean he was
the one to choose me rather than I choosing him. . . . I don't
know if I loved him as much as he loved me when we became
engaged but . . . Then love grew, in me as well, it became
something great and . . . well, you must understand him!

It wasn't easy for him to be my father's son-in-law! It
wouldn't have been easy for anybody. Let's not forget that he
too was a deputy in Parliament! At a certain point, he gave in.
He decided to leave Lucknow and live in Delhi, in my father's
house, with him and me. But, being a deputy in Parliament,
how could he meet people in the house of the prime minister?
He realized that right away, and so he had to find himself
another small house, and this wasn't convenient either. To be
a little here and a little there, a little with us and a little alone.
. . . No, life wasn't easy for him either.

O.F.: Mrs. Gandhi, have you ever had regrets? Were you ever afraid
of giving in?

I.G.: No. Never. Fear, any fear, is a waste of time. Like regrets.
And everything I've done, I've done because I wanted to do it.
In doing it, I've plunged in headlong, always believing in it.
Whether when I was a child and fought the British in the
Monkey Brigade, or when I was a girl and wanted to have
children, or when I was a woman and devoted myself to my
father, making my husband angry. Each time I stayed involved all the way in my decision, and took the consequences.
Even if I was fighting for things that didn't concern India. Oh,
I remember how angry I was when Japan invaded China! I immediately joined a committee to collect money and medi-
cines, I immediately signed up for the International Brigade, I
plunged headlong into propaganda against Japan. . . . A person like me doesn't have fear first and regrets afterward.

O.F.: Besides, you haven't made mistakes. There are those who say
that, having won this war, no one will be able to dislodge you
and you'll stay in power for at least twenty years.

I.G.: I instead haven't the slightest idea how long I'll stay, and I
don't even care to know, becuse I don't care if I remain prime

minister. I'm only interested in doing a good job as long as I'm capable and for as long as I don't get tired. I'm certainly not tired—work doesn't tire people, it's getting bored that's tiring. But nothing lasts forever, and no one can predict what will happen to me in the near or distant future. I'm not ambitious. Not a bit. I know I'll astonish everyone by talking like this, but it's God's truth. Honors have never tempted me and I've never sought them. As for the job of prime minister, I like it, yes. But no more than I've liked other work that I've done as an adult. A little while ago I said that my father was not a politician. I, instead, think I am. But not in the sense of being interested in a political career—rather in the sense that I think it necessary to strive to build a certain India, the India I want. The India I want, I'll never tire of repeating, is a more just and less poor India, one entirely free of foreign influences. If I thought the country was already marching toward these objectives, I'd give up politics immediately and retire as prime minister.

O.F.: To do what?

I.G.: Anything. As I told you, I fall in love with anything I do and I always try to do it well. And so? Being prime minister isn't the only job in life! As far as I'm concerned, I could live in a village and be satisfied. When I'm not governing my country any more, I'll go back to taking care of children. Or else I'll start studying anthropology—it's a science that's always interested me very much, also in relation to the problem of poverty. Or else I'll go back to studying history—at Oxford I took my degree in history. Or else . . . I don't know, I'm fascinated by the tribal communities. I might busy myself with them.

Listen, I certainly won't have an empty life! And the future doesn't frighten me, even if it threatens to be full of other difficulties. I'm trained to difficulties; difficulties can't be eliminated from life. Individuals will always have them, countries will always have them. . . . The only thing is to accept them, if possible overcome them, otherwise to come to terms with them. It's all right to fight, yes, but only when it's possible. When it's impossible, it's better to stoop to compromise, without resisting and without complaining. People who complain are selfish. When I was young, I was very selfish, now not any more. Now I don't get upset by unpleasant things, I don't play the victim, and I'm always ready to come to terms with life.

O.F.: Mrs. Gandhi, are you a happy woman?

I.G.: I don't know. Happiness is such a fleeting point of view— there's no such thing as continual happiness. There are only moments of happiness—from contentment to ecstasy. And if by happiness you mean ecstasy. . . . Yes, I've known ecstasy, and it's a blessing to be able to say it because those who can say it are very few. But ecstasy doesn't last long and is seldom if ever repeated. If by happiness you mean instead an ordinary contentment, then yes—I'm fairly contented. Not satisfied— contented. Satisfied is a word I use only in reference to my country, and I'll never be satisfied for my country. For this reason I go on taking difficult paths, and between a paved road and a footpath that goes up the mountain, I choose the footpath. To the great irritation of my bodyguards.

O.F.: Thank you, Mrs. Gandhi.

I.G.: Thank *you*. And best wishes. As I always say, I do not wish you an easy time, but I wish you that whatever difficulty you may have, you will overcome it.

New Delhi, February 1972

8

Ali Bhutto

The invitation was disconcerting. It came from Zulfikar Ali Bhutto, and there seemed no way to account for it. It asked only that I leave for Rawalpindi as soon as possible. I wondered why. Every journalist dreams of being summoned at least once by those who, when you go looking for them, run away or say no. But illogic is the stuff of dreams and leads to suspicion. Why did Bhutto want to see me? To entrust me with a message for Indira Gandhi? To punish me for having portrayed her with esteem and sympathy? The first hypothesis was immediately discarded. Bhutto had no need of a courier to communicate with his enemy—for that there were Swiss and Russian diplomats. The second hypothesis was soon discarded. Bhutto has the reputation of being a civilized person, and civilized people don't usually kill their invited guests. The third hypothesis, that he intended to let me interview him, filled me with proper astonishment. And, instead, this was just what Bhutto had in mind, after reading my article on the president of Bangladesh, the unfortunate Mujibur "Mujib" Rahman. As I found out when my curiosity won out over my suspicion and I decided to accept the invitation. But in accepting it, I let him know that being his guest would not keep me from writing about him with the same independence of judgment that I applied to everyone without distinction and that no amount of courtesy or flattery would ever be able to buy me off. Bhutto answered: certainly, all right. And this gave me my first impression of the man.

The man is unpredictable, bizarre, carried away by whims, by strange decisions. And, let's face it, highly intelligent. Intelligence of an astute, foxy kind, born to charm, to confuse, while at the same time nourished by culture, memory, flair. As well as by a great urbanity. At the Rawalpindi airport I was met by two officials who announced to me with considerable emotion that the president would receive me in an hour. It was ten in the morning, and I had had no sleep for about forty-eight hours. Not in an hour, I protested; I needed a good bath and a good sleep. Well, to someone else that would have been an insult. Not to him. He put off the meeting till seven-thirty in the evening, adding that he was expecting me for supper, and since intelligence combined with courtesy is the best instrument for seduction, it was inevitable that this meeting should be cordial.

Bhutto, wreathed in smiles, greeted me with open arms. He was tall, stocky, a little stout for such thin legs and delicate feet, and he looked like a banker who wants to get you to open an account in his bank. He seemed older than his forty-four years. He was beginning to go bald; his remaining hair was gray. Under his thick eyebrows, his face looked heavy: heavy cheeks, heavy lips, heavy eyelids. A mysterious sadness was locked in his eyes. There was something shy about his smile.

Like many powerful leaders, he too is weakened and crippled by shyness. He is also many other things and, as with Indira Gandhi, all of them in conflict among themselves. The more you study him, the more you remain uncertain, confused. Like a prism turning on a pivot, he is forever offering you a different face, and at the same moment that he gives in to your scrutiny, he withdraws. So you can define him in countless ways and all of them are true: liberal and authoritarian, fascist and communist, sincere and a liar. He is undoubtedly one of the most complex leaders of our time and the only interesting one his country has so far produced. The only one, moreover, capable of saving it, at least for a while. Anyone will tell you there is no alternative to Bhutto. If Bhutto goes, Pakistan will be erased from the map.

In this sense, he reminds you less of Indira Gandhi than of King

Hussein. Like Hussein, he is accused of leading a nation artificially born. Like Hussein he is in an earthenware pot squeezed among iron pots: the Soviet Union, India, China, America. Like Hussein, he is determined not to yield, and resists with the courage of a trapeze artist with no net to protect him. But in another sense, he reminds you of John Kennedy. Like Kennedy, he grew up in the kind of wealth for which nothing is impossible, not even the conquest of political power, cost what it may. Like Kennedy, he had a comfortable, happy, privileged childhood. Like Kennedy, he began his rise to power very early.

The fact is he comes from a family of aristocrats and landowners. He studied at Berkeley and then at Oxford, taking his degree in international law. At slightly more than thirty, he was one of Ayub Khan's ministers, though he detested him. At slightly less than forty, he was one of Agha Muhammad Yahya Khan's ministers, though he despised him. He arrived at the presidency with painful patience, without letting himself be bothered by the bad odor of certain associates.

Power is a more overwhelming passion than love. And those who love power have strong stomachs, and even stronger noses. They don't mind bad odors. Bhutto didn't mind them ever. He loves power. It is difficult to guess the nature of this power. His own response to it is ambiguous, he warns you against politicians who tell the truth or exhibit a boy-scout morality. Listening to him, you are almost led to believe that his ambition is a noble one, that he really intends to build a sincere and disinterested socialism. But then you visit his splendid library in Karachi, and discover that in the place of honor are sumptuous volumes on Mussolini and Hitler, bound in silver. From the tenderness with which they are kept, you conclude that their presence is not due to a book collector's idle curiosity. Doubt and anger arise in you. You ask him, and learn that his true friends were Sukarno and Nasser: two individuals perhaps moved by good intentions but certainly not two liberals. You're left perplexed. Is it his secret dream to become dictator, to be exalted one day by sumptuous volumes bound in silver? Mind you, this is the kind of question asked by Westerners ignorant of the tragedy of a country where freedom, democracy, and political opposition have never had any meaning and have always been replaced by hunger, injustice, and humiliation. But it is still a valid question, as ominous as the expression that fires up his gaze when something displeases him.

The following interview was conducted in five sessions, during the six days that I remained his guest and followed him on a trip through a few provinces. While strictly adhering to his words as recorded on tape, it is thus a mosaic of five different conversations. The first in Rawalpindi, the evening of my arrival. The second on the plane that took us to Lahore. The third in Hala, a city in Sind. The fourth and fifth in Karachi. I was always at his side, whether at the table or en route, and if I wanted to, I could do a portrait of him from my diary of those days. Bhutto, dressed in Pakistani fashion, in gray-green pajamas and sandals, who harangues the crowd in Sanghar where several years ago he escaped an assassination attempt, and the crowd is sullen; he shouts hoarsely into the microphone in Urdu, then in Sindhi, throws out his arms, offers himself with audacious insolence to other possible gunshots. And this is Bhutto the demagogue, avid for applause and authority. Or else Bhutto making people wait for hours in a courtyard in Hala; the city notables are there but he lingers in his room—he is writing. It is night when he finally arrives, advancing like a prince on the beautiful carpets, and like a prince he sits down and has me sit beside him—the only woman among so many mustachioed men, almost a well-calculated provocation. Thus seated, he receives in audience members of his party, governors, separatists, one by one, with a haughty signal of his finger; at the end he receives a poor man with a goat covered with tassels to be sacrificed in his honor.

And this is the aristocratic Bhutto, the Muslim Bhutto that no amount of Western culture will ever basically change—it is no accident that he has two wives. Or else Bhutto flying in a military helicopter, uncomfortable, wearing on his head a cap given him by Chou En-lai—his talisman. During the flight he gazes with tears in his eyes at the dry uncultivated fields, the mud huts where the peasants live a prehistoric existence. All of a sudden he clenches his fists and murmurs, "I must succeed, I must succeed." And this is the Marxist Bhutto, submerged up to his neck in the mirage of making Pakistan less unhappy and less hunger-stricken. Finally, the Bhutto who receives me in his houses in Karachi and Rawalpindi: explaining himself, pleading his cause, ruthlessly attacking Indira Gandhi, Mujib Rahman, Yahya Khan. His houses are furnished with exquisite taste, old Persian rugs and precious enamels, air conditioning, and photographs with inscriptions by his most powerful world colleagues, beginning with Mao Tse-tung. At dinner we drink wine, perhaps eat caviar; also present is his second wife, Nusrat, a beautiful woman with pleasant manners, and later his son comes in, a lively little boy with long hair. And this is the modern, refined, European Bhutto. Bhutto the brilliant speaker, author of books, who knows the English language better than Urdu and evokes the sympathy of any Westerner. A rash conclusion. As Walter Cronkite said when I asked him about Richard Nixon, Lyndon Johnson, Dwight Eisenhower, about the leaders he had interviewed in his long career as a television reporter: You cannot judge a head of state by seeing in him only the man. You shouldn't. Because the moment you discover that he too is only a man, with the virtues and defects and inconsistencies of a man, you inevitably like him and forget the rest.

This interview with Bhutto also unleashed a pandemonium. Not a journalistic one as in the case of Kissinger, but a diplomatic and even international one. For just as Bhutto had been offended to read that Indira called him an unbalanced man, so Indira was offended to read that Bhutto called her a mediocre woman with a mediocre intelligence, a creature devoid of initiative and imagination, a drudge without even half her father's talent, and said that the idea of meeting her, of shaking her hand, filled him with acute disgust. Needless to say, Indira had every reason to be offended. In judging her, Bhutto had been heavy-handed and too guided by hatred. I myself was actually embarrassed by it, and in my embarrassment had tried repeatedly to restrain him. "Aren't you being a little excessive, a little unjust?" But Bhutto had not taken my suggestion, and indeed had insisted on adding other perfidious remarks that I had not published, and my censorship had not done much good. The result was the dramatic, or rather ridiculous, consequences that I involuntarily caused.

Bhutto and Indira were supposed to meet at that time, to sign the peace agreement between India and Pakistan. Alerted by certain sentences reported in the New Delhi newspapers, Indira requested the complete text of the interview and had it transmitted by cable from Rome. Then she read it and announced that the meeting between herself and the prime minister of Pakistan would not take place. Bhutto lost his head and, not knowing where on earth to turn, turned to me. He sought me out again, through his ambassador to Italy. He traced me to Addis Ababa, where I had gone to see Haile Selassie. And here he made the most extravagant request of me.

I must write, he said, a second article and say that the interview with him, Bhutto, had never taken place because I had dreamed it up. I was to say that the opinions about Indira were not opinions uttered by him, but rather those that, in my imagination, I had thought he might utter. At first I didn't think I had understood. "What did you say, Mr. Ambassador?" "I said you should write that you invented everything, and particularly the part about Mrs. Gandhi." "But are you crazy, Mr. Ambassador? Has your prime minister gone crazy too?" "Miss Fallaci, you must understand, the lives of six hundred million people depend on you, they're in your hands." I cursed and told him to go to hell. But Bhutto did not give up and went on looking for me. Wherever I went I was pursued by an important Pakistani who begged me to disavow the interview, then reminded me that the lives of six hundred million people were in my hands. Vainly I replied that my hands were too small to contain six hundred million human beings, vainly I shouted that their demand was absurd and insulting. The nightmare ended only when Indira magnanimously decided to act as though Bhutto's error had never happened. And the two of them met to sign the peace accord.

It was amusing to watch them on television while they shook hands and exchanged smiles. Indira's smile was triumphant and ironical. Bhutto's displayed such discomfort that, even on the black-and-white screen, you seemed to see him blushing to the roots of his hair.

ZULFIKAR ALI BHUTTO: I must tell you why I was so eager to meet you. First of all, because you're the only journalist who has written the truth about Mujib Rahman. I enjoyed your article very much. And then because . . . look, it was much less enjoyable to read that I had something to do with the March suppression in Dacca.

ORIANA FALLACI: Something to do with? Mr. President, in Dacca they come right out and say it was you who wanted the massacre. You who wanted the arrest of Mujib. And that for this reason you stayed in the city until the morning of March 26.

Z.A.B.: To enjoy the spectacle from the windows of my suite on the top floor of the Hotel Intercontinental, drinking whisky and perhaps playing the lyre like Nero. But how dare they try to discredit me by an incident so barbarous and stupid? The whole business was conducted in such a stupid way. They let all the leaders escape to India and then they took it out on the poor wretches who counted for nothing. Only Mujib was arrested. Let's be logical. I would have done it with more intelligence, more scientifically, less brutally. Tear gas, rubber bullets, and I would have arrested all the leaders. Oh, only a disgusting drunkard like ex-President Yahya Khan could have sullied himself with an operation carried out so badly and bloodily.

Anyway, what interest would I have had in wanting such madness? Do you know that Yahya Khan's first victim was not to have been Mujib but myself? Many people in my party were in prison, and at the end of 1970, November 5, 1970, to be exact, he had said to Mujib, "Should I arrest Bhutto or not?" Look, the only reason why he reversed his schedule was that in West Pakistan he couldn't control the situation as in East Pakistan. Besides Mujib has never been intelligent—he let himself be backed into a corner.

But to conclude, the tragedy of March 25 caught me by surprise. Yahya Khan fooled even me. He had given me an appointment for the following day. And, days later, General Mohd Umar revealed to me that he'd resorted to this stratagem so that I'd stay in Dacca and "see the efficiency of the army." I give you my word of honor that all this is true.

O.F.: All right, Mr. President. But I wonder if history will ever have the exact version of what happened that terrible night and in the months that followed. Mujib Rahman . . .

Z.A.B.: Mujib, as you've seen, is a congenital liar. He can't help telling lies—it's something stronger than he. Mujib talks at random, depending on his mood and the disorders of his sick mind. For instance, he says there were three million dead.

He's mad, mad! And they're all mad, the press included, who repeat after him, "Three million dead, three million dead!" The Indians had let out the figure of one million. He came along and doubled it. Then tripled it. It's a characteristic of the man—he'd done the same for the hurricane. Look, according to Indian journalists, the dead that night were between sixty and seventy thousand. According to certain missionaries, there were thirty thousand. According to what I've been able to find out so far, there must have been something like fifty thousand. Mind you, too many. Even if the action was morally justified. I'm not trying to minimize things; I'm trying to bring them back to reality—there's quite a difference between fifty thousand and three million.

The same goes for the refugees. Mrs. Gandhi says ten million. It's obvious she started with that figure in order to legalize her offensive and invade East Pakistan. But when we invited the United Nations to check, the Indians were opposed. Why were they opposed? If the figure were exact, they shouldn't have been afraid of its being verified. The fact is it's not a question of ten million but of two. On the number of dead I may even be wrong, but not on the number of refugees. We know who left the country. And many were Bengalis from West Bengal, sent from Calcutta. It was she who sent them— Mrs. Gandhi. Since the Bengalis all look alike, who was to know?

And now let's talk about the other story: the women raped and killed. I don't believe it. Certainly there was no lack of excesses, but General Tikka Khan says that in those months he often invited the population to report abuses to him directly. He made his appeal with loudspeakers, and still he came to know of only four cases. Shall we multiply by ten and make it forty? We're still far from the senseless figures spread around by Mujib and la Gandhi.

O.F.: No, Mr. President. Go ahead and multiply by a thousand and even by ten thousand, and you'll come closer. If Mujib is talking at random when he says three million dead, Tikka Khan is joking when he says four cases. Mass atrocities took place, and how! I'm speaking as one who saw the corpses in Dacca. And by the way, you just used an awful expression, Mr. President.

You said "Morally justifiable." Or rather, "justified." Did I
understand you? Did you really mean to say that this massacre
was morally justified?

Z.A.B.: Every government, every country, has the right to exercise
force when necessary. For instance, in the name of unity. You
can't build without destroying. To build a country, Stalin was
obliged to use force and kill. Mao Tse-tung was obliged to use
force and kill. To mention only two recent cases, without rak-
ing over the whole history of the world. Yes, there are circumstances where a bloody suppression is justifiable and justified.
In March the unity of Pakistan depended on the suppression of
the secessionists. But to carry it out with such brutality on the
people instead of on those responsible wasn't necessary. That's
not the way to convince poor people who've been told that
with the Six Points there'll be no more hurricanes, no more
floods, no more hunger. I spoke out against such methods
more emphatically than anyone else, and when no one dared
do so.

O.F.: Nevertheless you've now put Tikka Khan, the general who
directed the massacre, at the head of the army. Right?

Z.A.B.: Tikka Khan was a soldier doing a soldier's job. He went to
East Pakistan with precise orders and came back by precise orders. He did what he was ordered to do, though he wasn't
always in agreement, and I picked him because I know he'll
follow my orders with the same discipline. And he won't try to
stick his nose in politics. I can't destroy the whole army, and
anyway his bad reputation for the events in Dacca is exaggerated. There's only one man really responsible for those
events—Yahya Khan. Both he and his advisers were so drunk
with power and corruption they'd even forgotten the honor of
the army. They thought of nothing but acquiring beautiful
cars, building beautiful homes, making friends with bankers,
and sending money abroad. Yahya Khan wasn't interested in
the government of the country, he was interested in power for
its own sake and nothing else. What can you say of a leader
who starts drinking as soon as he wakes up and doesn't stop
until he goes to bed? You've no idea how painful it was to deal
with him. He was really Jack the Ripper.

O.F.: Where is he now, Yahya Khan? What do you intend to do with him?

Z.A.B.: He's under house arrest in a bungalow near Rawalpindi, a bungalow that belongs to the government. Yes, I have a big problem on my hands with him. I've set up a war commission to study the responsibilities inherent in the recent conflict. I'm waiting to see the results, and that'll help me to decide. If the commission finds him guilty, I think there'll be a trial. The defeat we suffered is his—Mrs. Gandhi can rightly boast of having won a war, but if she won it, she should first of all thank Yahya Khan and his gang of illiterate psychopaths. Even to get him to reason was an impossible task—it only made you lose your temper.

In April, after that fine business in Dacca, he sent for me. He looked satisfied, sure of himself, by now convinced he had the situation in hand. He offered me a drink. "Well, you politicians are really finished," he said. Then he said that not only Mujib but I too was considered an agitator, I too was preaching against the unity of Pakistan. "I'm always under pressure to arrest you, Bhutto." I got so angry I lost all control. I answered that I would not let myself be intimidated by him, that his methods had led us to disaster; I threw away the glass of whisky and left the room. There I was stopped by General Pirzada, who took me by the arm. "No, come on, calm down, have a seat, go back in." I calmed down and went back. I tried to explain to him that there was a great difference between me and Mujib: he was a secessionist and I wasn't. A useless task. Instead of listening to me, he went on drinking, drinking. Then he got nasty and . . .

O.F.: Mr. President, can we go back a moment and try to understand how you arrived at that terrible March, morally justifiable or not?

Z.A.B.: Look here. On January 27 I had gone to Dacca to confer with Mujib. If you wanted to discuss matters with him, you had to make a pilgrimage to Dacca—he never condescended to come to Rawalpindi. I went even though it was just that day that my sister's husband had died; he was to be buried in the ancestral tomb in Larkana. And my sister was offended. In the elections, Mujib had obtained a majority in East Pakistan and I had obtained one in West Pakistan. But now he was insisting on the Six Points and we had to come to an agreement— Yahya Kahn was demanding that within four months we work out the Constitution, otherwise the Assembly would be dissolved and new elections called. To make Mujib understand this was a desperate undertaking—you can't expect brains from someone who doesn't have them. I argued, I explained, and he kept repeating dully and monotonously: "The Six Points. Do you accept the Six Points?" Good Lord, on the first, on the second, on the third I was even ready to negotiate. But the fourth anticipated that each province would make its own foreign trade and foreign aid arrangements any way it liked. What would happen to the sovereignty of the state, the unity of the country? Besides that, it was known that Mujib wanted to separate East Pakistan from West Pakistan and that he'd been keeping up connections with the Indians since 1966. So in January our talks had been interrupted and we come to March.

In the middle of March, Yahya Khan came to Karachi and told me he was going to Dacca—did I want to go too? Yes, I answered, if Mujib were ready to talk to me. The telegram informing me that Mujib was ready to talk to me was sent from Dacca by Yahya Khan himself. I left on March 19. On the twentieth I met Yahya and on the twenty-first I met Mujib, together with Yahya. A surprise: Mujib was all sweetness and light with Yahya. "I've come to reach an agreement with you, Mr. President, and I want nothing to do with Mr. Bhutto. I'll tell the press that I have met with the president and that Mr. Bhutto was there by chance," he said in a ceremonious tone. And Yahya: "No, no, Mujib. You must speak for yourself." And Mujib: "So many people are dead in the hurricane, so many people are dead." That's the way he is. All of a sudden a sentence engraves itself on his sick mind, even a sentence that has nothing to do with what you're talking about, and he goes on repeating it like an obsession. At a certain point I lost patience. How was I responsible for the hurricane? Had I been the one to send the hurricane? Mujib's answer was to get up and say that he had to leave to go to a funeral. And . . . oh, it's not worth the trouble.

O.F.: Yes, it is. Please, Mr. President, go on.

Z.A.B.: The fact is that when you talk about Mujib, everything seems so incredible. I don't understand how the world can take him seriously. Well, I got up too, to escort him to the anteroom, though he didn't want me to. In the anteroom there were three people: Yahya's aide-de-camp, his military secretary, and his political butcher, General Umar. Mujib began screaming, "Go away, everybody go away! I have to talk to Mr. Bhutto!" The three of them went out. He sat down and then: "Brother, brother! We must come to an agreement, brother! For the love of God, I implore you!" Astonished, I took him outside so no one would hear him. Outside, and in a particularly excited tone, he declared that I must take West Pakistan for myself, he East Pakistan, and that he had set up everything for a secret meeting. After dark he would send for me. I told him I didn't like this business. I hadn't come to Dacca to meet him like a thief under a banana tree and in the dark, I didn't intend to dismember Pakistan, and if he wanted secession, he had only to propose it to the Assembly, counting on his absolute majority. But it was like talking to a wall. I had to accept the compromise of resuming talks through our spokesmen. Which is what happened—without leading to anything, of course. In those days he was more deranged than ever—he lost his head over nothing. And so we arrived at the twenty-fifth.

O.F.: You didn't notice anything suspicious on March 25?

Z.A.B.: Yes. I felt a certain uneasiness, a strange sensation, which had come to a head. Every evening I went to Yahya to report that Mujib and I weren't making any progress, and Yahya showed no interest. He looked away or complained about the television or grumbled because he couldn't listen to his favorite songs—his records hadn't arrived from Rawalpindi. Then the morning of the twenty-fifth he said something that left me disconcerted: "There's no need to meet Mujib today. We'll see him tomorrow, you and I." Still I said, "All right," and at eight in the evening I reported everything to Mujib's envoy.

And he exclaimed, "That son of a bitch has already left." I didn't believe it. I telephoned the presidential residence and asked to speak with Yahya. They told me he couldn't be disturbed; he was at supper with General Tikka Khan. I telephoned Tikka Khan. They told me he couldn't be disturbed; he was at supper with Yahya Khan. Only then did I begin to worry, and suspecting a trick, I went to supper. Then to sleep. I was awakened by gunfire and by friends running in from other rooms. I ran to the window, and as God is my witness, I wept. I wept and said, "My country is finished."

O.F.: Why? What did you see from that window?

Z.A.B.: I didn't see any indiscriminate killing, but the soldiers were trying to demolish the offices of the *People*, an opposition newspaper that had its offices right in front of the Intercontinental. With their loudspeakers they were ordering people to leave. Those who came out were put to one side under the threat of machine guns. Other groups, on the sidewalk, were being kept at bay with machine guns and the hotel was surrounded by tanks. Anyone who tried to take shelter in it fell into the hands of the soldiers. That's all. That Mujib had been arrested I found out at eight in the morning, when I left. How did I take it? I was glad he was alive and I thought they might have maltreated him a little. Then I thought that his arrest might help to reach a compromise. They wouldn't keep him in prison more than a month or two, and in the meantime we'd be able to bring back law and order.

O.F.: Mr. President, Mujib told you, "You take West Pakistan and I'll take East Pakistan." That's just how it's turned out. Do you hate him for this?

Z.A.B.: Not at all. And I don't say it in the Indian fashion, that is hypocritically. I say it sincerely because, instead of hatred, I feel great compassion for him. He's so incapable, conceited, lacking in culture, common sense, everything. He's in no position to resolve any problem: either politically, or socially, or economically, or internationally. He only knows how to shout and put on a lot of airs. I've known him since 1954 and I've never taken him seriously—I understood from the very first moment that there was no depth to him, no preparation, that he was an agitator breathing a lot of fire and with an absolute lack of ideas. The only idea he's ever had in his head is the idea of secession. Toward someone like that, how can you feel anything except pity?

In 1961, during a trip to Dacca, I saw him again. He was in the lobby of my hotel; I went up to him and said, "Hello, Mujib, let's have a cup of tea." He was just out of prison, he seemed full of bitterness, and this time we were almost able to talk quietly. He said how East Pakistan was exploited by West Pakistan, treated like a colony, sucked of its blood—and it was very true; I'd even written the same thing in a book. But he didn't draw any conclusions, he didn't explain that the fault was in the economic system and in the regime, he didn't speak of socialism and struggle. On the contrary, he declared that the people weren't prepared for struggle, that no one could oppose the military, that it was the military that had to resolve the injustices. He had no courage. He never has had. Does he really call himself, to journalists, "the tiger of Bengal"?

O.F.: He even says that at his trial he refused to defend himself and that his behavior after his arrest was heroic. He was in a cell where there wasn't even a mattress to sleep on.

Z.A.B.: Come on now! He wasn't in a cell, he was in an apartment that's put at the disposal of important political detainees. In Lyallpur, near Mianwali, the Punjab prison. True, he wasn't allowed to read the newspapers and listen to the radio, but he had the entire library of the governor of Punjab at his disposal and he lived quite well indeed. At a certain point they even gave him a Bengali cook because he wanted to eat Bengali dishes. At his trial he defended himself, and how! He asked for the services of two eminent lawyers: Kamal Hussain and A. K. Brohi, his legal adviser and friend. Kamal Hussain was in prison but not Brohi, and to have Brohi means to have the best of the best. I'll tell you something else. At first Brohi didn't want to accept but Yahya Khan forced him, and he then presented himself at the trial with four assistants, four other lawyers. Paid for by the state, naturally. It cost a fortune, that trial. Well, Brohi has only one fault: he's a bit of a chatterbox. So every time he came back to Karachi from Lyallpur, he told about the conversations he'd had with Mujib and said it would be difficult to find him guilty—Mujib had put things in such a convincing way as regards his respect for the unity of Pakistan and his devotion to Yahya Khan. Mujib never tired of repeating that Yahya Khan was a fine man, a great patriot, and that he had been led astray by me—the only one responsible for his arrest. This was confirmed to me by General Pirzada, to whom I said, "Give him to me and you'll see that he'll call me a fine man, a great patriot, and insult you." Just what was to happen.

O.F.: But he was convicted and sentenced.

Z.A.B.: No. The special tribunal found him guilty and from then on it was up to Yahya Khan, as administrator of martial law, to decide on the sentence, which could have been five years or life imprisonment or the death penalty. Yahya decided nothing—the war had broken out and he had plenty of other things on his mind.

O.F.: Mujib told me they had dug his grave.

Z.A.B.: Do you know what that grave was? An air-raid shelter. They had dug it all around the walls of the prison. Poor Mujib. Being so fearful, he mistakes everything for a death notice. But I don't believe that Yahya was thinking of killing him. On December 27, when I was sworn in as the new president of the Republic, I met with Yahya Khan. He was desperate, drunk, he looked like the portrait of Dorian Gray. He told me: "The greatest mistake of my life has been not to execute Mujib Rahman. Do it yourself, if you like."

O.F.: And you?

Z.A.B.: I said that I wouldn't, and after thinking it over, I got ready to free Mujib. Having been condemned by everyone for the supposed atrocities of the army, Pakistan needed some sympathy—I thought the act of clemency would get much sympathy. Besides I thought the gesture would accelerate the return of our war prisoners. So I immediately sent an order to Lyallpur to bring Mujib to me in Rawalpindi. When the order arrived, Mujib got frightened. He began moaning that they'd come to take him out and execute him; he didn't calm down even during the journey or when he entered the bungalow I'd put at his disposal. A beautiful bungalow for important guests. When I arrived with a radio, a television set, and a bundle of clothes, he assailed me: "What are you doing here?" I ex-

plained I'd become president and he immediately changed his
tone. He threw his arms around my neck, he told me this was
the most wonderful news he'd ever had in his life, that God
was always sending me to save him. . . . (The other time too
I'd been the one to get him out.) Then just as I'd foreseen, he
began attacking Yahya, pausing only to ask me if he could
consider himself free. I saw him again twice before he went
back to Dacca by way of London. And both times he took out
his book of the Koran, he swore on the Koran that he'd keep
up relations with West Pakistan. He swore it also on the plane,
when I saw him off at three in the morning, and I almost succeeded in being moved. He swore and embraced me, he
thanked me, he repeated his eternal gratitude: "Don't worry,
Mr. President, I'll be back soon. I want to know your beautiful
country better, and you'll see me again soon, soon."

O.F.: Are you ever sorry you freed him?

Z.A.B.: No, never. He's a Pakistani like myself, whatever he may
say. And more than once we've suffered the same accusations,
the same persecutions—underneath it all there's a bond between us. I always remember him as I saw him one day in
January, when he clutched my arm and sobbed and begged,
"Save me, save me." I feel genuine pity for him. Besides, poor
Mujib, he won't last long. Eight months, at most a year—then
he'll be swallowed up by the chaos he himself wanted. You
see, Bangladesh today is a satellite of India. But it will soon
become a satellite of Russia, and Mujib isn't a communist.
Even if he were to manage all right, which is most unlikely, at
that point he'd find the Maoists on his back, who are the real
victors in this war. He has them on his back already.

Politically the Mukti Bahini count for nothing, lacking as
they do any ideological preparation, any indoctrination, any
discipline. Then socially speaking, they're a disturbance—they
only know how to fire in the air, frighten people, steal, yell *Joi
Bangla*. And you can't run a country by yelling *Joi Bangla*.
The Bengali Maoists, on the other hand . . . well, they certainly don't represent a very refined product—at most they've
read half of Mao's little red book. But they're an articulate
force and don't let themselves be used by the Indians, and I
don't even think they're against the unity of Pakistan. They'll

end by having the upper hand. Good Lord, it would take a genius to cope with such complex and frightful problems—just
imagine Mujib coping with them. And then that's such an unfortunate land. Hurricanes, floods, storms. One would say it's
born under an unlucky star, and let's not forget it's always
been the dregs of the world. You should have seen Dacca in
1947 and even in 1954! A dirty village where there weren't
even streets. Now that everything is destroyed, thanks also to
the dynamite of the Mukti Bahini, Bangladesh . . .

O.F.: I'm surprised you say Bangladesh.

Z.A.B.: Obviously I say it with anger and scorn. Obviously for me
it's still East Pakistan. But, rightly or wrongly, and even
though it's the result of a military action by the Indians, fifty
countries have recognized it. I must accept it. I'm even ready
to recognize it, if India gives us back our prisoners, if the massacre of the Biharis ends, if the federalists aren't persecuted. If
we're to reunite ourselves in a federation, we must first establish diplomatic relations. And I think that within ten or fifteen years Pakistan and Bangladesh can be reunited in a federation. Can and should, otherwise who will fill the vacuum?
West Bengal, which wants to separate from India? There's
nothing in common between the East Bengalis and the West
Bengalis. Between us and the East Bengalis, on the other
hand, there's religion in common. The Partition of 1947 was a
very good thing.

O.F.: Very good! To create a country with two stumps two thousand
kilometers apart and with India in the middle?

Z.A.B: Those two stumps stayed together for twenty-five years, despite all the mistakes that were made. A state isn't only a terri-
torial or geographical concept. When the flag is the same, the
national anthem the same, the religion the same, distance is
no problem. At the time when the Mongols unified India, the
Muslims of this part took a hundred days to reach the other
part. Now all they needed were two hours by air. Do you see
what I mean?

O.F.: No, Mr. President. I understand Indira Gandhi better when
she says that the Partition of 1947 was wrong and that wars of
religion are ridiculous in the 1970s.

Z.A.B.: Mrs. Gandhi has only one dream: to take over the whole subcontinent, to subjugate us. She'd like a confederation so as to make Pakistan disappear from the face of the earth, and that's why she says we're brothers, and so forth. We're not brothers. We never have been. Our religions go too deep into our souls, into our ways of life. Our cultures are different, our attitudes are different. From the day they're born to the day they die, a Hindu and a Muslim are subject to laws and customs that have no points of contact. Even their ways of eating and drinking are different. They're two strong and irreconcilable faiths. It's shown by the fact that neither of the two has ever succeeded in reaching a compromise with the other, a *modus vivendi*. Only dictatorial monarchies, foreign invasions, from the Mongols to the British, have succeeded in holding us together by a kind of Pax Romana. We've never arrived at a harmonious relationship.

You see, the Hindus are not the mild creatures that Mrs. Gandhi would like you to think. They have respect for their sacred cows, but not for Muslims. They've always mistreated and humiliated us. I'll never forget an episode that happened to me in 1944. I was on holiday with my parents in Kashmir. I was running up and down a hill, as boys do, and at a certain point I got very thirsty. So I went up to a man who was selling water and asked him for a drink. The man filled the cup, started to hand it to me, then stopped and said, "Are you a Hindu or a Muslim?" I hesitated to answer—I desperately wanted that water. Finally I said, "I'm a Muslim." Then the man poured the water on the ground. Tell that to Mrs. Gandhi.

O.F.: You two really can't stand each other, can you?

Z.A.B.: I don't even respect her. To me she's a mediocre woman with a mediocre intelligence. There's nothing great about her; only the country she governs is great. I mean, it's that throne that makes her seem tall, though actually she's very small. And also the name she bears. Believe me, if she were prime minister of Ceylon, she'd be nothing but another Mrs. Bandaranaike. And if she were prime minister of Israel . . . Come now, I wouldn't dare compare her to Golda Meir. Golda is far too superior. She has an acute mind, sound judgment, and she goes through much more difficult crises than those of Mrs. Gandhi. Also she came to power by her own talent. Mrs. Bandaranaike, instead, got there by the simple fact of being Bandaranaike's widow, and Mrs. Gandhi by the simple fact of being Nehru's daughter. Without having Nehru's light. With all her saris, the red spot on her forehead, her little smile, she'll never succeed in impressing me.

She's never impressed me, ever since the day I met her in London. We were both attending a lecture, and she was taking notes so insistently and pedantically that I said to her, "Are you taking notes or writing a thesis?" And speaking of theses, you know I can't believe she succeeded in getting that degree in history at Oxford. I completed the three-year course at Oxford in two years. And in three years she wasn't able to finish the course.

O.F.: Aren't you being a little excessive, a little unjust? Do you really think she could last so long if she wasn't worth something? Or are you obliged to think she's worth nothing because she's a woman?

Z.A.B.: No, no. I have nothing against women as heads of state, though I don't think women make better heads of state than men. My opinion of Mrs. Gandhi is impersonal and objective. It's not even influenced by the fact that she behaves so deplorably by not returning our war prisoners and not respecting the Geneva Convention. That's how I've always seen her: a diligent drudge of a schoolgirl, a woman devoid of initiative and imagination. All right, she's better today than when she was studying at Oxford or taking notes in London. Power has given her self-confidence and nothing succeeds like success. But it's a question of success out of proportion to her merits; if India and Pakistan were to become confederated countries, I'd have no trouble in carrying off the post from Mrs. Gandhi. I'm not afraid of intellectual confrontations with her. Having said that, I'm ready to meet her when and where she likes. Even in New Delhi. Yes, I'm even ready to go to New Delhi, like Talleyrand after the Congress of Vienna. The only idea that bothers me is that of being escorted by an honor guard from the Indian army and physical contact with the lady herself. It irritates me. God! Don't make me think of it. Tell me instead: what did Mrs. Gandhi say about me?

O.F.: She told me you're an unbalanced man, that today you say one thing and tomorrow another, that one never understands what's on your mind.

Z.A.B.: Ah, yes? I'll answer that right away. The only thing I accept from the philosopher John Locke is this statement: "Consistency is a virtue of small minds." * In other words, I think a basic concept should remain firm but, within that basic concept, one should be able to move back and forth. Now to one pole, now to the other. An intellectual should never cling to a single and precise idea—he should be elastic. Otherwise he sinks into a monologue, into fanaticism. A politician, the same. Politics is movement per se—a politician should be mobile. He should sway now to right and now to left; he should come up with contradictions, doubts. He should change continually, test things, attack from every side so as to single out his opponent's weak point and strike at it. Woe to him if he focuses immediately on his basic concept, woe if he reveals and crystallizes it. Woe if he blocks the maneuver by which to throw his opponent on the carpet. Apparent inconsistency is the prime virtue of the intelligent man and astute politician. If Mrs. Gandhi doesn't understand that, she doesn't understand the beauty of her profession. Now her father understood it.

O.F.: Indira Gandhi says her father wasn't a politician, he was a saint.

Z.A.B.: Oh, Mrs. Gandhi is wrong about her father! Nehru instead was a great politician—she should have half her father's talent! Look, even though he was against the principle of Pakistan, I've always admired that man. When I was young I was actually enthralled by him. Only later did I understand that he was a spellbinder with many faults, vain, ruthless, and that he didn't have the class of a Stalin or a Churchill or a Mao Tsetung. And what else, what else did Mrs. Gandhi say?

O.F.: She said it was you Pakistanis who started the war.

Z.A.B.: Ridiculous. Everyone knows they were the ones to attack us. November 26, on the eastern front. East Pakistan was perhaps not Pakistan? Let's be serious. If someone invades Palermo,

---

* Actually it was Emerson who said it: "A foolish consistency is the hobgoblin of little minds." (Translator's note.)

don't you conclude that Italy has been attacked? If someone
invades Marseilles, don't you conclude that France has been
attacked? Mrs. Gandhi pretends to forget that our counterattack in Kashmir, disputed territory, took place only on December 3. I remember seeing Yahya on November 29 and
reproaching him for our failure to counterattack. "You're behaving as though nothing has happened in the east. By delay-
ing action, you're playing India's game, you're making people
believe that East Pakistan and West Pakistan aren't the same
country," I told him. But he didn't listen to me. Four times
he changed his orders for a counterattack. The fourth time our
officers and soldiers were beating their heads against the tanks
in desperation. And Dacca? Let's withdraw into Dacca, I said;
we'll make a fortress out of it and hold out for ten months, a
year—the whole world will be on our side. But he was only
concerned that the Indians not conquer a little territory and
plant the flag of Bangladesh. And when he ordered Niazi to
surrender . . . God! I could have died a thousand times and
felt better. I was in New York, I remember. He'd sent me
there as a tourist and I'd found myself at that incredible session
of the UN. . . .

O.F.: And you'd made that scene.

Z.A.B.: A real scene, I admit. But I was convulsed with rage, with
disgust. The arrogance of the Indians. The fear shown by the
great powers, who wanted only to placate India. I wasn't able
to control my passion, and I made that speech in which I told
them all to go to hell. I wept too. Yes, I often weep. I always
weep when I discover something disgraceful, unjust. I'm very
emotional.

O.F.: Emotional, unpredictable, complicated, and . . . much
talked about. It seems to me the moment has come to take up
your personality, Mr. President. Let's talk a little about this
man who is very rich and yet a socialist, lives like a Westerner
and yet has two wives. . . .

Z.A.B.: There are many conflicts in me—I'm aware of that. I try to
reconcile them, overcome them, but I don't succeed and I
remain this strange mixture of Asia and Europe. I have a
layman's education and a Muslim's upbringing. My mind is
Western and my soul Eastern. As for my two wives, what can

I do about it? They married me off at thirteen, to my cousin. I was thirteen and she was twenty-three. I didn't even know what it meant to have a wife, and when they tried to explain it to me, I went out of my mind with rage. With fury. I didn't want a wife, I wanted to play cricket. I was very fond of cricket. To calm me down, they had to give me two new cricket bags. When the ceremony was over, I ran off to play cricket. There are so many things I must change in my country! And I was fortunate. They married my playmate off at the age of eleven to a woman of thirty-two. He always said to me, "Lucky you!"

When I fell in love with my second wife, I was twenty-three. She was also studying in England, and though she was an Iranian, that is, from a country where polygamy is the custom, it was hard for me to persuade her to marry me. I didn't have many arguments except for the two words, "So what, dammit!" No, the idea of divorcing my first wife never went through my head. Not only because she's my cousin, but because I have a responsibility toward her. Her whole life has been ruined by this absurd marriage to a boy, by the absurd custom in which we've been raised. She lives in my house in Larkana; we see each other every so often. She's almost always alone. She hasn't even had children—my four children are born of my second marriage. I've spent little time with her—as soon as I was an adolescent I went to the West to study. A story of injustice. I'll do everything I can to discourage polygamy—besides it causes no small economic problem. Often the wives are separated in different houses or cities, as in my case. And not everyone can afford it as I can. Though I'm not so rich as you say.

O.F.: No? . . .

Z.A.B.: No. To you, to be rich means to be a duPont or a Rockefeller. To us, it means much less. Here anyone who's rich owns a lot of land, but actually he's no richer than those European barons who own splendid crumbling villas and play the gigolo in order to live. Our land is dry and produces little. So let's say that instead of rich, I'm relatively rich, that I live well, that my sister lives well, that my brother lived well, that we've been to good schools but have never wasted a penny. I've never been a playboy. When I was a student in America and at Oxford, I never bought a car. I've always handled money wisely, for instance in order to go to Europe to meet interesting people and buy books. If you take a look at my library, you'll see where I put a good part of my money: in books. I have thousands of them, many of them old and beautiful— I've always immensely enjoyed reading. Like sports. Some people accuse me of being well dressed. It's true. But not because I squander my money on clothes—because I'm clean. I love to bathe and change my clothes; I've never been able to stand Indian and Pakistani princes who are dirty and stink. I own beautiful and comfortable houses. That's true too. But for a long time I didn't even have air conditioning. I like to entertain, but never silly or stupid people. I know how to dance, but only because I like music and because I hate to be a wallflower when others are dancing. Finally . . .

O.F.: Finally you have the reputation of being a lady-killer, a Don Juan. Is it true, Mr. President?

Z.A.B.: That's also very exaggerated. I'm a romantic—I don't think you can be a politician without being romantic—and as a romantic I think there's nothing so inspiring as a love affair. There's nothing wrong with falling in love and conquering a woman's heart—woe to men who don't fall in love. You can even fall in love a hundred times, and I do fall in love. But I'm a very, very moral man. And I respect women. People think that Muslims don't respect women. What a mistake. To respect and protect them is one of the first teachings of the prophet Mohammed. I, who don't call myself a champion of physical violence, once whipped a man. I whipped him ferociously, till the blood came. Do you know why? Because he had raped a little girl. And I was blind with rage this morning, when I read that some hundred students had attacked and stripped some girl students on the beach in Karachi. Scoundrels! I'll make them subject to martial law. And I say something else. If I were to ascertain that our soldiers really used violence on the women of Bangladesh, I'd insist on being the one to try them and punish them.

O.F.: Let's go on to something else, Mr. President. Let's go on to your Marxism and to how you can reconcile it with your privileges, even with your Muslim faith.

z.a.b.: I call myself a Marxist in the economic sense; that is, I confine myself to accepting Marxist doctrine so far as it concerns economics. What I reject in Marxism are its dialectical interpretation of history, its theories of life, the question whether God exists or not. As a good Muslim, I believe in God. Rightly or wrongly, I believe—faith is something that either exists or doesn't. If it does, it's useless to discuss it. It's in me, and I'm not ready to renounce it in the name of the ecclesiastical or philosophical aspects of Marxism. At the same time I'm convinced that to call oneself a Marxist and call oneself a Muslim are two things that can go together—especially in an underdeveloped country like Pakistan where I don't see any solution except scientific socialism.

I said Pakistan—I'm not raising any banners for international crusades; I'm not sticking my nose in the affairs of others. I concentrate on the reality of my country and that's all. No, not by a process of revolution—I recognize that. I would like to, since I can look you in the eye and swear to you I'm a revolutionary. But I can't afford sudden and bloody revolutions. Pakistan wouldn't be able to stand it; it would be a disaster. So I must proceed with patience, by reforms, measures that will gradually lead to socialism—nationalizing when possible, refraining from it when necessary, respecting the foreign capital of which we have need. I must take my time, be a surgeon who doesn't plunge his knife too deeply into the fabric of society. This is a very sick society, and if it's not to die under the knife, you have to operate with caution, waiting slowly for a wound to heal, for a reform to be consolidated. We've been asleep for so many centuries, we can't violently wake ourselves up with an earthquake. Besides, even Lenin, in the beginning, stooped to compromises.

o.f.: Mr. President, many people don't believe you. They say you're a demagogue seeking power and nothing else, that you'll do anything to hold on to your power, that you'll never give up your possessions.

z.a.b.: No? By the agrarian reforms I've made in these three months, my family has lost forty-five thousand acres of land. I personally have lost six to seven thousand. And I'll lose still more, my children will lose still more. God is my witness that I'm not playing with socialism, that I don't proceed slowly out of selfishness. I've felt no fear of giving up what I own ever since the day I read Marx. I can even tell you the time and place: Bombay, 1945. As for the accusation that I'm only out for power, well, this would be a good time to understand what we mean by the word power. By power I don't mean the kind Yahya Khan had. By power I mean the kind you exercise to level mountains, make deserts bloom, build a society where people don't die of hunger and humiliation. I have no evil platforms. I don't want to become a dictator. But so far I can say that I'll have to be very tough, even authoritarian. The broken windows I'm setting out to mend are often in splinters. I'll have to throw away the splinters. And if I throw them away too carelessly, I won't have a country, I'll have a bazaar.

Anyway look, you don't go into politics just for the fun of it. You go into it to take power in your hands and keep it. Anyone who says the opposite is a liar. Politicians are always trying to make you believe that they're good, moral, consistent. Don't ever fall in their trap. There's no such thing as a good, moral, consistent politician. Politics is give-and-take, as my father taught me when he said, "Never hit a man unless you're ready to be hit twice by him." The rest is boy-scout stuff, and I've forgotten the boy-scout virtues ever since I went to school.

O.F.: They say, Mr. President, you're a great reader of books about Mussolini, Hitler, Napoleon.

Z.A.B: Of course. And also books about De Gaulle, Churchill, Stalin. Do you want to make me confess I'm a fascist? I'm not. A fascist is first of all an enemy of culture, and I'm an intellectual enamored of culture. A fascist is a man of the right, and I'm a man of the left. A fascist is a *petit bourgeois*, and I come from the aristocracy. To read about a person doesn't mean to make him your hero. I've had some heroes, yes, but when I was a student. Heroes, you know, are like chewing gum—they get chewed, spit out, changed, and you like them especially when you're young. Anyway, if you care to know whom I've chewed the longest, here they are: Genghis Khan, Alexander,

Hannibal, Napoleon. Napoleon most of all. But I've also chewed a little of Mazzini, a little of Cavour, a little of Garibaldi. And a lot of Rousseau. You see how many contradictions there are in me?

O.F.: I see. And so, to try to understand you a little better, let me ask you who are the figures of our time to whom you've felt or feel close: those you've liked or who liked you the most.

Z.A.B.: One is Sukarno. He said I was cut from the same cloth. He worshiped me. And I worshiped him. He was an exceptional man despite his weaknesses—for instance his vulgarity with women. It's neither necessary nor dignified continually to show your own virility, but he didn't understand that. Furthermore he didn't even understand economics. The other is Nasser. Nasser too was a first-rate man, with Nasser too I got along very well. He loved me and I loved him. In 1966, when I was forced to leave the government, Nasser invited me to Egypt and received me with the honors of a head of state, then he said I could stay there as long as I needed.

Then, let's see . . . Stalin. Yes, Stalin. My respect for Stalin has always been deep, a gut feeling I'd say, just as much as my antipathy for Khrushchev. You may understand me better when I say I never liked Khrushchev, that I always thought him a braggart. Always swaggering, yelling, pointing his finger at ambassadors, drinking. . . . And always ready to give in to the Americans. He did a lot of harm to Asia, Khrushchev. And finally . . . I know, you're waiting for me to say something about Mao Tse-tung. But what do you want me to say about a giant like Mao Tse-tung? It's easier for me to talk about Chou En-lai. He's the one I know better, the one I've talked and discussed things with longer. Endless discussions, from dawn to dusk, for days, at least once a year. It's since 1962 that I've been going to China and meeting Chou En-lai. And . . . him, simply, I admire him.

O.F.: Mr. President, all these men have had to struggle a lot to gain power. But not you.

Z.A.B.: You're wrong. It hasn't been easy for me to get here. I've been put in prison, I've risked my life plenty of times. With Ayub Khan, with Yahya Khan. They tried to kill me by poisoning my food, by shooting at me. Twice in 1968, once in

1970. In Sanghar, two years ago, I was kept for an hour under the cross fire of assassins sent by Yahya Khan. One man died while shielding me, others were seriously wounded. . . . And let's not forget moral suffering; when you're born rich and become a socialist, no one believes you. Neither friends in your own circle, who in fact make fun of you, nor the poor, who aren't enlightened enough to believe in your sincerity. The hardest thing for me hasn't been to escape the bullets and the poison, it's been to get myself taken seriously by those who didn't believe me. The privileges in which I was born didn't put me on Aladdin's flying carpet. And if I hadn't had this vocation for politics . . .

o.f.: And how did this vocation start, how was it manifested?

z.a.b.: I've always had it, ever since I was a boy. But if we want to play at being psychoanalysts, we must say I owe it to my parents. My father was a brilliant politician—a pity he retired so very early, after having lost certain elections. He had a very high conception of politics, that of an aristocrat who's aristocratic to his finger tips, and he talked to me in such an inspired way. He took me around Larkana, he showed me the ancient temples, the splendid houses, the vestiges of our civilization, and he said to me: "Look, politics is like building a temple, a house. Or else he said it was like writing music, or poetry. And he mentioned Brahms, Michelangelo. . . . My mother was different. She came from a poor family and was haunted by other people's poverty. She did nothing but repeat to me: "We must take care of the poor, we must help the poor, the poor shall inherit the earth," and so forth.

When I went to America, her message had so sunk into my ears that I became a radical. I went to America to study at the University of California, where a great jurist of international law was teaching. I wanted to take my degree in international law. And that was the period of McCarthyism, of the communist witch-hunts—my choices were laid out. To get away from Sunset Boulevard, from the girls with red nail polish, I ran off to Maxwell Street and lived among the Negroes. A week, a month. I felt good with them—they were real, they knew how to laugh. And the day in San Diego when I wasn't able to get a hotel room because I have olive skin and looked like a Mexican . . . well, that helped. Then, from America, I went to England. And those were the years of Algeria, so I immediately took the side of the Algerians. But not by shouting slogans in front of Number 10 Downing Street. Maybe because I'm secretly a little shy, I've never liked to mix in the crowd and participate in turmoil. I've always preferred a discussion by writing, a struggle by the game of politics. It's more intelligent, more subtle, more refined.

O.F.: One last question, Mr. President, and excuse the brutality of it. Do you think you can last?

Z.A.B.: Let's put it this way. I could be finished tomorrow, but I think I'll last longer than anyone else who's governed Pakistan. First of all because I'm healthy and full of energy—I can work, as I do, even eighteen hours a day. Then because I'm young—I'm barely forty-four, ten years younger than Mrs. Gandhi. Finally because I know what I want. I'm the only leader in the Third World who has gone back into politics despite the opposition of two great powers—in 1966 the United States and the Soviet Union were both very happy to see me in trouble. And the reason I've been able to overcome that trouble is that I know the fundamental rule of this profession. What is the rule? Well, in politics you sometimes have to pretend to be stupid and make others believe they're the only intelligent ones. But to do this you have to have light and flexible fingers, and . . . Have you ever seen a bird sitting on its eggs in the nest? Well, a politician must have fairly light, fairly flexible fingers, to insinuate them under the bird and take away the eggs. One by one. Without the bird realizing it.

Karachi, April 1972

9

Willy Brandt

It will be up to history to decide to what extent Willy Brandt was a great statesman and a great man. But it was already clear that as a chancellor he was the only large figure in Europe. Everyone liked him. Everyone believed him. And everyone recognized in him the leader of a new Germany, a Germany that no longer inspired hatred or fear: much as it might arouse envy. He still has much to his credit. Not for nothing did they give him the Nobel Peace Prize. But his chief credit lies in having made us understand that the word German does not mean Hitler. He fought against Hitler since the age of fourteen—"by words and fists." He wrote against the Nazis, he came to blows with the Nazis, he fled from the Nazis—there is not the slightest stain on his democratic past. There was no need for him to kneel down in Warsaw. There was no need for him to read the psalm of forgiveness in Jerusalem. Still, he did so. And this to me seems no less significant than his *Ostpolitik*, his Europeanism, and his socialism, a humanitarian, liberal, modern socialism, as befits a man who rejects every shade of dogma. Furthermore, it was in this socialism that he grew up, became a journalist, a writer, the mayor of Berlin, and always took his stand. Let us not forget that Willy Brandt was the only head of state who spoke out with the same clarity and firmness against the Greek colonels and against the Soviet functionaries who are out to destroy their opponents.

His life has been exceptional from the moment of his birth, on December 18, 1913, in the city of Lübeck. His mother was a young, unmarried trade union worker. He never knew his father, and his father never acknowledged him. Only at about the age of thirteen did he hear his name, which sounded Swedish or Norwegian or Danish. In a book he writes, "The boy heard but was not interested. Or was he? An opaque veil extends over those years, gray as the fog in the port of Lübeck. Figures and faces merge like shadows that rise to the surface and disappear. . . . It is hard for me to believe that that boy called Herbert Frahm was myself."

He does not like to speak of his father. I was dumbfounded when he confessed he had always known who he was. "He was still alive after the end of the war. But not even then was I interested in meeting him." And one should not forget that the stigma of "illegitimate son" has caused him no small trouble in his political career. His opponents have exploited it shamelessly even in election campaigns. Especially Adenauer. But though this casts a dark shadow over our image of Adenauer, it helps us to understand Brandt. One is often distinguished from others for having suffered pain and humiliation—great dreams, sometimes even success, are often born of hunger and unhappiness. Perhaps if as a child he had been dandled on a father's knee, Willy Brandt today would not be Willy Brandt.

He does not much resemble his fellow countrymen. For twelve years he was Norwegian, and he admits candidly, or rather with reckless sincerity, that he still has Norway in his blood. "When, little more than a boy, you escape to a country whose culture and language you absorb, you lose one homeland only to find another. For me Norway was a second homeland." Is it still? The more you look at him and listen to him, the more you wonder where the German in him leaves off and the Norwegian begins. Or vice versa. He has a house in Norway and goes back there every year on vacation. His closest friends are in Norway. It was in Norway that he met both his first wife and his second, and his children are thus half Norwegian. He wrote better in Norwegian than in German, it is said, and this is something else for which Adenauer attacked him, calling him an interloper, a foreigner. He looks on passports with indifference—I'd say with a shrug of his shoulders. And isn't it extraordinary that a man so devoid of narrow-minded nationalism should represent the country that unleashed a world war in the name of nationalism? Brandt resumed his German citizenship only in 1946—to have chosen to do so honors the new Germany and the future Europe. I'm sure not to be mistaken when I say that in the final analysis he still represents Europe more than he does Germany, and, in that sense, his role isn't finished.

What a sorrow to have seen him resigning because of a dirty spy who lived next to him as a secretary; what a bitter blow to have seen him giving up because of the even dirtier blackmail that developed around him. When he proudly left his nation's helm, all of progressive Europe knew they had lost a battle; the defeat was not his alone. It was the defeat of all those who believe in peace joined with intelligence, freedom won with courage, and socialism achieved with patience. The only consolation is the thought that losing a battle is not losing a war. Men like him cannot be stopped; their seed has been sown. This man Brandt is not dead.

The following interview took place in his office in the Bunderkanzleramt on two occasions: Tuesday, August 28, and Monday, September 3. Seldom is an interview the portrait of a man in the way this one is. Not so much for what he says or doesn't say as for how he says what he does. He speaks in a precise, prolix, and severe manner. He almost never engages in remarks that might impair his dignity or makes admissions that would diminish his remoteness. If you try to probe his soul more deeply, he withdraws courteously and becomes silent. I tried again and again—it was useless. He opened the doors wide when I interrogated the politician; he closed them when I sought the man. Never have I encountered such modesty, such shyness. It is therefore hard for me to see him as others do—that is to say as a cheerful Teuton fond of women, wine, beer, and a good laugh. I can more easily identify him with the peasant of the fiord whom he describes in the interview. Tough, solid, hard as iron, and the enemy of unnecessary things. Even his politeness and the cordial way he receives you are devoid of anything unnecessary. A pity I wasn't able to talk to him alone. Present at the interview were his adviser Klaus Harpprecht, and the head of his press office, while a stenographer not in my employ to take notes operated a tape recorder placed next to mine. It seemed like a summit meeting, a council of state. It was he who wanted it this way. And, though at first it annoyed me, I was soon filled with respect. What a consolation to be among people who do things seriously.

ORIANA FALLACI: Frankly I don't know where to begin, Chancellor Brandt. I have so many things to ask you, including the story of your name, which is not the one you were born with. That was Herbert Frahm, and . . .

WILLY BRANDT: Yes, I started using the name Willy Brandt at the beginning of 1933—before leaving Germany and after the Nazis had come to power. I chose it as a *nom de guerre* with which to devote myself to clandestine activity against Hitler. But it was under that name that I went abroad, when I was nineteen. Under that name I began writing for the newspapers and publishing my books, under that name I went into politics and became an adult and came back to Germany at the end of the war. Everything is tied up with that name, and I never thought of taking back the one I was born with.

O.F.: Besides it was as Willy Brandt that you got married and became a Norwegian citizen. There, maybe that's where we should start. I mean the fact that for years you had been a citizen of another country. Except for Jews, there weren't many Germans who left Hitler's Germany.

W.B.: No, actually there were quite a few. If you take my own city, Lübeck, as an example, you'll find there were many who went away. And it goes without saying that almost all of them were older than I. Why did I leave Germany? Because if I'd stayed, I would have been arrested and sent to a concentration camp. At first I didn't have much chance of getting out. Even if I hadn't become an expatriate, I would have had to leave Lübeck. But not even by leaving Lübeck would I have been able to go to the university, and this is one contributing factor to my going away. When I'd finished school, I'd started working as a broker's agent, and it was interesting work for a year. But I wanted to study history, and in Hitler's Germany it was no longer possible to study history. So as soon as I got the chance . . .

A man who belonged to my group was supposed to escape

to Norway and open an office there to take care of some of the
problems connected with our resistance movement. It was all
arranged for a fishing boat to take him across, leaving from a
place not far from the house where I was living. I had to help
and I did so, but all the same the man didn't get away. He was
arrested and sent to a concentration camp. Then my Berlin
friends asked me if I wanted to go in his place. And I accepted. I had no idea it would mean staying away so long.
Many people thought that Nazism wouldn't last. They said
twelve months, at most four years. I didn't belong to the ranks
of the optimists, but I deluded myself into thinking that it
wouldn't last longer than the First World War. Instead it
lasted twelve years.

O.F.: That's just it, those twelve years you spent in Scandinavia—
for which your opponents have often reproached you. So let
me ask you this question: Are you sorry not to have participated directly, I mean in Germany itself, in the struggle
against Nazism?

W.B.: I showed, then and later, that I was willing to risk my life
whenever necessary. And even when it wasn't necessary. I
came back secretly to Hitler's Germany. I stayed several
months, before escaping again because they were about to
catch me. I went to Sweden, and to Norway, which was occupied by Hitler. So I've taken my risks. And looking at your
question from a rational standpoint, I'd say if I'd stayed in
Germany instead of expatriating myself, I probably wouldn't
have had the same opportunities to develop and prepare myself
for what I did in Berlin or later. I mean especially my European and international experiences. To be sure, you pay a
price for everything. And the price I had to pay was quite different from that paid by the majority of my countrymen. It
was the price of going away. Yes, it's true that to some people
that seemed a strange way of paying, and by this judgment
they supplied my opponents with the opportunity to start a
campaign against me. But I say to such people that it's just as
strange that so many Germans identify with me and have confidence in me. Did I say strange? I should have said wonderful. It's a wonderful thing that so many Germans have con-

fidence in a man whose life has been different from theirs. Not better. Different.

o.f.: Chancellor Brandt, I assume that in speaking of the price you paid you're also referring to the fact of being deprived of your German citizenship after your expatriation. Was it painful for you to lose your German citizenship and take on that of Norway?

w.b.: No.

o.f.: Why? Did you already like Norway so much?

w.b.: Yes. I considered it a second homeland. Because if one goes abroad as a young man and lands in a country where one feels at home and learns to speak the language well . . . I learned Norwegian very quickly, and I learned it well. I've said many times that I wrote Norwegian much better than I wrote German. And that was true, even if today it's not true any more. Besides, when the country that takes you in becomes a place where you make friends, when you absorb its culture to the roots, when all this is easy for you because you come from the Baltic . . . well, you feel that this separates you from your countrymen, but you also feel enriched by something you ordinarily wouldn't have had. Do I make myself clear? I mean you begin by losing one country and end by finding another. Nor is this something I'm discovering today, since I've always admitted it to be true. During the war I wrote in the preface of a book published in Sweden, "I work simultaneously for a free Norway and a democratic Germany. This means a Europe where Europeans can live." Anyway, to take on Norwegian citizenship for me didn't mean giving up Germany. Or I should say my conception of Germany.

o.f.: Then let me reverse my previous question. Was it painful for you to lose your Norwegian citizenship in order to get back your German?

w.b.: No. There are countries that don't confront you with such a choice. If I'd become an American citizen, I wouldn't have been able to hand back my passport, and at most I would have had to keep both nationalities. In Norway that doesn't happen. You're either a Norwegian citizen or you're not. So I turned in my Norwegian passport without any fuss, knowing full well that a passport has nothing to do with your attitudes or ties. I knew I'd keep going back to Norway, to see my friends and speak the language, and that in short my ties there wouldn't be broken just because of a passport. Many people have a passport that doesn't correspond to their nationality, and if you were to ask me, "So is it important to have a passport?" I'd answer, it's important primarily for crossing frontiers but the question of documents is often overrated. National identity is something else.

O.F.: So it was a search for national identity, for your mother country, that brought you back to Berlin after the war?

W.B.: No. I came back to Germany as a journalist, in the fall of 1945 and later in 1946. I came back to cover the Nuremberg trials and see a little of the country. I'd been asked to take over the editorship of a newspaper or news service in Germany, but nothing came of it. Then my good friend Halvard Lange, at that time the Norwegian foreign minister, had said to me, "If you don't go back to Germany within a year, why don't you join my ministry and go to Paris as part of the Norwegian embassy?" But just as I was about to accept, he changed his mind. "The prime minister and I think it would be better if you went to Berlin as a press attaché, with the job of supplying the Norwegian government with political information and evaluations." That's how it happened. And obviously the fact of my going to Berlin brought this process of identification to a head. Or rather, it obviously brought it to a head much sooner than whatever would have happened had I gone to Paris. Had I gone to Paris, I'd probably have joined some international organization. And, at least for a few years . . .

O.F.: . . . you would have gone on being a Norwegian citizen.

W.B.: Well, yes. At least for a while anyway. Later perhaps no. In fact, if I'd waited a little longer, there wouldn't even have been the need for me to request German citizenship again. By the terms of the Constitution of 1949, all I would have had to do was present myself in some office and say, "I'm here to regain the nationality that the Nazis took away from me." I, on the other hand, asked to become a German citizen again before there existed a new German state—in the spring of 1948. Yes . . . just imagine, the government of Schleswig-Holstein restored my nationality on a sheet of paper that still had the swastika printed on it! Yes, yes! They were so poor they didn't even have new official forms. They had to obliterate the swastika by scribbling over it in ink. I still have that document at home. I keep it as a souvenir of the way I went back to being a German citizen.

o.f.: That's amusing. But I can't believe that what brought you back to Germany was only chance and not sentiment.

w.b.: Nevertheless it's true. It wasn't a sentimental thing. No. I returned to Berlin for the simple reason that Berlin was interesting. It was the center of the conflict between East and West. It was the place to be. That this then accelerated my process of identification is another matter. And I don't mean only a process of political identification—I mean a process of identification with people living in poverty, in defeat. Berlin was a pile of ruins, but among those ruins the best qualities of the people came out. Yes, it's a phenomenon that often happens in adverse times, but it's always surprising. Oh, the morale of the Berliners was never so high as in the first postwar years. Even during the blockade it was never to be so high. And so my process of identification . . .

o.f.: But what do you mean by identification? What they call one's country?

w.b.: No. It wasn't the country that drew me back. It was the case of a people who, having passed through dictatorship and war and destruction, were trying to rebuild for themselves a life based on freedom. Yes, it was this that induced me to become a German again. It was the fantastic will to work that was in each of them, it was that capacity to accomplish something, that desire to help one another. . . . A desire we've lost by becoming rich. . . . It was in the air, like a feeling that everyone was sticking together to do something—despite the economic misery. Do you see what I mean? A question of human and moral values rather than a nationalistic fact. The more I think of it, the more I'm convinced it was those years in Berlin that implanted in me the idea of Europe. Or rather of the future of Europe.

o.f.: I keep wondering, Chancellor Brandt, if deep in your heart, or rather your mind, you're not more European than German.

w.b.: Well . . . It would be too much to expect a German chancellor who's almost sixty years old to admit to that. Especially
knowing that Europe hasn't moved as far as it should have.
No, you can't ask me to feel and behave more like a European
than a German. One shouldn't even ask me to give that impression. So let's say I try to be a good European when I assume the responsibilities of a German. To answer your question: no, I'm German.

o.f.: I see. But then—and I'm thinking of your visit to the Warsaw
ghetto—let me ask you: To what extent does the guilt complex
that your generation carries along with the word German
weigh on you?

w.b.: I make a distinction between guilt and responsibility. I don't
feel guilty myself, and I think it's neither just nor correct to attribute such a guilt complex to my people or my generation.
Guilt is something to be imputed to an individual—never to a
people or a generation. Responsibility is something else. And
even though I had left Germany very early, even though I'd
never been a supporter of Hitler—to put it mildly—I can't
exclude myself from a certain responsibility. Or coresponsibility. Yes, even if I'd dissociated myself from my people, I'd
still feel coresponsible for the advent of Hitler. In fact, we
must ask ourselves: why did he take power? And we can only
answer: not only because millions of people were stupid
enough to follow him, but also because the others were incapable of stopping him. Of course, I was young at that time.
And yet I too belong to that group of people who were incapable of stopping him.

In the life of a people, the crucial moment takes place when
the people allow power to end up in the hands of criminals.
And also when a people, having the opportunity, don't use it
to maintain the conditions necessary for a responsible government. Because afterward you can't do anything. Afterward it
becomes more and more difficult to throw out the criminals
who have taken power. In short, as I see it, coresponsibility
begins before and ends after. And even young people, unfortunately, find this coresponsibility on their shoulders. Not to the
same degree as their fathers, but . . . You mentioned Warsaw . . .

O.F.: Why did you kneel down in Warsaw, Chancellor Brandt?

W.B.: I didn't kneel because I had any guilt to confess, but because I wanted to identify myself with my people. I mean with the people from whom those who had committed such terrible things had emerged. That gesture wasn't only directed at the Poles. It was also directed at the Germans. Anyone who thinks I was only appealing to the victims of Nazism and their families is mistaken. I was also and primarily appealing to my own people. Because many of them, too many, have the need not to feel alone and to know we must bear this burden together.

O.F.: Chancellor Brandt, did you decide on that gesture on the spur of the moment, or had you already thought of it before?

W.B.: I hadn't thought of it before, but how can we know what our subconscious may have in mind? The idea was surely in my subconscious already, because, as I remember, I woke up that morning with the strange sensation that I wasn't just going to place a wreath of flowers and let it go at that. I saw intuitively that something else would happen. Even though I didn't know what. Then suddenly I felt the need to throw myself on my knees.

O.F.: And at Yad Vashem, during your last trip to Israel? Your gesture at Yad Vashem couldn't have been decided on at the last moment.

W.B.: You're right. Before going to Israel, I thought for a long time about what I could do. I'd heard that they call Yad Vashem the place of truth, the terrible truth beyond everything that the human mind can imagine. And I wanted to give some substance to this truth, because . . . Auschwitz showed that hell on earth exists. It seems to me I had already said it in Warsaw. And I think I've already said that when I was in Sweden I knew what was happening in Germany. I knew about it before most of those who were living in or outside of Germany.

So while I was getting ready for my trip to Israel, that sense of coresponsibility that I tried to explain to you before came over me again. And, as in Warsaw, I told myself that I wouldn't be able to limit myself to placing a wreath of flowers with a stony or emotional expression on my face. Once I was confronted by what had happened, I would have to react in some way to my own impotence. Do you see? I wanted to do

something, I didn't want to remain passive. I kept telling myself: there must really be some gesture I can make for the good
of the Germans and the Jews, a gesture to open the way to the
future. Oh, I don't want to speak lightly of reconcili-
ation—that doesn't depend on me. But the solution I found
seemed to me the right one because we have something quite
important in common with the Jewish people—the Bible. Or
at least the Old Testament. That's why I decided to read Psalm
103, verses 7 to 16: *They will flee at thy threats; they will be
terrified at the sound of thy voice. . . .* I decided to read it in
German, in the language of Martin Luther. Certain expressions were hard to understand, however. Especially for young
people. So, while flying to Tel Aviv, I studied the text and
compared Martin Luther's translation with the Jewish version
of the same words in German. I kept almost all of Martin
Luther's poetic expressions and added a few phrases from the
Hebrew Bible. I believe the Israelis understood what I wanted
to do. And for this I'll always be grateful to them.

O.F.: You were very eager to make that trip to Israel, weren't you?
Perhaps more than the trip to Warsaw.

W.B.: It was a question of two different things, since I knew nobody
in Warsaw and everything was new to me. On the other hand,
I'd already been to Israel in 1960 as mayor of Berlin; there I'd
even met Ben-Gurion and Eshkol. Then I had seen Golda
Meir several times at international socialist party congresses.
But . . . it's true, I was eager to make the trip last June
because I was going as the representative of my nation and
people. In short, not as Willy Brandt but as the representative
of a new Germany. To put it better, Jerusalem was not my
first or my last confrontation with the past. In fact, I'll also go
to Lidice when I visit Czechoslovakia. Jerusalem, however,
was the most important stop—the one that most completely
expressed our dark days. It represented the recognition of our
responsibilities as Germans; it reminded us that nothing of
what we did should be forgotten or swept under the rug. No, it
shouldn't. . . . It shouldn't. . . . Not that there's anything
left to confess, by now. By now everything is known. But to
recognize our responsibilities . . . Well, that not only serves

to cleanse our conscience but helps us to live together. Jews, Poles, Germans. Since we *must* live together.

O.F.: Still Golda Meir, when I interviewed her last November, told me she'd never set foot in Germany.

W.B.: I know. She's said it to others too. And I can't blame her for that. Nevertheless I've invited her officially, she's accepted both privately and in public, and I hope she'll come. I really do. I'm sure she's ready to come, and I like to think my visit to Israel may have helped to make the idea of setting foot in Germany a little easier for her. Golda is a great woman. A fascinating woman. A woman of almost Biblical stature. And everyone knows her qualities, which only old-fashioned people call masculine. Her strength of steel, for example, her shrewdness. Those are neither masculine nor feminine gifts—they're just gifts, that's all. And then Golda has such human warmth. . . . I say she'll come.

O.F.: That faith gives a very good picture of Willy Brandt. And speaking of faith, I'd like to take up again a subject we've barely touched on but which one can't avoid going into with you: Europe. Chancellor Brandt, you sounded discouraged when you referred to it a little while ago. Don't you ever have the suspicion that a united Europe is a utopia?

W.B.: No. A united Europe can be achieved. It's being achieved. Certainly it hasn't developed and won't develop in the way our American friends thought after the Second World War when they spoke of a United States of Europe. The Americans made the mistake of comparing the possibilities for unifying Europe with what had happened in the United States. A meaningless comparison. The United States is a melting pot whose realities are too different from ours, and to create Europe is another thing entirely. To create Europe means to maintain the values of national identity and then build over them the structure of a European government. And even though it's very slow, unfortunately, even though unfortunately it has no political sex appeal, even though it involves the obstacles of bureaucratic procedures, isn't that perhaps what's happening? Don't people move freely in Europe? Isn't there a level of trade such as we never had before in Europe? But of course Europe is being achieved! I'm more and more convinced of it whenever I compare the European Community of today with the one four or five years ago.

O.F.: But the Europe we call Europe is a very tiny Europe, Chancellor Brandt! It's not even half of Europe!

W.B.: Look, I would have been overjoyed if we'd been able to build a United States of Europe. If I myself could choose between a Europe entirely unified and a part of Europe unified, needless to say I'd choose the first. But it's not possible—we're not in the position to be able to choose between an imperfect solution and a solution that's more than perfect. We must work with a Europe divided in two, and even in three. We must work with a Western Europe, that is, one capable of moving toward a structure of common government. Then, through the policy of *détente* that has already begun, we must increase communication between Eastern Europe and Western Europe—despite the differences that exist between their social system and ours, between their political structure and ours. Oh, if someone were to offer me a way of uniting something more than Western Europe, I'd say, fine, wonderful, thank you. But it's not possible, it's not possible. Besides, there's that existing fact that I call the third dimension: Europe plus the United States. The United States as a part of Europe in the area of security. . . .

O.F.: So you're not thinking of a neutral Europe, capable of representing an equilibrium between the two great powers?

W.B.: No. I wouldn't look on Europe as a force placed between the two world powers. Aside from the fact that when one speaks of world powers, one should speak not of two but of three, and then one would have to speak of Europe as a fourth power, and add a fifth—Japan. . . . Aside from the fact that to speak of Europe as a fourth power wouldn't be exact, since if a united Europe were to begin trading, it would become the number one commercial power in the world. . . . No, I don't want to give the impression of aiming at a Europe that would maintain a policy of neutrality vis-à-vis the two blocs represented by America and the Soviet Union. Naturally I want a different relationship with the United States than the one with the Soviet Union. With the United States I want a partnership, even though at the same time I want an independent policy. Furthermore I believe that even the United States would like to see us behave in a more mature way than we have so far.

o.f.: But then . . . the reunification of Germany? Things being as they are, do you think you'll see the reunification of Germany?

w.b.: No. I don't think so. Look, I'll soon be sixty years old, as I've already told you. And I don't expect to become a Methuselah. Maybe, if I did expect to become a Methuselah, my answer would be more positive. Because I'd have to arrive at least at the age of 130, like certain old people in the Caucasus, to see the reunification of Germany. Not even within twenty or fifty years do I anticipate an isolated answer to the German problem. No, I can't even imagine an isolated answer to the German problem. I think a change in relations between the two Germanys will only come about as a result of a change in relations between the two Europes. So look, I'm not giving you an optimistic answer, but I give you an answer that includes the possibility that Europe may resolve the division between the two Germanys. But mark my words: if that should happen, I don't mean to say that we'll go back to forming a single German state. I mean to say the people of the two Germanys will decide to live a different relationship, under a roof different from the one they've lived under since the end of the Second World War.

o.f.: Chancellor Brandt, when you speak of Western Europe, you're obviously referring to a politically unified Europe. But what does this expression mean to you?

w.b.: It means three things. Because there are three things to be done. The first is economic integration. But that's already going on, since I think we're heading toward a common monetary system. Not in the sense that we must necessarily use the same money, but in the sense that there'll be a stable relationship among our currencies. Yes, yes, in some way we'll arrive at some form of a common European bank; in some way we'll arrive at economic and monetary union.

The second thing is what I call European social union. And when I say "social union," I'm not referring only to social policy in the old sense of the word, the sense used by trade unionists, and so forth. That too is important, but by social union I mean what a modern slogan called the "quality of life." In other words, I'm not referring only to an increase in productivity, since an increase in productivity is not a goal in itself. I'm referring to problems of the environment, working conditions, education. . . . One has to be fairly ambitious to bring about within ten years a unified Western Europe that socially will be the most progressive part of the world. Ten years are sufficient; in ten years we can do it. And then of course we'll be able to arrive at a common political structure, since that cannot exist without economic integration and social union. The third thing is to maintain our national identities. It would be a misfortune to give them up.

O.F.: Yes, but in this splendid Western Europe that you're ambitiously aiming at, what do we do with nondemocratic countries? What do we do, for example, with Spain and Greece?

W.B.: It's clear that no country can become a member of the European Community if it's not based on the institutions we have. Namely a government or parliament elected by the people, trade unions, and so forth. It's clear that if a country doesn't observe some minimum respect for the Declaration of Human Rights, it can't become part of our Europe. So it's a big problem. All the more so in that I've learned from experience that you almost never succeed in bringing freedom back in a country that's lost it. If you do succeed, it's almost always the result of a war—it seldom happens that a nation oppressed by dictatorship finds a way to liberate itself without a war. The speeches and actions of others help even less in liberating it. Boycotting its products, for example. . . . Refusing to go there on vacation. . . . It doesn't do any good. But history always has new developments up its sleeve, and sometimes satisfying ones.

Let's take Spain. I knew Spain during the Civil War, when as a young man I went there as a journalist. I stayed there about six months, especially in Barcelona and Catalonia, and I remember the tremendous hatred that divided the two sides. I remember the incredible poverty of the country people. Since then I've been back only once, to spend a vacation on

an island, and another time for half a day. That was when I
went to the United States by ship. I took the ship from Naples
and we stopped for half a day in Málaga, where I walked
around a little. Well . . . not that you could tell much from
the place, but what I saw seemed to me an extraordinary development. It was no longer the Spain I had known. So I
wouldn't be surprised if, within a generation, Spain were to
transform itself and enter into the European Community. It
could happen by a process of evolution.

O.F.: And Greece?

W.B.: Oh, the case of Greece is more complicated. When we talk
about Greece, we mustn't forget that things are not so simple
as our Greek friends insist when they state that up until 1967
there was a splendid democracy in Greece—a splendid democracy that all of a sudden became a military dictatorship. I
visited Greece in 1960, when Karamanlis was prime minister,
and I met Kanellopoulos, who today is very courageously in
the opposition. Ah, yes—a wonderful man, Kanellopoulos.
With strong ties to German culture as well. We've always kept
in touch during these years when he's had to face so many difficulties. . . . But the fact is that my press conference in
Athens was much different from those I'd held in other parts
of the world. Rather similar, I'd say, to those I'd had in countries of limited democracy. So it's not easy to foresee what will
happen in Greece. All I can hope is that the forces of freedom
and the future will be strong enough in that country. Because,
if they are, there's no doubt that they'll find many friends
abroad. The fact remains, however, that you don't regain democracy by arms. Arms serve only in the case of war. But I
think that the Greek people, if they want to, can regain their
freedom. They can if some special situation arises. Even without arms. And then even the help that their friends abroad are
able to give them will be useful.

O.F.: Good. And now let's go back to Willy Brandt. We've been
getting a little far from Willy Brandt, and . . . Chancellor, I
can't help but think of you as a journalist. You were a journalist for so long. What was journalism for you?

W.B.: Look, for me it was simply a way to earn a living. Writing has
always been easy for me—I began writing when I went to

school. To pay for my studies, I worked for a newspaper in
Lübeck, and in fact when I finished school, they wrote on my
diploma, "He will become a journalist." I didn't want them to
write "journalist"; I wanted them to write "*Zeitungs-
Schreiber*"—writer for newspapers. I was a young left-wing socialist and I objected to the use of foreign words in the German language. But they didn't listen to me and wrote "journalist." Anyway I never had any doubts, from the time I was a
boy, that someday I'd become a journalist. Even the study of
history was something I wanted to undertake in order to become a journalist. And when I thought of how I should organize my life, I always came to that conclusion. My dream was
to be the editor of a Lübeck daily and later a deputy to the
Reichstag in Berlin.

O.F.: So your final goal was politics, not journalism.

W.B.: Let's say political journalism plus politics.

O.F.: Politics or power? Somewhere I've read a sentence you're supposed to have said when you were mayor of Berlin: "Power is
the only way to do something sensible."

W.B.: I don't remember exactly, but it must have been something
like that. I said it during a friendly argument with my wife,
who was afraid that power was too important a responsibility.
Power . . . I don't like the word power. It's a word that gives
rise to misunderstandings. In my case, I'd prefer the word influence. But let's go ahead and say power—making it clear
that we mean it in the good sense. Well, it's obvious that to
achieve something, you must be in the position to achieve
something. And not necessarily the position of head of state,
though you can do a lot as head of state. Provided . . . Provided you remain so for a certain period of time.

O.F.: You've remained so, and you're prepared to stay there for a
good period of time. So I ask you: what is, what was your goal?
Why did you want power?

W.B.: Inside the country, to achieve a more modern way of life. I
mean a higher level of democratization and social equilibrium. I said social equilibrium, not equality. Outside, to show
that my nation could have good neighborly relations—both
with East and West. Perhaps I might say I was interested in
giving Germany a foreign policy because Germany had no

foreign policy. But it's bad to put it that way, since it doesn't explain that our foreign policy was still first of all that of a divided Germany and secondly of the Germany torn apart by the occupation. So it would be more correct to say I was anxious to have Germany settled in a European context, and with neighborly relations at home and abroad.

O.F.: I suppose you're referring first of all to your *Ostpolitik*, the opening toward the East. Chancellor Brandt, are you satisfied with what you've achieved by your *Ostpolitik*?

W.B.: Almost. When I look back, I find two or three points that I might have handled differently. But not too differently. All in all I'm fairly happy to tell myself that I hope I won't feel too self-satisfied as an old man. Oh, mind you, there's never a situation where you can tell yourself I-couldn't-have-done-better. Besides, a person seldom acts alone—what he does is generally the result of a vast process in which he finds himself involved. Still . . . before you arrived, I was here with my ambassador to the United Nations, and he was telling me some very flattering things about his contacts with the other ambassadors. Including those from Eastern Europe. They think I've done a lot and intend to give me a good reception during my upcoming trip to New York. Well, that pleased me. I mean I was very glad to know that they're not going to throw stones at me.

O.F.: They didn't throw stones at you even in Erfurt, when you went to East Germany. How did you feel in front of that crowd that applauded you so enthusiastically?

W.B.: I was very moved but also frightened. Frightened for them, for the risks they were taking by letting themselves go like that. I did nothing but make signs to them so they wouldn't get too excited. It was dangerous for them.

O.F.: That entitles me to ask you a question I'd like to put to every man or woman in power. Do you think that history is changed because one individual comes along instead of another? In other words, do you think that the Germany of today would be the same if Willy Brandt hadn't turned up?

W.B.: I think that individuals play a definite role in history. But I also think that it's situations that make one talent emerge instead of another. A talent that already existed, obviously. I'll

give you an example. If the Second World War hadn't broken
out in 1939, if the Allies hadn't been so unprepared, if after
the invasion of Norway and Denmark Hitler hadn't launched
his attack on Holland, Belgium, and France, what would have
become of Winston Churchill? Would he have been an exceptional man all the same, or wouldn't he rather have been a
somewhat querulous outsider with the habit of raising his
voice? What happened happened, and at the critical moment,
since Churchill was not too old, the British were able to rally
around him and have the advantage of his immense ability.
But what does this mean? Does it mean that Churchill's importance would have been the same even if those events had
happened five years later, or does it mean that Churchill's importance would have been less if those events had happened
five years later? No, it's not easy to know if, finding ourselves
in a certain situation, we're doing things that no one else
would be able to do. De Gaulle did things no one else in
France could have done. And still I say that a situation must
exist, and certain individuals must exist at the same moment
as that situation. If the individual and the situation meet, then
the mechanism is set off by which history takes one direction
instead of another.

O.F.: Strange that you cite De Gaulle, the man who delayed the
birth of Europe.

W.B.: De Gaulle was a great man, the only man capable of freeing
France from the inferiority complex that the Second World
War had caused it. The only one capable of making it a great
power *honoris causa*. If one looks on Europe with the concept
of a United States of Europe, then he was certainly not a sup-
porter. But the astonishing fact remains that, under him, the
European Community went forward instead of being dis-
mantled. He could have stopped it and instead he let it go on.
We mustn't put all the blame on him. And when we speak of
Ostpolitik . . .

O.F.: The *Ostpolitik* is Brandt, because it's Brandt who went to the
East.

W.B.: Yes, but I don't deny that someone else could have developed
a policy similar to mine. Even if I hadn't begun that policy in
1967 and 1968 when I was foreign minister, someone else

would have done it later. Albeit under less favorable conditions. It had to be done, otherwise Germany would have remained in a corner and in contradiction with the policy already undertaken by its most important allies. Namely the United States and France. Oh, believe me, the individual must be there but the situation must be there too.

O.F.: That's almost a Marxist argument. Chancellor Brandt, you were a Marxist as a young man, weren't you?

W.B.: I thought I was. But I'm not sure I worked hard enough to become one. Too bad. I should have. Because to be a Marxist as a young man is excellent preparation for becoming a good socialist as an old one.

O.F.: Anyway you were a left-wing socialist. Well, what's left in you of the socialism you dreamed of when you were a tempestuous and enthusiastic youth?

W.B.: Look, a good portion of that socialism has become reality. If I compare the conditions in which the people lived then and live now, I have to conclude that a good portion of material security has been achieved. What remains to be accomplished today is the permanent commitment of socialism. Not only as regards wages, which are important too, but as regards the strengthening of the human personality. I don't know if I make myself clear. One must know what to do with one's life. And . . . you see, as a young man I didn't know that socialism is a permanent commitment. I thought socialism was something to put into practice and then, if anything, to improve on. Instead it's much, much more. It's a way of combining freedom and justice and solidarity in a commitment that never ends. Socialism is like a sailor who very quickly learns to be a sailor, even if he's only a boy and has never seen the sea. Because on his first voyage, the sailor discovers that the horizon is not a boundary line. When the ship moves, the horizon moves too—always farther on, always farther on, until it becomes so many horizons that are always new. Oh, yes. That's how I see socialism—like a horizon we'll never reach and to which we always try to get closer.

O.F.: Chancellor Brandt, to what degree were you influenced by Scandinavian socialism? Or rather, were you influenced by it?

W.B.: Yes, of course. Take a country like Norway. A country that's been so important to me. One of the best experiences I've had has been to live in Norway, because in Norway the peasants have never been slaves. Never. The peasant movement remains at the base of their modern democracy and . . . that certainly influenced me. There I discovered the elements of liberalism without which humanitarian socialism can't exist.

O.F.: Chancellor Brandt, I know that your eldest son is a Maoist and . . .

W.B.: Oh, he wouldn't call himself a Maoist. He says he's a Marxist and perhaps a Marxist-Leninist. He's twenty-five years old now, an adult man, and he no longer represents the young rebels who call themselves Maoists. Even if his ideas are very different from the ideas of his father.

O.F.: The question I was getting ready to ask you still holds good though. Do you find in the young people of today a certain ingratitude, or a certain blindness to what has been done so that they could live in a better world?

W.B.: No. I wouldn't put it that way. Because young people today don't make the comparison between today's reality and yesterday's misery. The misery, for example, in which we were drowning during and after the war. Most of them weren't even born when we were drowning in that misery, and so they compare the reality of today with the possibilities of tomorrow. You see what I mean? They don't reason like ourselves, who put what we have today on one pan of the scales and on the other what we had in 1945 and 1946. Then we weigh it and say, "We've done well, we've done a good job." When I talk face to face with the young people of today, I defend what we've done. I say, none of you can take away our pride in having done a good deal. But I don't expect them to identify with my problems, since they aren't their problems. The result is I defend my times and they defend theirs. And this happens with my children too, with the advantage that we avoid arguments. We've never had very many, I must say, also because I've spent so little time with them . . . so seldom at home. . . . But when my eldest son, who lives in Berlin, comes to pay me a visit or spends his vacation with us, we don't quarrel. If it comes to analyzing the moral category in which each of us is engaged, I cut things short: "My problem isn't yours, and yours isn't mine."

O.F.: It's extraordinary that politics hasn't made you cynical, Chancellor.

W.B.: No, no. Never! You surely run the risk of becoming cynical when you achieve power. But I've always succeeded in controlling and then overcoming it.

O.F.: Even when Adenauer attacked you with such ferocity and stressed the fact that you were an illegitimate son, that you had taken Norwegian citizenship, that . . .

W.B.: Adenauer really behaved very badly with me. And yet, strangely enough, on the personal level, he never showed any hostility. Though he said all those ugly things about me, he had a kind of sympathy for me. And I, though I strongly disagreed with his methods and politics, had great respect for him. During the election campaign of 1961, and right in the middle of all that mudslinging, he called me to his office. Right here where we are now. Or rather, I was sitting where you're sitting now and he was sitting here where I'm sitting. Right away I said to him, "Mr. Chancellor, does it seem right to you, does it seem sensible, to carry on an election campaign the way you're doing?" He answered, "But, Mr. Mayor! I don't understand what you're talking about! Do you think I have anything against you? Not at all! If I had something against you, I'd call you aside and we'd talk about it." So I didn't react. Or not as I'd reacted in the campaign he'd launched against me in 1957 and 1958. Then the whole business was repeated in 1965, and this time I really got mad. I no longer wanted to run in the elections. I said to my party: "That's enough; I'm too heavy a burden for your shoulders. Better to leave the candidacy to someone else. I withdraw." And it was at that point that things began to go well for me. Sometimes you have to slow down or actually stop the automobile in order to pick up speed. In 1966 my party held its convention. It ended with unanimous support for Brandt, and . . .

O.F.: And Brandt became foreign minister, then chancellor, and then even won the Nobel Peace Prize. Chancellor Brandt, is it true that you cried when you received the news?

W.B.: No, that's an exaggeration. No. I'd heard that they would give me the prize, and when Ahlers, one of my assistants, handed me a sheet of paper with the news, I said nothing. I took the

paper, put it in a drawer, and went on writing some notes.
The Bundestag met that day and . . . Certainly I was moved.
But I didn't cry at all.

O.F.: Do you never cry?

W.B.: Very rarely since I've become an adult. Very rarely. I may
feel happy or unhappy or moved. Look . . . like most Nor-
dics, I'm sentimental. A romantic, if you like. So emotion
isn't alien to me, but I always try to conceal it. Or control it.
And I prefer to laugh. Especially when I drink a glass of wine
in the evening and am with my friends. I like to tell jokes. It's a
weakness of mine. I collect them all and often invent them.
The trouble is I often laugh at them more than the people
who are listening.

O.F.: That's all very nice, but it seems to me almost impossible that
you can speak of the Nobel Prize with such detachment. Not
many politicians receive the Nobel Prize and . . .

W.B.: That's because there aren't many good politicians, and because the committee has to be careful not to offend anyone. In
my case, they chose the right moment, namely, the moment
when they would have offended the least number of people. In
fact, despite the Nobel, I still have a lot of friends. Yes, I understand. You want to know if the Nobel was the greatest satisfaction of my life. No. It was something that encouraged me,
but I didn't react to it by dancing up and down. If I run
through the list of people who have won prizes, and even
when I think that the Nobel Prize is considered the most important, I . . . Anyway to give me the Nobel Peace Prize
wasn't like giving it to Carl von Ossietzky. They gave it to him
when he was in a concentration camp, and he was taken out
of that concentration camp only to be kept under arrest in the
hospital where he died. Ossietzky was a symbol, a martyr. I'm
really not a martyr and I wasn't suffering at all when I got the
prize.

O.F.: I'm seizing on the word suffering, Chancellor Brandt. And I'll
ask you something I've wanted to ask since the beginning of
this conversation. Have you suffered from the fact of not
knowing who your father was?

W.B.: No. I haven't suffered from it, no. If instead of did I "suffer,"
you were to ask me was I "affected" by it, then that's different.

And I say yes. But if it did affect me, that goes back such a long time that I've almost forgotten about it. I began so early to build my life by myself. I began so early to have a name of my own, mine only. It's no accident that I've always considered the name I carry as my real name. Literally. And then it's not correct to say I didn't know who my father was. I'll tell you something I've never told anyone. Anyone . . . I knew who my father was. I knew his name. But I never wanted to meet him. He was still alive after the end of the war. But not even then was I interested in meeting him.

O.F.: Why? Out of resentment? Out of respect for your mother?

W.B.: I don't know. I don't care to comment on my attitude. I give you the facts and that's all.

O.F.: I understand. And I suppose then that your mother has been very important in your life.

W.B.: Yes. When I was a child, a boy, yes. In fact, when they ask me "Why did you become a socialist?" I answer: through my mother. Even though she was very young, and though women were even forbidden to participate in political meetings, my mother was active in the trade union movement. And so not only was I born into socialism and trade unionism—that's where I grew up. With very strong roots. Do you see what I mean? It wasn't to my credit. It was to hers.

O.F.: Maybe you've become Willy Brandt just because you had no father and did have such a mother.

W.B.: That I don't know. I've never been to a psychoanalyst and I can't answer you. I can only say I've had the impression that, subconsciously, all this has had an influence. Yes, it must have had—but I don't know to what extent. Besides if I look at myself at all clearly, I can say that my attitude toward life has been influenced more by reading than by people. Aside from my mother, of course. To the question, "Which is the writer, the politician, the man who has had the greatest impact on you?" I find it very difficult to give an answer. Or rather, impossible. And I end up saying, "I've read a lot, I've read so much." I don't know even how to connect the effect of what I've read with the circumstances in which I was born and raised. But what's more significant is that I don't care about it. I'm not interested in bringing my unconscious to the surface.

O.F.: Chancellor Brandt, are you religious?

W.B.: Hm. . . . The way I interpret religion is completely nonorth-
odox, but I'm not an atheist—if that's what you want to know.
No, I'm not an atheist. I simply interpret what people call
God or transcendental problems in a different manner from
those who go to church. And I usually don't like to talk about
it, because . . . because . . . In short, it's against my nature
to reveal myself completely. I wouldn't succeed even if I tried.

O.F.: That I've well understood, Chancellor Brandt. I've never interviewed a man so reserved and modest as you. One can talk
with you about everything except Willy Brandt.

W.B.: You must remember that I come from the Baltic, that I'm
half sailor, and that those years in Norway had a great effect
on me. And so to absolve myself, I'll tell you a joke, a Norwegian one of course, that might have been invented just for
me. On a mountain above a fiord there lived two peasants.
Each one on his own. One day, one of the two peasants goes
to visit the other. He enters his house and says nothing. He
barely nods his head. Nor does the other one say anything. He
doesn't even nod his head. But he glances toward the sideboard, where there's a bottle of aquavit. The peasant who's
come to visit understands. He goes to the sideboard and takes
the aquavit; he takes two glasses. He puts them on the table.
He pours the aquavit. The two start drinking. They drink in
silence, slowly, one glass after another. There's not even a
grunt to interrupt this dumb show. But, at the last sip of
aquavit, the peasant who's come to visit raises his glass and
mumbles, "*Skoal.*" Then the other one explodes. "You stupid
bastard! Did we get together to drink or to talk nonsense?"

O.F.: I won't say *skoal* to you, Chancellor Brandt. But may I say
arrivederci and thank you?

Bonn, September 1973

Pietro Nenni

Locked in an ivory tower that hardly suits him, the grand old man now seldom participates in the political life to which he has dedicated over three-quarters of his more than eighty years and given everything a man can give. Even a daughter, dead in the extermination camp of Auschwitz after writing to her French comrades: *"Dites a mon père que je n'ai jamais trahi ses idées"* (Tell my father that I never betrayed his ideas). He leaves this ivory tower, which at times is his house in Rome and at others his villa in Formia, only to go to the Senate. They have made him senator for life, and he has accepted the office with great hesitation—he who was on the point of being elected president of the Republic. In the Socialist party of today he counts as a flag to be unfurled when convenient, and when not convenient to be folded up and put away in a drawer. He did not succeed in unifying it. He lost his battle and lost it badly, in bitterness and unconfessed disgust. Leaving the congress hall—it was 1968—he was heard to murmur, "Here Nenni has no more friends." A pity. He would still have had much to say, much to give. Age has imparted him only the image of a tired patriarch, for the rest he still is in excellent shape. He gets up every morning at seven and reads the newspapers while pedaling on his bicycle exerciser for a time equivalent to an excursion of five kilometers. He does not worry about his diet, nor deny himself a glass of wine or a coffee. He plays *bocce* with the enthusiasm of a

235

young boy. And the doctors look at him with incredulous stupor. But best of all, in this lion's organism, born not to surrender, the mind remains. It still functions for him like a computer.

He spends much of his time studying and writing. He is endlessly working on a book that is supposed to be his autobiography, but given his modesty in speaking about himself, will end by being something else. He wants to call it *Witness to a Century*. Many wonder if on arriving at the last chapter, someday, he will finally say what today he does not want to say or says unclearly: namely that his socialism is no longer the one of fifty years ago, nor even the one of twenty-five years ago. For now it is a socialism that rejects dogmas, programs, abstract formulas; in return it is nourished by a blind faith in freedom, in democracy, in man. Unpardonable heresies for a true Marxist. If you try to pin him down, he changes the subject. Or resorts to twisted arguments, vague admissions, which he then immediately withdraws. But the truth does not escape you: he has realized that the world is not ruled only by economics, that state capitalism is no different from private capitalism, and is in some ways still more despotic since it evades the laws of criticism, of the market, of competition. He has realized that the dictatorship of the proletariat is nothing but a catchword, that you can fight the Fiat company but not the state—as was shown by the workers massacred at Danzig and Szczecin, by the intellectuals thrown into prisons or madhouses in Moscow and Leningrad. "I feel more at ease in Stockholm than in Leningrad," he says. And that is the only uncompromising statement by which he dares to break his reticence. He has become enamored of Swedish socialism, which has not abolished private property but has given man more than what doctrinaire and scientific socialism has given. And, perhaps, his youthful love for an anarchism interpreted as the defense of the individual has re-emerged in him. Who can say how much torment such a discovery may have cost him and still does? Or how many sleepless nights, how much anguish, caused by his scruples toward those whose teacher he has been for two generations. Approaching the end of his life, he suffers a tragedy comparable to the tragedy of theologians who discover they no longer believe in God. Or no longer believe in the Church, even if they still believe in God.

I asked him to talk to me, out of his lucidity and wisdom, and to explain to me what is happening in the Italy of the 1970s. And this he did in a conversation that lasted several days and was broken up into several meetings. His health is not perfect; he has heart trouble and cannot endure prolonged exertion. So I met him in his house in Formia, where he goes for weekends or whenever else he can, or in his house in Rome, on the top floor of a building in the Piazza Adriana. We generally talked for a while in the morning, after he had played his *bocce* game, and stopped when it was time to go to lunch. We ate in a leisurely fashion, helped along by a good French wine, and then he took a nap. Toward four or five o'clock we resumed our conversation, slowly, like his way of speaking. He answered each question with exasperating slowness, separating one word from another as though he were dictating to a secretary, lingering over periods and commas, and paying no attention to the clock. And so dusk caught us, in this prolix process of words and ideas that nevertheless enchanted me to the point of forgetting to turn on the light. I'll always remember a session that ended in the dark, and neither of us had realized that darkness had fallen. We were in his study in Formia, a small room furnished only with a day bed, a desk, a bookcase, and two chairs. Pina, his housekeeper, came in and scolded us. "What's this? Do we sit around talking like the blind?" At other times twilight caught us in his study in Rome, which is just as small but somewhat resembles a sanctuary. Here, over the day bed, is a large portrait in oils of his dead wife and then there are the photographs of Vittoria, the daughter who died at Auschwitz. But not ordinary photographs from happy times: photos taken upon her entrance into the extermination camp, wearing a prisoner's striped gown, and with a number at the bottom. One full face and one in profile. I've always wondered why. Perhaps so as never to forget at any moment, and even less at the moment of closing his eyes in sleep or reopening them, the sacrifice of his daughter? Our meetings in the Rome study were primarily to go over and discuss the transcription of the dialogues recorded on tape in Formia.

It's not easy to interview Pietro Nenni, as anyone who has tried it knows. A journalist himself, instead of letting himself be interviewed, he would prefer to do the interviewing and then draft the article himself—so as to measure every sentence, every adjective, every comma, and perhaps immediately afterward to strike everything out and start all over again. He is never satisfied with what he writes. When he was the editor of *Avanti!*, the socialist daily, he forced himself to compose his pieces in type, against the clock, so as to keep himself from making corrections *in extremis.* So just imagine his being satisfied with what he says into a tape recorder. "I don't much care for that machine of yours, it's dangerous." If you interview him in successive stages, as I did, next day you find him submerged in a sea of slips of paper covered with scribbles, corrections, afterthoughts. Raising his wrinkled forefinger, he reads them, and unfailingly it is a new version of what he had told you: verified, expurgated, ruined. But rather than reading it, he dictates it to you, and having dictated it, adds supplementary changes. Copiously. "Cut out that *I.* It's not good to keep saying *I, I, I.* Cut out those *theys* and put *we.* It's not good to put the blame on others when it was also my own." You'd like to get angry and instead you're moved: he is such an honorable man, such a professor of honesty. And also such a professor of generosity: in judging others he is always afraid of offending them. He begged me not to write an opinion about Churchill, a man he never liked because of the contempt he showed for others, so as not to seem unjust. "After all, if it weren't for him, we wouldn't be here today to talk." Winston Churchill, Joseph Stalin, Charles de Gaulle, Mao Tse-tung, Nikita Khrushchev, John F. Kennedy, Richard M. Nixon, Antonio Gramsci, Filippo Turati, Enrico Malatesta, Queen Elizabeth—all have passed through his life and not superficially. "I remember Mao Tse-tung saying to me . . . I remember De Gaulle saying to me . . ." And the time he, a republican, was supposed to ride in the golden carriage of Her Royal Highness the Princess Margaret: "No, don't make me think of it." And the time they wanted to seat him next to the Greek ambassador at an official dinner. And he indignantly changed his seat. "Ah, what agony, what a pain. I felt sick to my stomach." To listen to him is a pleasure that should be taken as a gift. To write what you have listened to, on the other hand, is a torment that can only be taken as a punishment.

So when I sat down to compose this interview, I found myself faced with a problem of conscience: to compose it in my way or in his way, to recount everything he had told me before his afterthoughts or to report only what his excessive scruples had insisted on? No small problem when you respect a man to the degree that I respect him and at the same time believe in your own work as in a duty. And for several days I agonized over it, now deciding to do what he wanted and then deciding to disobey him. In the end I resolved the dilemma by a kind of compromise. Namely by composing the interview in the way that seemed right to me, while at the same time accepting some of his recommendations.

It worked. After reading the published interview, Nenni told me that I had betrayed neither his thoughts nor himself. And it was the beginning of a friendship in which I take the greatest pride. I like to see, reflected in myself, his ideas, doubts, uncertainties, and impossible dreams. It was also a great relief because, as Vittoria, his daughter who died at Auschwitz because she was his daughter, understood, above all he must not be betrayed, a crime many have committed. Far too many. Even at the moment when they should have been honoring him by electing him president of the Republic. He would have made a splendid president of the Republic, and it would have done us good to have him in the Quirinale. But they didn't let him, they didn't let us. His friends still more than his enemies.

ORIANA FALLACI: In an interview in *Europeo*, Arthur Schlesinger said of the Italians, "Who can ever understand you when you're the first not to understand yourselves?" Senator Nenni, I'm here to ask you to help us understand ourselves and what is happening today in Italy. You have the reputation of being a pessimist, I know. Still . . .

PIETRO NENNI: No, I'm a pessimist when it comes to evaluating immediate events—if you ask me what's going to happen tonight, I'll say it will probably be something unpleasant. But if you ask me what's going to happen in the years to come, then I become an optimist. That's because I believe in man, in his capacity to improve. It's because I consider man as the beginning and end of all things. Because I'm convinced that he, man, is always the decisive proof, and that only by changing man do you change society. In sixty-five years of participating in political struggles, my problem has always been that of improving myself as a man and of helping my comrades in arms to make the same effort. It's not impossible, if you understand man. And when Schlesinger says you can't understand the Italians, he's just making a wisecrack. They're no more incomprehensible than others, and no worse. It's only that they have great difficulty in rationalizing their collective life and in taking certain threats seriously. The unsuccessful coup by Valerio Borghese, for example. Obviously the danger is not Valerio Borghese in himself and for himself. The danger is the breakdown of the democratic state—a breakdown we encourage by doing and undoing things, thus running the risk of letting ourselves be overtaken by such phenomena as Valerio Borghese.

O.F.: You'll admit it's hard to take a Valerio Borghese seriously, or even a dictatorship headed by Valerio Borghese.

P.N.: You remind me of all the people who said, in the 1920–1922 crisis: "But you take this Mussolini too seriously! It must be because you were in jail with him. But how can a fellow like that take over the government? There's no man who can set up a dictatorship in Italy!" What does it mean, "There's no man"? You don't need an exceptional individual to make him the symbol of a situation! All you need is some fanatic, some supposedly harmless eccentric, some conceited type out for success. Besides what was Mussolini in 1920, and even in 1921 and twenty-two? He'd received four thousand votes in the elections of 1919—four thousand votes in Milan, a city he'd practically controlled since 1913, when he became editor of *Avanti!*. He was ready to run off to Switzerland; he had more faith in that possibility than in the idea of going to Rome and forming a government. And instead he went to Rome. As I was afraid he would. Because I knew that when adventurers, or rather *condottieri*, can operate within a sick society, anything becomes possible.

So it's irresponsible to smile and say, Where today is there a Mussolini? Where today is there a Hitler? Mussolinis get invented, Hitlers get invented. And to invent one all you need are a hundred newspapers to repeat daily, "He's a great man," a pope to declare, "He's the man of Providence," perhaps a Churchill to state, "He's the first man behind whom I sense the will of the Italians." As happened with Mussolini. So why can't one, in the same way, invent a Valerio Borghese, who is a former prince and colonel, a sinker of ships and ex-torpedo boat commander? Certainly his unsuccessful coup looks like a caricature of a *coup d'état*: you don't occupy Italy by occupying the Palazzo Chigi and the RAI radio and television station. Not unless there's complicity within the state, for instance support from the armed forces and the police, something that could happen today only on a very reduced scale and thanks to complicity at the top. Let's not forget that Mussolini took the train only after receiving the king's telegram inviting him to the Quirinale. But there's no king today in the Quirinale, there's Saragat. And anyway that's not the point. The point is . . .

O.F.: One moment, Senator Nenni. You're upholding a dreadful theory. You're saying there are similarities between the Italy of 1971 and the Italy of 1922. Is that so?

P.N.: Yes, to some extent. The Italy of 1971 is not the Italy of 1922, of course. At that time we didn't know fascism and now we know it only too well, nor are we ready to go through it a second time. But there's one point that shows striking similarities between the Italy of seventy-one and the Italy of twenty-two—the one I indicated to the Senate when I reminded it that what ruined us in 1922 was not the offensive strength of fascism. It was the weakness of the ruling political class. It was the petty divisions that promoted jealousy, spite, and false hopes among politicians. No one believed in the danger. Everyone waited. Giolitti was waiting in Vichy, pondering no one knows exactly what—maybe the awful words of Cromwell: "Things will have to get worse before we can expect them to get better." How many politicians today are thinking the same thing? And don't they also risk waking up one fine day, or rather one bad day, without being able to do anything more about it? Let's not forget that one night in 1967 the Athenians went to bed with their eyes and ears still full of popular demonstrations for old Papandreou, and woke up next morning with the colonels in power.

O.F.: But Italy is not Greece, Senator Nenni. And in Italy the left is strong.

P.N.: We were also strong in 1920—it's not enough to be strong.

One must know how to prevent certain things by making the
state, the government, the parliament function, and not go on
postponing, postponing, postponing—a practice to which
we've made too many concessions in recent years. For years
I've been warning against jealousy, spite, slowness, meanness.
For years I've been repeating what I now tell you: when you're
talking about fascism, better too much than too little vigi-
lance. They don't listen to me. These words of mine also fell
on deaf ears in the summer of 1964. In fact, the communists
at the time said I was talking about an "imaginary danger,"
and called it a "diversion to conceal the failures of the center-
left." And yet I was expounding real facts. Just think of what
we found out later about SIFAR * and certain military com-
mands. Look, how is it possible that in Reggio Calabria that
Franco Ciccio or Ciccio Franco or whatever his name is was
able to play the role of Masaniello? How is it possible that the
parties stayed away from Aquila? These were municipal revolts
and, mind you, they took as their target the headquarters of
the leftist parties and the government. Not the headquarters of
the MSI.* So the point to be examined, as I said, is not
Valerio Borghese, but rather what made Valerio Borghese
think that a sudden attack on the Palazzo Chigi and the radio
and television station could be transformed into a *coup d'état*
and receive the thanks of the state?

o.f.: Is there an answer?

p.n.: Of course there is! Here too, as in 1922, the fascists counted
on the help they'd get from the right. The classical right, the
eternal right, the right that has little voting strength but possesses economic power, and has leverage in the administration
and the armed forces. The right that would like to reabsorb the
moderate forces of the Christian Democrats. The right that
would like to re-establish a bourgeois order that's now in de-
cline. The right that makes use of the fascists as an element of
provocation because it needs disorder, that is, fear. Disorder is
always useful to the enemies of democracy. It's even useful to

---

* Servizio Informazioni Forze Armate della Repubblica; now called SID, Servizio
Informazioni della Difesa, military counterespionage organization. (Translator's
note.)

* Movimento Sociale Italiano, the neofascist party. (Translator's note.)

the communists, who can thus pose as defenders of legality, so just imagine how useful it is to the right. That's what our politicians don't understand when they play at making artificial reforms. That's what our youth groups outside Parliament don't understand when by their violence they help the reactionaries and the MSI.

O.F.: Senator Nenni, do you think it's right for the MSI to be in Parliament?

P.N.: No, I don't think it's right. Because the MSI was born with all the characteristics of a fascist party—to have accepted it was one more mistake by us Italians, who never take things too seriously. Yes, even in the case of the MSI our democratic state failed to keep its prerogatives: it did not apply Rule 12 of the Constitution, it didn't even apply the Scelba Law of 1952, which explicitly forbids the formation of organizations or parties that renew ties with fascism. Anyway I give only relative importance to the fact that in Parliament there's a party of the fascist type, since I see things in political terms. The fascists you can dissolve when and how you like—that's not enough to suppress them. To suppress them you have to pull up the social, political, and psychological roots that produce fascism. And these roots still haven't been pulled up in Italy, only cut at the surface.

O.F.: That's just what I wanted to get to, Senator Nenni: the predisposition the Italians show toward this disease called fascism. Fascism is first of all violence, contempt for democracy—therefore it doesn't only come dressed in black. Don't you think that these roots that have never been pulled up also flower into the violence of extremists on the left?

P.N.: Yes, the youngsters who call themselves Maoists, Trotskyites, neoanarchists indulge in violence, it's true. And so they offer examples, pretexts, they nourish hatred and fear, without realizing that they have nothing to gain by hatred and fear. But one shouldn't confuse them with the fascists. Fascism is not an extremist movement—it's fascism, that's all. Fascism is what we went through under Mussolini, under the Salò Republic. It doesn't want to advance the world, it wants to make it go backward. I mean, an act of Maoist violence and an act of fascist violence may be, yes, the same thing, but only roughly speaking. Morally and historically there's a great difference. The fascists are dangerous because they go back to a recent tradition of our country and have behind them the forces of reaction; the so-called Maoists are not dangerous because they don't go beyond a revolt that after all is childish. The ideas that inspire them are not despicable but utopian and outside Italian, or rather European, reality. We saw them explode in France in May 1968. What did they get by it? Just the opposite of what they were after. May 1968 was enough to bring about an involution of French society and bring it back to its conservative foundations. If today in France you have a Gaullism without De Gaulle, and it has power and keeps it, this is also owing to the youth movement that frightened so many people. I reminded the Senate of a sentence from Lenin: "Above all beware of arousing useless fear." These youngsters ought to take it to heart.

O.F.: And when they give a Nenni the raspberry, as in Turin? It was despicable the way they behaved with you on that occasion.

P.N.: Oh, no. It was a little incident of intolerance. I wasn't upset by it at all. One of their comrades had been arrested and they were protesting against anyone representing the authority of the government. For them I was the government, and responsible for the arrest. . . . Let's not forget that young extremists are the historical result of all the authoritarianism that you find in every social system, in every organized society. You're in trouble if at the age of twenty you reason with the mentality of someone eighty years old like me. Or even with the mentality of someone forty. Believe me, my indulgence toward them doesn't come from discouragement, it comes from a knowledge of history. In our society the phenomenon of youthful revolt comes and goes in precise cycles—at the beginning of this century the revolt of young people was one of the strongest movements. It was all there, even then, and on an international scale: antimilitarism, anticlericalism, futurism, the generation gap between parents and children. We too rebelled against our families, though in different terms. We too didn't accept the words of the peasant mother who shook her head and said, "Never mind, things have always been like this and always will." I remember it very well—I was one of the most outraged participants in that revolt.

O.F.: History repeats itself, after all, and Giambattista Vico is right.

P.N.: Of course he's right. History doesn't repeat itself in the same conditions but it repeats itself. At that time too there was extremist trade unionism, then too they resorted to wildcat strikes. The most typical demonstration was called the match strike, when they set fire to the crops. In Bologna, Parma, Modena. The class struggle, at that time, was mainly the struggle of peasants and day laborers. The culmination for us was Red Week, which I had the good fortune to direct alongside of Enrico Malatesta. I ended up in the Court of Assizes in Aquila as a result of it, accused of an attack on the state. Before Red Week, in 1909, we had tried a great international strike for the anarchist Francisco Ferrer. They shot him in Barcelona, for intention to commit a crime, and I was one of the sponsors of that strike in the city of Carrara, then anarchist and republican. In Forlì I also sponsored the strike against the war in Tripoli.

We believed in strikes as the means for obtaining the surrender of the capitalist forces, and also as a means for preventing war and guaranteeing peace among nations. . . . I repeat: these crises in which everything is called into question are recurrent crises. Sometimes they take cultural forms, sometimes social ones, but essentially they're the same thing. In my time we looked to Georges Sorel, to his *Réflexiones sur la violence.* Today they look to Mao's thoughts. Whether inspired by Mao or Sorel, the phenomenon always goes back to the same law. The law by which young people are a component in the development of societies. The boys and girls of today think they've invented the world. Youngsters always think that the world begins with them.

O.F.: Senator Nenni, your revolt emerged from a state of poverty and oppression that's not even comparable to that of today. So don't you feel that your violence was more justified than theirs?

P.N.: Undoubtedly. And your question reminds me of an article that's been written about the "moderate" Nenni—the man of

Red Week who today asks that violence be relinquished. This article acknowledged a logical continuity in me. It really is in me, my dear friend. Because today we have something to defend, and in my time we had nothing at all to defend. Or very little. Today freedom to think, to organize, to demonstrate exists—open to everyone. In my time it didn't exist. Today no one can stop you from transforming the present civil and social order. In my time you were stopped. In short, every struggle for freedom should include the defense of freedoms already gained, and when I look at the young people of today I'm sorry about only one thing: that they let themselves be ruined by the resurgent myth of violence. Violence is the midwife of history, yes—but only when you exercise it in the right conditions of time and place. Such conditions don't exist at present in our country. Violence is a response to abuses that leave you no other way to claim justice, yes—but we have other means of struggle against what survives of those abuses today. If these young people were to conduct their action on the plane of ideas, it would be much more effective. The trouble is that not all of them have ideas—many of these rebels are the industrialists and the bourgeoisie of tomorrow. Just as many of the rebels who exploded at the beginning of the century later became fascists, and even fascist ministers. Believe me, sometimes I wonder if their explosions in the streets and universities aren't a passing fashion, a way of letting off steam, a price paid to momentary resentments, rather than the considered rejection of a world to which in great part they belong.

O.F.: They spit on democracy, Senator Nenni. It's not unusual for them to spit on the Resistance. Through Mao they take as their model a society with which we have nothing in common. Now, you who have been to China and met Mao Tsetung . . .

P.N.: Yes, but it's not by brief contact with an unknown country that we get to understand a revolution, a system, or a man. I don't have much faith in such trips. You see, Khrushchev once told me that Stalin knew very little about Russia, and when he saw my astonishment, he explained, "We made films for him and then showed them to him. Scenes of city and country life—all concocted." And I answered jokingly, "The

same things you show us when we come to Russia." That's
how it is. We don't know much about the Soviet Union, even
after having been there. And we don't know much about
China after having been there. For instance, how can you get
behind the mystery of this recent phase of the Chinese revolution? Insofar as it can be seen as a libertarian revolt, it seems
to be something positive. But has it been only a matter of a
libertarian revolt? We'll find out in the future. As for Mao
Tse-tung, look: at the moment you approach Mao Tse-tung,
you're not approaching an ordinary man who has the features
of Mao Tse-tung—you're approaching the creator of a great
revolution and you're in a very special frame of mind. The
same thing happened to me with Mao Tse-tung as happened
to me with Stalin. Seen face to face, Stalin seemed like a
harmless and polite little man. He was so affable, he actually
gave the impression of being slipshod. But you never forgot he
was Stalin, one of the victors, if not the victor, of the Second
World War, the great leader of Russia.

O.F.: Let's go back to Mao Tse-tung. Did you like him?

P.N.: Of course! He may be the world figure I've liked the most.
But if I had to account for this choice, I wouldn't be able.
Because it's a matter of instinct. I suppose I liked him because
he comes from a peasant background. And I'm the son of
peasants, with no city or middle-class mixtures. Mao, what do
you want me to say about Mao? We were together for an afternoon, half of which was taken up by translation—we talked
about things through an interpreter. Not even Chou En-lai,
who's been a miner in Belgium and should know how to speak
French well, and who certainly speaks English, spoke to me
without an interpreter. Mao was cordial. He even asked me
what was Operation Nenni, about which there was a lot in the
newspapers at the time. So I explained to him that it was an
attempt at opening toward the Christian Democrats, so as to
encourage them to turn to the left, but he didn't express any
opinions. You can see some things don't enter into his frame
of reference. Then we talked about China's entry into the UN,
about mutual recognition by our two countries, about the
Catholic missions in China with regard to which there had
been some talk of massacres. He seemed to me very alive. And

I feel well with men who are alive. Which also goes and especially for Khrushchev. You see, the Soviet leaders are like stone walls. They never bring anything human into their talk—they shy away from pleasantries, they're always so pompous. Khrushchev instead was never pompous, even in front of a foreigner like me. He drank, he joked, he made fun of his collaborators. Speaking of Molotov, he said to me, "You know, that one's a mule!" Anyway I'd found out he was a mule myself when we'd met to discuss the Trieste problem. But what do these memories have to do with anything? Weren't we supposed to be talking about Italy and the Italians?

O.F.: Yes, and here's a question that many people would like to ask you. People are talking more and more about a council Republic composed of Catholics and communists. Do you think such a marriage is imminent, or rather possible?

P.N.: No, I don't much think so. The council Republic is a suggestive formula, like the one of "spaghetti with Chilean sauce." But I'd say even this formula is anything but imminent and probable. It's not based on solid realities. And too many factors are holding it back: a Socialist party aware of its role and its autonomy, the lay forces represented by such parties as the Republican party, the presence in Italy of cultural circles engaged in the defense of freedom. . . . It's obvious that to the Christian Democrats and the Communist party such a protest seems attractive. A two-party system, basically, is their political dream. It's obvious that there are currents engaged in an operation of this kind—even outside the Demo-christian and Communist parties there are those who delude themselves that a union of the "black priests" with the "red priests" would guarantee for several years a relative social peace, the preservation of the status quo. Didn't the same thing happen with me, with the opening to the left? There were many who believed that to open the doors of the government to the socialists would help to safeguard the status quo. But, I repeat, I have little belief in the possibility of such a deplorable event. No, no. It's too pessimistic to talk about it. I don't want to.

O.F.: Let's do it anyway. Even on the level of political fantasy. Senator Nenni, just what would a council Republic be? What consequences would it have for us?

P.N.: Clearly it would be the marriage of two integralist groups in agreement on one point: to remove from our midst all the forces that go back to the principles of democracy and freedom. Two integralist groups that are aware, yes, of certain problems but aren't aware of others that to me are fundamental: individual freedom, democratic life. With the council Republic we'd witness the division of power between two churches: to one church, the hegemony of the state; to the other church, the hegemony of the opposition. At the same time we'd see the eventual suppression and disappearance of every intermediary force capable of applying any restraint. In substance, the Socialist party would disappear as well as the bloc of lay forces. Also to disappear would be vast sectors, Christian in inspiration, that have made a broad contribution to the secular and democratic rebirth of Italy. I'm speaking in abstract terms, you understand, because each integralist group would have to reckon with us. Look, such a marriage tempts the imagination of foreign observers, the same as the formula of "spaghetti with Chilean sauce." Abroad, in fact, the problem of the communists in the government with or without the Christian Democrats is presented as the problem of Italy. I don't consider it *the* problem. I consider it *a* problem. And the solution of this problem is still in the hands of the communists.

O.F.: What do you mean?

P.N.: I mean that the clarification of their presence in a coalition whose common denominator is democracy depends on them. This is what it doesn't seem to me the communists have done. True, sometimes they've varied their methods and tactics. Just think of the switch they made in Salerno in 1944, with Togliatti's meeting with the king. True, they've made statements. They've taken risks. But the communist objective remains the conquest of power under the more or less totalitarian hegemony of their party. Then on an international level their historical position remains within the Soviet system, which is directed from Moscow even when they express reservations on what happened in Czechoslovakia and Poland, even when they know the Soviets were ready to intervene in Warsaw as they had intervened in Prague. In short, are the communists approaching a democratic and human socialism or not? Are they about to accept this revisionism of a socialism with a new face or not?

O.F.: Senator Nenni, do you think it can happen?

P.N.: I note that it hasn't happened in the last fifty years, and not even in the last ten. Quite a long period of time. We know that in the countries they govern, every revisionist attempt to have a socialism with a human face has been crushed by violence and terror. We know that Peking calls the Soviet Union a "paradise for a group of monopolist and capitalist bureaucrats as well as a prison for millions of workers." We know that Moscow returns the compliment by calling Mao Tse-tung "one of the greatest traitors of history, comparable only to Hitler." And on these basic conflicts the Italian communists have never clearly expressed themselves. So it's absurd to take for granted something that might happen and also might not, but anyway hasn't yet happened. Everything is possible, of course—the Italian communists have already been in the government. We were there together, from 1944 to 1947. And De Gasperi at the time was frightened by their moderation. He said to me, "Look, I can't deal with you politically because, when you offer me ten, Togliatti arrives and immediately offers me fifty." Would they do the same tomorrow? Who knows? Only by examining things vigorously can we give rise to the elements of a historical process that will keep the communists on the outside. So what I've been saying for years is still valid today: communists and socialists must each play their part. But the key issue in the Italy of today, believe me, is not that of the council Republic. It's not that of spaghetti with Chilean sauce. The key issue, or rather the key problem, is the crisis of the center-left. It's the weakness of the democratic state that this crisis involves.

O.F.: And that's what I wanted to get to, Senator Nenni. The center-left is one of your creations. But must we speak of crisis and failure?

P.N.: Failure? Must we consider this experiment a failure, or shouldn't we rather examine its crisis and the points from which strength be regained? True, there have been errors on our part. There have been contradictions, delays, culpable

slowness. Worse—there's been a degeneration in the oligarchi-
cal sense of power, a corruption in the relations between public power and private interests. There's been a weakening of
ideal values. That's the reason for the discredit that's fallen on
everything and everybody, for the lack of public confidence in
the political class. But if it's right to emphasize the errors of
the center-left, it's not right to condemn totally the work of the
center-left. All the more since this is just what the right and
the communists are thinking of abundantly. Don't forget an
important thing: the center-left has not only had to face the
sores inherited from fascism, it's also had to face new phenomena and problems that are troubling the entire world. Think of
what it's meant, in the entire world, the eruption on the public scene of a younger generation that evades the control tradi-
tionally applied by the schools and the family, so as to be the
maker of its own tomorrow. Think of the new needs of the
workers, of the tragedy they've discovered with automation:
man at the service of the machine instead of the machine at
the service of man. Think of the sexual revolution and the way
it's cut into family ties. . . .

O.F.: I agree. The center-left has found itself in power at the most
difficult moment, with the old rules collapsing, cultural values
changing, and humanity going through a crisis of growth. But
other countries too have found themselves going through the
same upsets, and still they've done something about it. And
today they don't have to use the sober words that you've rightly
used: degeneration of power, corruption, weakening of ideal
values.

P.N.: I know. In the German Federal Republic the little coalition of
social democrats and liberals has only a majority of five or six
votes. And, with those five or six votes, Brandt has been able
to take on problems of historical proportions, like the agreement with the Soviet Union on the mutual renunciation of
force, and the treaty with Poland. In Italy the center-left has a
majority of a hundred votes and every day it gets stalled in
front of some difficulty or other; for the most part difficulties of
an internal kind: groups large and small, each of which claims
a slice of power, the squandering of energies, the lack of
courage and initiative. I sometimes wonder if the generation

in the middle—namely the one between mine and the one now knocking at the door—hasn't arrived too easily at the summit of power. From the school cloisters to the power game, as the Frenchman Nobécourt said in his interview with *Europeo*. No, I don't pretend that behind every man there has to be what's behind many in my generation: the burden of the battle against fascism, the misfortune of having lived through the darkest tragedies of our century. Still . . .

O.F.: Still some little obstacle might not have been so bad for them—right, Senator Nenni? They've all been born ministers, as you exclaimed one day.

P.N.: But they have problems that give them no respite. Let's be just! Look at the exodus from the countryside, hundreds of thousands of families that burst pell-mell into the cities to find themselves abruptly in contact with another reality. Look at the dizzying growth of the schools: in eight years a student population that increases from less than two million to more than seven million, without adequate school facilities or teaching staffs. Look at tax reform, health, city planning, the regional governments to be organized. These are terrible problems and they're worse in Italy than elsewhere.

O.F.: Now will you admit to being a pessimist, Senator Nenni?

P.N.: No. Nothing is irreparably compromised. There's only one possibility before which we'd be defenseless: an economic, monetary crisis, a crisis of production combined with government instability. Then, yes, the dam would burst and swamp everything. But even this can be avoided—provided we roll up our sleeves, provided we carry out reforms, provided we stop dawdling with polemics on the new equilibriums in the sphere of some future historical process. I mean the one to be carried out in the next ten years. I'm neither a prophet nor the son of prophets but I say that this argument about the new equilibriums rests on an equivocation and on a very debatable prospect: the development of the communist party. By losing ourselves in certain worries we run the risk of pursuing an illusion and destroying what's been accomplished. We risk interrupting the contribution the Christian Democrats have made to a policy of social progress and driving them back into the arms of the right.

O.F.: Senator Nenni, your refusal to be pessimistic would be acceptable if the Socialist party were what you had imagined. But it's not. It's a divided party and one through which you can no longer determine events in the country. So I'm about to ask you a brutal, and perhaps a bad, question. When you succeeded in bringing about the unification, you said, "Now I can die in peace." And today?

P.N.: Today . . . I look on these things with great regret but also without any feeling of guilt. I lost the political battle, but one must be able to accept defeat. All the more so at the age of eighty, when a man doesn't have many chances for a comeback. To recognize defeat, however, doesn't mean to consider defeat as absolute and final. I've made my contribution, for whatever it's worth. And I'd make it again if I saw that republican institutions, the democratic freedom of the masses, were in danger. I think I've made an important contribution to certain achievements. My greatest victory was the Republic—no one wanted it with a commitment equal to mine. And if I haven't been successful in consolidating socialist unification, it's because I thought that it had a foundation in the consciousness and will of the militants. Because that consciousness and will haven't stood the test, the test of our relative lack of success in the 1968 elections, of the controversy over disengagement, of the argument over new equilibriums. What do you want me to say? It's a typically Italian phenomenon, this one of divisions, of schisms. No one waits for events to prove them right or wrong; everyone wants to be right immediately. So? I wanted a party conscious of its autonomy, dedicated to winning over the working masses again and the positions lost after the schism of 1947. I wanted a party capable of creating a socialist alternative within the sphere of the center-left. With this possibility gone, I can only hope that the center-left will regain awareness of itself and become deeply engaged in the politics of things.

O.F.: Senator Nenni, isn't it that the Italians are only comfortable with dogmatisms and churches?

P.N.: No, even if they're comfortable with power, since they still haven't liquidated the heritage of past centuries of servitude to foreigners and subordination to domestic tyranny. "I have a family to support. I have six children, eight children," they always tell you. And that's one aspect of that heritage, fed by social insecurity at many social levels. By saying "I have a family to support," they give up the struggle. Or else they give it up through a skeptical, corrosive intelligence that dissolves everything. An intelligence that's the enemy of concreteness. To criticize everything and everybody is a way of criticizing nobody—it's just a way of staying outside the struggle. And that's something we're very good at. But look, it's not correct to say the Italians are only comfortable with dogmatisms and churches. To oppression and compromise they react in lively fashion. Or rather let's say they always end by reacting. And that largely compensates for the negative heritage of a national, social, and political upbringing that's undoubtedly backward compared to other nations.

O.F.: Speaking of an intelligence that dissolves things, Schlesinger said, in that interview in *Europeo*, that the real tragedy of modern Italy was the death of the Action party.

P.N.: Schlesinger knew the leaders of the Action party and rightly esteemed it because it attracted men rich in moral and intellectual qualities—men who contributed in remarkable measure to the struggle against fascism, to the advent of the Republic, to the birth of the Constitution. But it was a party outside reality, fated not to stand up with time precisely because of the kind of intelligence we mentioned: the kind that dissolves everything and creates nothing. Besides it had the misfortune to arrive at the test of power after having lost its most inspiring figure: Carlo Rosselli. I knew Carlo Rosselli, many years before the fascists murdered him and his brother in France. It was in 1925, after I had written my comrades a letter upholding the necessity of giving our battle a European look and not wasting ourselves on such anarchist activities as assassination attempts. One morning a stranger knocked at my door. I let him in and he said something like this: "I'm Carlo Rosselli, professor at the University of Genoa. I've read your letter to the leaders of the party and I liked it very much. I'm a rich man; I don't have the economic problems that hinder so many of you. I've come to ask you if we can work together." We did work together. Together we founded *Quarto Stato*, the magazine to which some of the most worthy men of the future Action party were to contribute. But, I repeat, there was a dissolving spirit in their fine intelligence. And when the Action party died . . .

O.F.: . . . those worthy men dispersed into other parties and all of us ended by being contaminated by the dissolving spirit of their fine intelligence. You in the Socialist party first of all. Is that what you mean?

P.N.: Yes, but the difficulties of the Socialist party have been of a different kind. The Socialist party is a borderline party, with its political space being undermined from left and right—in such conditions it's hard to defend yourself. A small step to the left and you risk being sucked in by the communists, a small step to the right and you risk being taken for a moderate. You have to have clear ideas if you want to defend socialism and not fall into the orbit of one or the other.

O.F.: Senator Nenni, when you speak of socialism, what do you mean? Your socialism today is not that of fifty years ago.

P.N.: Yes and no. Because, you see, the socialism of fifty years ago was directed toward projects that were in part utopian, or still utopian. It experienced, and then some, the reality of daily struggle, the struggle of the workers and peasants, but it had no models for the "city of tomorrow." Today, instead, these models exist in concrete form. They exist in the two types of socialism that have been taking shape: the communist kind and the Swedish. The communist kind has achieved the abolition of private property, but it has done so in the context of a society closed to every breath of individual freedom and democratic life, through barrack societies where state oppression is fierce. The Swedish kind has led human freedom, equality among men, the democratic life of the masses, to the highest level so far achieved, but it hasn't broken the system of capitalist ownership. I feel more at ease in Stockholm than in Leningrad. I think that in Stockholm there's a new way of conceiving life that you don't find in Leningrad. Nevertheless the problem isn't resolved by an elementary choice—it's resolved by attempting a synthesis of the two experiments; I mean a system where the sociality of the means of exchange and production is combined with the greatest freedom for man. Because

basically what is man's principal objective? To achieve the
greatest freedom: freedom from all exploitation, from all tyranny. . . . But this discussion would be more suitable for a
study club than for an interview about Italy in the 1970s.

O.F.: I don't think so. It should interest many Italians of the 1970s.
It should interest all those who have realized that they're unable to accept scientific socialism, the dogmatic socialism that
imposes itself by the negation of freedom. But do you think
your socialism can be achieved?

P.N.: Yes, even if I don't know what concrete form it will take. And
I say this because I'm not bothered anymore by the disease of
setting up a future society in advance. It's a disease that hits
everybody, sooner or later, but of which I'm now free. Besides, isn't this socialism already being realized in Italy itself
and in a great part of the world? Look, in one century socialism has become the driving force behind every struggle for
freedom and equality, the impulse behind every battle for the
independence of men and nations. It's penetrated into the
most diverse societies, even those where it doesn't seem to
exist. It's transformed not only the conditions of life and the
relations of classes, but also the relations between men and
their way of thinking, of being. Why? Because, by becoming
concrete, the very concept of socialism has taken on new characteristics. And it's shown us that in democratic societies the
state tends to become the state for everyone. In communist
countries instead, no. The dictatorship of the proletariat was
conceived by Marx as an exceptional form of power to be exer-
cised during the transition from capitalist to socialist society.
But in communist countries the dictatorship of the proletariat
has become the dictatorship of the Communist party over society and the workers. And within the party it's become the dictatorship of the party machine over the party. In the party
machine it's become the dictatorship of a charismatic leader
like Stalin. In short, we've seen that even a proletarian revolution, if not sustained by the spirit of democracy and freedom,
can degenerate into bureaucracy, technocracy, police tyranny.
The mere abolition of capitalist ownership hasn't resolved the
problem of socialization and of self-management for the
means of production and exchange. It's merged into a state

capitalism that's no different from private capitalism, or rather is just as oppressive and alienating as private capitalism. The fact is that principles are always enticing when expressed by a formula. We never realize that when translated into reality they have unforeseeable effects precisely because they emerge from a formula.

o.f.: And to think that this formula, the dictatorship of the proletariat, has convinced so many Italians. Beginning with you. But didn't you realize these things the first time you went to Russia?

p.n.: Of course. In fact, even then I was a socialist and not a communist. But there was no need to go to Russia to realize these things. We socialists have always rejected the Soviet example. Before the Soviet Union became the equal of the United States on the level of military power, it's true we defended the Bolshevik revolution. But it was because we interpreted certain facts as difficulties owing to the backward nature of Russian society, difficulties that emerged from the process of industrialization in a predominantly peasant country. What's more, engaged as we were in the struggle against Nazi fascism, we had to seek the collaboration of the communists at home and the support of the Soviet Union in the international sphere. You'll say to me: How's that? What about the Moscow trials? And after those trials, the extermination of a great part of the Bolshevik group that had guided the October Revolution? Look, I wrote four articles in *Nuovo Avanti!* which we were publishing in Paris. In those four articles I denounced the Moscow trials and denied that they had any moral or juridical merit. But I didn't draw drastic conclusions from them, I didn't make them the reason for a resounding rupture. Why? Because we were in Spain together, we socialists and communists—exposed to the same risks, which isn't important, politically tied to the success or lack of success of the Spanish Civil War, and that's very important. We knew our victory would be a very hard blow against Nazi fascism, that our defeat would accelerate Hitler's race toward war. And the rifles we were shooting were Soviet rifles, the few tanks we had available were of Soviet make. There was only Russia to help us— France and England sympathized only with words. The shock came later. It came with Hungary. And it was a really violent shock. The only thing I had never believed was that a communist country could crush a people's movement with tanks, a movement that had exploded out of a need for freedom.

O.F.: And it was then that you returned your Stalin Peace Prize.

P.N.: "Returned" is a verb I don't like because it presupposes a theatrical gesture that doesn't go with my temperament. Let's put it this way: I'd received that prize in 1952, and when the crisis broke out in Hungary, parallel with the crisis in the Middle East, it seemed to me that the prize given me for peace ought to be used for peace. Therefore I donated the sum of money to the International Red Cross, for the Hungarian refugees and for the victims of the Anglo-French war in Egypt. But what good does it do to talk about it?

O.F.: It goes to show that in Italy there are still a few honorable men. And getting back to Italy, how do you see its place in the European context?

P.N.: To speak of Italy in the European context means to speak of Europe itself. And when Joseph Alsop says that Europe doesn't exist, Europe doesn't count, he's unfortunately speaking a bitter truth. I too think that the future of the world today is no longer decided in Europe. As furthermore it's not decided only in America. By now there's an Asian component that Europeans and Americans must take into account, and I'm not speaking only of China. I'm speaking of Japan, of India. Europe would have had an immense role in the world if it had realized its political and economic unity—the great idea that emerged from the Second World War. But twenty-five years have gone by and Europe has not been united nor is it about to be. The particular interests of individual states have prevailed over the community of interests, and, on the other hand, how can we fail to understand it in an Italy where not even the municipal particularisms between Catanzaro and Reggio Calabria, Aquila and Pescara, can be overcome? Particularism in the face of European unity began in England. Then it spread to France and became De Gaulle's historical error. From this standpoint, De Gaulle did great harm to Europe, and to France as well. True, he avoided painful trials—he was probably the only one who could have liquidated the terrible Algerian adventure. But taken all together, his action was a backward one. Backward in the area of freedom, of democracy, of foreign policy. And that Europe did not unite was also partly his fault.

O.F.: You knew him too, didn't you?

P.N.: Yes, I knew him immediately after the war, when we took up the subject of the peace treaty with Italy together. A complex man. I don't say fascinating, because he was too condescending in talking to people—that couldn't fail to be irritating. But on the problems of our frontiers I found him very open. On the Val d'Aosta, for instance, he had rejected the suggestions of the military men and politicians who demanded its annexation by France. He'd accepted the same suggestions on Briga and Tenda, he told me, because a "moral sanction" was necessary against Italy for having unjustifiably entered the war against France. Look, there's one Gaullism to which I'm faithful, and it's the one of June 18, 1940, when De Gaulle rebelled against the unconditional surrender of France. But there's a Gaullism I can't accept and it's the one of 1958: the survival of the monarchical conception of the state. That too produced De Gaulle's aversion for the unity of Europe. You'll tell me: But he said no to NATO. In order to say no to NATO, he should have said yes to European unity. By themselves, the individual European countries are no longer capable of withdrawing from the influence of one bloc or the other. If today the world is more or less divided up between the United States and the Soviet Union on the basis of the status quo, it's precisely because we weren't able to create a united Europe. On that I have no doubts.

O.F.: Senator Nenni, to what degree has your life been marked by doubt?

P.N.: To a great degree, always. I carry doubt inside me, sometimes even in exaggerated form. Once I had an argument with Gramsci about doubt. And it seems to me that Renan says, "Without the presence of doubt, we lose the exact evaluation of events and things; the mania for certainty is the approach to fanaticism." By the mania for certainty you end by not allowing the opinions of others. I instead have always been ready to listen to the opinions of others and to look for positive elements in them. Doubt suits me because it requires freedom and doesn't necessarily involve the loss of faith, of the will to fight. Even with all the inevitable mistakes.

o.f.: And the inevitable sorrows, the inevitable resignation, the inevitable bitterness. All things that you have had and have in abundance. Senator Nenni, have you ever wondered if it was worth the trouble?

p.n.: Never. Not even now when my life is almost over. When I look back and think of the ideals of my youth, of the price I've paid, I have no regrets. Because I believe I've simply done what I had to do, and because it's worth the trouble to fight for a more just humanity. It's worth the trouble, believe me. I've seen a good three generations grow up before my eyes: mine, that of my children, that of my grandchildren. Looking at them, I think: These decades of struggle haven't been in vain; today people are so much better off than they were in my time. Yes, life is infinitely less harsh today. There's no comparison with the world in which I was born, and let's not speak of the world in which my father and grandfather were born. We're at such a much higher level of civic life; we've achieved such formidable progress in every area. Even in that of freedom. You seem to me bewildered by this Italy, so full of ferment and discontent. And I understand you. In fact, I'll say more. Every bewildered person ought to be an alarm bell to which we ought to listen, while all too often, we don't listen to it. But look here. When you analyze sector by sector, bit by bit, thing by thing, it looks as though everything's about to collapse. Examining the whole, you realize the structure is on its feet.

o.f.: Then why such fears, such violence, such rejection of what's been done?

p.n.: Because once a problem is solved, another immediately arises. Or others. It's a characteristic of man. Man never accepts the status quo, he never arrives at saying, "I have no more problems." He'd be in trouble if he did. Everything would sink in the mud, become debased, and would come to lack the impulse that makes life acceptable. Namely, the constant search for something better. My dear friend, life should be looked at with the pessimism of intelligence, with the critical sense of doubt, but also with the optimism of the will. When there's a will, nothing is fatal, nothing is inevitable, nothing is unchangeable. I told you at the beginning: I believe in man. Man the creator of his own destiny.

O.F.: Thank you, Senator Nenni.

Rome, April 1971

II

Mohammed Riza Pahlavi

The shah was standing and waiting for me in the middle of the magnificent salon that serves him as an office. He made no reply to the little speech by which I thanked him for granting me the interview and in silence, very coldly, extended his right hand. His handshake was stiff. Still more stiffly he asked me to be seated. And everything took place wordlessly, without a smile. His lips were as sealed as a locked door, his eyes as icy as a winter wind. You might have said he was trying to reproach me for something, and I had no idea what it was. Or was he simply inhibited by shyness, by anxiety not to lose his regal tone? Once I was seated, he too sat down: legs together and arms crossed, torso rigid (because of the bulletproof vest, I suppose, that he always wears).

Thus rigid he stared at me, remote, while I related the incident that had happened at the gate, where his bodyguard had stopped me and almost made me late for the appointment. I finally heard his voice when he replied that he was very sorry but that certain mistakes happened out of an excess of zeal. It was a sad, tired voice. Almost a voiceless voice. His face was also sad and tired. Under his white hair, woolly as a fur cap, only his enormous nose stood out. As for his body, it looked so fragile under the double-breasted gray suit, so thin, that I promptly asked him if he felt well. Very well, he replied; he'd never felt better. The news that his health was in danger was devoid of foundation, and he had wanted to lose weight because he was getting a little too fat.

We had gotten off on the wrong foot, and it took a lot to warm up the atmosphere. Now that I think of it, I succeeded only when I asked if I might light the cigarette that I'd been craving for half an hour. "You could have said so before. I've given up cigarettes myself, but I like the smell of tobacco, the smell of smoke." At this point tea was brought in, served in gold cups with gold teaspoons. But almost everything in the place was gold: the ashtray that you didn't dare dirty, the box inlaid with emeralds, the knickknacks covered with rubies and sapphires, the corners of the table. And in that absurd and irritating glare of gold, emeralds, rubies, and sapphires, I sat for about two hours, trying to fathom His Majesty. Then, suspecting that I had fathomed nothing, I asked if I might see him again. He agreed, and our second meeting took place four days later.

This time His Majesty was more cordial. To please me, I suppose, he had put on a gaudy Italian necktie, and the conversation flowed easily, if somewhat ruffled on his side by the fear that I might be on his police blacklist. The fear struck him when I had qualified one of my questions by explaining that my book on Vietnam, *Nothing, and So Be It,* had been banned from the bookstores of Teheran during Nixon's visit. At this information he had jumped up as though pricked by a knife through his bulletproof vest. His look had become restless, hostile—for God's sake, was I therefore a dangerous character? Some moments went by before he decided to overcome the dilemma in the only way possible, namely, by relinquishing his excessive composure. Thus his smile opened up and, amidst smiles, we talked about the authoritarian regime in which he believes, of his relations with the United States and the USSR, of his oil policy. Yes, we talked about everything. Only after I had left did I realize that we had not spoken of the martial crisis that he was said to be going through with Farah Diba. He had only denied to me, with anger and indignation, that he had secretly remarried.

I also realized that I still knew very little about him, perhaps less than before; despite three hours of questions and answers, the man remained a mystery. So it is not easy for me to define his character.

It is, like Bhutto's, a character in which the most paradoxical conflicts merge to reward you for your pains with an enigma. He believes in prophetic dreams, for example, in visions, in a childish mysticism, and then goes on to discuss oil like an expert (which he is). He governs like an absolute monarch, for example, and then refers to his people in the tone of one who believes in them and loves them, by leading a White Revolution that would seem to be making an effort to combat illiteracy and the feudal system. He considers women as simply graceful ornaments, incapable of thinking like a man, and then strives to give them complete equality of rights and duties. Indeed, in a society where women still wear the veil, he even orders girls to perform military service.

So who is this Mohammed Riza Pahlavi who for over thirty years has been seated solidly on the most scorching throne in the world? Does he belong to the era of flying carpets or to that of computers? Is he a relic of the Prophet Mohammed or an adjunct of the Abadan oil wells? My suspicion is that he is a highly dangerous megalomaniac, because he combines the worst of the old and the worst of the new, not only to the detriment of his own people but of others as well, Europe in particular. Also, thanks to his foolish visions, he is too firmly convinced of being the reincarnation of Darius and Xerxes, sent to this earth by God to rebuild their lost empire.

In a brilliant short story of political fantasy, the writer Paul Erdman calls him insane and attributes to him the dream of provoking and winning the Third World War. History will tell if this judgment is excessive. But meanwhile the hypotheses formulated by Erdman seem to me entirely possible. Does not Mohammed Riza Pahlavi have at his disposal the most long-lasting oil wells existing in the world and an army that for the moment lacks only the atomic bomb? What is to keep him, with his oil and his army, from occupying, for example, Saudi Arabia and Kuwait, establishing himself on all the shores of the Persian Gulf, supplanting the United States and the Soviet Union, and neutralizing both? Has he not already begun his invasion of the West by trying to buy, among other things, Pan American and Fiat?

We Europeans were naïve, indeed superficial, in our underestimation of him, seeing him as a sad and harmless monarch who spent his time agonizing over the lack of an heir. In our superficiality and naïveté, we created a figure that did not exist, and relegated him, with his courtships, his engagements, his marriages, divorces, adulteries, and promenades in Rome and Saint-Moritz, to the pages of the scandal sheets. Nearsighted, incapable of seeing beyond this façade, we never took the trouble to put on our eyeglasses and see anything else. For instance, his country's prisons and concentration camps overflowing with political prisoners, the jail cells where they were tortured by medieval means, the courtyards of the barracks where they were shot dozens at a time, under a hellish, ruthless dictatorship where even to utter the word democracy was a mortal sin. We didn't even bother to count his oil wells, which were spreading like wildfire and increasingly fortifying his power at home and abroad. Today, in effect, we are paying the price for our myopia.

I will never forget Riza Pahlavi curtly raising his forefinger, while his eyes glared with hatred, to impress on me that the price of oil would go up, up, up, tenfold. And from the nausea I felt before that gaze and that finger, there remains to me today one small satisfaction: to have made him uncomfortable at the moment in which he understood that he had made a mistake in receiving me. ("You're not on the blacklist?" "I'm on everybody's blacklist.") Then, the pleasure of discovering that even this Majesty could behave without majesty. When the interview was published, Riza Pahlavi went all out to get me to disavow his remark that the price of oil would go up, up, up, tenfold. Indignantly I refused. He reacted by stating that I had invented it. And then a little later he went ahead and raised the price.

ORIANA FALLACI: First of all, Majesty, I'd like to talk about yourself and your position as king. There are so few kings left, and I can't get out of my head something you said in another interview: "If I could do it over again, I'd be a violinist, or a surgeon, or an archaeologist, or a polo player. . . . Anything but a king."

MOHAMMED RIZA PAHLAVI: I don't remember having said those words, but if I did, I was referring to the fact that a king's job is a big headache. So it often happens that a king gets fed up with being king. It happens to me too. But that doesn't mean I'd give it up—I have too much belief in what I am and what

I'm doing for that. You see . . . when you say there are so few kings left, you're implying a question to which I can only give one answer. When you don't have monarchy, you have anarchy or oligarchy or dictatorship. And anyway monarchy is the only possible way of governing Iran. If I've been able to do something, or rather a lot, for Iran, it's due to the small detail that I happen to be king. To get things done you need power, and to keep power you shouldn't have to ask permission or advice from anybody. You shouldn't have to discuss your decisions with anyone and . . . Naturally, I may have made mistakes too. I too am human. But I still believe I have a mission to carry out to the end, and I intend to carry it out to the end without giving up my throne. You can't foresee the future, of course, but I'm convinced the monarchy in Iran will last longer than your regimes. Or should I say that your regimes won't last and mine will?

O.F.: Majesty, how many times have they tried to kill you?

M.R.P.: Twice, officially. And then . . . God only knows. But what does it matter? I don't live with the obsession of being killed. Really. I never think about it. There was a time when I did. Fifteen years ago, for instance. I said to myself, Oh, why go to that place? What if they've planned to assassinate me and they kill me? Oh, why take that plane? What if they've planted a bomb and it goes off in flight? Not any more. Now the fear of dying is something I don't feel. And courage and defiance have nothing to do with it. Such equanimity comes from a kind of fatalism, from blind faith in the fact that nothing can happen to me until the day I've carried out my mission to the end. Yes, I'll stay alive until such time as I finish what I have to finish. And that day has been set by God, not by those who want to kill me.

O.F.: Then why are you so sad, Majesty? I may be wrong, but you always have such a sad and worried look.

M.R.P.: Maybe you're right. Maybe I'm a sad man at heart. But my sadness is a mystical one, I think. A sadness that comes from my mystical side. I wouldn't know how else to explain it, since there's no reason why I should be sad. I now have everything I wanted as a man and as a king. I really have everything, my life goes forward like a beautiful dream. Nobody in the world should be happier than I, and yet . . .

O.F.: And yet a cheerful smile on your part is rarer than a shooting star. Don't you ever laugh, Majesty?

M.R.P.: Only when something funny happens to me. But it has to be something really very funny. Which doesn't happen often. No, I'm not one of those people who laugh at everything silly, but you must understand that my life has always been so difficult, so exhausting. Just think of what I had to put up with during the first twelve years of my reign. Rome in 1953 . . . Mossadegh . . . remember? And I'm not even referring to my personal sufferings—I'm referring to my sufferings as a king. Besides I can't separate the man from the king. Before being a man, I'm a king. A king whose destiny is swayed by a mission to be accomplished. And the rest doesn't count.

O.F.: My goodness, it must be a great nuisance! I mean, it must be pretty lonely being a king instead of a man.

M.R.P.: I don't deny I'm lonely. Deeply so. A king, when he doesn't have to account to anyone for what he says and does, is inevitably very much alone. But I'm not entirely alone because I'm accompanied by a force that others can't see. My mystical force. And then I get messages. Religious messages. I'm very, very religious. I believe in God, and I've always said that if God didn't exist, it would be necessary to invent him. Oh, I feel so sorry for those poor souls who don't have God. You can't live without God. I've lived with God ever since the age of five. That is, since God gave me those visions.

O.F.: Visions, Majesty?

M.R.P.: Yes, visions. Apparitions.

O.F.: Of what? Of whom?

M.R.P.: Of prophets. Oh, I'm surprised you don't know about it. Everyone knows I've had visions. I even wrote it in my autobiography. As a child I had two visions. One when I was five and one when I was six. The first time, I saw our Prophet Ali, he who, according to our religion, disappeared to return on the day when he would save the world. I had an accident—I fell against a rock. And he saved me—he placed himself between me and the rock. I know because I saw him. And not in

a dream—in reality. Material reality, if you see what I mean. I
was the only one who saw him. The person who was with me
didn't see him at all. But no one else was supposed to see him
except me because . . . Oh, I'm afraid you don't understand
me.

O.F.: Indeed I don't, Majesty. I don't understand you at all. We
had got off to such a good start, and instead now . . . This
business of visions, of apparitions . . . It's not clear to me,
that's all.

M.R.P.: Because you don't believe. You don't believe in God, you
don't believe me. Many people don't. Even my father didn't
believe it. He never believed it, he always laughed about it.
Anyway many people, albeit respectfully, ask if I didn't ever
suspect it was a fantasy. My answer is no. No, because I
believe in God, in the fact of having been chosen by God to
accomplish a mission. My visions were miracles that saved the
country. My reign has saved the country and it's saved it
because God was beside me. I mean, it's not fair for me to
take all the credit for myself for the great things that I've done
for Iran. Mind you, I could. But I don't want to, because I
know that there was someone else behind me. It was God. Do
you see what I mean?

O.F.: No, Majesty. Because . . . well, did you have these visions
only as a child, or have you also had them later as an adult?

M.R.P.: I told you, only as a child. Never as an adult—only dreams.
At intervals of one or two years. Or even every seven or eight
years. For instance, I once had two dreams in the span of fifteen years.

O.F.: What dreams, Majesty?

M.R.P.: Religious dreams. Based on my mysticism. Dreams in
which I saw what would happen in two or three months, and
that happened just that way in two or three months. But what
these dreams were about, I can't tell you. They didn't have to
do with me personally; they had to do with domestic problems
of the country and so should be considered as state secrets. But
perhaps you'd understand better if instead of the word dreams I
used the word presentiments. I believe in presentiments too.
Some believe in reincarnation, I believe in presentiments. I
have continuous presentiments, as strong as my instinct. Even

the day when they shot at me from a distance of six feet, it was my instinct that saved me. Because, instinctively, while the assassin was emptying his revolver at me, I did what in boxing is called shadow dancing. And a fraction of a second before he aimed at my heart, I moved aside in such a way that the bullet went into my shoulder. A miracle. I also believe in miracles. When you think I've been wounded by a good five bullets, one in the face, one in the shoulder, one in the head, two in the body, and that the last one stuck in the barrel because the trigger jammed . . . You have to believe in miracles. I've had so many air disasters, and yet I've always come out unscathed—thanks to a miracle willed by God and the prophets. I see you're incredulous.

O.F.: More than incredulous, I'm confused. I'm confused, Majesty, because . . . Well, because I find myself talking to a person I hadn't foreseen. I knew nothing about these miracles, these visions . . . I came here to talk about oil, about Iran, about you. . . . Even about your marriages, your divorces. . . . Not to change the subject, but those divorces must have been quite dramatic. Weren't they, Majesty?

M.R.P.: It's hard to say because my life has gone forward under the sign of destiny, and when my personal feelings have had to suffer, I've always protected myself with the thought that a particular pain was willed by fate. You can't rebel against destiny when you have a mission to accomplish. And in a king, personal feelings don't count. A king never cries over himself. He hasn't the right. A king means first of all duty, and I've always had such a strong sense of duty. For instance, when my father told me, "You're to marry Princess Fawzia of Egypt," it didn't even occur to me to object or say, "I don't know her." I agreed at once because it was my duty to agree at once. One is either a king or one isn't. If one is a king, one must bear all the responsibilities and all the burdens of being a king, without giving in to the regrets or claims or sorrows of ordinary mortals.

O.F.: Let's skip the case of Princess Fawzia, Majesty, and take that of Princess Soraya. You chose her yourself as your wife. So didn't it hurt you to repudiate her?

M.R.P.: Well . . . yes. . . . For a while, yes. I can actually say that, for a certain period of time, it was one of the greatest sorrows of my life. But reason prevailed very soon, and I asked myself the following question: What must I do for my country? And the answer was find another spouse with whom to share my destiny and from whom to ask for an heir to the throne. In other words, my feelings are never focused on private matters but on royal duties. I've always trained myself not to be concerned with myself but with my country and my throne. But let's not talk of such things—of my divorces, and so forth. I'm far above, too far above, these matters.

O.F.: Naturally, Majesty. But there's one thing I can't help asking, since I think it ought to be cleared up. Majesty, is it true you've taken another wife? Ever since the day the German press published the news . . .

M.R.P.: Slander, not news, and it was spread around by the French press agency after it had been published by the Palestinian newspaper *Al Mohar* for obvious reasons. A stupid, vile, disgusting slander. I'll only tell you that the photograph of the woman who's supposed to be my fourth wife is a photograph of my niece, the daughter of my twin sister. My niece, who besides is married and has a child. Yes, some of the press would do anything to discredit me—it's run by unscrupulous, immoral people. But how can they say that I, I who wanted the law by which it's forbidden to take more than one wife, have got married again and secretly? It's unthinkable, it's intolerable, it's shameful.

O.F.: Majesty, but you're a Muslim. Your religion allows you to take another wife without repudiating the Empress Farah Diba.

M.R.P.: Yes, of course. According to my religion, I could, so long as the queen gave her consent. And to be honest, one must admit there are cases when . . . For instance, when a wife is sick, or doesn't want to fulfill her wifely duties, thereby causing her husband unhappiness . . . after all! You'd have to be hypocritical or naïve to think a husband would tolerate such a thing. In your society, when a circumstance of that kind arises, doesn't a man take a mistress, or more than one? Well, in our society, a man can take another wife. So long as the first wife consents and the court approves. Without those two conditions on which I based my law, however, the new marriage can't take place. So I, I myself, should have broken the law by getting married in secret?! And to whom?! My niece?! My sister's daughter?! Listen, I don't even want to discuss anything so vulgar. I refuse to talk about it another minute.

O.F.: All right. Let's not talk about it any more. Let's say you deny everything, Majesty, and . . .

M.R.P.: I deny nothing. I don't even take the trouble to deny it. I don't even want to be quoted in a denial.

O.F.: How come? If you don't deny it, people will go on saying the marriage has taken place.

M.R.P.: I've already had my embassies issue a denial!

O.F.: And nobody believed it. So the denial must come from you, Majesty.

M.R.P.: But the act of denying it debases me, offends me, because the matter is of no importance to me. Does it seem right to you that a sovereign of my stature, a sovereign with my problems, should lower himself to deny his marriage with his niece? Disgusting! Disgusting! Does it seem right to you that a king, that an emperor of Persia should waste time talking about such things? Talking about wives, women?

O.F.: How strange, Majesty. If there's one monarch who's always been talked about in relation to women, it's you. And now I'm beginning to suspect that women have counted for nothing in your life.

M.R.P.: Here I'm really afraid you've made a correct observation. Because the things that have counted in my life, the things that have left their mark on me, have been quite different. Certainly not my marriages, certainly not women. Women, you know . . . Look, let's put it this way. I don't underrate them; they've profited more than anyone else from my White Revolution. I've fought strenuously so that they'd have equal rights and responsibilities. I've even put them in the army, where they get military training for six months and are then sent to the villages to fight the battle against illiteracy. And let's not forget I'm the son of the man who took away women's veils in Iran. But I wouldn't be sincere if I stated I'd been influenced by a single one of them. Nobody can influence me, nobody. Still less a woman. Women are important in a man's life only if they're beautiful and charming and keep their femininity and . . . This business of feminism, for instance. What do these feminists want? What do you want? You say equality. Oh! I don't want to seem rude, but . . . You're equal in the eyes of the law but not, excuse my saying so, in ability.

O.F.: No, Majesty?

M.R.P.: No. You've never produced a Michelangelo or a Bach. You've never even produced a great chef. And if you talk to me about opportunity, all I can say is, are you joking? Have you ever lacked the opportunity to give history a great chef? You've produced nothing great, nothing! Tell me, how many women capable of governing have you met in the course of your interviews?

O.F.: At least two, Majesty. Golda Meir and Indira Gandhi.

M.R.P.: Who knows? . . . All I can say is that women, when they govern, are much harsher than men. Much crueler. Much more bloodthirsty. I'm citing facts, not opinions. You're heartless when you have power. Think of Catherine de Médicis, Catherine of Russia, Elizabeth I of England. Not to mention your Lucrezia Borgia, with her poisons and intrigues. You're schemers, you're evil. All of you.

O.F.: I'm surprised, Majesty, because it's you who appointed the Empress Farah Diba regent should the crown prince accede to the throne while still a minor.

M.R.P.: Hm . . . well . . . Yes, if my son should become king before the required age, Queen Farah Diba would become regent. But there'd also be a council with which she'd have to consult. I, on the other hand, have no obligation to consult with anyone, and I don't consult with anyone. See the difference?

O.F.: I see it. But the fact remains that your wife would be regent. And if you took this decision, Majesty, it means you think she's capable of governing.

M.R.P.: Hm. . . . In any case, that's what I thought when I took the decision. And . . . we're not here just to talk about this, are we?

O.F.: Certainly not. Besides I haven't even begun to ask you the things that interest me most, Majesty. For example, when I try to talk about you, here in Teheran, people lock themselves in a fearful silence. They don't even dare pronounce your name, Majesty. Why is that?

M.R.P.: Out of an excess of respect, I suppose. With me, in fact, they don't behave like that at all. When I returned from America, I drove through the city in an open car, and from the airport to the palace I was wildly applauded by at least a million people overcome with enthusiasm. They cheered, they shouted patriotic slogans, they were by no means locked in silence as you say. Nothing has changed since the day I became king and the people lifted my car on their shoulders and carried it for three miles. Yes, it was three miles from the house where I lived to the building where I was to take my oath to the Constitution. And I was riding in that car. After a few yards the people lifted the car like a sedan chair and carried it on their shoulders for a good three miles. What was your question supposed to mean? That they're all against me?

O.F.: God forbid, Majesty. I meant only what I said. Here in Teheran people are so afraid of you they don't even dare pronounce your name.

M.R.P.: And why should they talk about me to a foreigner? I don't see what you're referring to.

O.F.: I'm referring to the fact, Majesty, that many people consider you a dictator.

M.R.P.: That's what they write in *Le Monde*. And what do I care? I work for my people. I don't work for *Le Monde*.

O.F.: Yes, yes, but would you deny you're a very authoritarian king?

M.R.P.: No, I wouldn't deny it, because in a certain sense I am. But look, to carry through reforms, one can't help but be authoritarian. Especially when the reforms take place in a country like Iran, where only twenty-five percent of the inhabitants know how to read and write. You mustn't forget that illiteracy is drastic here—it'll take at least ten years to eliminate it. And I don't say to eliminate it for everyone—I say to eliminate it for those who today are under the age of fifty. Believe me, when three-quarters of a nation doesn't know how to read or write, you can provide for reforms only by the strictest authoritarianism—otherwise you get nowhere. If I hadn't been harsh, I wouldn't even have been able to carry out agrarian reform and my whole reform program would have been stalemated. Once that had happened, the extreme left would have liquidated the extreme right within a few hours, and it's not only the White Revolution that would have been finished. I had to do what I did. For instance, order my troops to open fire on anyone opposing the distribution of land. So to say that in Iran there's no democracy . . .

O.F.: Is there, Majesty?

M.R.P.: I assure you, there is. I assure you that in many ways Iran is more democratic than your countries in Europe. Aside from the fact that the peasants own their land, that the workers participate in the management of the factories, that the large industrial complexes are owned by the state instead of private individuals, you should know that elections here begin in the villages and take place at local, municipal, and provincial levels. In Parliament, of course, there are only two parties. But they're the ones that accept the twelve points of my White Revolution, and how many parties ought to represent the ideology of my White Revolution? Besides those are the only two that are able to get enough votes—the minorities are so negligible, so ridiculous in size that they wouldn't even be able to elect a deputy. And be that as it may, I don't want certain minorities to elect any deputies. Just as I won't allow the Communist party. The communists are outlawed in Iran. They only want to destroy, destroy, destroy, and they swear allegiance to others instead of to their country and their king. They're traitors, and I'd be crazy to let them exist.

O.F.: Maybe I explained myself badly, Majesty. I meant democracy as we understand it in the West, namely, a regime that permits anyone to think as he likes and is based on a parliament where even minorities are represented. . . .

M.R.P.: But I don't want that kind of democracy! Don't you understand? I wouldn't know what to do with such a democracy! It's all yours, you can have it! Your wonderful democracy! You'll see, in a few years, where your wonderful democracy leads.

O.F.: Well, maybe it's a little chaotic. But it's the only thing possible if you respect man and his freedom of thought.

M.R.P.: Freedom of thought, freedom of thought! Democracy, democracy! With five-year-old children going on strike and parading through the streets. That's democracy? That's freedom?

O.F.: Yes, Majesty.

M.R.P.: Well, not to me. And let me add: how much studying have you done in the last few years in your universities? And if you go on not studying in your universities, how will you be able to keep up with the needs of technology? Won't you become servants of the Americans thanks to your lack of preparation, won't you become third- or even fourth-rate countries? Democracy freedom democracy! But what do these words mean?

O.F.: Excuse me if I take the liberty of saying it, Majesty. But in my opinion they mean, for example, not removing certain books from bookstores when Nixon comes to Teheran. I know that my book on Vietnam was removed from the bookstores when Nixon came here and put back only after he'd left.

M.R.P.: What?

O.F.: Yes, yes.

M.R.P.: But you're not on the blacklist, are you?

O.F.: Here in Teheran? I don't know. It could be. I'm on everybody's blacklist.

M.R.P.: Hm. . . . And here I'm receiving you in the palace, and you're here sitting next to me. . . .

O.F.: Which is very kind of you, Majesty.

M.R.P.: Hm. . . . It certainly shows we have democracy and freedom here. . . .

O.F.: It certainly does. But I'd like to ask you something, Majesty. I'd like to ask you: if I were an Iranian instead of an Italian, and lived here and thought as I do and wrote as I do, I mean if I were to criticize you, would you throw me in jail?

M.R.P.: Probably. If what you thought and wrote went counter to our laws, you'd be put on trial.

O.F.: Really? And sentenced too?

M.R.P.: I think so. Naturally. But, between ourselves, I don't think you'd find it easy to criticize or attack me in Iran. What would you criticize or attack me for? For my foreign policy? For my oil policy? For having distributed land to the peasants? For allowing workers to share in profits up to twenty percent and to be able to buy stock up to forty-nine percent? For fighting illiteracy and disease? For having brought progress to a country where there was little or none?

o.f.: No, no. Not for that, Majesty. I'd attack you . . . let's see. I know: for the repression carried out against students and intellectuals in Iran, for example. I've been told the prisons are so full that new arrests have to be put in army camps. Is that true? But how many political prisoners are there in Iran today?

m.r.p.: I don't know exactly. It depends on what you mean by the expression political prisoners. If you're speaking of the communists, for instance, I don't consider them political prisoners because it's forbidden by law to be a communist. Therefore a communist to me is not a political prisoner but a common criminal. If then you mean those whose actions result in the death of old people, women, innocent children, it's all the more obvious that I don't even consider them political prisoners. To them, I show no mercy. Oh, I've always pardoned those who've tried to kill me, but I've never had the slightest pity for those criminals you call guerrillas or for traitors to the country. They're the sort of people who are capable of killing my son if only to plot against public safety. They're people to be eliminated.

o.f.: In fact, you have them shot, don't you?

m.r.p.: Those who have killed people, of course. They're shot. But not because they're communists—because they're terrorists. Communists are simply sentenced to prison, for terms that may vary from a few to several years. Oh, I can imagine what you think about the death penalty, and so forth. But, you see, certain opinions depend on the type of education one has had, on culture, on climate, and you shouldn't take it for granted that what goes for one country goes for them all. Take an apple seed and plant it in Teheran, then take another seed from the same apple and plant it in Rome—the tree that grows in Teheran will never be the same as the tree that grows in Rome. Here it's right and necessary to shoot certain people. Pietism is absurd here.

o.f.: While listening to you, I was wondering something, Majesty. I was wondering what you think of the death of Allende.

m.r.p.: Here's what I think. I think his death teaches us a lesson;

you must be one thing or the other, be on one side or the other, if you want to accomplish something and win. Middle-of-the-road compromises aren't possible. In other words, either you're a revolutionary or else you insist on law and order—you can't be a law-and-order revolutionary. Much less a tolerant one. And if Allende wanted to rule in accordance with his Marxist ideas, why didn't he organize himself better? When Castro came to power, he killed at least ten thousand people, while all of you said, "Bravo, bravo, bravo!" Well, in a certain sense he deserved the bravos since he's still in power. But then so am I. And I plan on staying there by showing that with force you can do a lot of things, and I'll even prove that your socialism is finished. Old, obsolete, finished. People were talking about socialism a hundred years ago; they were writing about it a hundred years ago. Today it no longer goes with modern technology. I achieve more than the Swedes, and in fact can't you see that even in Sweden the socialists are losing ground? Ah! Swedish socialism! . . . It hasn't even national-ized forests and water. I have.

O.F.: Again, Majesty, I don't understand. Are you telling me that in a certain sense you're a socialist, and that your socialism is more modern and advanced than the Scandinavian kind?

M.R.P.: Of course. Because that socialism means a system of social security for those who don't work and nevertheless receive a salary at the end of the month like those who do work. The so-cialism of my White Revolution, on the other hand, is an in-centive to work. It's a new, original socialism, and . . . be-lieve me, in Iran we're much more advanced than you and really have nothing to learn from you. But these are things you Europeans will never write—the international press is so infiltrated by leftists, by the so-called left. Ah, this left! It's even corrupted the clergy. Even the priests! By now even they're turning into elements whose purpose is only to destroy, destroy, destroy. And even in Latin American countries, even in Spain! It seems incredible. They abuse their own church. Their own church! They talk about injustice, about equality. . . . Ah, this left! You'll see, you'll see where it'll bring you.

O.F.: Let's get back to you, Majesty. So intransigent, so harsh, maybe even ruthless, behind that sad face. In the end so simi-

lar to your father. I wonder to what extent you've been influenced by your father.

M.R.P.: None at all. Not even my father could influence me. I've
told you, nobody can influence me! Yes, I was fond of my father. Yes, I admired him. But that's all. I never tried to copy
him, to imitate him. Nor would it have been possible, even if
I'd wanted to. As personalities we were too different, and even
the historical circumstances in which we found ourselves were
too different. My father started from nothing. When he came
to power, the country had nothing. Nor did he even have the
problems we have today on the frontiers, especially with the
Russians. And my father could afford to have good neighborly
relations with everyone. The only basic threat was represented
by the British, who in 1907 had divided Iran between themselves and the Russians, and wanted Iran to constitute a kind
of no man's land between Russia and their empire in India.
But later the British gave up this plan and things became fairly
easy for my father.

I, instead . . . I didn't start from nothing, I found a throne.
But no sooner was I on the throne than I found myself having
to lead a country occupied by foreigners. And I was only
twenty-one. That's not much, twenty-one, not much. Besides,
I didn't only have to keep the foreigners in check and nothing
else. I had to face a sixth column on the extreme right and extreme left—to exert greater influence on us, the foreigners had
created the extreme right and extreme left. . . . No, it wasn't
easy for me. Maybe it was more difficult for me than for my
father. Without counting the period of the cold war, which
lasted up until a few years ago.

O.F.: Majesty, you just mentioned the problems you have on the
frontiers. Which is your worst neighbor today?

M.R.P.: You can never tell, since you never know who your worst
neighbor is. But I'd be inclined to say that at the moment it's
Iraq.

O.F.: I'm surprised, Majesty, that you should cite Iraq as your worst
neighbor. I was expecting you to say the Soviet Union.

M.R.P.: The Soviet Union. . . . With the Soviet Union we have
good diplomatic and trade relations. With the Soviet Union
we have a gas pipeline. I mean we sell gas to the Soviet

Union. Technicians come to us from the Soviet Union. And the cold war is over. But the question with the Soviet Union will always be the same, and in negotiating with the Russians, Iran must always keep in mind the chief dilemma: to become communist or not? No one can be so crazy or naïve as to deny Russian imperialism. And though Russia has always had an imperialistic policy, the fact remains it's much more dangerous today because it's linked to communist dogma. I mean to say it's easier to face countries that are only imperialist than countries that are both imperialist and communist. There's what I call the USSR's pincer movement. There's their dream of reaching the Indian Ocean by passing through the Persian Gulf. And Iran is the last bastion for the defense of our civilization, of what we consider decent. If they were to try to attack this bastion, our survival would depend solely on our capacity and will to resist. So the problem of resisting comes up from now on.

O.F.: And Iran today is pretty strong militarily, isn't it?

M.R.P.: Very strong, but not strong enough to be able to resist the Russians in case of attack. That's obvious. For instance, I don't have the atomic bomb. But I feel strong enough to resist should the Third World War break out. Yes, I said Third World War. Many think the Third World War can only break out over the Mediterranean, but I say it can break out much more easily over Iran. Oh, much more easily! It's we, in fact, who control the world's energy resources. To reach the rest of the world, oil doesn't go through the Mediterranean, it goes through the Persian Gulf and the Indian Ocean. So if the Soviet Union were to attack us, we'd resist. And we'd probably be overcome, and then the noncommunist countries could hardly sit there with their hands folded. And they'd intervene. And it would be the Third World War. Obviously. The noncommunist world couldn't accept the disappearance of Iran, because it knows that to lose Iran would mean to lose everything. Have I made myself clear?

O.F.: Perfectly clear. And horribly. Because you talk of the Third World War like something that's going to happen in the near future, Majesty.

M.R.P.: I speak of it as something possible with the hope that it won't happen. As a possibility for the near future, I see instead a small war with one of our neighbors. After all, we have nothing but enemies on our frontiers. It's not only Iraq that's giving us trouble.

O.F.: And your great friend, Majesty, I mean the United States, is geographically remote.

M.R.P.: If you're asking me who I consider our best friend, the answer is the United States among others. Because the United States isn't our only friend—plenty of countries show us friendship and believe in us, in the importance of Iran. But the United States understands us better for the simple reason that it has so many interests here. Economic and therefore direct interests, political and therefore indirect interests. . . . I've just said that Iran is the key, or one of the keys, to the world. I need only add that the United States cannot shut itself up within the borders of its country, it cannot go back to the Monroe Doctrine. It's obliged to honor its responsibilities toward the world and thus to be concerned with us. And that does nothing to detract from our independence, because everyone knows that our friendship with the United States doesn't make us slaves of the United States. The decisions are made here, in Teheran. Not elsewhere. Not in Washington, for example. I get along with Nixon as I've got along with other presidents of the United States, but I can continue to get along with him only if I'm sure that he's treating me as a friend. In fact, as a friend who within a few years will represent a world power.

O.F.: The United States is also good friends with Israel, and you've expressed yourself lately toward Jerusalem in very harsh terms. Less harshly toward the Arabs, on the other hand, with whom it seems you want to improve relations.

M.R.P.: We base our policy on fundamental principles, and we cannot accept the idea that a country, in this case Israel, should annex territory through the use of arms. We can't because if this principle is applied to the Arabs, it may one day be applied to us. You'll tell me it's always been like this, that frontiers have always changed as a result of the use of arms and war. I agree, but that's no reason to recognize this fact as a valid principle. Besides everyone knows that Iran has accepted the UN resolution of 1967, and if the Arabs lose faith in the UN, how are you to persuade them that they've been defeated? What's to keep them from taking their revenge? Even from using the oil weapon? Oil will go to their heads. Besides it's already going to their heads.

O.F.: Majesty, you side with the Arabs but sell oil to the Israelis.

M.R.P.: Oil is sold by the oil companies, and so to anyone. Our oil goes everywhere—why shouldn't it go to Israel? And why should I care if it goes to Israel? It goes where it goes. And as for our personal relations with Israel, as you know, we have no embassy in Jerusalem but we have Israeli technicians in Iran. We're Muslims but not Arabs. And in foreign policy we take a very independent position.

O.F.: Does such a position foresee the day when Iran and Israel will establish normal diplomatic relations?

M.R.P.: No. Or rather, not until the question of the withdrawal of Israeli troops from the occupied territories has been resolved. And as for the possibilities of this question being resolved, I can only say that the Israelis have no choice—if they want to live in peace with the Arabs. It's not only the Arabs who spend enormous sums of money on war materials, it's also the Israelis. And I don't see how either the Arabs or Israelis can keep it up for long. Besides, new phenomena are beginning to occur in Israel—strikes, for example. How long will Israel go on nursing the terrible and fantastic spirit that inspired it at the time of its formation? I'm thinking especially of the new generations in Israel, and of the Israelis who come from Eastern Europe to find themselves treated differently from the others.

O.F.: Majesty, you said something a while ago that struck me. You said Iran would soon represent a world power. Were you perhaps referring to the forecasts of those economists who say that within thirty-six years Iran should be the richest country in the world?

M.R.P.: To say it will become the richest country in the world is perhaps going too far. But to say it will rank among the five greatest and most powerful countries in the world isn't going too far at all. Thus Iran will find itself at the same level as the United States, the Soviet Union, Japan, and France. I don't mention China because China isn't a rich country, nor can it become one if within twenty-five years it reaches the 1,400,000,000 inhabitants that have been predicted. We, on the other hand, in twenty-five years will be 60,000,000 at most. Oh, yes, we can expect great wealth, and great strength, whatever the communists may say. It's no coincidence that I'm getting ready to launch a birth control program. And here's the point I want to make: you can't separate the economy from other things, and once a country is rich economically, it becomes rich in every sense. It becomes powerful on an international level. Besides, when speaking of the economy, I'm not only referring to oil—I'm referring to a balanced economy that includes every kind of production, from the industrial to the agricultural, from handicrafts to electronics. We should have made the transition from carpets to computers— the result, instead, is that we've kept the carpets while adding the computers. We still make carpets by hand, but we also make them by machine. What's more, we make wall-to-wall carpeting. Every year we double our national production. Anyway there are so many signs that we'll become a world power. Ten years ago, for instance, when my White Revolution began, there were only 1,000,000 students in the schools. Today there are 3,100,000, and in ten years there'll be 5,000,000 or 6,000,000.

O.F.: You've just said that you weren't only referring to oil, Majesty, but we all know that it's thanks to oil that you have computers, and that it's thanks to oil that you turn out machine-made rugs, and that tomorrow's riches are also coming to you thanks to oil. Shall we finally talk about the policy you've adopted concerning oil and with regard to the West?

M.R.P.: It's simple. I have this oil and I can't drink it. But I know I can exploit it to the utmost without blackmailing the rest of the world and even by trying to keep it from being used to blackmail the rest of the world. Therefore I've chosen a policy of guaranteeing its sale to everyone without distinction. It hasn't been a difficult choice—I've never thought of aligning myself with the Arab countries that were threatening to blackmail the West. I've already said that my country is independent, and everyone knows that my country is Muslim but not Arab, therefore what I do is not to suit the Arabs but to help

Iran. Besides Iran needs money, and with oil you can make a lot of money. Oh, that's the whole difference between me and the Arabs. Because the countries that say "we won't sell any more oil to the West" don't know what to do with their money and so they don't worry about the future. Often they have a population of only six or seven hundred thousand inhabitants and so much money in the bank that they could live for three or four years without pumping or selling a drop of oil. Not I. I have these thirty-one and a half million inhabitants, and an economy to develop, a program of reforms to complete. Therefore I need money. I know what to do with money, and I can't afford not to pump oil. I can't afford not to· sell it to anyone.

O.F.: Meanwhile Qaddafi calls you a traitor.

M.R.P.: Traitor?!? Me a traitor, when I've taken the whole business into my hands and already dispose of fifty-one percent of the production that formerly belonged exclusively to foreign oil companies? I wasn't aware Mr. Qaddafi had addressed such an insult to me and . . . Look, I can't take this Mr. Qaddafi at all seriously. I can only wish him success in serving his country as I succeed in serving mine, I can only remind him that he shouldn't scream so much—the Libyan oil reserves will be exhausted in ten years' time. My oil, on the other hand, will last at least thirty or forty years. And maybe fifty, sixty. It depends on whether or not we discover new deposits, and it's very, very likely that new deposits will be discovered. But even if that shouldn't happen, we'll manage extremely well just the same. Our production is visibly increasing—in 1976 we'll be extracting as much as eight million barrels a day. Eight million barrels are a lot, quite a lot.

O.F.: In any case, you've made quite a few enemies, Majesty.

M.R.P.: That I still can't say. In fact, the OPEC hasn't yet decided not to sell oil to the West, and it may very well be that my decision not to blackmail the West will induce the Arabs to follow my example. If not all the Arabs, at least some of them. If not right away, in a short time. Some countries aren't in-dependent like Iran, they haven't the experts Iran has, and they don't have the people behind them as I do. I can dictate my own terms. They still can't. It's not easy to reach a point where you can sell your oil directly and be free of the oil companies that have had a monopoly for decades and decades. And if even the Arab countries were to follow my decision . . . Oh, it would be so much simpler, and safer too, if the Western countries were exclusively buyers and we direct sellers! There'd be no resentment, blackmail, rancor, hostility. . . . Yes, it may very well be that I'm setting a good example, and in any case I'm going ahead with it. Our doors are wide open to anyone who wants to sign a contract with us, and many have already offered to do so. British, Americans, Japanese, Dutch, Germans. They were so shy in the beginning. But now they're becoming ever more daring.

O.F.: And the Italians?

M.R.P.: We're not selling much oil to the Italians at the moment, but we may reach an important agreement with ENI * and I think we're on the way to doing so. Yes, we may become excellent partners with ENI, and anyway our relations with the Italians have always been good. Ever since the time of Mattei. Wasn't the agreement I signed with Mattei in 1957 my first success in breaking the old system of exploitation by foreign oil companies? Oh, I don't know what others say about Mattei, but I know I'll never be able to be objective in talking about him. I liked him too much. He was a very decent fellow, and a man capable of reading the future, a really exceptional personality.

O.F.: As a matter of fact, they killed him.

M.R.P.: Probably. But he shouldn't have been flying in that bad weather. The fog in Milan gets very thick in winter, and oil can really become a curse. But maybe it wasn't just the bad weather. And anyway it was a great shame. For us too. Well, I'm not saying that Mattei's death brought about a setback in our relations with ENI. No, no, since we're about to conclude a large deal. Mattei couldn't have done any better, since what we're about to do now is really the maximum. Still if Mattei had lived, we'd have reached this agreement years ago.

O.F.: I'd like to go back and clarify the point you mentioned before, Majesty. Do you or don't you think that the Arabs will end by

---

* Ente Nazionale Idrocarburi—National Hydrocarbon Authority. (Translator's note.)

carrying out their threat to cut off all sales of oil to the West?

M.R.P.: It's hard to say. Very hard, because one can just as easily say yes or no, with an equal chance of being wrong. But I'd be inclined to say no. To cut off oil to the West, to give up that source of profit, would be a very difficult decision for them. Not all the Arabs are following Qaddafi's policy, and while some may not need money, others certainly do.

O.F.: And meanwhile the price of oil will go up?

M.R.P.: It certainly will. Oh, most certainly! You can carry back the bad news and add that it comes from someone who knows what he's talking about. I know everything there is to know about oil, everything. It's really my specialty. And I tell you as a specialist that the price of oil will have to go up. There's no other solution. But it's a solution you Westerners have brought on yourselves. Or, if you like, a solution brought on by your overcivilized industrial society. You've increased the price of wheat by three hundred percent, and the same for sugar and cement. You've sent the price of petrochemicals skyrocketing. You buy crude oil from us and then sell it back to us, refined into petrochemicals, at a hundred times what you paid for it. You make us pay more for everything, scandalously more, and it's only fair that from now on you should pay more for oil. Let's say . . . ten times more.

O.F.: Ten times more?!

M.R.P.: But you're the ones, I repeat, who force me to raise prices! And certainly you have your reasons. But I too, if I may say so, have mine. Besides we won't go on quarreling forever—in less than a hundred years this business of oil will be finished. The need for oil is rising at an accelerated pace, the oil deposits are being exhausted, and you'll soon have to find new sources of energy. Atomic, solar, or something. There'll have to be many solutions; one won't be enough. For example, we'll even have to resort to turbines driven by the ocean tides. Even I'm thinking of building atomic installations for desalinating sea water. Or else we'll have to drill more deeply, look for oil at ten thousand meters below sea level, look for it at the North Pole . . . I don't know. I know only that the moment has come to take strong measures and not waste oil as we've always done. It's a crime to use it as we do today, crude. If

we'd only think that soon there won't by any more, if we'd
only remember that it can be transformed into ten thousand
derivatives, namely, petrochemical products. . . . For me it's
always a shock, for instance, to see crude oil used for electrical
generators, without paying any heed to the value lost. Oh,
when you talk about oil, the most important thing isn't the
price, it's not Qaddafi's boycott, it's the fact that oil is not ever-
lasting and that before we exhaust it we must invent new
sources of energy.

o.f.: This curse we call oil.

m.r.p.: Sometimes I wonder if that's not really what it is. So much
has been written about the curse we call oil, and believe me,
when you have it, on the one hand it's a blessing but on the
other it's a great inconvenience. Because it represents such a
danger. The world could blow up on account of this damned
oil. And even if, like me, you're fighting the threat . . . I see
you're smiling. Why?

o.f.: I'm smiling, Majesty, because you're so different when you
talk about oil. You light up, you vibrate, you concentrate your
attention. You become another man, Majesty. And I . . . I'm
going away without having understood you. On the one hand,
you're so ancient, on the other so modern and . . . Maybe it's
the two elements that merge in you, the Western and the
Eastern that . . .

m.r.p.: No, we Iranians aren't all that different from you Europeans. If our women wear the veil, so do yours. The veil of
the Catholic Church. If our men have more than one wife, so
do yours. The wives you call mistresses. And if we believe in
visions, you believe in dogmas. If you think yourselves superior, we have no complexes. Don't ever forget that whatever
you have, we taught you three thousand years ago.

o.f.: Three thousand years ago . . . I see now you're smiling too,
Majesty. You don't look so sad any more. Ah, it's too bad we
can't agree on the business of the blacklists.

m.r.p.: But can you really be on the blacklist?

o.f.: Majesty! As if you didn't know, you the King of Kings and
who knows everything! But I told you, it may well be. I'm on
everybody's blacklist.

M.R.P.: What a pity. Or rather, it doesn't matter. Even if you're on
the blacklist of my authorities, I'll put you on the white list of
my heart.

O.F.: You frighten me, Majesty. Thank you, Majesty.

Teheran, October 1973

12

Helder Camara

———◆———

His church was a poor church in the city of Recife, there in the north of Brazil where the only thing beautiful is the sea and, being close to the equator, it is always hot. That year it had never rained, and the drought had killed plants, children, hopes. It had killed nothing else because there was nothing else in Recife except dozens and dozens of baroque churches, coated by time with a black patina of dirt that no one thinks to clean. His church instead was clean, white as his good conscience. There the only dirt was the inscription in blood-red paint, which he had whitewashed over, but the paint showed through and the inscription was legible. It said, "Morte ao bispo vermelho." Death to the Red Bishop. It had been left there not long before by his persecutors, when they fired those machine-gun bursts at him and threw hand bombs. And since then the little church plaza was almost always deserted; many people were afraid to go near it. If you asked a policeman, "Por favor onde está a Igreja das Fronteiras?" he looked at you suspiciously and jotted down the license number of your taxi. It happened to me. The taxi driver was quaking with terror.

His house was attached to the church and hardly seemed the dwelling of an archbishop. Clothed in soft fabrics, covered with jewels, waited on by obsequious footmen, archbishops usually live in palaces with entrances on elegant streets. His instead could be reached by a street perpendicular to the little plaza, Rua das Fronteiras, and was enclosed by the low wall against which they had fired their machine guns. In this low wall you hardly noticed the little door with its green enamel paint, and the bell with no name. You rang the bell, some chickens fluttered, a cock crowed, and mingling with this noise a soft voice was heard: "I'm coming, I'm coming!" Then the door opened, cautiously at first, then widely, but still hesitantly, and there stood a little man in a black cassock. On the cassock a wooden cross suspended by a steel chain caught the eye. The little man was pale, bald, with a wrinkled face, a witty mouth, a little nose like a boiled chestnut, and the tired eyes of one who doesn't get much sleep. He had the innocuous, humble look of a parish priest.

He was not, he is not, a parish priest, and not even a little man. He is the most important man you can meet in Brazil, or rather in all of Latin America. And perhaps the most intelligent, the most courageous. He is Dom Helder Camara, the archbishop who defies the government and denounces the injustices, abuses, and infamies about which others keep silent, who has the guts to preach socialism and say no to violence. More than once he was up for the Nobel Peace Prize. Many call him a saint. If the word saint means anything, I too say he's a saint.

The Brazilian government does not think so. The Brazilian government is perhaps the most fascist, most sinister government that exists in Latin America. For those who oppose it by demanding freedom, its police inflict tortures that surpass any imagining. They use the *pau de arara*, or parrot's perch, which consists of a pole similar to the one on which parrots swing. Of iron or wood, it is inserted between the knees and the arm sockets of the naked victim, then hoisted up and held halfway between the floor and the ceiling. Here the victim remains hanging during the interrogation, and since his feet and ankles are bound tightly by cords, the blood circulation is stopped and the body swells as though about to explode, as though its weight had increased tenfold.

And then, for those opponents who demand freedom, there is the "hydraulic method," which consists of a flexible tube; the tube is introduced into the victim's nose and water poured into it while the mouth is held shut. Thus the victim feels he is drowning, and in fact it is a partial drowning—to be interrupted a little before the moment of death. And then, for those opponents who demand freedom, there are electric shocks to be applied to the ears, genitals, anus, and tongue. The charge is generally of 110 volts but may go up to 230, and it produces epileptic seizures, violent convulsions, third-degree burns, sometimes death, as has happened in a great many cases, including the one of a journalist who received a charge of 230 volts in the anus. He died at once.

Such tortures are inflicted on all those who fall into the hands of the DOPS, the Division of Public and Social Order, the Brazilian military criminal police. They are inflicted on liberals and communists, nuns and priests, guerrillas and students, even foreign citizens. The prisons in Brazil are full, and have been for many years. You know when you go in but you never know when you'll come out. If you come out alive, in eighty cases out of a hundred you come out mutilated—with a broken spine, paralyzed legs, crushed testicles, eyes and ears that no longer function. The literature on this infamy is endless. You can find it in the mimeographed sheets issued by resistance organizations, in American and European newspapers, in embassy dispatches. Even if the world often forgets, because Brazil is far away, because Brazil is a vacationland filled with sea, music, sambas, coffee, because it is not "convenient" to disturb the trade relations between democratic countries and dictatorships, even though the tragedy is public knowledge.

But beware of talking about it in Brazil, beware of making allusions to it or denouncing it. And most people keep silent. Helder Camara is the only one who dares to raise his voice, together with a small group of prelates who have not forgotten the Gospels. But he pays for it—God, how he pays! When in Paris he described the tortures inflicted on political prisoners in the jails of São Paulo, Rio de Janeiro, Belo Horizonte, Pôrto Alegre, Recife, they called him "traitor," "defamer," "demagogue." When he fired off his accusations from the little house in Rua das Frontieras, they fired back their machine guns and wrote *Morte ao bispo vermelho* on the wall. And so these infamous Brazilian authorities consider him a public menace, and keep careful watch on his every gesture, his every encounter.

The people instead worship him. They turn to him as to a father who never rejects them and is ready to receive them at any hour of the day or night. If he's not at home, it means he has gone to see an oppressed person in some prison, some hovel, some village where people die of hunger and thirst before reaching the age of forty and where death is a merciful liberation. If then he is not in Recife, it means he is traveling about the world, to shout out his message and his indignation, now in Berlin, now in Kyoto, now in Detroit, now in the Vatican—his emaciated arms raised to heaven and his fingers tensed claws reaching for God. Though nonviolent, he is a man who has chosen combat, cost what it may. And the fortresses he attacks are the fortresses of shame, privilege, dictatorship. He spares no one: neither Catholics nor Marxists, neither capitalist empires nor communist ones, but least of all does he spare the fascists, whom he thrashes with the anger of a Christ determined to drive the Pharisees from the temple.

Dom Helder Camara was born in Fortaleza, in the northeast of Brazil, in 1909. His father was a tradesman who dabbled in journalism and theatrical criticism, his mother a teacher in an elementary school. A *petit bourgeois* origin. And he never knew wealth— five other children in the family died a few months apart, of dysentery and lack of treatment. He went to the seminary very early, as a boy. His vocation burst out at the age of eight, he says—mysteriously and insistently. From then on he never conceived any other commitment for himself except that of a priest. He became a priest toward the age of twenty-two, when he became a fascist. Yes, for some time he was a fascist. "In every one of us sleeps a fascist and sometimes he never wakes up; sometimes instead he does." He tells it without shame, scourging himself by this admission, and the only justification he offers is when he explains that it was his bishop who asked him to become a fascist. One of those bishops clothed in soft fabrics, covered with jewels, waited on by obsequious footmen, and who live in palaces with entrances on elegant streets. One of those whose motto is God-Fatherland-Family.

Ah, yes, he knows the fascists well, Dom Helder does. He knew them long before he landed in this little church in Recife, in this little house where the hens flutter inside, and where he gets only four hours of rest out of twenty-four because at night they awaken him by continually telephoning insults to frighten him: "We're coming to get you now and kill you, you dirty communist." "Commend your soul to God because you won't live to see the morning, you ugly son of a bitch." But he says it doesn't matter; four hours of sleep a night are enough for him.

I interviewed him there, in the course of three days. We spoke in French, a language he knows well, and very often he seemed to me more like a political leader than a priest. He had the impassioned voice of a leader, the shining eyes, the sureness of one who knows he's believed. Every half hour he got up and went to make me a coffee. Then he came back with the coffee and cookies, taking the occasion to peer out into the street, to check that no one was there to daub the wall again or throw a bomb. I followed him with my gaze and thought of Camilo Torres, the young priest who had put away his cassock to shoulder a gun and had died in his first combat, a bullet in the middle of his forehead. I thought of Father Tito de Alencar, the young Dominican whom the DOPS had tortured in São Paulo with all the inhumanity of the Inquisition. Open your mouth and we'll give you the consecrated host before killing you. Then instead of the host, they gave him a charge of 222 volts on the tongue. I thought of all the priests and nuns who fill the prisons of Latin America and die in their sufferings, while the bishops clothed in soft fabrics, covered with jewels, and waited on by obsequious footmen collaborate with the generals in power and protect the executioners. In Brazil, in Chile, in Uruguay, Paraguay, Venezuela, Guatemala. And I came to the conclusion: "They won't give you the Nobel Peace Prize, Dom Helder. They'll never give it to you. You're too disturbing.

And indeed they didn't give it to him. In 1971 they gave it to Willy Brandt, and in 1973 when his name came up again, they gave it to Henry Kissinger and Le Duc Tho. And Le Duc Tho, thank heaven, refused it. Not Kissinger. As we all know.

ORIANA FALLACI: There's a rumor, Dom Helder, that Paul VI calls you "my red archbishop." And as a matter of fact, you can hardly be a convenient man for the Vatican. You must scare a lot of people inside it. Shall we talk about this a little?

HELDER CAMARA: Look, the pope knows very well what I say and do. When I denounce the tortures in Brazil, the pope knows it. When I fight for political prisoners and the poor, the pope knows it. When I travel abroad to plead for justice, the pope knows it. He's known my opinions for some time because we've known each other for some time. Since 1950, to be exact, when he was prosecretary of state for ordinary affairs. I don't hide anything from him; I never have. And if the pope felt it was wrong for me to do what I'm doing, if he were to tell me to stop, I'd stop. Because I'm a servant of the Church and I know the value of sacrifice.

But the pope doesn't tell me that, and if he calls me his "red archbishop," he does it jokingly, affectionately, certainly not the way they do here in Brazil where anyone who's not a reactionary is said to be a communist or in the service of the communists. The accusation doesn't touch me. If I were an agitator, a communist, I wouldn't be able to go to the United States and receive *honoris causa* degrees from American universities. Having said that, however, I should make it clear that by my ideas and speeches I don't pledge the authority of the pope—what I say and do is my exclusive personal responsibility. Which doesn't make me a hero—I'm not the only one to speak out. The tortures in Brazil, for instance, have been denounced first and foremost by the papal commission, which does pledge the authority of the pope. The pope himself has condemned them, and his condemnation counts for much more than that of a poor priest who doesn't scare anyone in the Vatican.

O.F.: A poor priest who's a prince of the Church, who's one of the most admired and respected men in the world. A poor priest to whom they're thinking of giving the Nobel Peace Prize. A poor priest who when he speaks of the tortures succeeds in filling the whole Palais de Sport in Paris and awakening the conscience of millions of people in every country. Shall we talk about this, Dom Helder?

H.C.: Well, it was like this. I was in Paris and they asked me to tell what was going on. I said sure, it's also a priest's duty to inform people, especially with regard to a country like Brazil where the press is controlled or subservient to the government. I began by reminding the French that I'd be talking about a crime quite familiar to themselves, who had been guilty of it during the Algerian war: torture. I added that such infamies also happened through the weakness of us Christians, who are too accustomed to bowing before power and its institutions or else to keeping silent. I explained that I wouldn't be telling anything new because it was no longer a secret that inhuman sufferings, like those of the Middle Ages, are inflicted on political prisoners in Brazil—irrefutable documentation had already been published everywhere.

Then I described the methods of torture—from electric shocks to the *pau de arara*. And I related incidents that I myself had checked. For example, the case of a student to whom they did such horrible things that he threw himself from the window of a police station. Luis De Ledeiros is his name. And the story goes essentially like this. As soon as I learned that Luis De Ledeiros was in the hospital, I rushed there together with one of my advisers. And I was able to see him. Quite aside from the attempt at suicide, he was in frightful condition. Among other things, they had torn out four of his fingernails and crushed his testicles. Those are two regular tortures, tearing out fingernails and crushing testicles. The doctor who was taking care of him confirmed this to me and said, "Go to the governor, he's a doctor, tell him to come here and examine the bodies of the tortured." It was just what I was looking for: to have in my hands, finally, a direct witness. I went immediately to the governor's palace, with my auxiliary bishop, and made the denunciation. Then I forwarded the denunciation to all the parishes, all the bishops, and to the conference of bishops.

O.F.: Some bishops don't believe it, Dom Helder, and they side with those who deny the tortures. How do you judge these men?

H.C.: How do you want me to judge them! By hoping that God will enlighten them, make them worthy of their responsibilities. I've always been for the pluralism of the Church, but when I see the ones who represent the putrid part of the Church, I get the urge to say what Pope John said to certain individuals: "Dear Father, don't you know you're really rotten? The spirit of God has never got to you, has it?" Good Lord, it was legitimate at first, or almost, to have doubts about the tortures. There was no proof. But to doubt it today is grotesque. Examples have been published in the report of the World Association of Jurists—with names, surnames, dates. And then how many priests are in prison? They're not the majority since it's more convenient to arrest a layman than a priest, to torture a layman than a priest, but there are still many and they're valuable witnesses if you can succeed in getting to them. I say "if" because today in Brazil when you go to prison, it becomes impossible to let anyone know and to get in touch with a relative or lawyer. But even that's not the worst thing—it's the silence of the press and citizens. Neither one nor the other dares speak out, and so it looks as though the people are in accord with the regime, that the victims are telling falsehoods or exaggerating. I can only hope that the scandal that's broken out in the world press and the intervention of the world Church will help to improve things.

O.F.: What happened to you, Dom Helder, after the statements you made in Paris?

H.C.: To denounce the tortures in Brazil is considered by the government a crime against the fatherland. And on this point too there's a certain divergence of views between me and the government. In fact, I consider it a crime against the fatherland not to denounce them. So I left Paris thinking, We'll see what happens to you, Dom Helder, when you get back to Brazil. Nothing happened. I went quietly through the police, the customs, and went home. True, there were attacks in the press. Curious, funny attacks. But I don't care about those, since I rarely read the newspapers, so as to avoid getting bitter. Besides it's useless to try to intimidate me; in my heart there are no doubts, and what's in my heart goes directly to my lips. I say to my flock, in my pastoral visits, in my sermons, the same things I'm saying to you. Nor can they drown me out, since in the exercise of my office I recognize no other authority but the pope. Of course, I'm forbidden to speak on the radio, on television, and since I'm not naïve I'm aware that sooner or later they might deprive me of my civil rights. For whatever those are worth, since in Brazil no one can exercise the vote, there are no elections. But on the whole I enjoy a certain freedom; they only bother me with threats.

O.F.: What kind of threats?

H.C.: Death threats, no? Machine-gun fire, bombs, telephone calls, and slander addressed to the Vatican. You must know that here in Brazil there's an extreme rightist movement called "Family and Security." They started using that to harass me some time ago. They approached people on their way to church and asked them, "Are you for or against communism?" The people said against, naturally, and so they collected signatures and then sent them to the pope, asking him to "throw out that communist Dom Helder." The pope never gave it any importance, and neither did I.

But then later there arose a clandestine movement, a kind of Brazilian Ku Klux Klan, a so-called Communist-hunting Command, or CCC. This CCC takes a particular interest in houses where suspected communists live, and it fires machine guns at us, or throws hand bombs, and writes insults on the walls. And they've paid their respects to me several times this way: twice here at home where they ruined the wall with machine-gun fire and made a mess on the wall of the church, once at the archbishop's palace, once at the Catholic Institute, once in another church where I'm accustomed to going. Always leaving the signature CCC. But they've never injured me. On the other hand, they shot a student I know in the spine and now he's paralyzed forever. A twenty-seven-year-old collaborator of mine, Henrique Pereira Neto, a sociology teacher at the University of Recife, who preached the Gospels in the *favelas*, the slums; we found him hanged to a tree and his body riddled with bullets. Things that in Recife are no longer surprising.

O.F.: No longer surprising?!

H.C.: No, like the telephone threats. I've got used to them by now. They call me at night, at hour or half-hour intervals, and say, "You're an agitator, a communist, get ready to die, we're on our way, and we're going to show you what hell looks like." What idiots. I don't even answer them. I smile and hang up the receiver. But why do you pick it up in the first place? you'll ask. Because it's my duty to answer the telephone. It could be someone who's sick, who needs me, who's asking for help. Am I a priest or not? During the world championship soccer matches they calmed down a little. For those days they only thought about the game. But then they started up again, and last night too they didn't let me pray or get any sleep.

Every half hour, ring-ring! "Hello, we're coming to kill you."
Idiots! They still haven't understood that it's no use killing me;
there are plenty of priests like me.

O.F.: Unfortunately not, Dom Helder. Rather there are very few.
But let's go back to that nickname of "red archbishop." What
are your political views today? Are you a socialist, as people
say, or not?

H.C.: Of course I am! God created man in his own image and like-
ness, because he was his cocreator and not because he was a
slave. How can we allow the majority of men to be exploited
and made to live like slaves? I don't see any solution in capitalism. But neither do I see it in the socialist examples that are
offered us today, because they're based on dictatorships, and
you don't arrive at socialism with dictatorship. Dictatorship we
have already—that's my *idée fixe.* Yes, the Marxist experiment
is amazing—I admit that the Soviet Union has had great success in changing its own structures, I admit that Red China
has shot ahead in a still more extraordinary way. But when I
read what's happening in the Soviet Union, in Red China, the
purges, the informers, the arrests, the fear, I find such a strong
parallel with rightist dictatorships and fascism! When I observe
the coldness with which the Soviet Union behaves toward underdeveloped countries, Latin America for instance, I find it
so identical with the coldness of the United States! I might try
to see some example of my socialism, perhaps, in certain
countries outside the Russian or Chinese orbit—Tanzania,
perhaps, Czechoslovakia before they crushed it. But not even
there. My socialism is a special socialism, a socialism that respects the human person and goes back to the Gospels. My socialism is justice.

O.F.: Dom Helder, there's no word so exploited as the word justice.
There's no more utopian word than justice. What do you
mean by justice?

H.C.: Justice doesn't mean assigning everyone an identical quantity
of goods in an identical way. That would be dreadful. It would
be as though everyone had the same face and the same body
and the same voice and the same brain. I believe in the right
to have different faces and different bodies and different voices
and different brains—God can afford the risk of being judged

unjust. But God is not unjust and wants that there be no privileged and oppressed, he wants for each to receive what's essential for living—while remaining different. So what do I mean by justice? I mean a better distribution of goods, both on a national and international scale. There's an internal colonialism and an external colonialism. To demonstrate the latter all you have to do is remember that eighty percent of this planet's resources are in the hands of twenty percent of its countries, namely in the hands of the superpowers or the nations that serve the superpowers. Just to give two small examples: in the last fifteen years the United States has earned a good eleven billion dollars on Latin America—that figure is supplied by the statistical bureau of Detroit University. Or just say that for a Canadian tractor Jamaica has to pay the equivalent of thirty-two hundred tons of sugar. . . . To demonstrate internal colonialism, on the other hand, all you have to do is think of Brazil. In northern Brazil there are areas that it would be generous to call underdeveloped. Other areas remind you of prehistory: people there live as in the time of the caves and are happy to eat what they find in the garbage. And what can I tell these people? That they have to suffer to go to Paradise? Eternity begins here on earth, not in Paradise.

o.f.: Dom Helder, have you read Marx?

h.c.: Sure. And I don't agree with his conclusions but I do agree with his analysis of capitalist society. Which doesn't give anyone the right to pin the label of honorary Marxist on me. The fact is that Marx should be interpreted in the light of a reality that has changed, that is changing. I always tell young people it's a mistake to take Marx literally; Marx should be utilized while keeping in mind that his analysis is of a century ago. Today, for instance, Marx wouldn't say that religion is an alienated and alienating force. Religion deserved that judgment but such a judgment is no longer valid; look what's happening with the priests of Latin America. Everywhere. Besides many communists know it. People like the Frenchman Garaudy know it, and it doesn't matter if people like Garaudy are expelled from the Communist party—they exist and they think, they incarnate what Marx would say in our time. What can I say? The men on the left are often the most intelligent

and most generous, but they live in a misunderstanding com-
pounded of naïveté or blindness. They can't get it into their
heads that today there are five giants in the world: the two capitalist giants, the two communist giants, and a fifth giant that's
a giant with clay feet, namely the underdeveloped world.
The first capitalist giant, there's no need to stress it, is called
the United States. The second is called the European Common Market, and it too behaves by all the rules of imperialism. The first communist giant is called the Soviet Union, the
second is called Red China, and only imbeciles delude themselves that the two capitalist empires are separated from the
two communist ones by their ideologies. They divided up the
world at Yalta and they go on dividing it up while dreaming of
a second Yalta Conference. So for the fifth giant with the clay
feet, for us, where is there hope? I don't see it either in the
American and European capitalists or in the Russian and
Chinese communists.

O.F.: Dom Helder, I must ask you an embarrassing question. There
was a period in your life during which you embraced fascism.
How was it possible? And how did you arrive later at such different choices? Excuse the ugly reminder.

H.C.: You have every right to remind me of that ugly memory and
I'm not ashamed to answer. In every one of us sleeps a fascist
and sometimes he never wakes up; sometimes instead he does.
In me he woke up when I was young. I was twenty-two, I was
dreaming even then of changing the world, and I saw the
world divided between right and left, that is fascism and communism. As an opponent of communism, I chose fascism. In
Brazil it was called Integralist Action. The integralists wore
green shirts instead of black ones like the Italians under Mussolini. And their motto was God-Fatherland-Family—a motto
that sounded fine to me. How do I judge this now? By my
youthful simplicity, my good faith, my lack of information—
there weren't many books to read, nor many sane men to listen to. And also by the fact that my superior, the bishop of
Ceará, was favorable and had asked me to work with the integralists. You know I worked with them till I was twenty-
seven? I began to suspect that that wasn't the right path only
when I arrived in Rio de Janeiro, where Cardinal Leme, who

didn't think like the bishop in Ceará, ordered me to abandon the movement.

I'm not embarrassed to tell you this, because any experience, any mistake, enriches you and teaches you—if nothing else, to understand others. To the fascists of today, I know what I'm talking about when I say there's not only fascism, there's not only communism; reality is much more complicated. But you want to know how I arrived at my choices today. The answer is simple: when a man works in contact with suffering, he always ends up being pregnant with suffering. Many reactionaries are what they are because they don't know poverty and humiliation. When did I get pregnant? Who knows? I can only say that my pregnancy already existed in 1952 when I was named bishop. In 1955, the year of the International Eucharistic Congress, it was already an advanced pregnancy. I gave birth to my new ideas one day in 1960, in the Church of the Candelaria, for the Feast of Saint Vincent de Paul. I got up in the pulpit and began speaking of charity understood as justice and not as beneficence.

O.F.: Dom Helder, some mean to arrive at that justice by violence. What do you think of violence as an instrument of struggle?

H.C.: I respect it. But here there's something that must be stated. When we speak of violence we mustn't forget that the number one violence, the violence that's the mother of all violence, is born of grievances. It's called injustice. So the young people who try to interpret oppression react to the number one violence with a number two violence, namely the current violence, and this provokes the number three violence, namely fascist violence. It's a spiral. I, as a priest, cannot and must not accept any of these three violences, but the number two violence I can understand—precisely because I know that one arrives at it through provocation. I detest those who remain passive, who keep silent, and I love only those who fight, who dare. The young people in Brazil who react to violence with violence are idealists whom I admire. Unfortunately their violence leads to nothing, and so I must add, if you start playing with weapons, the oppressors will crush you. To think of facing them on their level is pure madness.

O.F.: In other words, Dom Helder, you're telling me that armed revolt is impossible in Latin America.

H.C.: Legitimate and impossible. Legitimate because provoked, impossible because it'll be crushed. The idea that guerrilla warfare was the only solution for Latin America developed after Fidel Castro's victory. But Fidel Castro, in the beginning, didn't have the United States against him! The United States was taken by surprise with Cuba, and after Cuba, it organized antiguerrilla warfare in all the countries of Latin America, to prevent other Cubas. So today, in Latin America, all the military men in power are helped by the Pentagon in crushing anyone who attempts a revolution. Not only are there special schools for war where soldiers are trained under the harshest conditions, in the jungle, among the snakes, but where they're also taught political propaganda. That is, while their bodies learn to kill, their minds are persuaded that the world is divided in two: on one side capitalism with its values, on the other communism with its antivalues. These special forces, in short, are so prepared that anyone who tries to face them inevitably ends by losing.

O.F.: Like Che Guevara? Dom Helder, what's your opinion of Che Guevara?

H.C.: Guevara was, in Cuba, the genius of guerrilla warfare. He showed it in Cuba, since it was he and not Fidel Castro who carried off that extraordinary victory. I say extraordinary because I haven't forgotten, you know, what Cuba was like in the times of Batista! Others have, I haven't. But from a political standpoint, Guevara was much less of a genius, and his death shows that my argument is right. Then he chose Bolivia, namely a country with a very small privileged class and where the masses live below the human level—with neither the hope nor the awareness necessary for revolt. And it was a mistake because he couldn't be helped by those for whom he was fighting—those who have no reason to live don't even have a reason to die. He remained alone, and the experts in antiguerrilla warfare devoured him. No, Cuba can't be repeated, and I don't believe that Latin America has "need of many Vietnams," as Che Guevara said. When I think of Vietnam, I think of a heroic people who are fighting against a superpower, since I by no means believe that the United States is there to defend the free world. But I don't even think that Red China gives a damn about Vietnam and I ask, "Do you really delude yourselves that when that war is over, the Vietnamese people will come out the winner?"

O.F.: And Camilo Torres?

H.C.: The same. Camilo was a sincere priest, but at a certain point, while remaining a priest and a Christian, he lost any illusion that the Church knew or wanted to realize its beautiful texts. And he thought the Communist party was the only one capable of doing something. So the communists took him and sent him immediately into combat, where the danger was gravest. They had a plan in mind: Camilo would be killed and Colombia would catch fire. Camilo was killed but Colombia didn't catch fire. Neither the young people nor the workers stirred. And we go back to my statement of before.

O.F.: Dom Helder, would you also apply that statement to the young people who are carrying out guerrilla warfare in the cities of Brazil?

H.C.: Of course. Oh, I respect enormously the young Brazilians of whom you speak! I love them because they're daring, mature, because they never act out of hatred and think only of freeing their country. At the cost of their lives. They don't have time to prepare the masses, they're impatient, and they pay with their lives. I wouldn't like to discourage those young people but I have to. Is it worth while to sacrifice their lives for nothing? Or almost nothing?

Consider first of all the bank robberies they commit to get the money necessary to buy weapons. Weapons cost a disgusting price, to bring them into the cities is a mad undertaking— that risk, that sacrifice, isn't it therefore disproportionate? Now consider the kidnapping of diplomats, done for the purpose of freeing their comrades in prison. Every time an ambassador is released by the guerrillas in exchange for their comrades in prison, the police send out a dragnet and the empty cells fill up again. As well as the torture chambers. On one side they come out, and on the other they go in—what's the sense of it? The sense of making an exchange, of adding cripples to cripples, deaths to deaths? The sense of increasing the spiral of violence, of facilitating the fascist dictatorship?

My opposition, as you see, isn't based on religious motives but on tactical ones. It doesn't come from any idealism, it comes from an exquisitely political realism. A realism that applies to any other country: United States, Italy, France, Spain, Russia. If in any of these countries the young people were to pour out into the streets and attempt a revolution, they'd be annihilated in a flash. In the United States, for instance, the Pentagon would end up completely in power. We mustn't be impatient!

O.F.: Even Jesus Christ was impatient, Dom Helder. And he didn't offer a lot of tactical arguments when he defied the constituted authorities. In the history of the world those who have won have always been those who challenged the unchallengeable. And the young . . .

H.C.: If only you knew how I understand the young! I too was impatient as a young man—at the seminary I was such a dissenter that I wasn't allowed to become a Child of Mary.* I talked during the hours devoted to silence, I wrote poetry even though it was forbidden, I argued with my superiors. And the new generations of today fill me with admiration because they're a hundred times more disobedient than I was, a hundred times more courageous. In the United States, in Europe, everywhere. I know nothing about the young Russians, but I'm sure they too are trying something. Yes, I know that for the young people of today it's all much easier because they have more information, more communications, they have the road that my generation paved for them. But they use it so well, that road! There is in them such a thirst for justice, for revolt, such a sense of responsibility. They're exacting toward their parents, their teachers, their pastors, themselves. They turn their backs on religion because they've realized that religion has betrayed them. And they're sincere when they find sincerity, sensitivity. Some time ago some young Marxists came to see me, and with a certain arrogance they said they'd decided to accept me. Listen, listen, I said, so let's suppose I

* The Children of Mary was a pious organization, something like a devotional club. (Editor's note.)

don't accept you. That led to a heated, in fact harsh, discussion, but it ended in an embrace. I don't only love the young people of today, I envy them, since they have the good fortune to live their youth together with the youth of the world. But you can't stop me from being old and therefore from being wise, not impatient.

O.F.: Of course not. So let me ask you, Dom Helder, what solutions has your wisdom found for eliminating injustice?

H.C.: Anyone who has the solution in his pocket is a presumptuous fool. I have no solutions. I have only opinions, suggestions, which can be summed up in two words: peaceful violence. That is, not the violence chosen by young people with weapons in their hands, but the violence, if you like, already preached by Gandhi and Martin Luther King. The violence of Christ. I call it violence because it's not content with small reforms, revisions, but insists on a complete revolution of present structures—a society remade from top to bottom. On a socialist basis and without shedding blood. It's not enough to struggle for the poor, to die for the poor—we must give the poor an awareness of their rights, and of their poverty. The masses must realize the urgency of freeing themselves and not be freed by a few idealists who face torture like the Christians faced the lions in the Colosseum. To get yourself eaten by lions doesn't do much good if the masses stay seated to watch the spectacle. But how do we get them to stand up on their feet? you'll answer—this is a game of mirrors!

Well, I may be a utopian and naïve, but I say it's possible to "consciencize" the masses, and, perhaps, it's possible to open a dialogue with the oppressors. There's no man who's completely wicked; even in the most infamous of human beings you find valid elements—and what if we succeed in some way in talking with the more intelligent military men? What if we were actually to succeed in inducing them to revise their political philosophy? Having been an integralist, a fascist, I know the mechanism of their minds—it may even be that we'll succeed in convincing them that that mechanism is wrong, that torturing and killing don't kill ideas, that order isn't maintained by terror, that progress is reached only by dignity, that the underdeveloped countries don't defend themselves by putting themselves at the service of the capitalist empires, that the capitalist empires go arm in arm with the communist empires. We must try.

o.f.: Have you tried, Dom Helder?

h.c.: I will try. I'm trying now by talking to you in this interview. They'll have to understand too that the world is going forward, that the breath of revolt is not only blowing on Brazil and Latin America, but also on the whole planet. Good Lord, it's even blown on the Catholic Church! On the problem of justice the Church has already arrived at certain conclusions. And those conclusions are on paper, and signed. For it's true that many priests are talking about celibacy, but still more are talking about hunger and freedom. And then, you know, one must consider the consequences of the discussion about celibacy: there's a relationship between the various revolts; you can't demand a change in the outer structures if you don't have the courage to change the inner ones. The great human problems aren't the monopoly of priests living in Latin America, of Dom Helder. They're faced by priests in Europe, in the United States, in Canada, everywhere.

o.f.: They're isolated groups, Dom Helder. At the top of the pyramid we still have those who defend the old structures and the established authorities.

h.c.: I can't say you're wrong. There's an enormous difference between the conclusions signed on paper and the living realities. The Church has always been too preoccupied by the problem of maintaining order, avoiding chaos, and this has kept it from realizing that its order was more often disorder. I often wonder, without excusing the Church, how it's possible for serious and virtuous people to have accepted and go on accepting so many injustices. For three centuries in Brazil the Church found it normal for the Negroes to be kept in slavery! The truth is that the Catholic Church belongs to the mechanism of power. The Church has money, so it invests its money, sinks up to its neck in commercial enterprises, and attaches itself to those who hold wealth. It thinks in that way to protect its prestige, but if we want to sustain the role we've arrogated to ourselves, we have to stop thinking in terms of prestige. Nor should we wash our hands like Pontius Pilate; we must cleanse ourselves of the sin of omission and settle our debts. And reacquire the respect of the young people, if not their sympathy and maybe their love.

Away with that money, and enough of preaching religion in terms of patience, obedience, prudence, suffering, beneficence. Enough of beneficence, sandwiches, and cookies. You don't defend the dignity of men by giving away sandwiches and cookies, but by teaching them to say, I'm entitled to ham! We priests are responsible for the fatalism with which the poor have always resigned themselves to being poor, the underdeveloped nations to being underdeveloped. And by going on this way we prove the Marxists are right when they say that religions are an alienated and alienating force, namely the opium of the people!

O.F.: My goodness, Dom Helder! But does Paul VI know you say these things too?

H.C.: He knows, he knows. And he doesn't disapprove. It's just that he can't speak the way I do. He has certain people around him, poor man!

O.F.: Listen, Dom Helder, but do you really think that nowadays the Church can have a role in the search for and application of justice?

H.C.: Oh, no. Let's get the idea out of our heads that after having caused so much trouble the Church can allow itself such a role. We have the duty to render that service, yes, but without ostentation. Without forgetting that the most serious guilt belongs to us Christians. Last year I participated for a week in Berlin at a round table of Christians, Buddhists, Hindus, Marxists. There we discussed the great problems of the world, examined what we'd done, and concluded that religions have a great debt toward humanity, but that the Christians, or rather the Catholics, have the biggest debt. How do you explain that that handful of countries that have in their hands eighty percent of the world's resources are Christian countries and often Catholic? So I conclude: if a hope exists, it lies in the effort of all religions put together. Not in the Catholic Church alone or in Christian religions alone. By now there's not a single religion that has many possibilities. Peace can only be reached thanks to those whom Pope John called men of good will.

O.F.: They're a minority without any power, Dom Helder.

H.C.: It's the minorities that count. It's the minorities that have always changed the world, by rebelling, by fighting, and then by awakening the masses. Some priest here, some guerrilla there, some bishop here, some journalist there. I'm not trying to flatter you, but I must tell you that I'm one of the few people who like journalists. Who, if not the journalists, report injustices and inform millions and millions of people? Don't cut this remark out of the interview: in the modern world journalists are an important phenomenon.

There was a time when you came to Brazil only to talk about our butterflies, our parrots, our carnival, in short our folklore. Now instead you come here and raise the problems of our poverty, of our tortures. Not all of you, of course—there are also the thoughtless ones who don't care if we die of hunger or electric shocks. Not always with success, of course—your thirst for truth stops where the interests of the enterprise you serve begin. But God is good, and sometimes he sees to it that your bosses aren't very intelligent. Thus, with God's blessing, the news always gets through, and once it's printed it rebounds with the speed of a rocket directed at the moon, then spreads like a river overflowing its banks. The public isn't stupid, even if it's silent. It has eyes and ears, even if it has no mouth. And the day always comes when it thinks back on what it's read. I'm only waiting for it to read this ultimate truth: one mustn't say that the rich are rich because they've worked harder or are more intelligent. One mustn't say that the poor are poor because they're stupid and lazy. When hope is lacking and one inherits only poverty, it no longer does any good to work or be intelligent.

O.F.: Dom Helder, if you weren't a priest . . .

H.C.: You needn't bother to ask—I can't even imagine being anything but a priest. Just think, I consider the lack of imagination a crime, and yet I haven't the imagination to see myself as not a priest. For me, being a priest isn't just a choice, it's a way of life. It's what water is for a fish, the sky for a bird. I re-

ally believe in Christ; Christ to me is not an abstract idea—
he's a personal friend. Being a priest has never disappointed
me, nor given me regrets. Celibacy, chastity, the absence of a
family in the way you laymen understand it, all this has never
been a burden to me. If I've missed certain joys, I've had and
have others so much more sublime. If you only knew what I
feel when I say Mass, how I become one with it! The Mass for
me is truly Calvary and the Resurrection; it's a mad joy!

Look, there are those who are born to sing, those who are
born to write, those who are born to play soccer, and those
who are born to be priests. I was born to be a priest—I started
saying so at the age of eight and certainly not because my
parents had put the idea in my head. My father was a Mason
and my mother went to church once a year. I even remember
that one day my father got frightened and said, "My son,
you're always saying you want to be a priest. But do you know
what that means? A priest is someone who doesn't belong to
himself, because he belongs to God and to men, someone
who must dispense only love and faith and charity. . . ." And
I said, "I know. That's why I want to be a priest."

O.F.: Not a monk, however. Your telephone rings too often, and
that wall hit by the machine guns wouldn't be suitable for a
monastery.

H.C.: Oh, you're wrong! I carry a monastery inside myself. Maybe
there's little of the mystic in me, and even in my direct en-
counters with Christ I'm as impertinent as Christ would want.
But there always comes a moment when I isolate myself in the
manner of a monk. At two in the morning I always wake up,
get up, get dressed, and gather up the pieces I've scattered during the day: an arm here, a leg there, the head who knows
where. I sew myself back together again; all alone, I start
thinking or writing or praying, or I get ready for Mass. During
the day I'm a frugal man. I eat little, I detest rings and precious crucifixes, as you see; I rejoice in gifts that are right at
hand: the sun, the water, people, life. Life is beautiful, and I
often wonder why to sustain life one should kill another life—
whether it's a man or a tomato. Yes, I know that while chewing the tomato I make it become Dom Helder and thus ideal-
ize it, make it immortal. But the fact remains that I'm destroy-

ing the tomato—why? It's a mystery I don't succeed in fathoming and so I set it aside, saying never mind, a man is more important than a tomato.

O.F.: And when you're not thinking of the tomato, Dom Helder, doesn't it ever happen to you to be a little less of a monk and a little less of a priest? In short, to get angry with men who are worth less than a tomato and dream of at least hitting them with your fists?

H.C.: If that were to happen, I'd be a priest with a rifle on my shoulder. And I very much respect the priests with rifles on their shoulders; I've never said that to use arms against an oppressor is immoral or anti-Christian. But it's not my choice, it's not my road, it's not my way of applying the Gospels. So when I get angry, and I notice it by the fact that words no longer come out of my mouth, I stop and say, "Calm down, Dom Helder!" Yes, I understand, you aren't able to combine what I just said with what I said before: on one side the monastery, on the other politics. But what you call politics for me is religion. Christ didn't play the oppressors' game, he didn't give in to those who told him if you defend the young people who kidnapped the ambassador, if you defend the young people who rob banks to buy weapons, you're committing a crime against the fatherland and the state. The Church wants me to busy myself with the liberation of the soul, but how can I liberate a soul if I don't liberate the body that contains that soul? I want to send men to heaven, not puppies. Much less puppies with empty bellies and crushed testicles.

O.F.: Thank you, Dom Helder. It seems to me that about says it all, Dom Helder. But now what will happen to you?

H.C.: Bah! I don't hide myself, I don't defend myself, and it wouldn't take much courage to bump me off. But I'm convinced they can't kill me if God doesn't want it. If instead God does want it, because he thinks it's right, I accept that as his grace—who knows, my death could even help. I've lost almost all my hair, the little that's left is white, and I don't have many more years to live. So their threats don't frighten me. In short, it'll be a little hard for them, that way, to make me shut up. The only judge I accept is God.

Recife, August 1970

13

Archbishop Makarios

At a certain point I said to Makarios, "You remind me of Jane Austen's advice." Makarios smiled. "What advice of Jane Austen's?" "An intelligent woman should never let others know how intelligent she is." Makarios smiled again. "But I'm not a woman." "No, but you're intelligent, so intelligent that you're doing all you can to keep me from realizing it," I said. And then his gaze hardened, something in him arched, like the back of a cat preparing itself for combat. I too arched myself, waiting for the blow of his claws, and ready to give it back. The blow didn't come. With the same rapidity with which he had flared up, he regained his composure and went on with his story. "As I was telling you, I'm lucky. I know already what the newspapers will write when I pass to a better life. Last July I read such nice obituaries about myself. They gave me up for dead, remember? The cables to my ambassadors were nice too. The nicest came from Lord Caradon, the last British governor of Cyprus and a great enemy. I met Lord Caradon in London. We got to talking about the old days when we used to quarrel over the British bases on Cyprus. I told him those bases had been good for just one thing: to give me refuge after the *coup d'état* and help me leave the island." Every time his mind wanders and he forgets Jane Austen's advice, you're a little sorry. You want to shout at him, "Pay attention!" And it goes without saying that in this interview his mind often wandered. Almost always. Which is one of the reasons I like Makarios.

I hadn't liked him before. Once I had even tried to show him that I didn't, with the result that I had received his blessing. It was in Athens, at the time of the wedding of Juan Carlos and Sophia. He was staying at the Grande Bretagne, and I was staying there too. One evening he came down to the lobby, and as soon as he appeared, all dressed up like an icon, shining with gold and jewels, and gripping his pastoral scepter, the lobby became a chapel. Some bowed till their noses touched their navels, some knelt on the floor, some tried to kiss his hand or at least his vestments. The only erect head was mine, very visible besides, because I had remained seated on a high armchair. The chair was situated between the elevator and the exit, and he noticed me at once. And his eyes pierced mine like needles of indignation, surprise, sorrow. Who was I? How did I dare? However, he continued his solemn advance, and, as he passed in front of me, he imparted to me that blessing.

Needless to say, I could have done happily without it. To the mind of a layman, he is irritating to say the least. Let us not forget that he represents the most solid fusion of the temporal power with the spiritual. He is like a pope who sits in the Quirinale instead of the Vatican; he is the head of the Greek Orthodox Church on Cyprus and the president of Cyprus. So, you never know whether to address him as a religious leader or a political one, whether to call him Beatitude or President, Archbishop or Mr. Makarios. Nor does the fact that he was democratically elected help you to forget a bitter reality: he gets those votes thanks to his relationship with heaven. For the peasants of Cyprus, voting for him is almost a sacrament. While handing in their ballots with his name, even the communists make the sign of the cross. And yet, yet . . . he's one of the few heads of state before whom it's worth the trouble to get to your feet if not to kneel down. Because he's one of the few with brains. Along with brains, courage. Along with courage, a sense of humor, independence of judgment, dignity. A dignity that approaches regality, and God knows where it comes from. The son of an illiterate shepherd, he guarded sheep until the age of twelve.

Many people cannot stand him. They accuse him, for instance, of devoting or having devoted too much attention to women, of being in no sense an ascetic. I believe it. They also accuse him of governing through lies, intrigue, and opportunism. And this I don't believe completely unless by lies you mean Byzantinism, by intrigue, elasticity, by opportunism, imagination. His character cannot be judged by the yardstick we use in the West. He does not belong to the West. He belongs to something that is no longer the West but is not yet the East, something that sinks its roots into a culture that is sophisticated and archaic at the same time, and which has mastered the art of survival. He has the gift of survival, gained and regained through fast stepping, contortions, cleverness, lucidity, cynicism. Four times they tried to kill him. Four times he escaped. Twice they sent him into exile. Twice he came back. And only once did he seem to have lost for good—after the coup of July 1974. Instead, those who lost were those who were thought to have won—as a result of that coup, the Greek military junta fell and now finds itself under arrest. If I close my eyes on the subject of the archbishop-president, I can't help accepting Makarios and taking him seriously even when he tells me he's a socialist.

I interviewed him twice, for a total of six hours. The interview as written skips over such well-known incidents as the attempts on his life and his flight. I interviewed him in his suite in the Plaza Hotel in New York, where he had gone to keep an eye on Kissinger and the UN. No longer dressed up in gold and jewels, he wore a plain blue cassock and seemed older than his sixty-one years. His attitude was mild, deliberately humble. His voice was soft, deliberately suave. He said "he's a criminal" in the same tone with which he might have said "he's a good man." I wasn't bored for a minute, and indeed enjoyed myself. He knows how to be so brilliant. And at several moments I admired him. He cares so much about freedom. We parted friends. In the doorway, he whispered, "That advice of Jane Austen's . . . it goes for you too. What a pity you're a woman." And I answered, "What a pity you're a priest."

ORIANA FALLACI: An abrupt question, Beatitude: are you going back to Cyprus or not?

ARCHBISHOP MAKARIOS: Of course I'm going back. Certainly! I'll go back in November. At the latest, the end of December. The date depends entirely on me. I haven't gone back as yet because I was waiting for the Greek government to withdraw and replace the officers responsible for the coup against me. And also because I wanted to follow the UN debate on Cyprus from near by. I don't understand why there should be any doubt about my return—after all I didn't resign. Nothing and nobody is against my going back, except those who are afraid of being tried and punished, something I don't intend to do since it would hurt the unity of the country. Mind you, that doesn't mean I intend to let history have a distorted version of the facts. On the contrary, I want the world to know what happened. But I want to avoid any punishment, any revenge. I'll grant a general amnesty, and anyone who's anxious about my return can calm his fears. Besides it's only a question of a few individuals. The people support me today even more than before the coup. And they're eager to have me back. They're ninety-nine percent for me.

O.F.: Ninety-nine percent of the population includes the Turkish Cypriots. And I don't think they're so eager to have you back, Beatitude.

M.: Of course. I don't think either that the majority of the Turks are in favor of me. I'm sure Mr. Dektas, the Turkish vice-president, is anything but pleased with the idea of seeing me arrive. But this doesn't worry me, and anyway it won't be up to me to negotiate with Mr. Dektas and the Turkish community. That will still be done by Clerides, who's an excellent negotiator and knows Dektas better than I do. Oh, naturally it's understood that Clerides won't make any decisions without my consent. It's understood that when I speak of going back to Cyprus, I mean to go back as president. I'm the president, I'll go back as president, I'll never agree to go otherwise. And the question of whether I'll remain president for a long time or not concerns me alone. I'll make that decision when I'm back in Cyprus. I'm saying I don't exclude the possibility of retiring from the presidency after a certain period of time. I'll have to decide on the basis of the situation. Should a bad agreement be reached, for instance, I wouldn't care to stay as president. But this, I repeat, we'll see later on.

O.F.: What do you mean by a bad agreement?

M.: Turkey is going to insist on a geographical federation, and I will never accept a federation on a geographical basis. It would lead to a partition of the island and to a double *enosis*: half of Cyprus consigned to Greece and half to Turkey. It would mean the end of Cyprus as an independent state. I'm more than ready to discuss a federation, yes, but on an administrative basis not a geographical one. It's one thing to have areas governed by Turks and areas governed by Greeks; it's quite another to divide ourselves into two parts. It's one thing to group, for example, two or three Turkish villages and entrust them to a Turkish administration; it's quite another to shift more than two hundred thousand people from one end of the island to the other. The Turkish Cypriots are scattered all over Cyprus. How can you say to them, "Pack up your things, leave your house, your land, and move elsewhere because we're going to have a federation"?! It's inhuman, to say the least.

O.F.: Is this really what worries you, Beatitude? I mean the tragedy of the Turkish Cypriots? It doesn't seem to me that so far they've been the object of much concern. They've been treated like second-class citizens and . . .

M.: That's not true! It's not true! Though they're a minority, they've had a lot of privileges, and they've behaved as though they represented the majority. We haven't been the ones to mistreat them, it was their Turkish leaders, by forcing them to live in separate villages, blackmailing them, keeping them from co-operating with us even economically, and from progressing. They didn't even let them do business with us, or help us to develop tourism. They weren't our victims, they were their victims. Nobody can deny that a true democracy, and a good one, exists in Cyprus. In their newspapers the Turks could abuse me and insult me as much as they liked. They could come to see me at the archbishop's palace whenever they liked. The trouble is they were obliged to come secretly, without their leaders knowing it. In mixed villages we had no problem living together, in the past and at the time of the Greco-Turkish war as well. What you say isn't true.

O.F.: And is it true that you deprived them of many constitutional privileges, Beatitude?

M.: I deprived them of nothing. I simply complained about those privileges because they only served to hamper the functioning of the state. The Constitution provides that they be represented in the government at the ratio of thirty percent. And very often the Turkish Cypriots didn't have people capable of filling that thirty percent. There was, for example, a post that could have been filled by an intelligent Greek and it had to be given to an illiterate Turk just because he was a Turk. Once they voted against taxes. I tried to explain to them that a state can't survive if the citizens don't pay taxes, and they refused anyway. So I forced them to pay all the same. Was that an abuse? Another time, when I was about to go to Belgrade for the conference of nonaligned countries, Mr. Dektas tried to stop me from going by exercising his veto power. I told him, "Exercise it all you like. I'm going just the same." Was that an abuse?

O.F.: Beatitude, whether you're right or wrong, the reality today is different. The Turks occupy forty percent of the island and . . .

M.: And I don't accept it. Because I can't recognize a *fait accompli*, I can't legalize with my signature a situation created by the use of force. So-called realists advise me to negotiate a geographical federation with the Turks; they say I should be less rigid. Instead of holding on to forty percent of the island, they repeat, the Turks might be content with thirty percent. So be flexible. I don't want to be flexible.

O.F.: Flexible is a word dear to Henry Kissinger. Is he the one who says that?

M.: Kissinger has never clearly told me he was in favor of a geographical federation. He's never told me clearly what he's doing. He's always talked about a "solution acceptable to both sides" and always repeated "we don't want to say openly what we're doing to persuade Turkey." So I can't state the he's actually preparing the agreement that I reject, but I can tell you we're still in disagreement on many things. Many. If it wanted to, the United States could play a more decisive and precise role in this matter. Doesn't it supply economic aid and arms to Turkey? Isn't it the only one that could persuade or even force Turkey to be more reasonable?

O.F.: Beatitude, do you think that what happened in Cyprus would have been possible without the tacit authorization of Kissinger and the Americans?

M.: Ah! I think the United States and other countries knew in advance that the Turks were preparing the invasion of Cyprus. And perhaps they were fooled by the Turks, perhaps they fell into the trap when Turkey said it would be a limited operation—a police action to restore constitutional order in two days. Perhaps they understood only later what Turkey's real plans were. But all the same they could have prevented what happened. They could have stopped the continuous arrival of Turkish troops. I had a long discussion with Kissinger about it. And I expressed to him all my disappointment; I told him in no uncertain terms how dissatisfied I was with the attitude held by his country.

O.F.: And he?

M.: He answered that he didn't agree with me, that he had tried to persuade Turkey, that he had acted behind the scenes. But again he didn't want to explain clearly what he had done.

O.F.: Beatitude, many people feel that Kissinger's responsibility and that of the United States go well beyond the Turkish invasion of Cyprus. Let's not forget that the invasion took place following the coup carried out against you by the junta in Athens and that . . .

M.: Of course! The first chapter of this tragedy was written by the Greek military junta. Cyprus had been first of all destroyed by the intervention of Greece. Turkey came later, like a second evil. And I'm sorry to say so. I'm sorry because the present Greek government is behaving well toward me, in a frank and honest manner. I've not met Karamanlis or Averoff, but I've known Mavros. And I like Mavros. He's a good man. He's sincere, open, and that's more than enough for me. But the fact remains that Greece would not have regained its freedom if Cyprus hadn't lost its own. The fact remains that Turkey would never have dared intervene if the previous government, the junta, hadn't offered it the pretext. The Turks had been threatening to invade us for such a long time, and yet they'd never done it. They'd never found an excuse.

O.F.: Yes, but don't you think the United States and the CIA had something to do with that *coup d'état*? There are rumors that

the CIA wasn't exactly unhappy about the attempts on your
life.

M.: As regards those attempts, I don't believe it. Before the last one,
in fact, it was people at the American embassy in Nairobi,
during a trip I took to Africa, who informed me my life was in
danger. They came to me and said, "We know that when you
go back they'll try to kill you. Be careful." A few days later, in
Cyprus, they confirmed the information to me, adding that
the attempt would take place within two weeks. As indeed
happened. As for the *coup d'état*, on the other hand . . . I
don't know. Kissinger told me, "It wasn't in our interests to
have that *coup d'etat* against you." I suppose I ought to believe
him, but should I? There are plenty of indications that show
just the opposite of what Kissinger told me, and still I have
nothing to go on. I've even asked for information from Athens;
I've tried to find out more. No use. I have to keep my idea
without being able to offer any proof that it's correct. Kissinger
added, "Naturally we were following the situation and it was
known to us that neither Ioannides nor the rest of the junta
liked you. But we had no concrete information as to 'the day'
when the *coup d'état* against you would take place."

O.F.: Maybe it was helped along by the letter you wrote to Gizikis
in July.

M.: Let's say that that letter speeded things up. If I hadn't written it,
the coup would have happened all the same, a month or two
later. As Kissinger admits, it had been more than decided on;
all that remained was to set the date. I was too big an obstacle
to *enosis*, and they were too anxious to have *enosis*. Every time
we were on the point of reaching an agreement between Greek
Cypriots and Turkish Cypriots, officials in Athens intervened
by shouting about *enosis*. "We don't care about your local
agreements, our goal is *enosis*." I remember one of these officials who came to me one day and said, "You must declare
enosis. Anyway it will take three or four days before the Turks
can send troops to Cyprus. In the meantime the United States
will intervene and keep them from invading the island. In a
week *enosis* will be a *fait accompli*." Maybe they really believed that annexation to Greece was a viable alternative. Anyway they expected me to take orders from Athens, they wanted

me to obey like a puppet, and that's absolutely impossible with my temperament. I obey only myself.

O.F.: So you too were expecting the coup.

M.: No. I never thought they'd be so stupid as to order a coup against me. In fact, to me it seemed impossible that they wouldn't consider its consequences. I mean Turkish intervention. At the most I thought they might do such a thing by making a deal with Turkey, that is, authorizing Turkey to intervene so that Greece could then respond, to be followed by partition and double *enosis*. I went on thinking so even after the coup, when I got to London. It took some time for me to realize that Ioannides had simply acted out of a lack of intelligence. And yet I knew him. In 1963 and 1964 he had been in Cyprus as an officer of the National Guard, and one day he came to see me, accompanied by Sampson, in order to "explain to me secretly a plan that would settle everything." He had bowed to me, he had kissed my hand most respectfully, then: "Beatitude, here's the plan. To attack the Turkish Cypriots suddenly, everywhere on the island. To eliminate them one and all. Stop." I was flabbergasted. I told him I couldn't agree with him, that I couldn't even conceive the idea of killing so many innocent people. He kissed my hand again and went away in a huff. I tell you, he's a criminal.

O.F.: Do you find Papadopoulos better?

M.: I'd say yes. If I had to choose between Papadopoulos and Ioannides, I'd choose Papadopoulos. At least he's more intelligent, or, if you prefer, less stupid. I met him for the first time when he came to Cyprus, shortly after his coup, as minister for the presidency, and no one can say that at that time I was paying him any great consideration. But I saw him again a couple of times in Athens, when I went there to discuss the problem of Cyprus, and I must say that on those occasions he seemed to me much smarter. In any case, supplied with common sense. Well, Papadopoulos was suffering from megalomania, and besides I don't know what he really thought about Cyprus. On the other hand, he was capable of controlling many situations simultaneously, and he was head and shoulders above his collaborators. I don't even think he hated me, in the beginning.

He started hating me later, in the last two years. And maybe only in the last year.

O.F.: And you, Beatitude, are you capable of hating?

M.: Well, let's say that the feeling we call hatred is part of human nature. You can't stop anyone from feeling it once in a while. And though I don't like to admit it, since I must preach love, there are moments when . . . well, when . . . All right, let's say that I don't like certain people. Why are you smiling?

O.F.: Because you make me think of certain Renaissance popes who led their armies in war, and I can't understand to what extent you're a priest. So I conclude that maybe you're not a priest at all, but a big politician dressed as a priest.

M.: You're wrong. I'm a priest first and then a politician. Better still, I'm not a politician at all. I'm a priest, first of all a priest, above all a priest. A priest who has been asked to be head of state and consequently a politician. But one would say you don't much like that.

O.F.: No, and I'm dismayed by it. In the world I live in, the struggle of laymen consists precisely in not allowing the spiritual power to be confused with the temporal power, and in keeping a religious leader from becoming a political one.

M.: In my world, on the other hand, it's fairly common. And all the more so in Cyprus, where the archbishop, like the bishops, is elected directly by the people, with universal suffrage. In other words, in Cyprus, the archbishop isn't only a representative and administrator of the Church, he's also a national figure. The ethnarch. And then, in my opinion, the Church should interest itself in all aspects of life—the Christian religion doesn't confine itself to taking care of the moral progress of men, it's also concerned with their social well-being. I see no conflict between my position as priest and my position as president. I see nothing scandalous about my holding both the temporal and spiritual power. Besides I don't lean on a party; I'm not the leader of a political party who goes around asking people to elect him. I simply serve the people in the two capacities that they insistently and almost unanimously offered me. As I explained many years ago to another layman, Prime Minister George Papandreou, I'm strong because I'm weak. Because I have neither a party nor an army nor a police force behind me. And because I don't even know the rules of politics. Because I follow certain principles that are Christian principles and not games, tricks, political maneuvers.

O.F.: Oh, come off it, Beatitude! You, who are a past master in the most Byzantine game of compromise. You, who are considered the most brilliant specialist in intrigue and calculation.

M.: No! I don't use those methods, I don't! I yield to compromises, of course, but never to anything that's not clear and honest. I'm not a saint. But I'm an honest man, and I don't believe politics has to be dishonest. I don't think that in order to have success, it's necessary to indulge in deceit. Do you know why my people love me? Do you know why they forgive all the mistakes I make? Because they understand that those mistakes are caused by bad judgment, not by bad intentions. You must not confuse me with the popes of the past, and in fact, if you were to ask me, I have a very negative opinion of them. I really try to bring Christian teachings into the maze of the office that's been entrusted to me and which I accepted. I'll give you an example. In Cyprus we have capital punishment, and as head of state, I'm the one who has to put his signature on death sentences. But executions in Cyprus are very rare, because every time a condemned man appeals to me, I let him off. Everyone in Cyprus knows the death penalty is nominal, that I always suspend executions. Those popes went to war, but I don't accept war, I consider it a madness that's destined to end someday, to be remembered with disbelief. I don't accept bloodshed.

O.F.: Excuse me, Beatitude, but you were the one who actually said, at the beginning of the struggle for the independence of Cyprus, "Much blood will have to flow."

M.: I can't possibly have said it that way. Maybe I said, "The road to freedom is irrigated with blood," something like that. Maybe I said, "We'll have to die," but not, "We'll have to kill." I was in favor of sabotage, yes, but on condition that it didn't cost the blood of innocent people. All that killing took place when I was in exile and couldn't do anything to stop it. Oh, I'm not the terrible person you think!

O.F.: We'll see. But now let's forget about Cyprus and talk about you. First of all, why did you become a priest?

M.: I always wanted to be a priest. Ever since I was a child. I was barely thirteen when I entered the monastery. But the reason is hard for me to explain. Maybe I'd been impressed by my visits to the monasteries around my village. I liked the monasteries so much. Life there was so different from the kind we led in the village, and I sometimes wonder if for me the monastary wasn't a way of escaping the sheep, the poverty. My father was a shepherd. And he always wanted me to help him look after the sheep, and I didn't like looking after the sheep. In fact, he used to complain and say, "I can't expect anything from my elder son! If I need help when I'm an old man, I'll have to turn to my younger son!" He said it so often that in the last years of his life, when I was already archbishop, I liked to tease him: "Do you remember when you used to grumble and say you couldn't expect anything from me?" He was very religious, like everyone in the family, but he couldn't understand why on Sunday morning I left the sheep to run to the monastery and help the priest say Mass. I was twelve years old when I told him I wanted to take that path, and he got angry. But I wasn't scared, I was so sure that nothing would be able to stop me.

O.F.: And your mother?

M.: I don't remember my mother very well. She died when I was very small; I don't even have a picture of her. In those days, the poor didn't get their pictures taken, especially in the mountains of Cyprus. About my mother, I only remember the day she got ill. There was only one doctor in the whole district, and my father set out on foot to look for him. He had no idea in what village he might find him, and went wandering around for hours, and finally he came back dragging the doctor like a sheep. The doctor used the same pill for all illnesses. Aspirin, I guess. He gave my mother the pill, and she died soon after. I remember the funeral. I remember the nights I slept with my father, because with him I could cry better. And I remember the night when he too started crying, and I said, "If you'll stop crying, I'll stop too." And then I remember my grandmother taking me away, and the relatives saying to my father, "You're young, you should get married again. Also for the children." Besides myself, there was my little brother, and my little sister who had just been born. And one day they brought me home to meet my new mother—Father had got married again. My new mother was a woman in the middle of the room, and she kept whispering, "Come in, come in!" I didn't want to go in because I didn't know her. But then I went in and soon I loved her. She was nice. She's still alive, and still nice, and I still love her. Very much. Oh, it's so difficult, and also so easy, to tell you where I come from. My father couldn't read or write. Neither could my mother, nor my grandmother, nor my stepmother. I think my father resigned himself to the idea of letting me go into the monastery because there I would learn to read and write. When he took me there, he kept urging me: "Be obedient, study . . ."

O.F.: Were you disobedient then too? You just told me that you only obey youself.

M.: I was shy. I was so shy that in school I didn't even have the courage to get up and show that I'd studied the lesson. When the teacher called on me, I blushed and my tongue got paralyzed. But not even then was I able to obey. Take the story of the beard. When I was twenty years old, the abbot of the monastery ordered me to let my beard grow. And a novice isn't obliged to grow a beard. I refused, and he got angry. "Either you obey or out you go." "All right, I'll go." Then I packed my bag—I knew exactly what would happen. "You mustn't go! Stay." "All right, I'll stay." "But grow a beard." "No, no beard." "Look out or I'll beat you." "Beat me." He started beating me, and while he was beating me, he yelled, "Will you let it grow?" "No." "Now will you let it grow?" "No." Finally he sat down, exhausted. "Please. Let it grow a little. Just a little, so I won't lose face." "No." "Just the little bit needed to make people ask whether you have one or not." I smiled. "This little bit?" "Yes." "Like now?" "Yes." "Not even a millimeter more?" "Not even a millimeter more." "All right." And a compromise was reached without my giving in to obedience.

O.F.: Revealing, I'd say.

M.: It's my strategy. It always has been. I mean, I've always enjoyed the game of pushing myself to the edge of the abyss and then stopping so as not to fall. You see what I mean? It's not that I stop at the last moment because I realize the abyss is there; I calculate to the millimeter that I can go that far and no further. The others, naturally, think I'm about to fall, to commit suicide. Instead I go along very quietly, knowing I'll put on the brakes. It was the same with the abbot. I hadn't the slightest intention of leaving the monastery; I liked it too much. But I knew that by making him believe the contrary and taking his beating, he'd give in and accept a compromise that for me was a victory.

O.F.: And has there been any case when your calculations didn't work, when destiny decided for you?

M.: I don't believe in destiny. Everyone makes his own destiny. At the most there exist unforeseen circumstances, which one must know how to take advantage of. I, for instance, hadn't foreseen that I'd become bishop at the age of thirty-five and archbishop at thirty-seven. . . . But that's a story worth telling. After seven years in the monastery, three of which were spent studying at the high school in Nicosia, I was sent to Athens to take my degree in law and theology. There I was caught by the war, the Italian and then the German occupation, a tough as well as adventurous period. After the liberation, however, I got a scholarship in the United States and went to Boston. I liked America—they'd given me, among other things, a small Greek Orthodox parish. I decided to stay there for five years instead of the three that had been arranged and take my teaching degree in theology. And here the plan failed. Two years had barely gone by, in fact, when I received a cable from Cyprus informing me that a certain district wanted to elect me its bishop. I was alarmed. I didn't want to leave America, I didn't want to go back to Cyprus. Cyprus meant nothing to me except a vague geographical knowledge. And a limited one at that, since all I had seen were the mountains where I was born, the monastery where I'd grown up, and the school in Nicosia where I'd studied. Do you know I was eighteen when I saw the sea for the first time? I cabled back: "Many thanks but I don't want to become bishop stop."

O.F.: Are you telling me you weren't ambitious?

M.: Of course I was! No priest can be happy if he doesn't succeed in an ecclesiastical career. But my ambitions were different. The fact is that no sooner had I sent my reply when a second cable arrived: "Elections held. People elected you unanimously." It was 1948, the eve of the struggle for independence. Sadly I took a plane to Athens, and I remember that there I kept asking everybody, "Will I find a taxi at the Nicosia airport?" Then I took the plane from Athens to Nicosia and . . . I've already told you that in Cyprus the election of a bishop is something very democratic. The people participate in it spontaneously, enthusiastically, and without tricks. But I didn't tell you that it arouses a mad fanaticism. And I can't stand fanaticism. In any form. So you can imagine how I felt when, going out to look for a taxi, I saw this incredible crowd fanatically shouting my name. I recovered myself if only to utter what was to be my first political statement: "You wanted me. So I shall dedicate myself to the Church and to Cyprus. And I'll do everything I can to help Cyprus win its freedom and break the chains of colonialism." Then I saw myself lifted up and taken to Larnaca, the district where I'd been elected. And from that moment on, Cyprus became my life.

O.F.: A good life, Beatitude. A lucky life, let's face it.

M.: A tough, difficult life, full of assassination attempts, of risks, anxiety, and exile. I was in the Resistance against the British. Still it's true that two years later, when the archbishop died, I was triumphantly elected in his place, thus becoming the youngest head of a Church in the whole world. It's true that I liked it. But it doubled my political commitment and cost me exile. To get rid of me, the British sent me to the Seychelles and . . . Of course, when I look back on it today, that exile seems anything but tragic. Actually it wasn't an exile, it was a vacation. I was given a nice house where I was served and respected. The landscape was marvelous, so marvelous that I wanted to see it again, and I went back as a tourist and even bought a little piece of land near the same house, which the owner, unfortunately, didn't want to sell. The British treated me well and didn't keep me there long—just eleven months. But at that time I didn't know it and thought they'd keep me for at least ten years or forever. I had no idea what was going

on in Cyprus, I had no radio, no newspapers, and I couldn't
speak with anyone. And . . .

O.F.: And?

M.: Well, all right, I'll tell you. I wasn't born for the contemplative
life. I can stay shut up for a week in this suite in the Plaza, but
on the eighth day I have to go out, see people, do something,
live. You'll object: didn't the monastery teach you anything?
Well, our monasteries aren't very strict—those who stay inside
them do so by choice and not because they're forced to. And
no one says I should go back and live in a monastery. I prefer
to do what I'm doing and . . . why should I go back to a
monastery?

O.F.: So I was right to compare you with those popes. Besides I've
never believed in the picture some people paint of you: ascetic, vegetarian . . .

M.: I'm not a vegetarian! I like vegetables but I also eat meat. One
of my most painful memories is a certain official dinner that
was offered me in India. The waiter came over and asked me,
"Are you vegetarian?" I thought he was asking if I liked vegetables and I answered yes. Then he put a flower beside my plate
and for the whole meal served me nothing but vegetables. I
was consumed with envy seeing the others devouring chicken,
fish, steaks. In fact, now whenever they put a flower in my
hand, I get suspicious.

O.F.: But I was referring to other flowers, Beatitude. It seems you
were once at a party where a dancer did a wild belly dance,
and you're said to have remarked, "The beauty of woman is a
gift of God."

M.: I don't know that incident. It's true, I love popular dances, I
like folklore . . .

O.F.: No, no, I wasn't talking about folklore. I was talking about
belly dancing. I was trying to ascertain that you're not one of
those priests who pray from morning to night and . . .

M.: I'm usually a very simple man. At the same time, however
. . . What should I say? . . . When necessary . . . I make
certain . . . adjustments. I like to walk, for instance, to run,
to climb mountains, to keep in shape. Also because I like
sports and I dislike fat people. So whenever I can, I take an excursion, I walk in the woods. . . . Under my robe, you see, I

wear trousers. If I always dress this way, in robes, even at home, it's because my people are used to seeing me in a cassock and I can't disappoint them. But cocktail parties bore me, and so do worldly things. . . .

O.F.: I still haven't made myself clear, Beatitude. Maybe it's better to call things by their right names. I was referring to women, to the rumors that you're very fond of women. They even say that in Cyprus you have two, well, two wives.

M.: Come now. In the Orthodox Church, bishops and archbishops can't marry. Only priests can. But then they don't become bishops.

O.F.: I know. I said "wives" to be polite.

M.: . . .

O.F.: Isn't it true you're very fond of women?

M.: . . .

O.F.: All right, let's change the subject. They also say you're not a sincere man, that a word of truth never comes out of your mouth. Do you think a head of state should be permitted to tell lies?

M.: No, this is something I can't accept. I'm so incapable of telling lies, any lie, that when I can't tell the truth, I prefer to keep silent. Silence is always better than lies. Look, during the Resistance struggle, the British arrested me several times. After being arrested, I was interrogated, and naturally I couldn't deny what I was doing. And then everyone knew I had contacts with Grivas. So, in order not to lie, I answered, "I can't say anything. I don't want to say anything. I refuse to answer." And I kept silent.

O.F.: Just what you did with me when I asked you about women.

M.: What did I say?

O.F.: Nothing.

M.: The perfect answer.

O.F.: I'm beginning to like you, Beatitude. And at this point it pains me to insist on the ugly things they say about you. For instance, that you rule through favors, and that you're very rich, and that . . .

M.: I possess nothing. Absolutely nothing except that little piece of land in the Seychelles. I haven't a penny in any bank in the world. I have nothing but a kind of salary, which I can use as I like, but it's very small. I administer the properties of the Greek Orthodox Church in Cyprus, it's true, and as archbishop I can dispose of anything that belongs to the archbishop's palace, but I'm not authorized to use a single cent for myself. Theoretically, even my linen belongs to the archbishop's palace. As for favors, I help many people, it's true. But my friends less than anyone. And my relatives still less. My brother is my driver. That doesn't seem to me a great career; also when you stop to think of the attempts that are made on my life. I stay in good hotels when I travel, it's true. But do you know why? Because I have friends all over the world and they're anxious to pay for me. In London, for instance, after the *coup d'état*, I went to the Grosvenor House, where I always go. The next morning Charles Forte, whom I'd known from Cyprus where he wanted to open a hotel, came to me and said, "Do you know I'm the owner of the Grosvenor House?" I hadn't known. "It will be an honor for me to have you as my guest for as long as you care to stay in London." And so I didn't pay. In fact, he even wanted me to be his guest in New York, at the Pierre, another hotel he owns. I didn't accept because I didn't want to take advantage of him.

O.F.: Yes, but then why do they call you the Red Archbishop?

M.: I've never understood where that came from. Maybe from the fact that I've never made anticommunist propaganda. Or the fact that I follow a policy of nonalignment. Most of the nonaligned countries are accused of being leftist-oriented and even of looking to the Soviet Union.

O.F.: Are you a socialist, Beatitude?

M.: If you're referring to Swedish socialism, not Soviet socialism, I can say I really have nothing against socialism. Among all social systems, it's the closest to Christianity, to a certain Christianity, or at least to what Christian teaching should be. Christianity doesn't favor any social system—it recognizes that any social system, from the capitalist one to the communist, can contain something good. But if I had to choose the best system, or the most Christian system, I'd choose socialism. I said socialism, not communism. And let me add that, in my opinion, the future belongs to socialism. It will end by prevailing, through a kind of osmosis between the communist countries and the capitalist ones. Spiritually it's already happening. The socialist, that is, egalitarian, spirit is permeating all human relationships. Today equality is an almost spontaneous feeling.

o.f.: You're an optimist, Beatitude.

m.: I always have been. And never at random. In the last thirty years a great change has happened in the world. Thirty years ago who would have imagined that colonialism would be over and that war would no longer be accepted as a means for subjugating a country? Who would have imagined that social hierarchies would no longer be accepted with conviction, that the word socialism would no longer be frightening?

o.f.: But if you believe in socialism, how can you administer a church that's one of the richest in the world?

m.: Never so rich as the Catholic Church. And anyway the Church isn't a reactionary force; it doesn't represent the capitalist world. If it often goes to the right, the fault is only of its representatives. And the representatives of the Church aren't the Church; the representatives of religion aren't religion. When you think that not even the priests, bishops, archbishops, and theologians have been able to uproot religion from the hearts of men! I may be too ˙optimistic, but even the Catholic Church leads me to make a positive judgment. It's changed so much in recent years, thanks to Pope John. In 1961, when I was asked to stop in Rome on a state visit, I was invited by the pope. And naturally I had a great desire to go, but still I wondered if I should. Our lack of understanding goes back so far. Not only had I never met a Catholic bishop, I'd never met a Catholic priest! I told myself that the other heads of the Orthodox Church would be offended. But soon after that the patriarch of Constantinople, Athenagoras, met with Paul VI in Jerusalem.

o.f.: Did you feel at ease with the pope?

m.: It was interesting. A pity all that protocol.

o.f.: And who are the leaders with whom you've felt at ease?

m.: Let's say that some leaders, not many, have impressed me, and that others have left me indifferent. They were considered great men, but they were only men at the head of great countries. Among those who impressed me, I'd put Jack Kennedy.

That childish face of his was really nice; it had a dignity of its own. Besides Kennedy was simple, human. Along with Kennedy, I'd put Tito. But Tito and I are friends; I like to think he has the same affection for me that I have for him. . . . He's such a dynamic man, full of clear ideas. And generous besides. "Anything you need, just let me know," he always says. I liked Nasser too. I remember meeting him at the first conference of nonaligned countries, in Bandung in Indonesia. It was the first time he'd left Egypt, the first time he'd flown in a nonmilitary plane, and he was so excited. I found that touching. As for Castro . . . I don't know. He has certain qualities necessary for a leader. With me he behaved . . . well, he behaved like Castro. Golda Meir is a very strong, interesting woman, but we disagree about too many things. We've met twice and we didn't exactly throw our arms around each other. Sukarno . . . he didn't impress me. Nixon even less. An ordinary man, very ordinary. And then . . . what do you want me to say? I like Constantine. Not because I'm a monarchist—I saw him coming into the world, I saw him grow up, I like him. But I can't say that because I shouldn't be making political propaganda for him.

O.F.: And Mao Tse-tung?

M.: I wouldn't say I have much in common with him. And I don't know how to define the impression he made on me. His health, when I met him last May, really wasn't good and . . . Let's put it this way: in China he's a kind of god. His fingerprints are everywhere, obsessively, and I've already told you that I hate fanaticism. I feel more at ease with Chou En-lai. Besides I've known him for nineteen years, since the Bandung Conference. Chou En-lai is so intelligent, so pleasant, with him you can even joke. He prepared a fabulous welcome for me—hundreds of thousands of people in the streets of Peking, a million in Shanghai. I kept saying to him, "You want to make me feel like somebody!" We also had fun when he started talking about our two countries, about the role they'd play in history. He kept repeating, "Our two countries . . ." Finally I interrupted and exclaimed, "Will you do me a favor? Will you stop talking about our two countries, about their historical roles? I feel ridiculous. How can you compare a little island of five hundred thousand inhabitants with a China of eight hundred million? What historical role can we have in common, we two? I'm a mosquito next to an elephant!" Mao Tse-tung was there too. He tried to smooth things over by saying that mosquitoes can sometimes give a lot of trouble, while elephants are innocent. But that didn't go down with me. And I still kept my inferiority complex.

O.F.: Do you often feel that inferiority complex?

M.: Ah, yes. If it's not inferiority, it's uneasiness. During my visit to the Soviet Union, for instance, I stayed inside the Kremlin. Every morning I said to myself, "Good Lord! An archbishop inside the Kremlin!" Podgorny was nice and polite; he did nothing but smile at me, but he didn't succeed in making me forget the paradox. To get out of it, I combined my state visit with a visit to the Russian Orthodox Church. And that was worse. The coronation ceremony for the new patriarch of Moscow was taking place just then, and the crowd was as numerous as in Peking, as in Shanghai. It was very hard for me to behave as though I really felt important. Look, there's only one time when I lost that inferiority complex.

O.F.: When?

M.: When I visited Malta.

O.F.: We can offer you San Marino.

M.: They've never invited me. But I've felt comfortable in Africa too. Oh, it's extraordinary the number of babies and streets that have been named after me in Africa! In Tanzania I did nothing but meet little black Makarioses, and the same in Zanzibar, though Zanzibar is Muslim. In Mombasa there's a Makarios Avenue. And in Nairobi . . . Ah, Nairobi was the best of all, because in one week I baptized five thousand people. I'd been invited by Kenyatta, another leader who's impressed me very much, and all of a sudden I had an idea. I asked, "How many people could I baptize if I stayed here a week?" They said, "As many as you like." "Even fifty thousand?" "Even fifty thousand." Well, fifty thousand was too much. I said, "Let's do five thousand." The first contingent arrived in two days, coming on foot from very distant villages. And naturally I should have baptized them in the river. But I didn't want to run the risk. The water is polluted and I'm a hygienist. So I threw them all into a swimming pool, adults and children, and . . . For a week I did nothing but fill that pool. It was amusing because there's a Catholic mission there that's not too well liked because of its old ties with colonialism, and to baptize even a single person those poor missionaries have to sweat like hell. Help women give birth, nurse babies, and what have you. For me instead it was quite simple. I didn't have to do any of those awful things, and the result is that in Africa I have at my disposal the largest concentration of black Orthodox Christians. Naturally they understood nothing about what it means to belong to the Greek Orthodox Church. You meet some fellow on the street and ask him, "What religion do you belong to?" And he answers, "To Makarios's religion!" But it's all right just the same and . . . Look, I'll always live in Cyprus. As I told you, Cyprus is now my life. But if I couldn't live in Cyprus, I'd live in Africa.

O.F.: And now I begin to understand something about you, Beatitude. Good-bye, thank you, and see you again in Cyprus.

M.: See you again in Cyprus. Come when you like. I'll receive you as president.

New York, November 1974

14

Alexandros Panagoulis

———◆———

That day he had the face of a Jesus crucified ten times and he looked older than his thirty-four years. His pale cheeks were already furrowed by wrinkles, his black hair already showed wisps of white, and his eyes were two pools of melancholy. Or rage? Even when he laughed, you didn't believe his laugh. Besides, it was a forced laugh that hardly lasted—like a burst of gunfire. His lips immediately locked themselves again in a bitter grimace, and in that grimace you looked in vain for a reminder of his health and youth. He had lost his health, along with his youth, the moment he was tied for the first time to the torture table and they had said to him, "Now you're going to suffer so much you'll be sorry you were ever born." But you understood at once that he wasn't sorry to have been born; he had never been sorry and never would be. You understood at once that he was one of those men for whom even dying becomes a way of life, so well do they spend their lives. Neither the most atrocious tortures, nor the death sentence, nor three nights spent waiting to be shot, nor the most inhuman prison, five years in a concrete cell one and a half meters by three, had broken him.

Two days earlier, coming out of the Boyati prison with the pardon granted by George Papadopoulos along with an amnesty for three hundred political prisoners, he had not uttered a single word that might have helped him to be left in peace. In fact, he had declared contemptuously, "I didn't ask for it, that pardon. They imposed it on me. I'm ready to go back to prison right now." Indeed those who loved him feared for his safety, now, as much and more than before. Out of prison he was too disturbing for the colonels. Tigers on the loose are always disturbing. Those in power shoot at tigers on the loose or else they set a trap to put them back in the cage. How long would he remain in the open air? This was the first thing I thought that Thursday, August 23, 1973, on seeing Alexandros Panagoulis.

Alexandros Panagoulis. Alekos to his friends and to the police. Born in Athens in 1939, son of Athena and Basil Panagoulis, who was an army colonel decorated in the Balkan War and in the First World War and in the war against the Turks in Asia Minor and in the civil war that lasted until 1950. Second of three brothers, democrats and antifascists all. Founder and head of Greek Resistance, the movement the colonels never succeeded in destroying. Author of the plot that on August 13, 1967, failed by a hairbreadth to cost Papadopoulos his life and bring down the junta. For this he had been arrested, tortured incessantly until the trial, where they had discovered that he was not an executor of orders but the leader of Greek Resistance, the movement that made up most of the opposition; and for this he had been condemned to death—a penalty that he himself had asked for in a defense speech that for two hours kept the judges spellbound. "You are the representatives of tyranny and I know you'll send me before the firing squad. But I also know that the swan song of every true fighter is his final gasp before the firing squad." That unforgettable trial. Never before had an accused been seen so transformed into an accuser. He arrived in the court with his hands handcuffed behind his back. The police took off the handcuffs and locked him in a vise that held him by the shoulders, the arms, the waist, but he jumped to his feet all the same, pointing his finger and shouting his contempt.

So as not to make him a hero, they did not execute him. And it goes without saying that he became one all the same, because sometimes it is easier to die than to live as he lived. They transported him from one prison to another, saying, "The firing squad is waiting for you." They came into his cell and beat him almost to death. And for eleven months they kept him handcuffed, day and night, even though his wrists had begun to fester. Then periodically they kept him from smoking, from reading, from having a piece of paper and a pencil to write his poems.

He wrote them all the same, on tiny pieces of onionskin from packages of the gauze they put on his wounds, using his blood for ink. "A match for a pen / blood that has dripped on the floor for ink / the package from some forgotten gauze for paper / But what do I write? / Maybe I only have time for my address / Strange, the ink has coagulated / I write you from a prison / in Greece." He even managed to send them outside the prison, those beautiful poems written with his blood. His first book had won the Viareggio Prize and he was now a recognized poet, translated into Italian and French, and on whom critics wrote essays, sententious literary analyses. But more than a poet he was a symbol. The symbol of courage, of dignity, of the love for freedom.

All this troubled me, now that I was in his presence. How do you greet a man who has just come out of a tomb? How do you speak to a symbol? And I was nervously biting my nails—I remember it perfectly. I remember it because I remember everything from that Thursday, August 23. The landing in Athens. The fear of not finding him though I had let him know of my arrival. The search for Aristofanos Street, in the Glifada quarter, where his house was. The taxi driver who finally found the house and began to shout and make the sign of the cross. The sultry day, my clothes sticking to my skin. The crowd of visitors who thronged the garden, the terrace, every corner of the house. The other journalists, the voices, the shoving. And him, sitting in the midst of chaos with the face of Christ.

He looked very tired, indeed exhausted. But as soon as he saw me he sprang up like a cat, and ran to embrace me as though he had always known me. Anyway, if he hadn't always known me, we already knew each other. In those periods when he was allowed to read a few newspapers, he was to tell me, my articles had kept him company. And he had given me courage by the simple fact of existing, of being what he was. So my worry about having to face a symbol instead of a man vanished. I returned his embrace, saying "ciao," he replied "ciao," and there were no other words of welcome or felicitation. I simply added, "I have twenty-four hours to stay in Athens and prepare the interview. Immediately afterward I must leave for Bonn. Is there a corner where we can work quietly?" He nodded silently and then, plowing his way through the crowd of visitors, led me into a room where there were many copies of one of my books in Greek. Besides these, there was a bouquet of red roses that he had sent to me at the airport and that had come back because the friend charged to welcome me had not been able to find me. Touched, I thanked him brusquely. But he understood my brusque tone because, for a moment, the melancholy look disappeared from his eyes and his pupils showed a flash of amusement that dismayed me again. It was a flash that made you divine a host of tender and vehement feelings in conflict among themselves, a soul without peace. Would I be able to understand this man?

We began the interview. And immediately I was struck by his voice, which was beguiling, resonant, almost guttural. A voice to persuade people. The tone was authoritative, calm, the tone of one who is very sure of himself and allows no replies to what he says since he has no doubts about what he says. He spoke, that is, like a political leader. While speaking, he smoked his pipe, which he almost never took from his mouth. You would have said his attention was concentrated on that pipe, not on you, and this imparted to him a certain harshness that was intimidating since it was not a recent harshness, that is to say ripened by physical and moral agony, but an innate one and thanks to which he had been able to triumph over physical and moral agony.

At the same time he was considerate, polite, and he left you almost dumbfounded when, by a sudden veering—you know, the way a motorboat veers when it is proceeding directly and then suddenly turns to go back—his harshness broke into sweetness, as melting as the smile of a child. The way he poured you a beer, for instance. The way he touched your hand to thank you for some remark. This changed the features of his face, which, no longer sorrowing, became disarmed. His face was not handsome with its small, strange eyes, its large and still more strange mouth, its forehead too high, and, finally, those scars that ruined everything. On the lips, on the cheekbones. And yet quite soon he seemed almost handsome—an absurd, paradoxical handsomeness, and independently of his beautiful soul.

No, perhaps I would never understand him. I decided from that first meeting that the man was a well of contradictions, surprises, egotism, generosity, illogicality, which would always enclose a mystery. But he was also an infinite fountain of possibilities, and a personality whose worth went well beyond that of a political personality. Perhaps politics represented only a moment in his life, only a part of his talent. Perhaps, if they didn't kill him soon, if they didn't put him back in the cage, we would one day hear about him for heaven knows what other things.

How many hours did we stay there talking in the room with the books and flowers? It's the one detail I don't remember. You're not aware of time passing when you listen to what he had to tell. The story of the tortures, first of all, the origin of his scars. He had them all over his body, he told me. He showed me those on his hands, on his wrists, his arms, his feet, his chest. Here they were exactly where the wounds of Christ were—at the level of the heart. They had inflicted them on him, in the presence of Papadopoulos' brother, Constantine, with a jagged paper knife. But he showed them to me with detachment and no self-pity, stiffened by an excessive, almost cruel self-control. All the more cruel when you realized that his nerves had not emerged intact from those five years of hell. And this was revealed by his teeth when he bit his pipe; it was revealed by his eyes when they dimmed into lamps of hatred or mute contempt. Pronouncing the names of his torturers, in fact, he isolated himself in impenetrable pauses and failed even to answer his mother when she came in to ask if he wanted more beer or coffee.

His mother came in often. She was old, dressed in black like the widows in Greece who do not give up their mourning, and her face was a network of wrinkles as deep as her suffering. Her husband dead of a broken heart while Alekos was in prison. Her eldest son disappeared. Her third son in prison. Furthermore she had been in prison herself, for four and a half months. But they hadn't succeeded in breaking even her. Neither by threats nor by blackmail. In a letter to a London newspaper, she once wrote of her sons: "Trees die on their feet."

At a certain point Eustace, the youngest brother, freed by the amnesty only a few hours earlier, came into the room. Eustace, whom everyone called Stathis, seemed different. Prison had not impaired his youth, his health, his cheerfulness. He was a handsome boy with laughing eyes and prancing legs, the look of a baseball player.

He embraced Alekos without mawkishness, but so violently as to make his bones crack, then sat down to one side to listen; he almost tried to minimize his presence. You guessed him to be overwhelmed by his admiration for Alekos, his love for Alekos. It was for Alekos that in 1972 he had left Rome where he had taken refuge, and had returned secretly to Greece. He wanted to organize for him another escape attempt, and for this he had been arrested, tortured, and condemned to four years and nine months. Plus four and a half years as a draft dodger. However, he had been in prison before, for instance in 1967, and you lost no time in discovering that he was made from the same dough, or rather the same rock, that he was the third pillar of this extraordinary family.

Ah, if only we had also seen George arrive from the garden! But George was not to arrive. No one knew anything more of George, the eldest brother who had followed his father's career and attained the rank of captain. In August of 1967 George had refused to remain in the Greek army, and like Alekos had deserted. He had fled across the Evros River to Turkey, and arriving in Istanbul had sought asylum in the Italian embassy. To our shame, the Italian embassy had refused him asylum, beating about the bush over the necessity of informing the Turkish government, then the Italian government, and so on. George had fled again, this time to Syria, and in Damascus he once again appealed to the Italian embassy, which behaved in the same way. Nevertheless, an embassy more deserving of respect, a Scandinavian one, had taken him in, and there he had remained for a month, until the day he went out into the street and the Syrian police discovered him without a passport. Now fleeing from the Syrian police, he had reached Lebanon. From Lebanon he would have liked to embark for Italy, but did not do so since the Arab countries recognized the Greece of the colonels.

He had preferred to cross over into Israel, a country that did not have diplomatic relations with the Greece of the colonels, and to go to Italy on a ship from Haifa. And instead, in Haifa, the Israelis had arrested him. George had trusted them, he had told them who he was, and they had arrested him all the same, to turn him over to the Greek government. They did not even give him the benefit of a trial; they simply loaded him on the *Anna Maria*, a Greek ship that plied between Haifa and Piraeus. And at this point all trace of him was lost. It seems that George was still in the cabin before the ship entered the straits between Aegina and Piraeus. But when the ship was approaching port, the cabin was found empty. Did he escape by jumping ship? Was he hurled by someone from the ship? His body was never to be found. Every so often the sea gave up a corpse, the authorities summoned Athena to see if she recognized it, and Athena answered, "No, that's not my son George."

At some hour in the evening we interrupted the interview. The crowd of visitors had dispersed, and Athena had offered me hospitality for the night. She had also prepared a dinner, set out on the best tablecloth, and so we ate: myself, she, Alekos, Stathis, a friend. Alekos seemed less tense, less solemn, and soon opened a door to his infinite surprises, letting himself go in a facetious conversation. He called his cell, for example, "my villa in Boyati," describing it as a very luxurious place, with outdoor and indoor swimming pools, golf courses, private cinemas, dazzling salons, a chef who sent for fresh caviar from Iran, odalisques who danced and polished his handcuffs. In this paradise he had once gone on a hunger strike "because the caviar wasn't fresh and wasn't gray." And then, in the same tone, he gave examples of his "widely known friendships" with Aristotle Onassis, Stavros Niarchos, Nelson Rockefeller, Henry Kissinger, or described his "personal jets," and the yacht that the day before he had "borrowed from Princess Anne of England."

I couldn't believe my eyes and ears. Was it possible that in the concrete tomb he had been able to salvage his sense of humor, his capacity to laugh? Not only possible, but undeniable. "You can't understand Alekos," Stathis confided to me at one point, "if you don't know his habit of making fun of people. He's always been like that." However, after dinner when we resumed the interview, Alekos returned to being serious and nervously biting his pipe. We spoke, this time, until three in the morning, and at three-thirty I fell exhausted on the bed they had prepared for me in the living room. Over the bed was a photograph of Basil in his colonel's uniform, and the frame was crowded with gold, silver, and bronze medals, evidence of the various campaigns he had fought up until 1950. Beside the bed was a picture of Alekos when he was an engineering student at the Polytechnic University and member of the central committee of the Youth Federation of the "Union of Center" party. An intelligent and witty little face, at that time without mustaches, and which was no help to me in fathoming a mystery. Then I remembered having seen, in the next room, pictures of the three brothers as children. I got up and examined them. The one of George revealed an elegant and solemn little boy, politely seated on red velvet. The one of Stathis revealed a somewhat less elegant, less solemn little boy, but likewise seated politely on red velvet. The one of Alekos showed a tiger cub with an angry scowl who, standing erect on the red velvet, seemed to announce with anarchistic independence, "No, and I mean no! I won't sit on that thingamajig!" His little knitted outfit hung loosely to show that he didn't give a damn about his outer appearance, and so it was useless for his mother to scold him or plead with him; he was going to do as he liked all the same. And almost as though to show his rejection of advice, orders, and the interference of others, his right hand rested proudly and provocatively on his hip; his left was holding up his pants at the point where he had lost a button.

How long did I stay there studying those photographs? This I really don't remember. But I remember that at a certain point my attention was attracted by something else: a rectangular object covered with dust. I took it in my hand with the sensation of penetrating a secret, and discovered it was a seventeenth-century Bible, with a document attributing its ownership to Alekos Panagoulis. But it was a three-hundred-year-old document, and this Alekos was an ancestor who had fought as a guerrilla against the Turks. I was to find out later that, from the seventeenth century to 1825, the Panagoulis family had supplied nothing but heroes. Some had been named Jorgos, that is George, like the young Jorgos who died in the battle of Faliero in 1823. Others had been named Stathis. But most of them had been named Alekos.

Next morning I left for Bonn. And it goes without saying that it was not a final departure. Seeing me off at the airport, Alekos had made me promise to come back, and a few days later, while he was in the hospital, I returned to discover things that helped a little to clear up the secrets of his elusive personality. First of all, the long poem that he had dedicated to me. It was entitled "Voyage" and told of a ship that had left on an endless voyage, a ship that never yielded to the temptation or the need to dock in any port, approach any shore, or drop its anchor. The crew protested, at times implored, but the captain resisted as he would have resisted a storm, and continued to follow a light.

The ship was himself, Alekos. And also the captain was himself, also the crew. The voyage was his life. A voyage that would end only with his death, since the anchor would never be dropped. Neither the anchor of love, nor the anchor of desires, nor the anchor of a deserved rest. And no argument, no flattery, no threat would be able to induce him to do otherwise. So if you believed in that ship, if you cared about that ship, you must not try to hold it back, nor to stop it by the mirage of green banks and earthly paradises. You should let it go on the mad voyage that had been chosen, and that amidst his host of contradictions was the fixed point of an absolute consistency. "Even Odysseus at the end rested. He reached Ithaca and rested," I remarked after reading the poem. And he answered, "Poor Odysseus." Then he handed me another poem that began as follows: "When you landed in Ithaca / what unhappiness you were to feel, Odysseus / If you had more life ahead of you / why arrive so soon?" I think I really became his friend that day, listening to him in the hospital.

Indeed I went other times to Athens, and never mind if each time the Greek authorities were less pleased. While not daring to deny me an entrance permit, the police filled out forms about me that they never filled out for anyone, and during my stay in Athens they scrupulously occupied themselves with my person. Hardly a difficult thing to do, since I lived in the house in Aristofanos Street, where the telephone was tapped and four policemen in uniform, heaven knows how many in civilian clothes, kept watch on every door, every window, the street itself, twenty-four hours out of the twenty-four.

Psychologically, it was as though Alekos were still in prison and I were there with him. Once he accompanied me to Crete, for five days. And for five days we were constantly followed, spied on, provoked. At Heraklion, where we had gone to visit Knossos, the police cars followed us bumper to bumper. We went into a restaurant to eat, and they planted themselves there to wait for us. We went into a museum, and they planted themselves there. Then often we saw them coming from the opposite direction, because they were equipped with radios and had changed shifts. A nightmare. At the Xania airport I was insulted by an agent in civilian

clothes. On the plane that took us back to Athens, we were relegated to the last two seats and kept under surveillance for the
whole trip. Back in Athens, they wouldn't even allow us the pleasure of a supper in Piraeus without a policeman soon arriving to
dog our heels. They even harassed us at the funeral of a democratic
minister who had died of a heart attack, and needless to say, Papadopoulos never granted the interview that according to the Greek
embassy in Rome he had been ready to give me. What a pity. It
would have been amusing to ask Mr. Papadopoulos what he understood by democracy. And also by amnesty.

It would have been still more amusing to tell him that Alekos,
wherever he went, was welcomed like a national hero. People
stopped him in the street, embracing him and even trying to kiss
his hand. Taxi drivers let him get in even at forbidden points. Car
drivers stopped traffic to greet him. And not seldom, in bars, they
didn't want him to pay the check. In short, everyone was for him
and with him, and only those who were in the service of the colonels were against him. And I followed this extraordinary phenomenon, finally understanding a little the difficult creature who was the
object of it. Understanding better, for example, his disgust and
unhappiness, his thirst for a peace that would never be achieved
and that manifested itself through explosions of desperate and de-
spairing rage, heedless audacities, mad telephone calls to Dimitrios
Ioannides, the strong man of the regime, daring him to arrest him
again.

Or else following in him the craftiness of Odysseus, the shatter-
ing intuitions of Odysseus, whom he increasingly resembled in
every sense. And the tears that filled his eyes when he looked at the
Acropolis, to him the symbol of everything in which he believed.
And his dark silences. And the outbursts of joy that brought back
all of a youthfulness regained for a few hours, for a few minutes.
And the sudden boyish laughter, the unforeseeable jokes immediately canceled by those about-faces of mood. And the exaggerated,
indeed puritanical modesty with which he refused women when
they offered themselves to him with love notes, open invitations,
cunning stratagems. Besides, neither of his past adventures in love
nor of his present sentiments did he ever confide anything to anybody: "A serious man doesn't do that." Shy, stubborn, proud, he
was a thousand persons inside a single person whom you could

never cease to absolve. What a joy to hear him say, in connection with his assassination attempt, "I didn't want to kill a man. I'm not capable of killing a man. I wanted to kill a tyrant."

In the meantime, he had asked for a passport. But it was not even easy for him to obtain the documents necessary for the request. In every office where he applied he found underhand Kafkaesque obstacles. At the Glifada municipal office, for instance, there was no record of his having been born. Suddenly his name was missing from the register. Athena's name was there, Stathis' name, but not his. He laughed about it, with poorly concealed bitterness. "I wasn't born, you see. I was never born." But one morning he came back, jumping with joy. "I was born! I was born!" Who can say why they changed their minds.

A week later, it was a Monday, they gave him the passport—valid for a single round-trip journey. And three hours later, we left, on an Alitalia flight for Rome. But not even our departure was a civilized one. Once past the customs, the police, the baggage examination, we came down into the waiting room and immediately a flock of policemen in civilian clothes surrounded us—a provocation. Then the flight was called and we reached Gate 2. We presented our embarkation cards. They pushed us back. "Why?" Alekos asked. Silence. "We have regular passports and regular embarkation cards. And we've completed all the formalities." Silence. All the other passengers had gone through, boarded the bus, got off the bus, and boarded the plane. The plane was awaiting only us. And we couldn't even approach the boarding ramp. What was worse, we were given no explanation, nor was any given to the Alitalia employees who were escorting us like VIPs.

Ten minutes, fifteen, twenty, twenty-five, thirty . . . I still haven't understood why, after thirty minutes had gone by, they let us go on board. Maybe they had telephoned to the chief of public security. Maybe he had informed Papadopoulos and Papadopoulos had decided that it wasn't a good idea, from the international standpoint as well, to make the mistake of preventing our departure at the last minute. But I haven't understood something else: I haven't understood why, once the doors were closed, the plane was held for another forty minutes on the runway. There were no problems with the control tower that day. There was only a great embarrassment on board. An embarrassment that vanished, however, once we were in the sky. The bluest sky in the world.

In Italy he was received as a hero, as a symbol. And also in France, in Germany, in Sweden, wherever he went in Europe to keep his struggle alive, to ask for help against the dictatorship in Greece. Only the United States did not receive him at all. They steadily refused him a visa. He dreamed of going to Washington to thank the senators and congressmen who had helped to save his life, to explain to them why he went on fighting for freedom. He also wanted to accept the invitation of some universities that wanted him to read from his poems. But when he asked for the visa, something shameful happened. It happened first in a room of the American consulate in Milan. I was there. "Where have you been the last five years?" the vice-consul asked. "At Boiati!" Alekos answered in surprise. "Where is Boiati?" "Next to Athens! The military prison! The one where I was held for five years after the death sentence!" So I intervened: "Sir, I thought you had recognized Mr. Panagoulis, the hero of the Resistance in Greece who was condemned to death and not executed because of the intervention of all the democratic governments of the world, including the personal intervention of Lyndon Johnson." The vice-consul became pale. His eyes filled with terror, he grabbed the passport where he had already put the visa, though unsigned, and for almost an hour he refused to give it back to its owner. He finally did when I threatened to call the Italian police and have him arrested for robbery. But then he stamped an enormous CANCELLED that soiled the page like an insult, and this was the beginning of many insults to come: The insult of the American ambassador in Rome, Mr. John Volpe, who never answered the protests that I wrote him. (Volpe is the man who grants visas to any Italian fascist who wants to visit America and have his contacts in Washington, including Giorgio Almirante, who is on trial for reconstruction of the Fascist party in Italy.) The insult of the American general consul in Rome, a woman, who wrote Panagoulis a brutal letter to endorse the behavior of the vice-consul and praise it, explaining that no visa could be granted to a man who had attempted to take the life of a head of state, therefore a man guilty of a breach of such-and-such Immigration Rules, which meant that Mr. Panagoulis had commited a crime of "moral turpitude." The insult of Henry Kissinger himself, who personally denied the visa in spite of the intervention of senators and congressmen. The insults of all those who, like Henry Kissinger and his ambassadors, shake hands with the dictators and consider it "moral turpitude" to fight them.

Many things have happened since then. In November 1973 resistence to the dictatorship found its voice in a students' revolt at the Polytechnic—only to be silenced by their massacre. As a result, Papadopoulos fell, only to be replaced by even more vicious tyrants. Under Ioannides' leadership, the new colonels dared to attempt that which even Papadopoulos had studiously avoided: the conquest of Cyprus and assassination of Archbishop Makarios. Faced with the prospect of war with Turkey, the colonels were forced to resign, and democracy was resumed with the return of Karamanlis. It was July 1974, and Alekos, who had continued the struggle from his exile in Italy, was finally able to return home. He had made several clandestine trips while the dictatorship was still in power and he chose August 13, the anniversary of his attempted assassination of Papadopoulis, as the day he would officially return home.

Three months later, November 17, the anniversary of the day on which his death sentence had been handed down, Alekos was elected to serve as deputy to the Greek parliament. Together with the other sixty members of the Union of Center Party, he serves in the opposition. In addition to his political activities, the seriousness of his interest in literature was confirmed by the release of a new poetry collection, *I Write from a Prison in Greece*. Alekos has entered a new world whose heavier responsibilities have broadened and matured him. (Someday, someone will have to tell of the noble position he took in Papadopoulos' trial, when he opposed the death penalty for the ex-dictator. Alekos argued that such a sentence would be just only when the suppression of freedom has forced upon the citizen the moral right and duty to act as prosecutor, judge, and executioner. When freedom has been restored, killing is reduced to mere personal vengeance.)

And because of these trips I have made this interview the concluding one in this book. By that I want to demonstrate my choice for those who oppose power and fight against it. So here is the interview I had with Alexander Panagoulis at the end of August 1973 when we met for the first time. It should be read keeping in mind that it took place only two days after his release and that the man has much more to say. Perhaps, and it may be crazy to say it but I like to say it all the same, he still has everything to say.

In what sense, I don't know. In fact, I repeat, it is possible that politics is only one aspect of his talent and personality. And I would not be surprised if his activities were to undergo a turn at some point. True, he carries the stigmata of the tribune and the leader, nor does it seem to me that it will be easy for him to free himself of them. But his authentic culture is based on literary culture, his authentic vein is the poetic vein, and it is no accident that he likes to repeat, "Politics is a duty, poetry is a need." In the mystery that surrounds him and will perhaps always surround him in my eyes, only one point seems clear to me: he will never find what he is seeking. Because what he is seeking does not exist. It is a dream called freedom, called justice. And weeping, cursing, suffering, we can only pursue it, telling ourselves that when a thing does not exist, one invents it. Haven't we done the same with God? Is it not perhaps the destiny of men to invent what does not exist and fight for a dream?

ORIANA FALLACI: You don't look happy, Alekos. But why? You're finally out of that hell and you're not happy?

ALEXANDER PANAGOULIS: No, I'm not. I know you won't believe me, I know this will seem absurd and impossible to you, but I feel more irritated than happy, more sad than happy. I feel as I did last Sunday when I heard those hurrahs coming from the cells of the other prisoners, and I didn't know the reason for the hurrahs, and thought: It must have to do with an amnesty. Papadopoulos is making his proclamation, so he's getting ready to put on a show with an amnesty that will impress the naïve. By now he can afford to be less afraid. Or rather, pretend to be less afraid. It doesn't cost him much to let some of us go. I thought "some of us" because I didn't think he'd free me too. And when I found out on Monday morning, I didn't feel any joy. None whatsoever. I said to myself: if he's decided it's all right to free me too, it means his plan is more ambitious; it means he's really counting on legalizing the junta within the framework of the Constitution and seeking recognition from his old opponents. Coming in my cell, the prison commandant had announced the pardon to me: "Panagoulis, you've been pardoned." I said, "What do you mean, pardoned? I didn't ask anyone for pardon." Then I added, "You'll soon realize it's easy to put me in but hard to get me out. Before I get to Erythrae, you'll have put me in again." Erythrae is a suburb of Athens.

O.F.: You told him that?

A.P.: Sure. What else could I say? Should I perhaps have said thank you, very kind of you, give my compliments to Mr. Papadopoulos? Besides Tuesday was worse. You know, there's a special procedure for reading the amnesty decree to the prisoner—a kind of ceremony with a platoon presenting arms, the others standing at attention, and so forth. So, around noon, Prosecutor Nicolodimus arrives for the ceremony, and they take me out of my cell and lead me in front of the commandant's quarters, where everybody is standing up, and so forth. I see a chair and immediately sit down. Dismay, surprise. "Panagoulis! On your feet!" orders Nicolodimus. "And why?" I answer. "Why do you have to read a piece of paper that you call a presidential decree but for me is only the piece of paper of a colonel? . . . No, I won't get up. No!" And I stay sitting. The others on their feet, at attention, and so forth, and me sitting down. I wouldn't have given up that chair even if they had chopped me to pieces. They had to celebrate the ceremony while I sat there with my legs crossed. I never stopped provoking them. When the lieutenant colonel came to get me, about two in the afternoon, I provoked him too. "Panagoulis, you're free. Take your things." "I don't take anything. Take them yourself. I didn't ask to leave."

O.F.: And he?

A.P.: Oh, he said the same thing as the others. "Once you're outside, you won't say that. You'll discover the *dolce vita* and change your mind." Then they took my bags and carried them to the gate like porters. It was amusing because in one of those bags they were carrying like porters I had hidden the last poems I'd written and the little saws I used to saw the bars. They're tiny saws, look. But they work. Seventeen times they found these saws on me, and yet I was always able to get more of them, and when I left Boyati I had about ten. I kept them here, see? And the next time . . . I'm always expecting them to come back and get me to take me back there. And you want me to be happy!

O.F.: And yet, once you were outside, when you saw the sun and your mother, it must have been wonderful.

A.P.: It wasn't all that wonderful. It was like going blind. It had been so many years since I'd been outside that concrete tomb, so many years since I'd seen the sun and open space. I'd forgotten what the sun was like, and outside there was a very strong sun. When I felt it on me, I had to close my eyes. Then I reopened them a little, but only a little, and with my eyes half-closed I went forward. And by going forward, I discovered space. I no longer remembered what space was like. My cell was a meter and a half by three; I could only take two and a half steps in it. At the most three. Rediscovering space made me dizzy. I felt myself spinning inside like a merry-go-round, and I staggered and almost fell. Besides even now, if I walk for more than a hundred meters, I get tired and disoriented.

No, it hasn't been wonderful. And I don't care if you don't believe it. Or I do care and never mind. I made a terrible effort to go forward in all that sun, all that space. Then all of a sudden, in all that sun, in all that space, I saw a spot. And the spot was a group of people. And from that group of people a black figure detached itself. And it came toward me, and little by little it became my mother. And behind my mother another figure detached itself. And this one too came toward me. And little by little it became Mrs. Mandilaras, the widow of Nikoforos Mandilaras, murdered by the colonels. And I embraced my mother, I embraced Mrs. Mandilaras, and afterward . . .

O.F.: Afterward you cried.

A.P.: No! I didn't cry! Not even my mother cried! We're people who don't cry. If by chance we cry, we never cry in front of others. In these years I've cried only twice: when they murdered Georghadjis and when they told me my father was dead. But no one saw me cry—I was inside my cell. And then . . .

then nothing. I went home with my mother and Mrs. Mandilaras and the lawyer. And at home I found a lot of friends. I
was with my friends until six in the morning, then I went to
bed in my own bed, and don't ask me if I felt moved at sleeping in my own bed. Because I didn't feel moved.

Oh, I'm not insensitive, you know! I'm not! But I'm hardened. Much hardened, and what else do you expect from a
man who for five years has been buried alive in a concrete
tomb, without any contact with the world except with those
who beat him, insulted him, tortured him, and even tried to
murder him? True, they didn't execute me after pronouncing
that death sentence. But they buried me all the same—alive
instead of dead. And for that I despise them. It was their right
to execute me, since I made that assassination attempt, and
how! But they had no right to bury me alive instead of dead.
That's why I feel nothing but rage toward those clowns who
now allow me to sleep in my bed.

O.F.: Alekos, don't say such things. Do you want to go back to
prison?

A.P.: If we were to look at things logically, I should really have been
taken back before arriving in Erythrae. I'm ready to go back to
prison at any moment. From this moment on. Since yesterday, since the day before yesterday, since the moment I was
blinded by that sun. I'll tell you something else: if my going
back to prison would do any good, I'd be happy to go back.
Because for what reason should they take me back to prison?
For what I say to others or to you? But isn't it my right to say
what I think under a democratic regime, and doesn't Papadopoulos insist that Greece is a democracy? Papadopoulos has
every interest in keeping me outside and showing the world
that he cares nothing about what I say. And if he wants to go
about harming me intelligently, he has to make me fall into
some trap. But that he's already tried.

The day after my release some big kid came here saying he
was a student, though just from his haircut you could tell right
away that he belonged to the military police. He told me he
had killed an American who'd been taken as a hostage to free
Panagoulis, some time ago, and then asked me for some machine guns. I yelled and threw him out, and then telephoned

immediately to the military police. I tried to get the chief, one of those who had tortured me. He was out, and so I said to the receptionist, "Tell him that if he sends me another one of his *agents provocateurs*, I'll beat the hell out of him." My God! They weren't able to break me in prison—just imagine them being able to break me now.

O.F.: Alekos, aren't you afraid of being killed?

A.P.: Who knows! Since they want to look like liberals, democrats, it wouldn't even be to their advantage to kill me—for the moment. But they might be thinking about it. In March of 1970, immediately after the murder of Polycarpos Georghadjis, the hero of the war of liberation in Cyprus and minister of Archbishop Makarios, they tried it. It was about seven in the evening and I was in the fifth day of a new hunger strike. All of a sudden I heard a whistle and my straw mattress caught fire. I threw myself on the floor; I shouted murderers, bastards, beasts, open the door. But it was more than an hour before they took me out, or rather before they opened the door. An hour during which the mattress went on burning and burning . . . I couldn't see any more, I couldn't breathe. When the prison doctor came, a young second lieutenant, I was in a coma.

As I found out later, he wanted to take me immediately to the hospital, but they didn't let him, and for two days I stayed between life and death in my cell. The doctor made a desperate effort to save me and succeeded in transferring me to the hospital. The men of the junta showed themselves to be completely indifferent. Very often I fainted and I couldn't speak because my throat hurt and even breathing was painful. After forty-eight hours that young second lieutenant got some older medical officers to come and see me, and when they saw what condition I was in, they were furious. The chief of the medical officers said it was a crime to keep me in the cell, and telephoned to his superiors to protest. If it's true what I heard later, he also called the commander in chief of the armed forces, who's now vice-president of the pseudo democracy, Odysseus Anghelis. He told him that their refusal to have me transferred to a hospital was a criminal act and that he would denounce them. And it was thanks to him that they finally ad-

mitted me. In the hospital they found ninety-two percent car-
bon dioxide in my blood and they said I wouldn't have lasted
more than two hours—even if I'd gone beyond the two hours,
in any case, I wouldn't have survived. And . . . But do you
know why they freed Theodorakis?

O.F.: Theodorakis? No.

A.P.: Because I was about to die. That Frenchman was in Athens.
That Servan-Schreiber. And it seems he'd come to take me
away. They wouldn't have handed me over to Servan-
Schreiber, of course, even if I'd been well. And besides there
was the fact that I was in a state of coma as a result of their attempt to murder me. So, in anticipation of the scandal that
would have broken out with my death, they gave him Theodorakis. Amusing, isn't it? I don't mean by this that I wasn't
happy about the release of Theodorakis. He had suffered so
much in prison. But . . . the story is still amusing.

O.F.: Interesting. But how did you come to have proof that they'd
tried to murder you?

A.P.: A few days before, they had taken away my mattress to "dust"
it. That happened very seldom, every three or four months.
And when they brought it back to the cell, the guard came to
me. The guard was a friend. He said, "Alekos, did you hide
anything in your mattress?" "No, nothing. Why?" I answered.
"Because I saw Corporal Karakaxas poking around inside it as
though he were looking for something." I didn't give any importance to the matter at the time, but still the first thing I
thought when the mattress caught fire was that they'd put
phosphorous or plastic or something inside it. And the first
name that came to mind was Karakaxas. Naturally they accused me of setting myself on fire. But when I reminded them
that six days before they'd taken my cigarettes and matches,
they realized they were in trouble. Major Kutras of the military police came to me and said, "If you don't tell anyone
what happened, you have my word of honor that we'll release
you and let you go abroad."

Since I refused even to discuss such an offer, after ten days
they threw me back in the cell, and from that time on even
my mother's visits were forbidden. As for my lawyer, I never
saw him in five years. I never received his letters, he never

received mine. And even that's not all there is to be said about their illegal and criminal treatment of me. They were obviously afraid I'd reveal the attempted murder and so all my mail ended up on the prison director's desk. Even the letters I wrote to Papadopoulos. I wrote to Papadopoulos as the moral leader of the junta, to express to him all my disgust and contempt. They should have had the courage to publish them, those letters, or at least to make them public. I sent so many of them, to all addresses. And then I wrote to the president of the Constitutional Court. I sent him telegrams to let him know what they were doing to me and to tell him I was ill. But not even he ever received my telegrams and . . .

O.F.: And how are you now, Alekos?

A.P.: Less well than I look. My health isn't good. I always feel weak, exhausted. Sometimes I have breakdowns. I had one yesterday, another when I was just out of prison. I can't walk—three steps and I have to sit down. And aside from that, a lot of things are wrong—in my liver, my lungs, my kidneys. They've taken me to the clinic and the first results haven't been reassuring—Monday I have to go back.

All those hunger strikes, for instance, weakened me. You'll say but why also inflict those hunger strikes on yourself? Because during interrogations a hunger strike is a means of keeping your head. You show them, I mean, that they can't take everything away from you since you have the courage to reject everything. I'll try to explain. If you refuse to eat and you attack them, they get nervous and the fact of being nervous doesn't allow them to apply a systematic form of interrogation. During torture, for instance, if the man being tortured keeps up a provocatory and aggressive attitude, systematic interrogation is transformed into a personal struggle by the tortured man himself. Understand? I mean that with hunger strikes, the body is weakened and this won't allow the interrogation to be continued, since it's useless to interrogate or torture someone who loses consciousness. These conditions are realized after three or four days without food or water, especially if you lose blood because of the wounds inflicted by the tortures. So they're forced to transfer you to the hospital and . . . Oh, even my memories of the hospital are painful. They tried to feed me with a plastic tube put up my nose. I suffered a lot, even when I had the feeling I was gaining time. And then . . .

O.F.: And then?

A.P.: Then, from the hospital, they took me back to the torture room and started torturing me again. Then I started a new hunger strike, and again I provoked them, again I was contemptuous, aggressive. So their system failed again. And again they were forced to take me to the hospital, where again they tried to feed me through a tube in the nose. Oh, even the behavior of some doctors was disgusting. My torturers continued the interrogation in the hospital, but in a less consistent way since there they couldn't use their methods. I gained time, I repeat, and that was important to me. In short, it would have been impossible for me to give up hunger strikes. They were too indispensable a weapon.

O.F.: During the interrogations, I understand. . . . But later, Alekos, in prison?

A.P.: Even in prison I had no better way to express my disgust, my contempt, and to show them they couldn't break me. Even if I was now a convict. By rebelling through hunger strikes, I had the feeling of not being alone and I felt I was offering something for the cause of Greece. I thought if I kept a steady, courageous attitude, the soldiers and guards and the officers themselves would understand that I was there to represent a people determined to win. Besides many of the hunger strikes I went on in prison were provoked by the way they behaved with me. They wouldn't even let me have a newspaper, a book, a pencil, a cigarette. And in order to have a newspaper, a book, a pencil, or to smoke a cigarette, I refused to eat. For days on end. I went on one strike that lasted forty-seven days, one that lasted forty-four, one forty, one thirty-seven, two thirty-two, one thirty, five between twenty-five and thirty . . . I went on so many. And despite this, they never stopped beating me. Never. I took so many beatings in that cell. They broke my ribs when they beat me with iron rods; they've barely healed. . . .

O.F.: When did they beat you for the last time?

A.P.: If you're talking about a serious beating, on October 25, 1972, on the thirty-fifth day of a hunger strike. Nicholas Zakarakis, the director of the Boyati prison came in, and I was lying on the straw mattress. I didn't have any more strength; I could hardly breathe any more. All the same he started insulting me and all of a sudden he said that I'd been paid to assassinate Papadopoulos and that I'd put the money in Switzerland. Then I just couldn't keep silent. I gathered what little voice I had left in my throat and yelled, "*Malakas! Dirty malakas!*" *Malakas* is a bad word in Greek. Zakarakis reacted with such a rain of blows that it still hurts when I think of it. Usually I defended myself. But that day I couldn't lift a finger and . . . Also on March 17 they'd beaten me. They'd tied me to the cot and beaten me for an hour and a half. When Dr. Zografos lifted the sheet and saw my body, he closed his eyes in horror. It was a body as black as ink, one bruise from head to foot. They'd beaten me especially on the lungs and on the loins, and so for two weeks I spat blood and urinated blood. So how can you expect me to feel well now? Besides the business of urinating blood also comes from something else they did to me during the interrogation.

O.F.: I won't ask you about it, Alekos.

A.P.: Why not? Anyway it's something I also told at the trial and which I informed the International Red Cross about. It was Babalis, one of my torturers, who did it to me. While I was tied naked to that iron bed, he put an iron wire up my urethra. A kind of needle. Then while the others were shouting obscenities, he heated the end of the wire that was sticking out red-hot with his cigarette lighter. It was awful. You can say, "After all, they didn't use electric shocks on you." No, they don't know how to do it. But they did that thing to me, and when you talk about torture, how do you decide which is the worst? To stay handcuffed for ten months, ten months I say, day and night, isn't that perhaps a torture? Ten months, day and night. Only beginning in the ninth month did they free my wrists, for a few hours. Two or three hours in the morning, at the insistence of the prison doctor. My hands were swollen, my wrists were bleeding, and in some places they had running sores. . . .

I succeeded in informing my mother, who filed an official

written accusation with the prosecutor general. And that accusation is proof, because if my mother had written a falsehood, wouldn't they have indicted her? Didn't they indict Mrs. Manganis when she revealed that her husband, Professor George Manganis, had been tortured? They put her in prison too, that great lady, though she'd told the truth. They could afford to because in her case it was difficult to prove the accusations. But in my case, no. They couldn't imprison my mother—the proofs existed. And were obvious. They were the wounds and scars I carried on my whole body.

If I had to make a list of the tortures . . . Look at these three scars on the side of the heart. I got them the day they broke my left foot with the phalange. Naturally they always used the phalange on me, which consists in beating you on the soles of your feet until the pain arrives at your brain and you faint. I even stood that fairly well. But that day Babalis went all out and broke my left foot. Five minutes later Constantine Papadopoulos came in. You know, Papadopoulos' brother. He put his pistol to my head and shouted, "Now I'm going to kill you, I'm going to kill you!" and he started hitting me. While he was doing that, Theofiloyannakos hit me over the heart with an iron paper knife with a jagged point. "I'll stick it in your heart, I'll stick it in your heart!" That's how I got these three scars.

O.F.: And these scars on your wrists?

A.P.: Oh, these I got when they pretended to open my veins. Nothing serious. They only cut me superficially. Anyway, you know, I have scars all over my body. Ever so often I discover one and say: Now when did I get that? After three weeks of torture, I didn't pay any attention to them any more. I felt my blood dripping somewhere, my flesh opening up somewhere else, and just thought: Here we go again. They usually began their tortures by whipping me with a metal cable. It was Theofiloyannakos who whipped me. Or else they hung me from the ceiling by my wrists and left me there for hours. It's hard to take because after a while the upper part of the body becomes as though paralyzed. I mean, you can't feel your arms and shoulders any more. You can't breathe, you can't cry out, you can't rebel in any way and . . . They knew all this, of course, and when I reached that point they beat me on the loins.

Do you know what I could never get used to? Suffocation. Theofiloyannakos * did that to me too, holding my nose and mouth with both his hands. Oh, that was the worst of all. The worst! He held my nose and mouth for one minute, watching the clock, and he let me take a breath only when I was turning blue. He stopped doing it with his hands when I succeeded in biting him. I almost bit off his finger. But then he switched to using a blanket and . . . Another thing I couldn't stand were the insults. They never tortured me in silence. Never. They shouted, shouted. . . . In voices that were no longer voices but roars. . . . And then the cigarettes crushed out between the testicles.

Listen, why do you only want to hear about these things from me? It's not right. They didn't just do it to me. Go to Military Hospital 401, if you can, and ask to see Major Mustaklis. With him, during his interrogation, they used the *aloni*. Do you know what the *aloni* is? It's when the torturers stand in a circle, then they put you in the middle, and they all hit you at once. They beat him on the spine and the back of his neck. He's still completely paralyzed. He lies in bed like a vegetable and the doctors pronounce him "clinically dead."

o.f.: I'd like to ask you something, Alekos. Before all this happened, could you stand physical pain?

a.p.: Oh, no! No. The least little toothache bothered me immeasurably, and I couldn't stand the sight of blood. Just to see people suffer made me suffer. I admired people who were able to tolerate physical pain and couldn't see how they did it. Man is really an extraordinary creature, a sea of surprises. It's incredible how a man can change, and it's wonderful how a man can show himself to be capable of bearing the unbearable. That rhetorical proverb, "The steel is tempered by the fire," is really true, you know. The more they tortured me, the harder I got. The more they tortured me, the more I resisted. Some say that under torture you call on death as a liberation.

---

* The chief of the torturers, now condemned to twenty years in prison. (O.F.)

It's not true. At least not for me. I'd be lying if I said I was never afraid, but I'd also be lying if I said I ever wanted to die. Dying was the last idea to enter my head. I thought only of not giving in, of not talking, and of rebelling. If you only knew how many times I hit them myself! If I wasn't tied to the iron table, I kicked and bit them. It was very useful because they got more furious than ever and beat me harder till I fainted. I always wanted to faint, because fainting was like resting. Then they started again, but . . .

O.F.: Excuse me, Alekos. I'm curious about something. But did you know that the whole world was concerned with you and was protesting about you?

A.P.: No. I only realized it the day they came in my cell waving newspapers and shouting "Russian tanks have entered Czechoslovakia! Now nobody'll have the time or wish to be concerned about you!" And then I realized it when they showed me to reporters, after my first escape attempt. There were so many, from so many countries. And I said to myself, "But then they know!" And I felt something like a caress on the heart. And it seemed to me I was less alone. Because the most awful thing, you know, isn't to suffer. It's to suffer alone.

O.F.: Go on with your story, Alekos.

A.P.: I was saying that when they insulted me, "criminal, bastard, traitor, fag," other unrepeatable vulgarities, I insulted them back. I yelled frightful things. For instance: "I'll fuck your daughter!" But coldly, without losing my head, you see what I mean? I'm very emotional, but with rage I get cold. One day they sent me an officer who was an expert in psychological interrogation. You know, one of the ones who says, "My dear boy, it's better that you talk." Seeing he was so polite, I asked him for a glass of water. He had it brought to me. But as soon as I had the glass in my hand, instead of drinking out of it, I broke it. Then with the broken glass, I threw myself on those scoundrels. I cut two or three of them before they jumped on me and threw me to the floor, on the pieces of glass, and one piece almost cut off half my right little finger. I also cut the tendons, you see. I can't move this finger any more. It's a dead finger. Then you know what that beast Babalis did? He called the doctor, and without freeing my wrists, which were tied

behind my back, he had him take stitches in my little finger.
Like that, without an anesthetic. God, how it hurt! That day I
screamed. I screamed like a madman.

O.F.: Listen, Alekos, weren't you ever tempted to talk?

A.P.: Never! Never! Never! I never said anything. Never. I never
implicated anyone. Never. Since I had taken all the responsibility myself for the attempt on Papadopoulos' life, they
wanted to know who would have taken over the responsibilities
of the government if the attempt had been successful. But they
didn't get a word out of me. One day when I was lying on the
iron bed and really couldn't take any more, they brought in a
Greek named Brindisi. He had talked, and now he was crying.
Crying, he said, "Enough, Alekos. It's no use any more. Talk,
Alekos." But I answered, "Who's this Brindisi? The only Brindisi I know is an Italian port." The same day they brought in
Avramis. Avramis was a member of Greek Resistance, an ex-
police officer, a brave and honest man. I denied that I knew
him, I denied that he belonged to Greek Resistance. Theofiloyannakos yelled, "You can see he knows you. And he's already admitted it. Admit the same thing and we'll get this
business over with." I said, "Listen, Theofiloyannakos. If I
were to get my hands on you for just one hour, I'd make you
confess anything. Even that you raped your mother. I don't
know this man. You've tortured him and now he says what
you want him to." And Theofiloyannakos: "Whether you talk
or not, we'll say that you've talked."

Listen, even under the most atrocious tortures I never betrayed anyone. Anyone. And this is something even those
animals respect. The direction of my tortures was entrusted to
the chief of police, the then Lieutenant Colonel and now
Brigadier General Ioannides. One night, seeing me spit blood,
he shook his head and said, "It's no use. No use insisting. It
happens once in a hundred thousand times that someone
doesn't talk. But this is that case. He's too tough, this Panagoulis. He won't talk." Ioannides has always said, "The only
group we can be sure we haven't decimated is Panagoulis'
group. This tiger broke his handcuffs." Well, maybe it's not
nice for me to tell you this. Maybe you'll get the idea I'm a
fop and write that I'm self-satisfied and stuff like that. But I

must tell you all the same, because after all it's a great satisfaction. Isn't it?

O.F.: Of course it is. And now I'd like to know something else, Alekos. After suffering so much, are you still capable of loving men?

A.P.: Of still loving them? Of loving them more, you mean! God damn it, how can you ask such a question? You don't think I identify humanity with the brutes in the Greek military police? Why, that's only a handful of men! Doesn't it mean anything to you that in all these years they're always the same ones? Always the same ones! Listen, bad people are a minority. And for every bad man, there are a thousand, ten thousand good ones—namely their victims. The ones you have to fight for.

You can't, you shouldn't, see things so black! I've met so many good people in these five years! Even among the cops. Yes, yes. But just think of the soldiers who risked their lives to smuggle my letters, my poems, out of prison! Think of all those who helped me when I tried to escape! Think of the doctors who had me taken to the hospital, and when I was in the hospital ordered the guards not to keep me tied to the bed by my ankles. "I can't do that," the guards said. And the doctors: "This isn't a prison! It's a *hospital!*" What about that fellow Panayotidis who participated in the tortures and always spat on me? One day he came up to me all embarrassed and said, "Alekos, I'm sorry. I did what they ordered me to do. I would have done it even if they'd told me to do it to my father. I haven't the courage to rebel. Forgive me, Alekos." Oh, man . . .

O.F.: Do you mean man is fundamentally good, man is born good?

A.P.: No. I mean that man is born to be good, and is more often good than bad. And listen, to accept men, all I have to do is think of something that happened when I was in the hospital after they tried to kill me by setting fire to my mattress. There was an old cleaning woman in that ward. You know, one of those old women who mop floors and clean toilets. One day she came by and stroked my forehead and said, "Poor Alekos! You're always alone! You never speak to anyone. I'll come back tonight and sit beside you, and you can tell me about things, all right?" Then she went toward the door and there she was grabbed by the guards, who took her away. She didn't come back that night. I waited for her but she didn't come back. I never saw her again. I never found out what happened to her and . . .

O.F.: Are you crying, Alekos? You?!

A.P.: I'm not crying. I don't cry. I'm moved. Kindness moves me. Goodness moves me. And so I'm moved. Understand?

O.F.: I understand. Are you religious, Alekos?

A.P.: Am I? No. I mean, I don't believe in God. If you talk to me about God, I can only say that I agree with Einstein: I believe in Spinoza's God. Call it pantheism, call it what you will. And if you talk to me about Jesus Christ, I can say that's all right with me, because I don't consider him the son of God but the son of man. The sole fact that his life was inspired by the wish to alleviate human suffering, the sole fact that he suffered and died for men and not for the glory of God, is enough to make me consider him great. The greatest of all the gods invented by man. You see, man can't leave the idea of love out of consideration because he can't live without love. I've received so much hate in my life but I've also received so much love. As a child, for instance. I was a happy child because I grew up in a family where we all loved each other. But it wasn't just a question of family. It was a question of . . . how should I say? Of discoveries.

For instance, during the Italian occupation we took refuge on the island of Leukas where there were a lot of Italian soldiers. They always called me "little one, *piccolo, piccolo, piccolo!*" and then gave me presents. A chocolate, a biscuit. My father, an army officer, didn't want me to accept those presents and insisted I throw them away. But my mother said, "Pick them up and say thanks." My mother knew they weren't doing it to insult me but to be kind. She knew they weren't bad soldiers but good men. I've been less happy since growing up. It's hard to feel completely happy when you realize that others don't always care about the things you care about. And when I saw the indifference of my contemporaries for the problems of life, I . . . well, I wasn't able to be happy any more. Like today.

O.F.: It's curious, Alekos. You talk like a man who can't even conceive the idea of trying to kill someone.

A.P.: Before April 21, that is before the coming of the colonels, I couldn't even conceive the idea of killing. I wouldn't have been able to harm my worst enemy. Anyway, even today, the idea of killing is repugnant to me. I'm not a fanatic. I'd like for everything here in Greece to change without spilling a single drop of blood. I don't believe in justice applied in a personal way. Still less do I believe in the word revenge. Even for those who've tortured me, I don't conceive the word revenge. I use the word punishment and imagine only a trial. For me it would be enough to see them sentenced to one day of prison in the cell where I spent five years. I care too much about law, rights, duty. In fact, I've never challenged Papadopoulos' right to have me tried and sentenced. What I always protested was the way they carried out the sentence, the beatings they gave me, the cruelties they inflicted on me, the concrete tomb where they kept me without even allowing me to read and write. But when someone does what I did, the attempted assassination I mean, he doesn't go against the law. Because he's acting in a lawless country. And the answer to lawlessness is lawlessness. See what I mean?

Look, if you're walking in the street and not bothering anyone, and I come up and start slapping you, and you can't even report me because the law doesn't protect you, what are you to think? What are you to do? Mind you, I was talking about slaps, nothing more. A slap doesn't even hurt, it's only an insult. But there should be a law that forbids me to slap you! A law that forbids me even to give you a kiss if you don't want it! And if this law doesn't exist, what do you do? Don't you have the right to react and maybe even kill me so that I won't bother you any more? To take justice into your own hands becomes a necessity! Or rather a duty! Yes or no?

O.F.: Yes.

A.P.: I'm not afraid to say it: I know what hatred is too. I love love so much, and I'm full of hatred for anyone who kills freedom, those who killed it in Greece, for instance. God damn it, it's hard to say these things without sounding rhetorical, but . . . There's a sentence that turns up often in Greek literature: "Happy to be free and free to be happy." So when a tyrant dies a natural death in his bed, I . . . I can't help it, I'm overcome with rage. Overcome with hatred. In my opinion, it's an honor for the Italians that Mussolini came to the end he did, and it's shameful for the Portuguese that Salazar died in his bed. Just as it'll be shameful for the Spaniards when Franco dies of old age.

God damn it! You can't let a whole nation be transformed into a herd of sheep. And listen, I'm not dreaming of utopia. I know very well that absolute justice doesn't exist, that it'll never exist. But I know there are countries where a process of justice gets applied. So what I'm dreaming of is a country where those who get attacked, insulted, deprived of their rights, can demand justice in a court. Is that too much to ask? Bah! It seems to me the least a man can ask. That's why I get so angry with the cowards who don't rebel when their fundamental rights are violated. I wrote on the walls of my cell: "I hate tyrants and cowards disgust me."

O.F.: Alekos . . . this is a difficult question. What did you feel when they sentenced you to death?

A.P.: At that moment, nothing. I was expecting it, I was prepared for it, and so I didn't feel anything except an awareness that by dying I'd be contributing to a struggle that would be carried on by others.

O.F.: And were you sure they would shoot you?

A.P.: Yes. Absolutely sure.

O.F.: Alekos . . . this question is still more difficult. And I don't know if you'll want to answer. What does a man think when he's about to be shot?

A.P.: I've wondered myself. Many times. And I tried to say it in a poem I wrote in my head the morning when they came to find out if I was asking for pardon and I answered no. . . . It's a poem that gives a pretty good idea of what I was thinking at that moment. It goes like this: "As / the branches of the trees hear / the first blows of the ax / so / that morning / the orders / reached my ears / At the same moment / old memories / that I thought dead / flooded my mind / like sobs / rending sobs of the past / for a tomorrow that wouldn't arrive / The will / that morning / was only a wish / Hope? / it too was lost / but not for a moment was I sorry / that the platoon was waiting." And look, as far as I know, there are three writers who've explained it in a way similar to what I felt. One is Dostoevsky in *The Idiot*. Another is Camus in *The Stranger*. The third is Kazantzakis in the book where he tells of the death of Christ. What Dostoevsky says, I knew—I'd read *The Idiot*. But I hadn't read *The Stranger*, and when I did, much later in Boyati, it disturbed me to discover that I'd thought the same things while I was waiting for the hour of execution. I mean, all the things you'd like to do if they weren't about to cut off your head. To write a poem, for example, or a letter. To read a book, to create a little life for yourself in that little cell. A life just as wonderful because it's life. . . . But I was especially disturbed to read the version that Kazantzakis gives on the death of Christ. There's a moment in that book when Christ closes his eyes, on the cross, and sleeps. And dreams a dream that's a dream of life. He dreams that . . . But I don't want to talk about it. It's not good to talk about it.

O.F.: It doesn't matter, since I've understood anyway that you were dreaming of making love to a woman. In Kazantzakis' book, Christ dreams he's making love to Martha and Mary, the sisters of Lazarus. Yes . . . ten minutes of sleep to dream of life. . . . It's right like that, it's beautiful like that. But how did you spend the rest of that night?

A.P.: The cell was a bare cell, without even a cot. They'd put a blanket on the floor for me, that's all. I was handcuffed. Always handcuffed. So for a little while I lay there handcuffed on the floor, then I got up and started talking to the guards. My guards were three noncommissioned officers. Young, about twenty-one. They looked like nice guys and they weren't hostile; in fact they looked as though they were sad about me—depressed at the thought that in a little while I'd be shot. To cheer them up, I started talking about politics. I spoke to them as I would have spoken to students during a demonstration. I explained to them that they shouldn't remain passive, they should fight for freedom. And they listened to me with respect. I even recited a poem I'd written: "The Three Deaths." You know, the one that Theodorakis has set to music. While I was reciting, they wrote the verses on their cigarette packages.

Then those three were relieved by three others, also conscripts, and among them was one who sang in the choir of a church. I let myself play a cruel joke. I asked him to sing me what he sang for the funeral Mass. He sang it to me. And still joking, I told him, "Some of those words I don't like. And when you sing for me, at my funeral Mass, you mustn't say them. For example, you mustn't call me servant of the Lord. No man is anybody's servant. No man should be anybody's servant. Not even of the Lord." And he promised that for me he wouldn't sing those words, he wouldn't call me servant of the Lord. So we stopped that cruel game and went on to sing some other songs by Theodorakis.

O.F.: Alekos . . . what does a man feel when they tell him that they're not going to shoot him after all?

A.P.: They never told me the death sentence was suspended. For three years they never told me. And in Greece a death sentence is valid for three years. At any moment, during those three long years, they could have opened the door of my cell and said, "Let's go, Panagoulis. The firing squad is waiting for you." The first morning, I was expecting to be shot at five, five-thirty. Even the grave was ready. When I saw that five-thirty had gone by, and six, six-thirty, seven, I began to suspect there was something new. But I didn't think the execution had been suspended—I thought it had been delayed for a few hours. Maybe the helicopter had been held up, maybe the prosecutor had had to take care of some red tape. . . . Then, around eight, a squad came to the door of my cell. And I said to myself: Here we go. But someone gave an order and the squad disbanded. Right after that they told me they wouldn't shoot me that morning because it was the Feast of the Presentation of the Virgin, so there wouldn't be any executions. They'd shoot me next day, November 22.

I started waiting for dawn again, and the second night was like the first, and at dawn I was ready again. An officer came and said, "Sign the request for pardon and you won't be shot." I refused, and just as I was refusing, I heard another officer giving a curt order to the soldiers outside. And I thought: Here we go. Here we really go this time. Instead nothing happened, and in the afternoon they took me away from the Aegina prison. They took me to the military port and there, with Patrol Boat P-21, they took me to the office of the military police. The place where I'd been interrogated. Here there was an officer and he said to me, "Panagoulis, the newspapers have already reported your execution. Now we'll be able to interrogate you as we please. We'll make you tell anything we like, and you'll die under torture. And nobody will know it because everyone thinks you've been executed." It was only a malicious threat, however—they didn't torture me that day. At dawn on November 23, they put me in a car and said, "Panagoulis, no more fooling around. We're taking you to be executed." Instead they took me to Boyati.

O.F.: Alekos, I wonder how you've managed to keep a clear mind after having been five years alone and buried inside a concrete box not much wider than a bed. How did you do it?

A.P.: Simply by rejecting any idea of having been defeated. Besides I never felt defeated. That's the reason I never stopped fighting. Every day was a new battle. Because I wanted every day to be a new battle. I never allowed myself to fall into inertia. I thought of my oppressed people and my rage was transformed into energy. It was just this energy that always helped me to think up new ways to escape. I didn't want to escape for the sake of escaping, I mean so as not to be in prison. I wanted to escape to continue my struggle, to be with my comrades again. I had come into the struggle determined to give my all, and my desperation came from my certainty that I'd given too little, that I'd done too little.

When Greece had been overwhelmed by the dictatorship, I'd said to my friends, "My only ambition is to give my life to put an end to this dictatorship, my only wish is to be the last one to die in this battle. Not so as to live more than others but to give more than others." And today, in all sincerity, I can say the same thing to my friends and I don't care if our enemies know it. On the contrary. I certainly don't delude myself that I'll be alive the day when victory will be celebrated, but I believe with all my heart that that day will be celebrated. For that to happen, however, I must go on fighting. And this idea, together with the idea of escaping, helped me not to go crazy in those five years.

O.F.: But how did you plan to escape from that tomb?

A.P.: In the most incredible ways. First of all, I thought of a way to send messages to my comrades. . . . Even knowing there was little possibility of my succeeding in escaping, the idea never left me. Never. My principle was the same as today: better to fail than to lull yourself into inertia. Now I'll tell you about two attempts that failed but that to me seem amusing. One night the guards open the door of my cell, at the same time as always, and they don't find me inside. As I'd foreseen, those idiots get panicky and start shouting, panting, mutually accusing each other, looking for me on the walls, on the ceiling, and not thinking of looking for me in the only place where I could have been hiding: under the cot. I was under the cot, and it was fun to listen to them. "You're the one who came in the cell this morning!" And the other: "You're the one who had the keys!" "Well, let's not fight about it! Let's try and find him!" And away they go, out of the cell, to give the alarm—leaving the door open.

So I rushed out of the cell and ran in the dark, for some fifty meters. I stopped against a tree. From this tree I reached another tree, then the shadows of the kitchen, and then the prison wall. People were yelling all over the yard: "Alarm, alarm." I yelled too: "Alarm canceled. Canceled!" I hoped someone would hear it and believe it. Now all I had to do was get over the wall. I was just about to when a soldier saw me and grabbed me.

O.F.: How did you feel when they grabbed you?

A.P.: I certainly wasn't happy about it. But I didn't get angry; I just thought: It doesn't matter. Next time it will go better. The next time was with a pistol made of soap. I'd made it myself, using soap and pieces of bread, and then I'd painted it black with the tips of burned matches. You know, one match at a time, as though it were a brush. The barrel I'd made with the tinfoil from cigarette packages and it looked just like a metal barrel. One night they came in my cell as usual to bring me my food and . . . I pointed my pistol at them. There were three of them. They got so scared that the one holding the tray let it drop. The other two looked paralyzed. And the whole business was so funny that I couldn't keep it up—the impulse to laugh was too strong. You won't believe it, but if I hadn't given in to the desire to laugh, maybe I would have succeeded in escaping. But I had the consolation of having had a little fun. And that's something.

O.F.: But how many times did you try to escape, Alekos?

A.P.: Many times. Once, for example, by digging through the wall of my cell with a spoon. It was October 1969, and at that time I'd succeeded in getting them to put a toilet in the cell. And then, by a hunger strike, I even got them to let me put a curtain in front of the toilet. I chose that place to make the hole—the curtain acted as a screen. I worked on it for at least two weeks, and on October 18 the hole was ready. So I tried to slip through it but I couldn't get all the way through because I had too many clothes on. I had to take them off, throw them out through the hole, and then slip through the hole again. That spoiled everything. A guard went by, saw the clothes, and gave the alarm. They immediately pounced on me. Right away the interrogation began. They didn't want to believe that I'd dug through the wall with nothing but a spoon. They tortured me to find out how I'd done it. Oh, you can't imagine how they tortured me!

After the tortures they took me back to my cell and even removed my cot. I went back to sleeping on the ground, handcuffed, and with nothing but a blanket. Two days later Theofiloyannakos reappeared. "How did you do it?" "You know, with a spoon." "That's impossible, it's not true!" "And what do I care if you believe it or not, Theofiloyannakos?" And that was the beginning of more kicking and beating. Then, two weeks later, there even came a general: Phaidon Gizikis. All nice and polite. "You can't complain, Alekos, if they keep you handcuffed. After all you dug a hole in the wall with a spoon!" And I: "You're not really going to believe those imbeciles? You're not really going to take the story about the spoon seriously? After all, a wall isn't a custard pudding!" That hurt his feelings. And for having teased him like that, I had to go back on a hunger strike. They didn't want to give me back my cot, or take off the handcuffs. But they took them off, finally, and gave me back the cot after forty-seven days of living on nothing but a few drops of coffee. I even wrote a poem about it.

O.F.: Which one?

A.P.: The one called "I Want." "I want to pray / with the same
strength with which I want to curse / I want to punish / with
the same strength with which I want to pardon / I want to
give / with the same strength with which I wanted to in the
beginning / I want to overcome / since I cannot be overcome."

But now I'll tell you about another attempt. The one I
made at the end of February 1970. In January they had transferred me to the military police training center in Goudi and
one of the guards was a friend of mine. Right away I started
planning another escape. My cell had two locks. I asked my
friend to go to the market and buy as many locks as he could,
similar to those two. Along with the locks, the keys. He
brought me back about a hundred of them. One by one we
tried them, and one was the one we were looking for. But it
opened only one lock, of course. So we had to find the second
one too. I told him to go back to the market and buy other
locks. He did, and two days later, February 16, he was my
guard—from eight to eleven in the morning, from ten to mid-
night at night. We spent the morning trying the new locks,
and so we found the key that opened the second lock.

I was mad with joy—I would get away that night. Or rather,
we would get away. He certainly couldn't stay there after my
escape. Everything was ready. It seemed impossible to fail.
And instead . . . Instead two hours later, about eleven in the
morning, they came to get me and took me back to Boyati.
Where they had built me a special cell. In reinforced concrete. I now understood that the transfer to Goudi had been
only so as to build me a new cell. A secure cell, in reinforced
concrete.

O.F.: The cell you were in until the other day?

A.P.: Yes. And they locked me in it. The first time I tried to escape
from this new cell was June 2, 1971. Then they transferred me
again to the military police center, but there too I tried to escape—on August 30. That was the escape that got the most
publicity, since Lady Fleming was involved in it, and afterward there was that trial. You see, the secret is not to resign
yourself, never to feel yourself a victim, never to behave like a
victim. I've never played the victim—not even when I was

wasting away with hunger strikes. I always thought up new ideas for escaping, and I always appeared to be in a good mood or aggressive. Even when I was dying of sorrow. Sorrow. . . . Solitude. . . . I also told about that in the book of poems that won the Viareggio Prize. Look, solitude can be overcome by imagination. How many lives I've given birth to in my mind trying to overcome solitude. And how intensely I lived each life through my imagination.

O.F.: But once, Alekos, you did succeed in escaping.

A.P.: Yes, with George Morakis, who all because of me has been sentenced to sixteen years in prison and can't even benefit from this amnesty since they consider him a deserter. He was a young noncommissioned officer, George Morakis, and he spontaneously offered me his help. Oh, my escape with Morakis was so amusing. I was dressed like a corporal and was carrying in my hand a bunch of keys for all the cells. When we got to the last door, I threw the keys to the little soldier on guard and said, "Open the door, goldbrick." The soldier didn't recognize me. He snapped to attention, opened the door for us, and I even told him not to make a lot of noise asking who-goes-there in case we came back. You understand, there was always the possibility of not being able to make it and of having to sneak back in if we didn't succeed in getting over the wall.

The last door let us out on the actual military field—to get out of there all we had to do was climb the wall. Even though the wall was very high and surmounted by barbed wire. I bent over, Morakis got on my shoulders and got up the wall. Then he reached down, I grabbed his arms, and away we went. Out for a stroll through the streets of Athens. Too bad they caught us, four days later. They arrested me in the house of a traitor, Takis Patitsas. He had had connections with Greek Resistance, this Patitsas, since 1967. He worked in a travel agency and had supplied us with a certain number of stolen passports. They had wanted to know about him too when they tortured me during the interrogation, and naturally I hadn't talked. In fact, Patitsas was never arrested.

After my escape I went to his house full of trust. I only meant to stay there a few days. Just long enough to get information and make contact with my comrades in my Greek Resistance group. He received me with hugs and kisses, but the next day he left the house where I was his guest and only reappeared after forty-eight hours. We talked, we ate together, and next morning he left, saying he was going to work. Instead he didn't go to work. He went to the police station and handed over the keys. That's how they caught us, by opening the door with Patitsas' keys. As a reward he got five hundred drachmas. About seventeen dollars. Let's talk about something else, if you don't mind.

O.F.: Yes, let's talk about something else. Let's talk about Papado-poulos.

A.P.: Listen, I can't take this Papadopoulos seriously. He's a type you can't understand unless you examine his history. A history that shows right away how dishonest, mentally sick, and what a liar he is. For six years he's told nothing but lies, and how many times, to vomit out my disgust, I wrote to tell him so! You know, those letters that I gave to the prison director. In each one I called him comical, a ridiculous clown, a buffoon, a criminal, and mentally sick. And don't think that I was exaggerating or carried away by anger. All these things are abundantly clear from his biography.

He was the captain who participated in the 1951 *coup d'état*, which failed however, with the brigantines *Cristeas* and *Tabularis*. And he who, as lieutenant colonel, was secretary of the commission that drew up the famous Pericles Plan by which they tried to falsify the results of the 1961 elections. When the democratic government ordered an investigation of the Pericles Plan, that idiot replies that he didn't know Greek syntax and so couldn't have been the one responsible. You'll find this information in official documents, published besides in all Greek newspapers at the time.

It's he who at the beginning of 1963 carried out a sabotage of his own department and then personally tortured some of his soldiers to get them to confess that it was communist sabotage. He was head of the Office of Propaganda and Psychological Warfare, and everyone knows he was the one who ordered the murder of Polycarpos Georghadjis. Everyone knows he was the one behind that incident where they tried to murder me in prison. That he's a ridiculous man anyway, you can also judge from the fact that he's extended the amnesty to the torturers. Isn't that an admission that torture existed? And isn't it tantamount to encouraging more torture?

O.F.: Yes, but it doesn't keep him from being in power and staying there.

A.P.: Listen, if you're saying that all this doesn't exclude his capacity to stay in power, let me make an observation. When I was in Rome I saw a film with Mussolini speaking to the crowd from the Palazzo Venezia. I was astonished and wondered how the Italians had managed to put up for so many years with such a ridiculous man who spoke in such a ridiculous way. And yet Mussolini was a powerful dictator and in his way capable. Does stealing power and keeping it keep anyone from being ridiculous? The difference between Papadopoulos and Mussolini is that, for better or worse, Mussolini had popular support. Papadopoulos doesn't even have that. His power is based on the junta and nothing else, namely on ten officers who control the entire army. He's the little leader of a little clique.

Moreover he acts in bad faith. He doesn't present himself like Franco, who says, "I am the master. Period." He presents himself by talking about revolution and then even about democracy. Democracy! What the hell kind of democracy is a democracy where one goes up for election alone, without even having the decency to invent an opponent or an opposition? You can say: But you're out of prison because of Papadopoulos' amnesty. But don't you understand that it's a trick, a mockery? Don't you understand that behind this action of his there's a hidden stratagem to extend the tyranny?

O.F.: What do you think of Constantine, Alekos?

A.P.: I've always been a republican, of course, and I'm certainly not the one to feel sorry about Constantine. Besides, Constantine created the conditions for having himself thrown out of the country when he forced Papandreou to resign, in July 1965. But I don't care to emphasize whether I like Constantine or not. I'm only interested to see if Constantine can be useful in the struggle against the junta. Perhaps he can. Because Constantine may still have some influence in certain sections of the army, especially among the officers. Perhaps, the situation being what it is, we can't ignore him. And we can't deal with the problem of him, at the moment. By now he's an enemy of the junta. And by now he has no other choice but to remain an enemy of the junta.

O.F.: Alekos, but you don't suppose that Papadopoulos let you all out so as to overthrow him?

A.P.: Of course not. But he doesn't think that he's capable of being overthrown. And that's his mistake because the resistance in Greece is a reality. People are joining in it, albeit in a passive way for now. They're joining in, for instance, by refusing the dictatorship unanimity. The task assumed by the whole Greek political world is that of following the popular will. And that task shows up by not helping Papadopoulos to legalize his regime. I'm sure no respectable politician in Greece will participate in the farce of the elections. You must understand that we can overthrow him. Papadopoulos didn't come out of a civil war like Franco—he came out of a *coup d'état*. When Franco came to power, his opponents were decimated. Defeated. The last democrats left Spain like El Campesino.

Here it's different. Here no one has been defeated. No one has been decimated. And all it will take for the dictatorship to end is for the Greek people not to go to sleep as the Italian people did. The people always tend to sleep, to resign themselves, to accept. But it doesn't take much to awaken them. Who knows! Maybe I lack realism, information, and even logic. But if you're going to talk about logic, I say when has logic ever made history? If logic were to make history, the Italians wouldn't have let themselves be seduced by Mussolini, and Hitler wouldn't have existed, and Papadopoulos wouldn't have come to power. He controlled only a few units in all of Attica, and some units in Macedonia. And when you talk about politics . . .

O.F.: But what is your political ideology, Alekos?

A.P.: I'm not a communist, if that's what you want to know. I never could be, since I reject dogmas. Wherever there's dogma, there's no freedom, and so dogmas aren't for me. Whether religious dogmas or sociopolitical ones. Having said that, it's hard for me to make a distinction and say that I belong to this or that other ideology. I can only tell you I'm a socialist—in our times it's normal, I'd say inevitable, to be a socialist. But when I talk about socialism, I'm talking about a socialism applied in a regime of total freedom. Social justice can't exist if freedom doesn't exist. For me, the two concepts are connected.

And this is the kind of politics I'd like to participate in, if Greece only had democracy. This is the kind of politics that's always attracted me. Oh, if I belonged to a democratic country, I really think I'd go into politics. Because what I'm doing now and what I've done so far isn't politics—it's only a flirtation with politics. And I like to flirt, yes, but I like love much better. In democracy to be in politics becomes as beautiful as to be in love with love. And that's my trouble. You see, there are men who are capable of politics only in time of war, that is in dramatic circumstances, and there are others capable of politics only in time of peace, that is in normal circumstances. Paradoxically, I belong to the latter. All things considered, between Garibaldi and Cavour I prefer Cavour. But you must understand that ever since the moment the junta took power, neither I nor my comrades have been making politics. Nor will we until the moment when the junta is overthrown. We mustn't, we can't, unless we have an operating force. And this operating force is the resistance, namely the struggle.

O.F.: Alekos, you say that paradoxically you belong to the Cavourians. Truly paradoxically, since as a political figure you became famous through a rather Garibaldian assassination attempt. Alekos, do you ever curse the day you made that attempt?

A.P.: Never. And for the same reason for which I never feel any repentance. Look, it would have been enough for me to say at the trial that I repented, and they wouldn't have condemned me to death. Instead I didn't say it, just as I don't say it now, because I've never changed my mind. And I don't even think I'll change it in the future. Papadopoulos is guilty of high treason and of many other crimes that in my country are punished with the death penalty. I didn't act like a mad fanatic and I'm not a mad fanatic. Both I and my comrades acted as instruments of justice. When tyranny is imposed on a people, the duty of every citizen is to kill the tyrant. There's no need to repent and our struggle will go on until justice and freedom are re-established in Greece. I, or rather we, have set out on a road on which there's no turning back.

O.F.: I know. Tell me about the attempt, Alekos.

A.P.: It was a well-prepared attempt, down to the last details. I had thought of everything. I would have to open the electrical switch of the two mines from a distance of about two hundred meters. The two mines were well placed. I had made them myself. They were two good mines. Each one contained five kilos of TNT and a kilo and a half of another explosive material, C-3. I had placed them at a depth of one meter to the two sides of the little bridge that Papadopoulos' car would have to cross going along the coastal road from Sounion to Athens. The explosion was to expand in an arc of forty-five degrees and open a circular chasm about two meters in diameter. A single explosion would have been enough, the explosion of a single mine to hit the target, provided the car went by at the right moment.

But it was the fault of the comrade who had put it in the trunk of the car that the fuse turned out to be so tangled and knotted that all I could salvage of it was some forty meters. The fact is it wasn't possible to open the switch at that distance, because I wouldn't have had any place to hide myself. The only place where I could have hidden was between eight and ten meters from the bridge. I had to try just the same. I could see right away the drawbacks and dangers of such a position. The most serious was that I couldn't see the highway very well. I had made many trials, before the attempt, and had chosen the position at two hundred meters because I'd noted that when the car was between me and the bridge, I saw it half hidden by a billboard. At that moment I would have opened the switch. Instead from the new position I didn't have a good view of the highway, so I couldn't perceive the car at the moment when I should have to light the fuse. The other drawback of this position was that from there it would be almost impossible to get away. Along the highway, every fifty or a hundred meters, there was a patrolman. And farther on, several police cars. Besides one not more than ten meters away.

O.F.: So you would have had to jump in the sea from there?

A.P.: Exactly. And a fast motorboat was waiting for me, hidden some three hundred meters away. I could see right away that to escape wasn't just almost impossible but impossible. I decided to go through with it all the same. I lit the fuse and jumped right in the water. I swam under water for twenty or thirty meters. Then I came up for air. I realized immediately that they hadn't seen me jump in the sea. Cops were running from all sides toward the point of the explosion. I swam a little more and then came out of the water to try to get to the motorboat across the rocks and so more quickly. I was running bent over, with my head down. And all of a sudden I saw the motorboat leaving. The plan stipulated that it would wait for me five minutes, no more. Still I didn't despair.

The plan had an alternative: if the motorboat hadn't been able to come, or else if it had to leave without picking me up, I was to hide in the rocks until late that night. There were several cars that would wait for me in different places, and after leaving my hiding place in the dark, I would have been able to reach one of them. Of course it would be uncomfortable, since all I had on was a pair of bathing trunks, but that wasn't too much of a problem. So I hid inside a little cave and stayed there for two hours. Two hours during which the coastal and military police kept looking for me all over. And it was during those two hours that I became optimistic—so far they hadn't found me, and so they'd never find me.

Then something happened that I can only call fate. Just above the cave where I was hiding, there was standing a police officer. I heard him say, "He's not here, let's take a look behind those bushes and then look for him on the other side." But just as he was starting toward the other side, he fell backward and . . . he fell right in front of me. He saw me right away. In a split second they were all on top of me. Hitting me, asking me, "Who are you? Where are the others? Who was it got away in the motorboat? Talk, talk!" And blows . . . and more blows . . . I pretended to be a mute and didn't answer any of their questions. . . . Then they took me up to the road and shoved me in a car and . . .

o.f.: Don't go on, if you don't want to. That's enough.

a.p.: Why? In the car, I was about to say, there was the minister of public security, General Zevelekos, and Colonel Ladas. A cop who'd known me for some time exclaimed, "It's Panagoulis!" So the officers thought I was my brother George. Captain George Panagoulis, whom they'd been looking for since August 1967. They started yelling, "We've got you, Captain! Now we're going to kill you!" It would take another thirty hours before they realized their mistake. During those thirty hours they used on me all the most brutal, most infamous interrogation methods. They said to me, "We've arrested Alexander, in Salonika! And right now Alexander is suffering even more than you!" They also asked me about officers whom, naturally, I didn't know. They asked me, for instance, about General Anghelis, who at that time was commander in chief of the armed forces. They wanted to know if he was involved in the plot and tortured me to find out. They were carried away by panic and did awful things to me, but their interrogation was anything but systematic—they were hysterical. When they finally understood that I was not George but Alexander, they became so ferocious they doubled the tortures.

o.f.: Don't think about it any more, Alekos. Maybe it's dreadful to say so, but that's the way it had to be. Because today you're a symbol to whom even your enemies look with admiration and respect.

a.p.: You sound to me like the ones who say, "Alekos, you're a hero!" I'm not a hero and I don't feel like a hero. I'm not a symbol and I don't feel like a symbol. I'm not a leader and I don't want to be a leader. And this popularity embarrasses me. It disturbs me. I've already told you: I'm not the only Greek who suffered in prison. I swear to you, I'm only able to tolerate this popularity when I think that it helps as much as my death sentence would have helped. And so I look on it with the same detachment with which I accepted my death sentence. But, even putting it that way, it's a very uncomfortable popularity. It's unpleasant. When you all ask me "What will you do, Alekos?" I feel like fainting. What should I do so as not to disappoint you? I'm so afraid of disappointing all of you who see so many things in me! Oh, if only you could succeed in not seeing me as a hero! If only you could succeed in seeing in me only a man!

O.F.: Alekos, what does it mean to be a man?

A.P.: It means to have courage, to have dignity. It means to believe in humanity. It means to love without allowing love to become an anchor. It means to struggle. And to win. Look, more or less what Kipling says in that poem entitled "If." And for you, what is a man?

O.F.: I'd say that a man is what you are, Alekos.

Athens, September 1973